terms the Jewish situation in those areas of Jewish life and culture in which they are thoughtful authorities. Beginning with a historical survey by Jacob R. Marcus to provide background, there follow essays in the economic, philanthropic, cultural, organizational, religious, and every other important phase of Jewish life. They point out the facts, and also submit the resultant problems. They avoid the temptation to prophesy, but each essay encourages further discussion. The book concludes with an evaluative summary by its editor.

Every reader of this book will no doubt learn much and draw significant conclusions from this highly stimulating compilation of essays. For though each contributor to the volume limits himself to one theme, the whole describes a people whose experience during the past generation constitutes a very significant chapter in the evolution of the American dream and American reality.

Each of the essays is interesting, important and revealing. Each can and should form the topic of more than one evening's discussion, whether in one's parlor or adult class. The entire volume is nothing less than a challenge to the American Jewish community. It shows what we have achieved—and it is no mean achievement. It also shows what there is still to be done, which, if accomplished, will make the American Jewish community a blessing to itself and to America as a whole.

THE AMERICAN JEW

The American Jew

A REAPPRAISAL

EDITED BY Oscar I. Janowsky

The Jewish Publication Society
of America

PHILADELPHIA
5727—1967

THE
JACOB R. SCHIFF
★ LIBRARY ★
OF JEWISH
CONTRIBUTIONS TO
AMERICAN DEMOCRACY

Number 22 in The Series

TO

HORACE STERN

former Chief Justice of the Supreme Court of Pennsylvania
whose distinguished public career included many years
of devoted interest in the Jewish Publication Society
fifty of them as one of its officers

"For Thou dost bless the righteous; O Lord,
Encompass him with favor as with a shield."
(Psalms 5.13)

Preface

Who and what is an American Jew?

This question has recently aroused considerable discussion, and persons of diverse points of view have sought clarification in Jewish religious ideals and practices, in historical traditions, in the dispersion of the Jews with its consequences of minority status, intermittent persecution and gnawing insecurity, and in other conditioning factors. This book seeks a partial answer to the question: "What is an American Jew?" by addressing itself to a related question: "What is American Jewry?" It attempts to identify this group; to explain how it became what it is today, and how it functions through its institutions and services; to analyze the special features which distinguish it as a group in demographic, economic and social patterns, in religion and education, in currents of thought and cultural expression, in philanthropic motivation, and in conceptions and efforts to further its continuance and welfare. In a word, this is a study of the American Jewish community.

The word "community" as applied to American Jewry may arouse some misgivings. Sociologists who identify the term with a village, town, tribe or nation would not characterize the Jews as a community. However, a recent study classified no fewer than ninety-four definitions of the term "community" as employed by sociologists,[1] and not a few of the latter would cover the Jewish group. In this book, the term community is applied to two related groupings: the "American Jewish Community" refers to the American Jews who have a sense of belonging together and who maintain institutions and provide services in pursuit of their common interests; the "local Jewish community" defines the Jewish group of a town, city or region.

American Jewry in all of its ramifications is too comprehensive a subject for effective treatment in one volume. Emphasis has therefore been placed on the Jewish community and its institutions, rather than on the problems and gropings of the individual Jew, and on the inner life of the Jews rather than on minority-majority relationships. Anti-Semitism has been noted briefly, but its full analysis has gratefully been left to the specialist in abnormal psychology. We are concerned here with the efforts of Jews who are more or less identified with the internal affairs of American Jewry.

Emphasis on some areas, however, does not necessarily mean total exclusion of others. The reader will find excellent chapters on demographic and social patterns, on Jews in the American economy, and on some intergroup relationships. Similarly, cultural expression has brought into focus the attitudes of some "negative" Jews. Finally, American Jewry has not been treated as an abstract concept. The authors have been mindful that American Jewry consists of human beings whose needs the community and its institutions are meant to serve.

The frame of reference of these studies is historical and sociological, while the treatment of subject matter is descriptive and evaluative. Each subject is dealt with in some detail, covering basic data, recent trends, and where relevant, problems and needs. Past developments are surveyed, present aims and achievements are appraised, and currents of change are analyzed and evaluated. The approach is dynamic rather than static.

In level and style, the book has aimed to be both scholarly and popular. It is meant neither for the reader of digests and captions, nor for the specialist. Its wide range has precluded exhaustive treatment of the various subjects; but an effort has been made to avoid shallow generalizations, apologetics and sensationalism.

Documentation has been included and placed at the end of the book. The main purpose of the footnotes is to facilitate verification and to encourage further reading. Instead of long bibliographical lists, each author has included a more selective "bibliographical note" as a guide to the most useful books on the subject. This book, then, is meant to serve not as an ornament of scholarship, but as an instrument for clarification and enlightenment and as a basis for understanding and participation.

Editing this volume has involved a number of difficulties. I am aware that the division into segments of a subject like the American Jewish community must in large measure be arbitrary. For example, the long chapter devoted to Jewish culture has been limited to literature and the arts; but other subjects, treated in separate chapters, might well have been included under a broader definition of culture.

The allocation of space to the various subjects may likewise appear arbitrary: because of the variety of cultural expression, and because of the crucial role of Jewish education, these topics have been assigned more space than the other segments of this book. Limitations of space have imposed upon me the onerous duty of constraining the specialists who have contributed to this volume. The most difficult problem has been to induce these able and busy scholars to accept the arduous assignments and to write their essays in a relatively short time. I am grateful to my associates for their cooperation, for yielding graciously to the restrictions of space, and for their generosity in making necessary revisions.

In a composite volume on American Jewry the dangers of repetition and overlapping are especially marked. The subjects of community organization or community services, for example, might have ranged over the entire field. To minimize this possibility, I discussed in person with all but a few of the authors the contents of the entire book and prepared draft outlines of the contents of all but a few of the chapters for the consideration of the contributors. The latter also received a memorandum, including a table of contents and outlining the nature of the book, its orientation and emphasis, treatment of subject matter, the audience to whom it is addressed, and other relevant matters.

A number of the authors, as well as the editor, are indebted to various libraries and to individuals whose studies were used to good advantage. I am personally grateful to Dr. Solomon Grayzel, editor of the Jewish Publication Society, and to Professor Jacob R. Marcus, chairman of the Committee on American Jewish History, for allowing me a free hand in editing. Thanks are due to Mr. Lesser Zussman, executive director of the Society, for his efficient management of the business aspects of this volume.

Although this book has been prepared and published under the sponsorship of the Jewish Publication Society of America, the views expressed in it do not necessarily represent those of the Society or its Publication Committee. Each author bears sole responsibility for his or her opinions and interpretations.

OSCAR I. JANOWSKY

The City College of the
City University of New York
June, 1963

Contents

Contributors to This Volume

HASYE COOPERMAN heads the department of Literature at the New School for Social Research, where she teaches Comparative Literature as well as a course in Yiddish Literature. She is the author of several volumes of criticism and poetry.

ABRAHAM G. DUKER is Director of Libraries and Professor of History and Social Institutions at Yeshiva University. He is also an editor of *Jewish Social Studies* and former president of the College of Jewish Studies in Chicago. He has taught at various institutions of higher education and has written extensively on modern East European and American history.

JUDITH K. EISENSTEIN has taught music and music education at the Teachers Institute of the Jewish Theological Seminary and at the College of Jewish Studies (Chicago). She is the author of song books and composer of a number of sonatas. Her articles have appeared in Jewish and musical magazines.

ARTHUR HERTZBERG is the rabbi of Temple Emanu-El in Englewood, New Jersey, and serves as lecturer in Jewish History in the Graduate Faculty of Columbia University. He is the author of several books, among them *The Zionist Idea* (1959) and *Judaism* (1961), and co-author of *The Outbursts That Await Us* (1963).

OSCAR I. JANOWSKY, professor of History at CCNY and former director of graduate studies, is the author of works on minority rights and related subjects. He directed and wrote *The JWB Survey* (1948). During 1952–1957 he was chairman of the Commission for the Study of Jewish Education in the United States and (with U. Z. Engelman) director of the study from 1952 to 1955. He edited *The American Jew: A Composite Portrait* (Harper Bros., 1942).

MILTON R. KONVITZ is professor of Industrial and Labor Relations and professor of Law at Cornell University. He has held fellowships from the Guggenheim Foundation, Ford Foundation, Fund for the Republic, and the Institute for Advanced Study at Princeton. He is the author of numerous works on civil liberties and civil rights, including *Fundamental Liberties of a Free People* (1957), and *Civil Rights in Immigration* (1953). He is president of the Hebrew Culture Foundation.

CHARLES S. LEVY is associate dean and professor of Social Work at the Wurzweiler School of Social Work, Yeshiva University. He held social group work supervisory and administrative positions in the National Jewish Welfare Board, in youth and in community service organizations.

JACOB RADER MARCUS, Adolph S. Ochs Professor of American Jewish History at the Hebrew Union College-Jewish Institute of Religion in Cincinnati and director of the American Jewish Archives, has published a number of works on Jewish—particularly American Jewish—history. Among his writings touching on America are the two-volume *Early American Jewry;* a documentary source book—*American Jewry: Documents, Eighteenth Century;* and the three-volume *Memoirs of American Jews: 1775–1865.* His *Jew in the Medieval World* is now available in a paperbook edition.

NATHAN REICH is professor of Economics at Hunter College and chairman of the board of directors of YIVO. He was an assistant editor of the *Encyclopedia of the Social Sciences* (1930–1934). Among his publications are *Canadian Pulp and Paper Industry* (1927); *Labor Relations in Republican Germany* (1938); and *A Profile of German Labor Relations* (MS).

JOSEPH J. SCHWARTZ, a scholar in Semitics and Semitic literature, has devoted many years to public service. He was executive director of the Brooklyn Federation of Jewish Charities, held high office in the JDC, served as executive vice-chairman of the U.J.A., and has been vice president of the Israel Bond Organization since 1955. He is a past president of the National Conference of Jewish Social Welfare and a past vice president of the New York State Conference on Social Work. He assisted in the preparation of the Harrison Report to President Truman.

JUDAH J. SHAPIRO is secretary of the National Foundation for Jewish Culture. He served formerly as director of the Department of Cultural and Educational Reconstruction of JDC and the Conference on Jewish Material Claims Against Germany. He is also a former national director of the B'nai B'rith Hillel Foundations.

C. BEZALEL SHERMAN has for years observed developments in American Jewish life both as student and participant. He was cultural director of the Labor Zionist Organization, and he held high positions with the Anti-Defamation League of B'nai B'rith, the Jewish Labor Committee, the American Jewish Congress and the Jewish Agency. Among his published works are *The Jew Within American Society* (1960); *Labor Zionism in America* (1956); and *Jews and Other Ethnic Groups in the United States* (1948, in Yiddish).

EISIG SILBERSCHLAG, author of several books of poetry and a book of essays on contemporary world literature in Hebrew, has edited *Hatekufah* with Aaron Zeitlin, translated the entire corpus of Aristophanic comedy from Greek into Hebrew, and contributed to numerous Hebrew and English periodicals. He is dean of the Hebrew Teachers College of Boston.

MARIE SYRKIN is editor of *Jewish Frontier,* associate professor of Humanities at Brandeis University, and a prolific writer. Among her books are, *Your School, Your Children* (1944); *Blessed Is the Match* (the story of Jewish resistance under the Nazis— 1947); *Nachman Syrkin: A Biographical Memoir with Selected Essays* (1961); and *Golda Meir: Woman with a Cause* (1963).

JUDD L. TELLER is a lecturer, contributor to leading periodicals and author of a number of books, including *Scapegoat of Revolution* (1954); *The Kremlin, the Jews and the Middle East* (1957); and *An Informal Biography of the Jewish People* (1963).

BEATRICE I. VULCAN is a social worker—MSS Smith College School for Social Work and candidate for the doctorate at the Columbia University School of Social Work. She has served as social worker, director of social work or country director with the American Red Cross, UNRRA and JDC in the South Pacific, Europe and North Africa.

HAROLD WEISBERG is associate professor of Philosophy and dean of the Graduate School at Brandeis University.

ALFRED WERNER is a noted art critic and author of *Modigliani the Sculptor* (1962); and *Jules Pascin* (1962). He has also written texts for books on Utrillo, Dufy, Henri Rousseau, and Vlaminck, and edited writings by da Vinci, Dürer, Rodin, and Gauguin. He has taught at Wagner College and lectured widely. He is a contributing editor to *Arts Magazine* and U.S. correspondent of *Pantheon*.

EDWIN WOLF, 2ND, is librarian of The Library Company of Philadelphia. He is co-author of *The Jews of Philadelphia* and of *Rosenbach, a Biography*. He is a former president of The Federation of Jewish Agencies of Philadelphia; president of The National Foundation for Jewish Culture; and chairman of the Publication Committee of The Jewish Publication Society.

THE AMERICAN JEW

Background for the History of American Jewry

JACOB RADER MARCUS

HERDER called the story of the Jew "the greatest poem of all time," and it is a fact that American Jewry may lay claim to a fabulous history. In 1649, when the Pilgrims still walked the land, there was one Jewish businessman in Boston. As late as 1880 —that is, still within living memory—no more than 300,000 Jews called this country home; today there are about 5,600,000. Fifty years ago most Jews were immigrants and very few attended schools of higher learning; today a majority of Jewish youth is exposed to college, and five of America's eleven Nobel Prize winners, in the years 1959 to 1962, were Jews.

AMERICAN JEWRY BEFORE 1920

The Coming of the Immigrants

As far back as the medieval Crusades, and as late as 1648, European Jews, driven out of their native lands in Western and Central Europe, moved eastward into the Slavic realms. With the dawn of the modern age and the rise of an Atlantic civilization in the mid-seventeenth century, with the coming of mercantilism and the Industrial Revolution, with the beginnings of colonial empires in the New World, the Jews of Europe began to move westward. The farthest "frontier" fringe of Jewish settlement was first established in Dutch-ruled New Amsterdam in 1654. The first arrivals were Sephardim, or Spanish-Portuguese Jews, in quest, for the most part, of new economic opportunity. Some—but actually only a few—were religious émigrés. A few hundred Sephardim, at the most, came to these shores, and by 1720 they no longer constituted a majority among American Jews. Intermingled with them ever since their very first day on American shores were Ashkenazim: German and East European Jews. Ashkenazim and Sephardim banded together to establish tiny Jewish communities in the tidewater towns of Newport, New York, Philadelphia, Charleston, Savannah, and, finally, Montreal, Canada.

By the 1820's the trickle of Germans had become a steady stream, crossing the mountains and flowing westward. Major Mordecai Manuel Noah could even dream then of a colony for Europe's poor and oppressed Jews—a haven at the western terminus of the Erie Canal, soon to become the most popular highway to the interior of the continent. By 1840 the newcomers had established little synagogues and communities in at least five towns of the trans-Allegheny West; by 1849 they were among the Argonauts in California, and in the next generation they had spread out into the trans-Mississippi plains and prairies. There was hardly a town of size in the whole country that did not shelter a Jewish shopkeeper or a modest congregation. By the 1850's and the 1860's, when the Central European immigrants were still coming in substantial numbers, East European Jews began to pour in, thrust from their native Russia by the hard times that had followed the breakdown of agrarian feudalism and the birth pangs of industrial capitalism. The Russian pogroms of the 1880's and the Czar's effort to crush the impending social revolution ultimately drove over 2,000,000 East European Jews to these shores. Today they and their descendants are settled mainly in two megalopolises: in the Atlantic "supercity" reaching from the Potomac Valley to the New Hampshire border, and in the

Pacific colossus which strides from San Diego to the northern shores of San Francisco Bay.

Political Rights

The twenty-three Brazilian Jewish refugees who landed in New Amsterdam in the late summer of 1654 were denied even the most elementary economic and religious rights by Governor Stuyvesant and the Dutch West India Company. But these restrictions could not endure, for the Jews—because they were "population" and, even more, because they commanded economic skills—were needed in the "wilderness." By the time the Dutch flag was lowered over the Hudson a decade later, the Jews had wrested the right to settle, own land, and do business, but it was not until the 1690's, under English rule, that they were accorded the privilege of holding public religious services and selling at retail. It was not until the adoption of the Federal Constitution in 1789 that Jews were permitted to hold public offices of honor and responsibility. Still, federal rights, in those days of decentralized government, had little impact on the status of the Jews in the thirteen original states. It would take a century before New Hampshire Jewry finally achieved full enfranchisement—an event that would not come to pass until the centennial year of 1876, just a hundred years after the Declaration of Independence. By the twentieth century, however, as state-imposed disabilities gave way to federally defended rights, nearly every office of public trust in America had had its Jewish holders. Oscar S. Straus, a former ambassador, served in the President's Cabinet as Secretary of Commerce and Labor in 1906, and a decade later Louis Dembitz Brandeis was appointed an associate justice of the United States Supreme Court.

The Right to Do Business

The United States was the first country in the modern Diaspora to enfranchise the Jew—a grant which, whatever else it secured to him, also enabled him to do business without let or hindrance. Lacking economic rights, the Jew would have been little attracted to America. During the Sephardi period, from the 1640's through the 1840's, most American Jews were petty shopkeepers, dealing in hard goods, soft goods, and wet goods: hardware, dry goods, and liquors—all under one roof. A handful were farmers, some were artisans, a few were wealthy merchants and merchant-shippers, fur entrepreneurs, land speculators, and candle manufacturers. By the fifth decade of the 1800's, the new immigrants crossing the mountains were largely storekeepers. Those who were successful became merchants on a large scale: department store owners, bankers, and early investors and executives in the railroad and insurance industries. Some, though not many of the native Jews, had turned to the professions of law, medicine, and engineering; one of the United States Army's outstanding ordnance experts in the ante-bellum period was a native-born North Carolinian engineer, Major Alfred Mordecai. No other business, however, attracted the successful businessman like garment manufacturing; by 1843 a Jew had written a brochure on the subject, and by the time the East European immigrants began to swarm ashore at Castle Garden, Jews of German background already dominated the industry.

The older generation of native and German Jews, frightened by the onrush of the new immigrants and perhaps unduly apprehensive about their own status, made every effort to disperse the "Russians" into the interior. But the humble East Europeans were often better economists than their would-be mentors. They gauged the economic trends more accurately than the millionaire Jews of Wall Street, for they knew by the 1890's that the last frontier had been reached, that there was no place for the rural peddler, and that the future lay with the city and the factory—with America's rapidly emergent industrialization: they insisted on remaining in the eastern metropolitan centers, entered into the clothing industry as laborers, and after thirty years of sweatshops and blundering efforts to improve themselves, created four "Jewish" labor unions whose social and economic policies are still among the most enlightened and exemplary of the organized crafts. Many of the Russian and Polish garment workers emerged from the sweatshops and factories to become highly successful apparel manufacturers.

Religion

Though most of the Jewish labor leaders and many of their followers were anti-religious in the early days, this attitude toward

religion was not characteristic of the American Jew. The first
Sephardim who came here in the middle 1600's were devoted
religionists and with little delay set about reconstituting the Euro-
pean-type religious community to which they were accustomed.
Its central institution on these shores was the synagogue, and
traditional loyalties, combined with the moral pressures exerted
here, impelled newcomers to affiliate themselves. Despite the
Germanic origins which prevailed among them, by the 1720's the
immigrants of those early days were content to join—and, in
some instances, even to establish—Spanish-Portuguese congregations, so that the Sephardi rite became typically American and was
accepted by all Jews until the early 1800's.

The domination of the Orthodox Sephardim began to wane
in the 1820's and 1830's, when the new, post-Napoleonic arrivals
created their own Orthodox Ashkenazi conventicles. But Sephardi
Orthodoxy began losing ground even among the older, well-established families, whose desire to integrate more closely with the
relatively liberal American culture led some of them, as early as
1824, to reject Orthodoxy and the authority of the traditional
Law. Thus Reform Judaism came to birth in Charleston, South
Carolina, probably the largest and certainly the most cultured
Jewish community in the United States at that time. By the 1840's,
Reform, as an aspect of acculturation, was in full swing. The
movement was particularly strong in "the West," the Ohio and
Mississippi valleys, and it was there, in 1873, that the Reformers
led the way in establishing the first real nationwide and enduring
American Jewish institution, the Union of American Hebrew Congregations. Two years later, the Union created the Hebrew Union
College in the Queen City of the West, Cincinnati. Yet, despite
its early start and excellent organization and discipline, Reform
was never to become a majority movement even in its palmiest
days. Reacting indignantly to the sharp break with traditionalism
that Reform formulated at the Pittsburgh Conference in 1885,
the native-born Americanized Orthodox, mostly "Germans," abandoned the Union which they had supported, and a year later
established the Jewish Theological Seminary Association. Thus
was Conservative Judaism organized as a separate religious denomination in this country. Not an East European movement, even

though the Russian and Polish immigrants had already organized dozens of their own synagogues a decade or two before that time, Conservatism represented an effort on the part of the well-Americanized Orthodox to maintain themselves in the community.

The Russian, Polish, Lithuanian, Galician, Roumanian, and Hungarian masses who poured in after the pogroms of the 1880's opened hundreds of new synagogues, fortified Orthodoxy and *kashrut,* and preserved the age-old Hebrew liturgy. Their vernacular, however, was Yiddish, and here, on these shores, they were soon to create a vigorous and appealing Yiddish literature. Because of their Messianic traditions and the oppression they had experienced under Russian rule, they were ardently ethnocentric and sympathetic to Jewish nationalism. Zionism, the new Messianism of the 1880's and 1890's, was generally as acceptable to them as it was distasteful to their Americanized predecessors.

Social Welfare

The immigrant East European *shuls,* and the Orthodox German and Sephardi synagogues which had preceded them, were not only places of prayer and worship, but hearths of education and centers of social welfare. The roots of present-day social philanthropy go back to the first American Spanish-Portuguese synagogues, which provided for the local and itinerant poor, advanced free loans, nursed the sick, buried the dead, pensioned the unfortunate, aided the old, and even collected money for the Jews of Palestine. Like the earlier Sephardim, the German immigrants of the nineteenth century were Europe-oriented, transplanting and practicing here their ancestral tradition of pious works. From the 1820's on, however, the Ashkenazi immigrants preferred to protect themselves and the later arrivals by creating their own mutual aid and benevolent societies. Most of those new organizations divorced themselves from direct synagogal control, thus initiating the secularization of American Jewish charities. Even in the days before the Civil War, the existence of rival philanthropic organizations led to waste and inefficiency and brought about the beginnings of a federation movement, but it was not until the 1890's that federations became effective and began to include even the East European self-help societies. By World War I the federations were taken into the Community Chests, and thus received aid not from Jews alone, but from the urban community at large.

Jewish Education and Culture

The Sephardi synagogue-community, beginning with the seventeenth century, was concerned with education. In addition, there had undoubtedly been private Jewish teachers since the 1600's. By 1731 New York Jewry supported an all-day or parochial school whose curriculum was confined to Hebrew. Later, secular subjects were taught in Portuguese and in English, but English quickly became the sole language of instruction. The Central European pioneers of the nineteenth century continued the all-day school tradition—in German and in English—till about the time of the Civil War when the public school system became firmly established. Ever since 1838, religion had been taught primarily in the synagogal "Sunday School," patterned after Protestant counterparts, and those congregational Sunday schools, plus an occasional afternoon Hebrew school, were to remain typical until the twentieth century. After 1910, the afternoon schools, under the influence of the new bureaus of Jewish education, were organized so as to affect a synthesis of Hebrew lore, American pedagogy, and Zionistic ethnicism. American Jewish education was consequently re-Judaized and improved, and this approach to the instruction of Jewish children was, by the 1930's, adopted even by the Reformers of the Union of American Hebrew Congregations.

The Jewish religion and the Hebrew language are, of course, central to Jewish culture, but few advances were made in those areas until the second quarter of the nineteenth century. The Sephardim, however, merely by maintaining their Jewish identity, had held the fort till the arrival of Central and East European Jews in larger numbers, and it is noteworthy that Gershom Mendes Seixas, American Jewry's first native-born clergyman, had a working knowledge of Hebrew. Still, it remained for a German immigrant, Isaac Leeser, the *hazzan,* or minister, at Philadelphia's Sephardi Mikveh Israel, to lay the groundwork for the American Jewish cultural system. From 1830 to 1868, Leeser furthered Sunday Schools and all-day schools, produced textbooks, prepared

English translations of the traditional prayerbooks and the Hebrew Bible, created the first Jewish publication society, established a national Jewish monthly magazine, *The Occident,* helped organize the first union of congregations in the form of the Board of Delegates of American Israelites, and in 1867—a year before his death—even established a theological seminary, Maimonides College. It was Leeser's short-lived college that spurred on another immigrant, Bohemian-born Isaac M. Wise, of Cincinnati, to create the Hebrew Union College in 1875, and, a decade later, the memory of Leeser's efforts had its influence on the anti-Reform leaders, who in 1887 established the Jewish Theological Seminary in New York. These seminaries and the others that followed became, and still are, the nurseries of Jewish learning and scholarship in this continent. The crowning literary achievements of America's new Jewish learning at the turn of the century were the twelve-volume *Jewish Encyclopedia,* and *The Holy Scriptures,* as the Jewish Publication Society called its translation of the Hebrew Bible.

After two generations of lingering affection for their original German vernacular, the German-Jewish immigrants on these shores began to employ English almost exclusively. The first generation of East Europeans, equally devoted to their own mother tongue, nurtured a lively Yiddish literature, daily press, and theatre. Yiddish floated in a world of its own, giving emotional, intellectual, and spiritual sustenance to the millions of East European immigrants who yearned for the familiar culture of their old homeland. Yiddish proved to be a transitional culture on these shores, but it performed an effective service in enabling the newcomers to survive spiritually until they and their children could take deep root in American soil.

American Jewry until the 1920's constituted, by and large, an immigrant community and as such was concerned primarily with the struggle for existence rather than the acquisition of secular learning. The Sephardim and ante-bellum Germans, too, had rarely been distinguished for their general education and academic achievements, even though they had in their midst some notable lawyers, an occasional playwright, and a few fine physicians. It was, for the most part, not until after World War I that the chil-

dren of the East Europeans began to make their mark in the
world of literature and the fine arts.

THE EMERGENCE OF AN AMERICAN JEWISH COMMUNITY

In 1920, even though there were over 3,500,000 Jews in this
country, one could not speak of a genuine American-Jewish community. Such a community simply did not exist. Instead, there
were *two* separate Jewish communities eyeing one another warily
—the native, or "German," and the immigrant, or "Russian." No
one national American-Jewish community had developed as an
organic structure; there was not even one organized *local* American Jewish community, for practically all Jewish institutions were
still autonomous. The sources of conflict between the two large
"communities" were many and varied. The East Europeans regarded their usually wealthier and more prestigious coreligionists
of German origin with envy; the Germans looked down on the
"newcomers" with disdain. The Orthodox and the Reformers dis-
trusted each other, while both looked askance at the religious indifference of the Jewish labor union leaders. The five decades
between 1880 and 1930 were filled with conflicts between the elite
and the masses, between political conservatives and liberals, dem-
ocrats and socialists. Immigrants and natives were arrayed against
each other. The East Europeans, who wanted one central, all-embracing national American Jewish community—which, if only by
sheer weight of numbers, they could hope to control—struggled
against the Germans, who wanted decentralization and the right
to go their own way—by which they hoped to undermine challenges to their traditional leadership.

Yet, though they were not conscious of it, the two hostile forces
were wedded in a higher unity. Before 1820 the disciplined synagogue-community had claimed—indeed demanded—the loyalty
of all Americans who called themselves Jews. Even after the 1820's
—after the pull of American liberalism, permissiveness, and assimilation had drawn many away from the synagogue—Jews were
still joined by a consensus: the consciousness of a common past,
a common tradition, and a similar way of life. This sense of kinship remained very strong, and unfailingly obliged Jews to help
one another here and abroad.

Since 1820, therefore, American Jewry has been held together, if not by the synagogue, then by socio-cultural bonds and by the nourishing influences of a powerful subterranean current of religion and religious institutions. During the 1920's, ambivalence and hostility permitted only a tenuous unity, but a more closely integrated unity was to arise in the next decade. The quota laws, cutting American Jewry off from the intensely Jewish East European reservoir, made intra-Jewish assimilation here inevitable, so that Americanization could begin to move forward at a rapid pace even for the first-generation immigrants. The Jewish melting pot—intra-marriage—began to boil. The rise of Nazi anti-Semitism and its American imitators welded all Jews together, if only through resentment and shock and despair. Intense Jewish sympathies and loyalties were engendered by Zionism, which recommended itself increasingly as an effective defense against the burgeoning anti-Semitic threat. The new, ethnically motivated Jewish education, which had been taking shape since 1910, made children proud of their heritage, while the herculean efforts of Jews throughout America after World War II to salvage Europe's decimated Jewry and strengthen the Palestinian community made American Jews realize that, whatever their lineage, they were indeed brothers. And when authority in the power structure was finally shared with the wealthy sons and grandsons of East European immigrants—as happened in the 1930's and the 1940's—unity became a practical possibility.

By the 1920's then—antagonisms notwithstanding—an integrated, united, local American Jewish community was at least in the process of becoming. The age of Jewish fusion had begun. The "Spanish-Portuguese," the "German," the "Russian" Jew was disappearing; soon there would be only "American" Jews. A new "American" Jewish community had begun to emerge.

INTEGRATION

Political Rights

The American Jew is both American *and* Jew. As an American with roots going back to the seventeenth century, he insists on his rights. Ever since the 1650's he has been compelled to fight for the achievement or maintenance of his economic, civil, and political liberties. The past never lacked oppressions; prejudice was rarely less than vocal. As early as 1793—only a decade after the Revolution—Jonas Phillips, a Revolutionary veteran, was fined for refusing to be sworn on the Sabbath. Governors ignored Jewish sensibilities in Thanksgiving Proclamations; Jewish children in the public schools were—and often enough still are—compelled to submit to Christian religious indoctrination; legislators imperiled the Jewish future through continual efforts to "baptize" the Constitution, as Isaac M. Wise put it, and make the United States a "Christian" nation; newspapers slandered Jews *as Jews* well into the twentieth century. Against many of these disabilities, the Jew has fought successfully and still continues to fight—for himself and for other elements in American life—by sponsoring fair education, fair economic, and fair accommodation laws and practices. The new approach of today is really the old Jewish socialistic approach of half a century ago: protect all groups, and the American people as a whole, through effective social action procedures. Aroused by the waves of racism and anti-Semitism that threatened them in the 1920's and 1930's, American Jews in all large towns spontaneously began creating local defense agencies representing the entire range of what was still an inchoate Jewish community. These were the Jewish community relations committees, dedicated to the fight against anti-Semitism and to the furtherance of better relations with the preponderantly Gentile world in which Jews lived.

Economic Life

Though there is today no area of economic activity without its Jewish participants, it has never been easy for the Jew to fit into the "normal" occupational pattern—a fact due, in large part, to a past which compelled Jewish preoccupation with certain forms of commerce. Even today the considerable antagonism he often encounters in banking, insurance administration, transportation, utilities, and in many "heavy" industries helps maintain a Jewish preponderance in garment manufacturing, merchandising, trading, the service industries, and the professions. In the new consolidated community that he is in the process of creating, he has established his own vocational bureaus to offer special help to fellow Jews and to advance their economic integration. In a world of commerce and rapidly proliferating automation, the American Jew seeks a white-collar job; in the smaller towns, he is frequently self-employed. His desire to conform, coupled with the overwhelming pull of the environment, and an almost obsessive passion for anonymity in business life, has led the Jew to adapt himself completely to the American social pattern in dress, language, demeanor, and even the name he bears. Moses has given way to Murray, and as soon as Murray becomes a Jewish stereotype, a new name beginning with "M" will be found.

General Culture

American Jews have made tremendous, almost fantastic strides in their absorption of general culture since 1914. In the professions, in music, in painting and sculpture, in the academic world, and particularly in the area of the sciences, Jews are often highly distinguished and, in numerous instances, pre-eminent—and this despite the fact that they constitute but a meager three percent of the American population. Though noticeable reinforcements in the sciences have come, especially since the 1930's, from the arrival of European Jewish refugees, some of them already Nobel Prize winners in Europe, native-born Jews who excel are not uncommon. Some of the best known of America's litterateurs are the children of Jewish immigrants; Jewish journalists and publicists are among the leaders of the general American press. With cultural and social integration has, of course, also come intermarriage—and, in some instances, complete assimilation and loss of Jewish identity. The intermarriage rate for the Jewish community as a whole is rapidly approaching the ten percent mark.

JUDAIZATION AND COMMUNALITY

The Voluntary Suburban Ghetto

Politico-economic integration, cultural assimilation, and even a growing rate of intermarriage by no means pose a real threat to the survival of the contemporary American Jew, for there are many compensatory and countervailing forces and influences. Jewish cohesiveness, Jewish sympathies, the feeling of intra-Jewish kinship—these are stronger today than they have ever been. Ever since World War I, American Jews, as a whole, have been moving out to the suburbs, congregating together there to create voluntary physical and psychological havens, or "ghettoes," but in the best sense of the term. Motivated, on the one hand, by apprehensions and anti-Jewish social pressures, real or imaginary, and, on the other, by the pull of Jewish communality, Zionism, and an ethnocentric religious education, the Jews of today cluster together around their Jewish institutions. To promote their survival as Jews, they are fashioning a rather compact form of Jewish settlement—reminiscent, in some respects, of the medieval-type society—with a full complement of Jewish institutions, religious, educational, eleemosynary and social, all held together loosely by a Jewish community council. This development of an ethno-religious enclave has characterized the direction of Jewish life in America since the 1930's.

The Reacceptance of the Synagogue by Jews

Synagogue affiliation has again become *de rigueur* for American Jews—especially in the suburbs, where many today join synagogues for social, educational, and "folkist" reasons, if not out of a sense of piety. It is deemed un-American not to belong "to the church or synagogue of your choice," and the typical suburban Jew is in this, as in other respects, very much a conformist. But the new suburban world beyond the core city is the scene for other departures from past norms. The Orthodox in suburbia are fighting a gallant, but losing struggle to retain their majority status in the Jewish group. Together with the Classical Reformers, who have outlived their integrationist day, they are fast giving way to the Neo-Reformers and Conservatives who, sharing an appetite for *yiddishkeit,* are slowly drawing closer to one another. Jewish religious loyalties, which are not only tolerated but encouraged by the American ethos, are further reflected in the decline of most of the bureaus of Jewish education as overall school entities and by the growth and strengthening of congregational afternoon and week-end religious schools, whose curricula and instructional standards are better—more Jewish and more thorough.

A new factor on the scene has been the reappearance of the colonial and mid-nineteenth-century parochial—full-day—schools. Reinstituted, in large part, by refugee Orthodox leaders after World War II, they have found rapid acceptance by the Conservatives, and even the Neo-Reformers are not immune to their appeal. Should the Catholics ever win their struggle to secure public money for their parochial schools, the Jewish all-day schools, fortified by similar governmental grants as well as by Jewish welfare fund money, are likely to flourish in larger numbers.

Social Welfare Trends

In the new Jewish suburban "community" slowly being pieced together by need and a subconscious romanticism, the most powerful component is the Jewish welfare fund. Through a united Jewish appeal, this common fund-raising effort has, since the 1920's, provided the money for overseas relief, for Israel, for national health, civic defense, and other needs, as well as for local requirements not covered by Community Chest contributions. Prosperity and government aid have combined to reduce the urgency of Jewish-provided financial relief for the sick, the aged, underprivileged children, and needy families. The inevitable coming of "socialized medicine" and increased government aid to health institutions will probably divert Jewish philanthropies to other forms of social amelioration in the Jewish community. The social welfare agencies of the coming generation are likely to concern themselves far more with strengthening and saving the Jewish family through psychological and psychiatric services and with developing viable, possibly even exemplary, forms of geriatric services.

Leisure

The new suburban spiritual and emotional refuge has already developed its own forms of leisure. The colonial Jews of Newport relaxed in a card-playing and eating club; the German immigrants of the nineteenth century created eating, drinking, and music clubs of their own, while their children established literary and social institutions which they called young men's Hebrew literary associations. Though submerged by the waves of immigration from Eastern Europe, the Hebrew literary associations reappeared

almost immediately as settlement houses preaching Americanization. In the last generation the settlement houses have in turn disappeared, even in the core areas, but they have been resurrected
in the suburbs as beautifully furnished Jewish community centers,
deluxe playgrounds of middle-class youth. Supplemented in downtown urban areas by the older eating clubs, and in the more "posh"
suburban pastures by elegant country clubs, the community center
functions not only as a recreational institution, but, in many instances, as a force for general American culture, especially in the
fine arts and in the drama. Its Jewish influences are, thus far at
least, negligible except in an associative sense.

Coordination in the Oncoming Community

There is no lack of "togetherness" in contemporary American
Jewish life. The middle-class American Jews who live in the fluid,
wandering expanses of suburbia dwell together, often worship together, commonly receive their Jewish education together, and
almost invariably swim and play golf together. As much as the
medieval Jew—and perhaps even more so—the Jew of the on-
coming twenty-first century has the assurance, vital for survival,
that he can always live and enjoy himself among Jews and that
they will provide for him no matter what happens. He is assured
of prenatal care in a Jewish clinic and, though it may be cold
comfort to him, he can be reasonably confident that he will die in
a Jewish hospital or home for the aged and that a synagogue will
annually recite commemorative prayers for him long after his
death!

Still, though this community and its institutions constitute a
growing, impending reality, "togetherness" is conspicuously ab-
sent where coordinating agencies for religion, education, defense,
and social welfare are concerned. Here centrifugality is the usual—
and wasteful—rule. To tie these various communal agencies together, to avoid duplication and overlapping, to effect planning
and direction—this remains one of the challenges of the future. The
challenge has not gone unnoticed, for an overall council was created in some cities as early as the 1930's. This marked the beginning of the Jewish community council "movement," which as
yet has little influence in most towns. Once, however, the power

groups that dominate the Jewish welfare funds accept the idea of a common council, see the advantages in working for it, and surrender some of the prerogatives which are traditionally theirs by virtue of their larger gifts, there is no question that the community council will rise to power as a force for purposeful planning in the Jewish community of the next generation. This will come, because it is certain that a new federated Jewish community, more or less democratically motivated, is emerging on the American scene.

There are no gains without losses, of course, and there will be a loss in diversity of expression. Because it requires a medium of communication, this emergent federated community—or its Jewish welfare fund—will create, as in some localities it already has created, a local weekly magazine, impressive in format, rich in content, beautifully printed, and reaching every Jew who has ever contributed to a communal agency. Unfortunately, however, the need or hunger for communal peace is likely to preclude a vigorous editorial policy where dissent and controversy are concerned. The new successful community newspaper will not—perhaps cannot—be an organ expressive of differences in opinion; its dedication to information, education, and harmony cannot but doom it to fashioning a community of bland conformists.

THE RISE OF A NATION-WIDE JEWISH COMMUNITY

History is not without some logic. People create the institutions they need in order to survive. That explains the development of local Diaspora Jewish communities ever since the Jews were exiled to Babylon in the sixth pre-Christian century. But the local Jewish community, whether in present-day America or in ancient Babylonia, is not an island. It cannot live Jewishly by and for itself alone. To effectuate its purposes, to defend itself, and to move forward, it requires the spiritual, cultural, intellectual, and political support of a supra-local, or national, Jewish community. Just as municipal or state governments are federated into a state or a national entity, so the work of individual Jewish communities must be coordinated and planned, with smaller units organized into larger bodies, in order to further American Jewry as a whole.

The need for more effectual local and national organization has become especially compelling in the wake of the two global wars which spelled an all but total destruction for European Jewry. Before the Nazi holocaust, American Jewry was little more than a spiritual colony of Europe; but now the Jews of the United States have fallen heir to the mantle of world Jewish leadership— whether or not they are prepared for the task and whether or not they wish it—for America's Jews constitute the only sizable Diaspora Jewry still free and still surviving. *Noblesse oblige* has now been added to all the other reasons driving American Jewry to organize on a local, regional, and—above all—national level. For now, not only is such organization essential if the community is to function smoothly—and the community is a corporation of almost 5,600,000 units—but it is no less essential if the community is to fulfill the ineluctable obligation that history has imposed on it: to help all Jews everywhere in the world.

A nation-wide Jewish community has been of very slow growth in the United States. This fact is no departure from the norms of Diaspora experience, for the Jews of the last 2,000 years never succeeded in forging a truly effective national organization. Problems of slow communication, governmental opposition, Jewish factionalism, and the objections of local Jewish vested interests have everywhere in the past inhibited such a development. Yet a national communal attitude has been evolving in America since the 1840's. A ritual murder accusation in far-away Damascus aroused and united American Jewry, at least emotionally, in 1840, and in answer to a nascent consciousness of larger common needs, continual, if unsuccessful, efforts were made to conjoin all of American Jewry throughout the 1840's and the 1850's. It was only in 1859 that American Jews came together in an embryonic nation-wide organization—in response to the *cause célèbre* of Edgar Mortara, an Italian-Jewish child "legally" abducted by the Papal authorities in Bologna. The plight of a Jewish mother, bereaved of her son, shocked even Catholic monarchs. The Jews of the French Empire were sufficiently agitated to create the Alliance Israélite Universelle, while the indignant members of America's minuscule Jewish community—numbering about 100,000— organized themselves into the Board of Delegates of American

Israelites. Primarily a civic defense and overseas relief agency, the Board was never able to establish its authority and in 1878 was absorbed by the younger, more powerful Union of American Hebrew Congregations as the Union's Board of Delegates on Civil and Religious Rights.

The Union of the 1870's, made possible by the appearance of the telegraph and the railroad, still remains the closest approach American Jewry has ever made to a national representative body. At its inception, it set out to include and speak for all American Jews, whatever their religious preferences. It was not, initially, a "Reform" institution. Through its Board of Delegates, it reached beyond purely congregational concerns into the areas of defense and relief, and even attempted to settle the early East European Jewish immigrants in colonies on the western plains. But, as a national overall coordinating agency, the Union failed to command the support of even all the native-born in the community. It made no serious, sustained effort to cope with the problems of the East European immigrant masses; the latter in turn ignored the Union.

The failures of the Union and the aspiring B'nai B'rith—both of them essentially midwestern organizations—left a vacuum into which the financially powerful eastern Jewish bankers, merchants, and lawyers rushed. From their vantage point, particularly in New York City, the numerical hub of American Jewry, the eastern magnates assumed the role of self-appointed standard bearers. For the most part devoted men who loved Jews and Judaism, they undertook to give the amorphous immigrant Jewish masses an effective leadership, and they won their spurs in the protest against Russian brutality after the Kishinev massacre of 1903. Three years later they organized the American Jewish Committee and offered American Jewry a vigorous, disciplined and highly paternalistic leadership as well as a program of Americanization. Soon the American Jewish Committee, aided by the Union of American Hebrew Congregations and the B'nai B'rith, renewed the fight— ultimately successful in 1911—to abrogate the Russo-American treaty of 1832, because the Czarist regime had refused to honor the passports of American Jews.

In 1908, the Committee attempted, by itself, to organize the immigrant Jews of New York City and other urban centers into *kehillot,* or overall local communities, which would govern nearly every phase of the lives and activities of the newcomers. This effort failed, but the idea of adapting the European *kehillah* or *Gemeinde*—an authoritative, all-inclusive community—to American forms of autonomous living persisted. In later years, it would be resuscitated when the "Russians" felt strong enough to rebel against the competent and well-meaning "Germans" who presumed to speak for them.

The outbreak of World War I led to a temporary truce between the competing groups within American Jewry. Only a few months after the war began, the Orthodox, the Jewish labor unionists, and the American Jewish Committee buried their differences and banded together in an American Jewish *Joint* Distribution Committee to help the Jews of Eastern Europe, caught between the Russian and German-Austrian armies. One of the most important developments in the entire course of American Jewish history, this common effort for relief united all the Jews in America and was, within a generation, to create a national American Jewish consensus.

One would think that, having worked together on various problems—Czarist oppressions, immigrant aid, and the like—since 1903, the two dissimilar communities, the "German" and the "Russian," would by the time of World War I have begun to merge. It was just then, however, that each body, feeling sure of itself, made a determined effort to assume, or to retain, hegemony in the emerging national American Jewish community. The test came in 1915, when the "immigrants" insisted on calling a democratically elected Jewish Congress which would labor, at the war's conclusion, to secure minority rights for the oppressed Jews of Eastern Europe and to effect some form of Jewish autonomy in Palestine. The "natives" initially opposed the Congress, but overwhelmed by Jewish public opinion after a bitter struggle, they accepted their defeat graciously and loyally joined in a temporary Congress uniting American Jewry. The Congress sent delegates to Versailles to lobby at the Paris peace conference in 1919. The following year, according to plan, the Congress disbanded, each group going its own way under the leadership either of the American Jewish Committee or of the newly formed permanent American Jewish Congress.

The "immigrants" soon found that, despite their numbers and the victory they had won during the war in forcing the "natives" to meet with them in a common congress, they could not dominate American Jewry. The Committee's defeat in 1916 had already alerted its supporters and followers to the fact that their hitherto undisputed leadership of American Jewry was a thing of the past. But the final decision—and compromise—came through historic forces over which neither party had any control. History decreed that, after the gates of immigration began closing in 1921, the two groups would find themselves cast into a common melting pot out of which one monochromatic American Jewish community would inevitably emerge.

Two rival American Jewries could not, in any case, maintain themselves in an age of expanding technology. The telephone, the intercity and interstate highway, the automobile, the airplane— these have become a guarantee and a promise of the ultimate creation of a merged and unified American Jewish community. Rapid transportation and instantaneous communication, annihilating time and space, have swept away the conditions which inhibited unification. Today, in the 1960's, it takes less time for a California delegate to fly to a meeting in New York than it took his grandfather to travel by train from Baltimore or Boston. Today every Jew is his brother's neighbor. Physically and emotionally, American Jews have become one entity. And this oneness is further advanced today by congeries of national agencies that for decades have been knitting all American Jews tightly together. The Jewish Telegraphic Agency, for instance, feeds news—the *same* news —to over a hundred American Jewish weeklies. The Synagogue Council of America—as persistent as it is as yet ineffective—attempts to express the common aims and needs of religious Jewry, Orthodox, Conservative, and Reform. The various rabbinical colleges—with their newly established branches in Los Angeles, now the second largest community in the United States—are nurseries of a common American Jewish culture, and their efforts are supplemented by the Jewish "secular" colleges that are now capturing the imagination of American Jewry. A Hebrew press persists, three

Yiddish dailies still appear in New York City, and major organizations like the American Jewish Committee, the American Jewish Congress, the Zionist groups, and the B'nai B'rith publish magazines that appeal to Jews of culture, academic background, and philosophic training. Even the New York general press—*The Times* and *The Post*—supplements the Jewish newspapers by giving full coverage to Jewish news both here and abroad. Common news makes for community of sentiment.

The cultural stirrings in American Jewish life are evident in organizations like the Jewish Publication Society; the American Jewish Historical Society, and the American Jewish Archives, both of which collect and disseminate American Jewish historical materials; the Yivo Institute for Jewish Research, rich in Yiddish lore; the B'nai B'rith, with its Hillel Foundations and educational programs; the National Jewish Welfare Board, which sponsors national book and music programs; and the American Association for Jewish Education, which is making a valiant effort to raise the level of Jewish elementary education throughout the country. There is a widespread youth movement, without equal in Jewish communities elsewhere in the world. Through the B'nai B'rith and the Jewish community centers, but primarily through the indefatigable efforts of the Jewish religious denominations, a knowledge of Jewish life and history, of the Hebrew language and the religious heritage, is being assiduously cultivated, especially in summer camps, which are exerting a spiritual influence on the Jewish youth of this country.

Welding American Jewry together is inevitably a slow and often painful process, for Jewish life abounds with negative factors which are almost as important as—if not more important than—positive factors in ensuring unity. Outer pressures are and always have been no less crucial than inner urges. In the 1940's, the various local Jewish community relations committees that had emerged out of the fight against Judeophobic prejudice joined together to represent American Jewry in its struggle with anti-Semitism, religious bigotry, and the reactionary forces intent on denying minority groups their constitutional rights to political, religious, and civil liberty. This new nation-wide self-defense group, the National Community Relations Advisory Council, was formed in 1944 by the Council of Jewish Federations and Welfare Funds, which realized, from its successes with a common Jewish welfare fund and a united Jewish appeal, that only through union could American Jewry cope with threats to its security. But it was not only the obvious need to reduce duplication of effort and wasteful expenditure that moved the Council of Jewish Federations and Welfare Funds to press for a single, common national defense agency. It was also the Council's consciousness of the fact that the American Jewish Conference, a new "Congress" called a year earlier, in 1943, could not and would not command the loyalty of American Jewry. The Jewish masses, at least, hoped that the American Jewish Conference, like the historic "Congress" of 1915–1920, would attempt to cement together all Jews in this land, give them an effective and permanent national leadership, and work for a larger measure of opportunity in Palestine. But, as the Council of Jewish Federations and Welfare Funds understood, the Conference could not but founder on the question of sovereignty for Palestinian Jewry and on the fears of some of the national agencies that their vested interests would suffer in a "national assembly" like the Conference.

Even the National Community Relations Advisory Council did not succeed in holding the various defense agencies together, and at the outset of the 1960's there were still three large bodies working separately toward the same goals and employing the same techniques of social action. Today the Council of Jewish Federations and Welfare Funds, its elite character notwithstanding, is the closest approach to a truly national agency uniting all Jews, for it embraces the federations, welfare funds, and community councils—whatever they call themselves—of practically every organized Jewish communal social agency in the United States. Ultimately the National Community Relations Advisory Council is again likely to include the American Jewish Committee and the Anti-Defamation League of B'nai B'rith and again to give direction to a united defense effort. This drive toward cooperation, merger, and union, which is part of the centripetal tendency in nearly every phase of American life, will in the future bring about a common effort on the part of all national Jewish agencies, not merely those dedicated to the fight against disabilities. Eventually most American Jewish nation-wide bodies will forge either a Congress of Community Councils or a Consultative Council of National Agencies in order to give intelligent guidance to the emerging national community, in the same way that the community council is attempting to coordinate the work of the local agencies.

TODAY AND TOMORROW

American Jewry and the Rise of a United World Jewry

The creation of an overall national American Jewish "Congress" or "Council," whether composed of local delegates, of national societies and agencies, or of notable individuals, would not only give needed leadership to American Jewry, but would also provide help and guidance to World Jewry. In this respect, the American Jew would be reflecting the aspirations of the United States government which, on a much larger scale, is attempting to influence all nations on all continents. The United States as a world power is reaching out everywhere to protect and further its international pre-eminence in commerce and politics. Hopeful that its politico-economic ideals of representative democracy in a modified capitalistic system will find acceptance among the old and new nations of the world, the American republic is determined to maintain the political hegemony which it has exercised for a generation since the fall of the British Empire.

Though American Jewry, in its relation to the Jews of the world, can have no political, industrial, or economic ambitions, it has resolved, since the Hitlerian destruction of European Jewry and the ensuing deterioration of Jewish life in Asian and African lands, to reach out and help its fellow-Jewries. This obligation is incumbent upon American Jewry by virtue of its inescapable tradition of assuming responsibility for its coreligionists, by virtue of the historic role of leadership thrust upon it, and by virtue, finally, of its sympathies and its wealth. In the last decade, consequently, the Zionists, the American Jewish Congress, the B'nai B'rith, and the American Jewish Committee have each created separate international committees and are working with their own overseas affiliates to salvage what they can of Old World life and to restore it to some semblance of its former stability. The economic arm of this effort at world rehabilitation for Jewry is the American Jewish Joint Distribution Committee; its prime agency in the new Republic of Israel is the Jewish Agency for Israel.

There are even individuals and groups working to integrate the efforts of American Jewish national agencies and the national agencies of all other Jews abroad into one world-wide organization dedicated to the religious and cultural survival of the Jewish people, and to the defense of their civic and political liberties in all lands. The sponsors of this proposed world-wide agency are particularly anxious to protect the State of Israel against the political enemies who have vowed its destruction. If such an overall Jewish international agency were ever to arise, it would probably be led by American Jews—at least as long as the United States continued to exercise hegemony in the world. The creation of such a world Jewish body, in which American Jewish personalities would play a leading part, becomes ever more feasible logistically in a generation soon to enjoy the use of supersonic passenger planes requiring but two and one-half hours to fly from New York to London.

The New Jew and the New Prospect

This generation is witnessing the rise and consolidation of the local community, the stirrings of an overall national advisory agency, and still vague but nonetheless promising *tentatives* to bring about an American-led international union of all Jews everywhere corresponding to the feeling of kinship that Jews bear one another. A new Jew is thus emerging here on American soil.

He is and will continue to be a completely acculturated American, indistinguishable in his physical appearance, language, and dress from his fellow-citizens. The typical young man—or woman —of the coming generation will be a college graduate, a white-collar worker, and, frequently, self-employed. Politically he will ally himself with the most liberal and democratic party, for he has found, even in this last half of the twentieth century, that eternal vigilance is still the price of liberty.

He will also have some conception of his historic relationship to the Jewish people of the past. It is a fact that even today the average Jewish religious school student, who has read one or two of the many textbooks on the subject, can boast a better and more systematic knowledge of Jewish origins and history than his parents and grandparents ever could—even though he is no Hebraist and is not likely to be one. And because he knows more, he is more sympathetic; with knowledge have come loyalty and devotion, not in parochial but in broad universal terms, to the ideals of his people and to the welfare of even the most distant of Jewries. This growing sense of kinship and the "style" of American life in general will bring the majority of Jews back into the synagogue. Some will come only to associate with their fellows. Others will seek education for their children and for themselves. Some will remain to pray, and in a world where science reaches out to embrace the infinite, they will reverently identify themselves once again with the spiritual ideals of their fathers.

What is actually in process in this generation, on the eve of a new century, is a blending of Americanism and Judaism. Like the historic mergers of Hellenism and Judaism, Arabic and Jewish culture, German methodology and Jewish lore, the new American Jewish synthesis will be expressed in the vernacular; like Philo's Greek commentaries, or Maimonides' Arabic *Guide,* or Zunz's German monographs, it will take a literary form. It will constitute, in effect, a fusion between the Jewish intellectual heritage and the various currents of thought prevalent in contemporary and future America. When, ultimately, books of enduring value begin to appear, works embodying the best in both cultures, books of such lasting worth that they will merit translation into other languages, including Hebrew, then we shall have witnessed the birth of another Golden Age in Jewish life. Barring a "historical accident," such a development is inevitable on this soil.

II

Demographic and Social Aspects

C. BEZALEL SHERMAN

INTRODUCTION

IT is extremely difficult to chart the development of the demographic and social aspects of American Jewry, because the Jewish community has long neglected to compile and study the necessary basic information. Even today we lag behind many smaller Jewish communities, including neighboring Canada, in this respect. In part, this may be explained by the fact that the census of the United States Government does not inquire into religious identification. However, the American-Jewish community, had it so desired, could have evolved its own methods of ascertaining the basic facts; but no such desire has been manifested in the past by the Jewish bodies that had the means to undertake investigations. This shortcoming, however, was not the reflection of a feeling that there was something in Jewish life that was better left unrevealed. Jewish leadership was simply inhibited by the mistaken notion that public study of the position of the Jews as a group would run counter to the American principles of political equality and separation of Church and State, and would, therefore, affect adversely their status within American society.

The Jewish leaders of previous generations could conceive of no utilitarian purpose that would be served by research into the demographic, economic and social aspects of the Jewish people; the Jews of America, they thought, were doing quite well, both as Americans and as Jews, without such investigations. Nor were objective factors lacking to retard the study of Jewish life in this country. Tidal waves of immigration and rapid socio-economic mobility kept the Jewish community in a state of flux. Conditions changed from day to day, and it would have been difficult for researchers to keep up with the shifting scene, even if funds for research and trained personnel had been plentiful. And neither the money nor the researchers were available.

The situation has been undergoing a gradual change for the better during the past quarter of a century. The Jewish population, still highly mobile, has begun to assume features of permanent consolidation. Among the Jewish community relations agencies, the awareness has been growing that accurate information about the composition, occupational distribution, and social structure of the Jewish population is essential for their proper functioning. Furthermore, small cadres of Jewish social scientists have appeared who realize that the Jewish community offers an excellent field for scholarly observation. Among these are a number of young rabbis who have utilized their communities as subjects for doctoral dissertations. A number of valuable monographs have thus been produced, and these constitute sources for the comprehensive history of American Jewry which is yet to be written.

It is, however, in the area of practical Jewish activities, centering in welfare campaigns, that the study of the Jewish community has made its greatest strides. Jewish fund-raising has assumed such proportions in the past three decades that it has become necessary for the direction of successful campaigns to marshal much more information than was formerly available about the anatomy of the local Jewish communities. Research has, therefore, become not just a matter of scholarly curiosity, but an imperative need. Responding to that need, Jewish federations, welfare funds, and community councils throughout the land have embarked upon the study of their constituencies, with the result that we now have over thirty surveys of local Jewish communities.

With respect to methodology, these surveys leave much to be desired. They are uneven qualitatively, and since they have been undertaken independently by the individual communities for a variety of reasons, they do not always offer a solid basis for comparison. Nevertheless, they provide the best information we have, and in the aggregate they do shed much light on contemporary Jewish life in this country.

The decennial census of the United States Government presents another source of important information, although it does not, as mentioned before, contain questions relating to religion (except for the informal survey carried out in 1957 to which frequent reference will be made in the following pages). In this connection, we must single out the work of Nathan Goldberg of Yeshiva University, whose painstaking probings into the census figures have unearthed data of immense importance. The questions relating to mother tongue, included in the United States census since 1910, but omitted in 1950, also yield much information, if related and interpreted properly. In all, we now have a body of material which gives a fairly close portrayal of actual conditions and permits us to make generalizations that have considerable factual support.

THE DEMOGRAPHIC SITUATION

Size and Distribution of Jewish Population

The number of Jews now living in the United States is estimated at about five-and-a-half million, representing about three percent of the total American population. This estimate is substantiated by the community studies, by the statistics abstracted from the United States Census, and by a number of surveys carried out by public institutions, including one conducted in New York City by the Health Insurance Plan (HIP) in 1952, and that of Morris C. Horowitz and Lawrence J. Kaplan carried out under the auspices of the Federation of Jewish Philanthropies of New York in 1958. We may regard the estimate of about five-and-a-half million as reasonably well grounded and make it the point of departure for our demographic considerations.

We also now have more authentic material on the distribution of the Jewish population in the United States, although accurate figures are still not available. The Jews are the most urbanized ethnic group in the country, which is what might be expected from a group that came here with a highly urbanized background. However, it should be remembered that the country as a whole is becoming increasingly and rapidly urbanized. In the early 1880's, when the massive East European immigration began, the cities and towns accounted for only 29.5 percent of the American population, with 70.5 percent living in rural areas (places with a population of less than 2,500 each). In 1960 the figures were almost the exact opposite: 30.1 and 69.9 percent, respectively.

In 1957, the United States Bureau of the Census conducted an informal survey designed to gain information on the religious distribution of the American people. The survey, which was based on a sample embracing 35,000 households in 330 areas, 1,100 or about three percent of them Jewish, found, among other things, that the urbanized areas of 250,000 or more inhabitants accounted for 87.4 percent of the Jews in the country, about 54 percent of the Roman Catholics, and about 25 percent of the white Protestants.[1] This finding is very close to that of the National Opinion Research Center, which reported on the basis of surveys it conducted in 1953 and 1955 that 84 percent of the Jews, 45 percent of the Roman Catholics, and 23 percent of the Protestants lived in the metropolitan areas of 1,000,000 population or more.[2]

The following table, based on the 1957 survey, shows a similar pattern in the regional distribution of the Jewish population:

TABLE I

ESTIMATES OF REGIONAL DISTRIBUTION OF PROTESTANTS, CATHOLICS AND JEWS IN PERCENTAGES

| Region | Protestants | | Roman Catholics | Jews |
	Total	White only		
Northeast	16.8	17.1	46.0	69.1
North Central	30.4	32.1	28.0	11.9
South	38.3	35.1	13.9	7.7
West	14.5	15.8	12.1	11.3
Total	100.0	100.1	100.0	100.0[3]

It will be noticed that the gap between the Jews and Roman Catholics is not nearly so wide as between the Jews and the Protestants, who, as the earliest settlers, spread over a wider area. This is especially true in the south and west, where metropolitan areas of 1,000,000 and over are still few.

Here we have a clear indication that Jewish geographic concentration follows a definite pattern: it is largest where *general* concentration is largest and where immigration accounts for most of the population growth. The Jews gravitate to the urban centers which also prove attractive to other groups. The nine cities accounting for 70 percent of the Jewish population in the United States—Boston, Chicago, Cleveland, Detroit, Los Angeles, New York, Philadelphia, Pittsburgh and San Francisco—are also the largest centers for concentration of other ethnic groups. The difference between Jews and non-Jews is in the *degree* of concentration rather than in the *trend toward* concentration. Compared with some other ethnic groups, the Jews are not far ahead in their rate of urbanization.

A glance at Table II will show that the nine states which accounted for 85 percent of the total number of Jews in the United States in 1960 also accounted for 70 percent of the persons listed in the government census as "Foreign White Stock," a category embracing immigrants, their native-born children, and Americans of mixed parentage, i.e., persons with one parent born outside the United States. This category resembles in considerable measure the three generations comprising the overwhelming majority of the Jewish population.

Since the mid-1920's, when immigration from abroad was reduced to a trickle, the shifting of the Jewish population has been largely the result of inner migrations; and here, too, we find the Jews moving with the general tide. They flock to the industrial and commercial centers which attract migrants of other faiths as well. The Jewish population has increased in cities where the general population has also grown by influx from other parts of the country; and it has declined or remained stationary in areas that have registered no general gain of population. By way of illustration, let us take a few cities from different regions.

Los Angeles has attracted an enormous number of migrants

TABLE II

PERCENTAGE OF AMERICAN JEWISH POPULATION AND OF THE
FOREIGN WHITE STOCK CATEGORY IN NINE STATES IN 1960[4]

State	% of Jewish Population	% of Foreign White Stock
California	9.6	11.3
Connecticut	1.8	2.0
Illinois	5.4	7.3
Massachusetts	4.1	6.1
Michigan	1.9	5.7
New Jersey	5.9	6.3
New York	45.8	19.0
Ohio	2.9	4.5
Pennsylvania	8.2	7.5
	85.6	69.7

from all over the country since World War II; proportionately, it has attracted an even larger number of Jews, overtaking Chicago and Philadelphia to become the second largest Jewish community in the United States. A population study made in 1951 placed the number of Jews there at 323,000; another study conducted in 1959 brought the estimate up to 391,000 for an increase of 21 percent in eight years. San Francisco, on the other hand, which has increased little from internal migration, saw the Jewish community rising from 41,000 in 1939 to 46,000 in 1959—an increase of 14 percent in two decades.

Florida has drawn a great number of migrants from the north in recent years, and we find the Jewish communities in that state growing apace. Miami–Miami Beach more than doubled their Jewish population between 1948 and 1960, overtaking, with their 80,000 Jews, such old communities as St. Louis, Newark, Baltimore and Pittsburgh, which have not drawn migration during the same period. Washington D.C., another center of growth from internal migration, tripled its Jewish population, reaching a total approximating that of Detroit. Detroit had registered considerable growth during and after World War I, but barely held its own numerically after World War II, when the city no longer attracted large numbers of white migrants from other parts of the country.[5] The same pattern obtains in the smaller communities. Cities like Passaic and Paterson, important textile centers in the past, with a proportion of Jews to the total population surpassed only in New York City, have hardly changed in a quarter of a century. Passaic had 10,900 Jews in 1937 and 12,000 in 1948; Paterson with 20,000 Jews in 1948 had 24,000 in 1960. On the other hand, cities like Houston and Dallas, boom towns in terms of recent internal migration, became significant Jewish communities during that same period; the estimates for 1960 are 17,000 and 18,500, respectively.[6]

New York City, inhabited by about 45 percent of the Jews of this country, remains the colossus of American Jewry. However, in line with the general decrease of its white population, the Jewish population has also declined. The decline is total, affecting the entire city, if we accept the figures based on the HIP estimates;[7] it is confined to the boroughs of Manhattan, the Bronx, and Brooklyn, and is more than offset by the increase of the Jewish population in Queens, according to the estimates based on the so-called Yom Kippur method which Morris C. Horowitz and Lawrence J. Kaplan employed in their latest survey[8] (see Table III).

TABLE III

ESTIMATES OF JEWISH POPULATION OF NEW YORK CITY

Borough	Yom Kippur Method		HIP Study	
	1950	1958	1950	1957
Manhattan	331,000	339,000	350,000	293,000
Bronx	519,000	493,000	530,000	432,000
Brooklyn	920,000	854,000	940,000	794,000
Queens	223,000	423,000	280,000	408,000
Staten Island	4,000	6,000	10,000	10,000
Total	1,997,000*	2,115,000**	2,110,000	1,937,000

Source: A. Chenkin, "Jewish Population in the United States, 1960," *American Jewish Year Book*, vol. 62, 1961, p. 54.
 * 1,996,000 in Chenkin's table
 ** 2,114,000 in Chenkin's table

Chenkin's latest estimate is a Jewish population of 1,836,000 in New York in 1960, with the boroughs of Manhattan, the Bronx, and Brooklyn showing further decline, and Queens increasing its Jewish population.[9] This situation is similar to that prevailing in other large cities. Cleveland is now said to have a Jewish suburban periphery without a large city center; and in Chicago the loss of Jewish population by emigration would have been considerable had not many thousands of Jews settled in what might be termed suburbs within the northwest limits of the city. The trend toward the suburbs, too, has been a general American phenomenon since World War II to which the Jews have conformed. They have *de*concentrate old districts of residence only to *re*concentrate in new areas. They thus continue to live in aggregations now covering wider areas.

Effects of Decline of Immigration

The immigration of Jews from other lands, which in the past was the most significant factor in the growth of the Jewish community, is now practically at an end, as is immigration generally. The average annual immigration of Jews during the years 1899–1914 was 92,850; between 1920 and 1959 it was reduced to 18,000 a year; and during the decade 1950–1959, the average dropped to a little over 8,400 a year.[10]

The nature of Jewish immigration has likewise changed. Jewish immigrants no longer enter the tailor shops; nor do they move into slum areas. They do not swell the ranks of the Yiddish-speaking sector. The many thousands of Jews who have arrived since the 1920's and declared Yiddish as their mother tongue have contributed very little to arrest the catastrophic decline of the Yiddish press, theater and book market. The new immigrants have sought to learn English quickly, and they have yet to make their mark in Jewish communal life.

As the period of mass immigration recedes, American Jewry grows in homogeneity. In the ten communities studied before World War II—Buffalo, Chicago, Cincinnati, Minneapolis, New London, Norwich, Passaic, Pittsburgh, San Francisco, Trenton—the native-born comprised about two-thirds of the Jewish population. The proportion has risen considerably since then, with a community rarely showing less than 70 percent native-born. In 1937–1938, the American-born element constituted 63 percent of the Jews of Passaic, Pittsburgh and Trenton; the percentage rose to 74 during the years 1949–1953. San Francisco with 56.2 percent native-born Jews in the mid-1930's had 71.5 percent in 1959. The proportion of American-born in Los Angeles increased from 68 percent in 1951 to 75 percent in 1959. In 1953, New Orleans had 81 percent native-born Jews, while Jacksonville, Washington D.C. and Charleston, W.Va. had 85 percent each. We may therefore safely assume that the American Jewish community is now at least three-quarters native-born.

There are indications that as the Jewish community becomes more native, its geographic stability increases. The community studies that include information on length of residence in the given areas indicate that the bulk of the Jewish population remains in the states of birth or early settlement.

The Jewish Family

Since the turn of the century, the Jewish family has been smaller than the average throughout the western world. Income and education have affected the size of the Jewish family, like that of the family in general, in inverse proportion: the higher the income and education, the lower the birth rate. There also appears to be a close correlation between orthodoxy in religion and the size of the Jewish family; that is, fundamentalist Jews tend to have more children than those of liberal religious inclinations.

The lower Jewish birth rate has long been recognized as a well-established fact. As early as 1889, John S. Billings, surveying 10,600 Jewish families, found that the birth rate among Jewish women, 15–49 years of age, was only 70 percent that of the general population.[11] The figures compiled by Nathan Goldberg from various sources showed that Jewish immigrant women had fewer children than Christian immigrant women;[12] and the evidence of the 1957 survey confirmed the fact that in recent years, too, the Jews have had fewer children than either the Roman Catholics or the Protestants.

To be sure, the birth rate among the Jews has risen since World War II, along with the general rise in the country; but it has not been as high as among non-Jews. Jewish women as a rule marry at a later age than non-Jewish women, and they complete their families at an earlier age. During the period 1943–1957, the fertility rate among Jews was 80.1 percent that of Roman Catholics and 83.1 percent that of Protestants.[13]

Among Jews of the blue-collar category, the birth rate has been essentially the same as that of the white-collar category, whereas in the non-Jewish community there has been a wide difference between the two categories, with the blue-collar groups showing a much higher fertility. Nathan Goldberg sees a definite relationship between Jewishness and a low birth rate. It is his view that the uncertainties and tensions of living in a Gentile world discourage Jews from raising large families. He also regards the high premium which Jews place on education as an inhibiting factor, because Jewish parents are unwilling to have more children than they can properly provide for, especially with respect to education. Be that as it may, there is no doubt that the Jewish family has for decades been consistently smaller than the non-Jewish.

A comparison between the Jewish and general populations of the cities studied showed the former with a higher proportion of children under five and persons over 65. However, children under 14 constituted only 22.2 percent of the Jewish population; they constitute 26.7 percent of the white Protestant population and 27.7 percent of the Roman Catholics.[14]

In assessing demographic factors, due attention should be paid to the attitudes of the people concerned. A study conducted in 1956 in the metropolitan areas of Chicago, Detroit, Los Angeles, New York, Philadelphia, Pittsburgh, and San Francisco–Oakland throws interesting light on the subject. A sample of 1,165 couples, 116 of them Jewish, all in their first marriage with their second child having been born about six months prior to the interview, were asked how many children they desired to have to complete their families. The answers produced the following results: Roman Catholics 3.6, Protestants 3, Jews 2.7.[15] Another study showed 80 percent of the Jewish respondents, 20–39 years of age, approving the use of contraceptives, as against 55 percent of the Protestants and 39 percent of the Roman Catholics of the same age range.[16]

If the present trend continues, there is every reason to expect the proportion of the Jews in the total population to decline. Indeed, it is questionable whether the Jewish community will be able to hold its own numerically, let alone expand in the future. "The lowest rates of fertility shown are for Jewish and Presbyterian women," writes Donald J. Bogue after analyzing the figures of the 1957 census. And he continues: "These groups are 20 to 25 percent below the general population for fertility and are scarcely reproducing themselves."[17] Significantly enough, these two groups are also among the first three groups in educational attainments in this country, as will be shown later.

The marital bond, traditionally strong among Jews, appears to have retained much of its force in the United States, for the rate of divorce has been considerably lower than in the general population. Table IV, compiled by Nathan Goldberg, compares the divorce and separation rate for the country as a whole, as evidenced in the United States census of 1950, with figures for the Jews gleaned from the Jewish population studies of New Orleans, New York City, Pittsburgh, and Washington D.C.

TABLE IV

DIVORCE AND SEPARATION RATE AMONG GENERAL AMERICAN POPULATION AND THE JEWS OF NEW YORK CITY, NEW ORLEANS, PITTSBURGH, AND WASHINGTON D.C.[18]

Age	Males		Females	
	Jewish	Non-Jewish White	Jewish	Non-Jewish White
25–34	1.8	2.3	2.1	4.5
35–44	0.3	4.1	3.2	6.8
45–54	0.3	5.0	5.2	6.1
55–64	1.2	4.2	4.0	4.3
65 over	1.2	3.5	2.0	1.7

Jews have a higher rate of divorce and separation only in the age range of 20–24, confirming that the most satisfactory marriages are generally those effected when the mates are older and more mature.

Health

Data on the health status of American Jews are so scant as to discourage any attempt at generalization. It is generally known that Jews have a high incidence of longevity and a low rate of mortality, especially among infants. A survey of several neighborhoods in New York City revealed that in 1932, Jews had an infant mortality rate of 40 per thousand, compared with 57 per thousand for the general population. In 1925, Jewish boys under five had a mortality rate of 16.4 per 1,000, while the general population had a death rate of 21.7 per 1,000.[19] This may in part explain the higher percentage of children under five in the Jewish population.

A comprehensive study made by David M. Liberson showed that in New York City the Jews had a death rate of 9.9 per 1,000 in 1953, while the non-Jewish death rate was 10.5 per 1,000. Comparing the age at death of the Jewish decedents with that of the non-Jewish white decedents, he concluded that "the average age at death of Jews in 1953 was . . . over 66.5 and about two years higher than that of persons of other groups." In 1931, 68 percent of the Jewish decedents were below the age of 65; in 1953 the percentage of such decedents was reduced to 40. The corresponding figures for white Catholics and Protestants were 72 and 46 respectively.[20] As for mental health, it is even more difficult to arrive at anything resembling a pattern regarding the relative position of the Jews *vis-à-vis* the country at large.

At the request of this author, Dr. Renate G. Armstrong, a psychologist at the Westchester Division of the New York Hospital* and an observer of the effects of religion on mental patients, prepared a summary of the available material on the prevalence of mental disorders among Jews. The summary included the recent Midtown Manhattan Study conducted by Leo Srole and his associates.[21] There seems to be general agreement among psychiatrists and psychologists that, while organic and functional psychoses are less widespread among Jews, the latter have a higher proportion of neuroses than is to be found in the country as a whole. Alcoholism, on the other hand, is almost non-existent among Jews. Their positive attitude toward psychiatric treatment, and the

* Now with VA Hospital, Northport, N.Y.

stronger family ties existing among them may explain why Jews tend to seek more out-patient care than non-Jews.

Religion, according to a number of social scientists, may have an effect on the cause and progress of emotional disturbance. Thus Armstrong, drawing upon her own experience with mental patients, posits the possibility that Jewishness, with its concomitant strains due to anti-Semitism and non-acceptance by the dominant groups—strains felt strongest by escapist and self-hating Jews—may be the original or main cause in many of the difficulties bringing on mental breakdown. This is an interesting but as yet unproved theory. On the basis of the available data, one can only conclude that the ethnic and religious aspects of American Jews are not the dominant agents in the incidence and types of mental disturbance among them. The degree of acculturation, of socio-economic status and of urbanization appears to have the greatest influence on the frequency of mental illness and emotional problems among all ethnic groups in the United States.

Intermarriage

The data on the extent of intermarriage among Jews has been greatly enriched by the 1957 survey. The evidence of that survey that the American Jews have an intermarriage rate of 7.2 percent confirms fully the estimates drawn from an analysis of the statistics produced by the Jewish population studies. For greater accuracy, we should place the rate at between seven and ten percent,* a rate at least six times as high as the 1.17 percent Julius Drachsler found among the Jews of New York City in the first decade of the present century.[22] This would still be the lowest rate among the Jews of the Western world.

However, the total figure of seven to ten percent obscures several important factors. When the situation is studied in depth, we discover that the rate of intermarriage is not evenly distributed throughout the country; that it is higher in some cities and lower in others, depending on the size of the local Jewish community

* This figure covers the total population, including large and smaller communities and first generation American Jews as well as those more acculturated. For the younger generation, the rate of intermarriage is considerably higher. See E. Rosenthal, "Studies of Jewish Intermarriage in the United States," *American Jewish Yearbook*, 1963, pp. 3–53 (editor).

and the degree of its acculturation. Thus we find that the Jews of Iowa had an intermarriage rate of 31 percent in 1953. In Charleston, West Virginia, 84 of 367 married couples among the Jewish population, or 22 percent, had non-Jewish spouses. In San Francisco the proportion of Jewish families with non-Jewish members increased from less than 10 percent in 1938 to 17 percent twenty years later. In Washington D.C., 11.3 percent of 27,000 Jewish households had either a gentile husband (7.8%) or a gentile wife (3.5%) in 1956. A survey conducted in New Orleans in 1938 showed that one in every seventeen Jewish families had a non-Jewish member. Another survey made fifteen years later found non-Jewish members in 10 percent of the Jewish households.[23]

The general figures on intermarriage likewise fail to reveal that the rate is higher among the native-born, college-or-university-trained Jewish youth—precisely the group to whom American Jewry must turn for leadership. Moreover, since the proportion of this group in the total Jewish population is constantly rising, it is not unreasonable to expect the rate of intermarriage to mount to a point of serious concern to those who are interested in the perpetuation of the Jewish community.

A counteracting factor, however, must be noted. This factor was observed by Julius Drachsler more than forty years ago and has been substantiated by a number of studies since; namely, that as a group achieves social and economic equilibrium, the inclination of its members to marry outside the circle tends to taper off. If this holds true for the Jewish group, then we should expect the growing stability of the Jewish community to serve as a brake on intermarriage. There is no question that but for this growing stability the number and proportion of intermarriages would by this time have been higher. The surge in congregational affiliation and the extended network of Jewish country clubs and recreational facilities, both the result of greater Jewish communal consolidation, have had the effect of narrowing the potential of intermarriage. Surely the conversion of Christian spouses to Judaism must in large measure be attributed to the strengthening of Jewish institutional life in this country. The number of such conversions is not known, but that it is not negligible is indicated by the fact that rarely does one find a synagogue without some members who were born non-Jewish. That the Jewish community loses more than it gains from intermarriage goes without saying.

SOCIAL ASPECTS

Acculturation

We now have sufficient demographic data to conclude that American Jewry constitutes a community that is growing more indigenous in relation to American society and more homogeneous in its internal composition and structure. Its social problems are those of a minority group that wishes to conform to the way of life shaped by the dominant groups without totally losing its own individuality. The American Jew thus lives in two cultures. One identifies him with the totality of the American community, and induces a separateness from the Jews of the rest of the world; the other draws him to the latter, creating needs and interests apart from his fellow citizens. He is thus within and outside the mainstream of American life at the same time. This situation, inherent in the very place he occupies in the fabric of American society, explains the ambivalence characterizing Jewish social development in this country. This ambivalence finds its clearest crystallization in the discrepancy between the class position which the American Jew should occupy in terms of his economic progress, and the status he enjoys in terms of social prestige. External discrimination and internal cohesiveness combine to deprive him of the social standing to which he is entitled by virtue of his economic position and the degree of his acculturation. The social consequences of this situation call for elucidation.

Fully integrated into the processes of American government, the Jews have also organically woven themselves into the fabric of American culture. Although more than 90 percent of them owe their presence here to immigration since the last quarter of the nineteenth century, they have achieved a level of education which makes them the peers of the descendants of the earliest settlers. Figures assembled since the beginning of the century demonstrate that the Jews have consistently achieved higher standards of education than the general population. From the 1953 study of New Orleans, we learn that 82.8 percent of the Jewish youth, 21–24 years of age, received a college education, as against 25.5 percent of the total white population of that city. According to the HIP survey, the Jews of New York City, in 1952, had a median attainment of 10.3 school years, compared with a median of 9.6 years for the non-Jewish white population. The survey made by the Jewish Community Council of Washington showed the Jews at a higher educational level than the general population, whose educational standards were also unusually high. For the country as a whole, we have the decennial surveys of the Vocational Service of B'nai B'rith, showing that while the Jews represented only three percent of the American population, they provided nine percent of the enrollment in the colleges and universities of the land. The same surveys showed that in the mid-1950's, 62 out of every 100 Jews of college age were enrolled in institutions of higher learning, while only 27 out of every 100 non-Jews were similarly situated.[24]

Even more instructive from the point of view of the social position of the Jews are the conclusions Donald J. Bogue has drawn from an analysis of United States census figures:

Two religious groups stand out above all others as well-educated; those with Jewish and those with Episcopalian religious preferences. A third group, the Presbyterian, had attained an educational level considerably above the average.[25]

The educational attainments of the heads of households in the major religious groups are shown in Table V:

TABLE V

EDUCATIONAL ATTAINMENT OF HOUSEHOLD HEADS AMONG
MAJOR AMERICAN RELIGIOUS GROUPS IN 1955

Group	High School (4 yrs.)	College 1–3 yrs.	College 4 or more yrs.
White Protestant	22.4	10.8	9.1
Roman Catholic	22.5	9.0	6.8
Jewish	28.5	10.8	21.8

Source: Donald J. Bogue, *The Population of the United States* (Glencoe, Illinois, 1959), p. 702.

The median of school years completed by the heads of households in 1955 was as follows: White Protestants 9.5, Roman

Catholics 9.4, Jewish 11.4.[26] The Jews have been very mobile, educationally even more than economically, but the mobility has not brought with it the social advancement other groups of equal, or even inferior, achievements have scored. As Donald Young has put it: "probably no other white minority group which has sufficient money and cultural polish to fit into the accepted standards of vacation life is absolutely barred from the ordinary summer resort."[27] This was written in 1932, and the situation has since changed for the better in many areas of societal relations. The rich Jew is no longer "absolutely barred" from the ordinary summer resort, but the distance between his financial means and "cultural polish" on the one hand, and his social status on the other, has basically remained the same. In Young's words, he "has to create his own social classes, although many individuals mingle freely with Gentiles on all levels."[28]

The sharp edge between social classes within the Jewish community is blunted, for inasmuch as even the wealthiest and oldest groups remain frozen at a certain point in the general social scale, the later arrivals have the opportunity to overtake them. In this sense one may speak of the Jewish population as constituting a mono-class community. Not that there are no social and economic distinctions or barriers among the various strata of the Jewish community, but in the social structure of American society the Jews figure as a single group regardless of their inner divisions. With the number of Jewish blue-collar workers steadily diminishing and the number of white-collar workers constantly rising, with the professional taking his place alongside the merchant, financier, and industrialist in Jewish and civic affairs, the growing middle class character of the Jewish community becomes a leveling process, affecting not only status but mental attitudes and spiritual values as well. To this leveling process social discrimination from without contributes mightily.

The patterns of acculturated middle class living among the third generation Jews residing in the newest sections of the larger cities differ sharply from the patterns that prevailed in the old immigrant ghettos, but the tendency toward concentration persists among them, as a result of internal desire and external avoidance. Nor has the trend toward the suburbs changed the situation radically. The lines between Jew and non-Jew in social contact are, if anything, more sharply drawn in suburbia than in the urban centers. To be sure, there is more civic and cultural cooperation in the suburbs, especially in school work and adult education, but in personal relations, it is the old story: Jews keep to their own and so do non-Jews. The closer geographic proximity in which Jews and non-Jews live in the suburbs is in itself a somewhat separating factor, from a social point of view, in that it furthers group organization on religious lines. This explains why interest in congregational affiliation and Jewish education is, as a rule, greater among young Jews in suburbia than in the cities, affecting profoundly the intra-group relations within organized Jewish religion.

The Congregational Structure: Social Aspects

A generation ago the majority of the American Jews were to be found outside the Synagogue; today the situation is reversed. It is estimated that some two-thirds of the Jewish population are now congregationally affiliated. The Synagogue thus offers a fruitful field for observing social changes in American Jewish life.

The Jews are much closer to the Protestants than to the Catholics in their congregational pattern. Numerous studies have revealed a clear-cut status design in the Protestant church structure, with the Episcopalians, Presbyterians and Unitarians on top of the pyramid and the Baptists, Methodists, Lutherans and other denominations at the base. The denominational lines, Vance Packard contends, have so hardened in recent years as to create a near-caste stratification in organized Protestantism. He quotes Liston Pope's warning: "unless a drastic transformation comes about in the churches, and especially in their idea of what a true Christian Church really is, they will probably continue for the most part to adapt to class divisions and even to intensify them—as they have done in the past."[29]

In Jewish religious life, the process has been reversed. Social prestige and financial position were the determining factors in the selection of a congregation in the past. The more assimilated families of the upper classes belonged to the Reform temples. A step below them were the middle class families who had achieved a considerable degree of acculturation but were no more than a generation removed from the East European mass-immigration period. They, as a rule, joined the Conservative synagogues. On the lowest social levels were the members of the Orthodox *shulen,* comprising immigrants or children of immigrants who lagged in their accommodation to American conditions. This gradation has left its impress and still exists, but it has been reduced to a minimum in the large cities and has lost practically all meaning in the suburbs. Prestige-wise, in physical appearance and in the qualifications of their spiritual leaders, there is today little to distinguish a Reform congregation from a Conservative, or a Conservative from a modern Orthodox one, in the new districts of Jewish residence. Membership in any one of them, if not a result of chance, is a matter of familial attachment; and the demands upon the members in terms of religious practice are no greater in one synagogue than in the other. Differentiation among them is more often based on institutional loyalties than on ideological views.

Three factors have combined to create this situation. It is, first of all, the result of a tremendous shift of the Jewish population, which has completely altered the congregational scene. Very few indeed are the surviving old synagogues that have not undergone the metamorphosis from Orthodox to Conservative or Reform. On their part, the Reform temples, the houses of worship of the German-Jewish elite in years gone by, have abandoned their aristocratic exclusiveness as a result of a mass-influx of members with East European background. In the second place, because of the leveling process described above, all Jewish religious groups have been drawing their constituents from more or less the same milieu in recent years, with no markedly higher status attaching to one congregation than the other in the eyes of the outside world. To the extent that the attitude of the gentile to the Jew is the same, whether he is identified with Reform, Conservatism or Orthodoxy, the various synagogues have no particular appeal to specific classes within the Jewish community itself.

Finally, Jewish congregations show the effects of adaptation to the religious patterns prevailing among the non-Jewish urbanized middle and upper classes. These, according to H. Richard Niebuhr, manifest a tendency to turn from a transcendental faith to a cultural religion, or as Mordecai M. Kaplan would have it, from a supernatural religion to religion as civilization. However regarded, what we see is in essence a process of secularizing religion. This process penetrates all denominations, including the fundamentalist sects of the various faiths. A committee of prominent Presbyterian churchmen, headed by Henry P. van Dusen, president of the Union Theological Seminary, complained in a recent report that the American people were becoming more religious and more secular at the same time. August B. Hollingshead, in a study of a community he called "Elmtown," found that "the church is a community facility like the school, the drug store, the city government and the bowling alley" to most of the youth.[30] Investigators of other communities have come up with similar findings.

The Synagogue has gone even further along the road to secularization than its Christian counterparts. The disparity between the number of members and the number of worshippers attending services, except for the High Holidays, is tremendous. The synagogues themselves are branching out into all sorts of secular activities, so much so that they come into conflict with other Jewish institutions and, at times, even with private business establishments. No wonder that in many a case it is difficult to pin down the exact religious identification even of some rabbis. At a national conference of Hillel directors held in 1959, Benjamin M. Kahn, national director of the B'nai B'rith Hillel Foundations on the college and university campuses, had this to say about the affiliations of the rabbis employed by or applying for positions in Hillel Foundations:

The majority do designate themselves as Orthodox, Reform or Conservative. Yet several men hyphenate their self-definition, using such syncretic terms as Orthodox-Conservative, Conservative-Reconstructionist, Liberal-Traditionalist, Conservative-Reform.[31]

In 1958, the Miami Chapter of the American Jewish Committee conducted a survey to determine the attitudes of the Jews of Dade County, Florida (which includes the Miami area), toward their Jewishness. The survey was based on a sample of 240 Jews, equally divided between men and women and ranging in age from 30 to 79. Of the sample, 48 percent were members of Conservative congregations, 28 percent belonged to Reform temples, and 14 percent to Orthodox synagogues. The 240 Jews were asked: "Regardless of your actual affiliation and membership, would you describe yourself as an Orthodox, Conservative or Reform Jew, or as none of these?" The report states that "about a quarter of each group described themselves as something other than the branch of Judaism of the congregation to which they belong."[32] In another survey conducted by a chapter of the same organization in a southern city fictitiously called "Southville" (which has a Jewish population of 3,000 families), only 4 percent of the 285 respondents were affiliated with the Conservative synagogue, compared with 53 percent affiliated with a Reform temple and 41 percent with an Orthodox synagogue. However, 40 percent of the Orthodox affiliates declared themselves to be Conservatives.[33]

While the Synagogue is undergoing a process of secularization, Jewish secularism is being "religionized." It would, therefore, be as fallacious to deny completely a religious motivation to the increase in congregational affiliation as it would be to interpret it exclusively in terms of religious revival.

All surveys and population studies that deal with the attitudes of the Jews toward their group existence in this country report that the Jews regard themselves as constituting primarily a religious community, whose ethnic character stems from the fact that the Jewish religion is the faith of the Jewish people exclusively. The philosophy of Classical Reform, still echoed by the American Council for Judaism, which denied the Jews of the world the status of a people, is rejected by the vast majority of American Jewry. The new Jewish generation accepts the concept of Jewish peoplehood, but it cannot comprehend a Jewishness that is completely divorced from the Jewish religion. Jews regard the Synagogue as the center of Jewish identification and see it as the institution in which American patterns of living and the search for Jewish self-expression converge.

Thus, the Jews, while increasingly adopting as their own the norms of behavior and scales of values of the dominant groups in American society, find in the Synagogue a preferred agency for Jewish "otherness." Membership in a synagogue is one of the forms of separateness which is desired from within and sanctioned from without. This may explain why American Jewry has made its most original contributions to the culture of the Jewish people in the field of religion. All Jewish religious groups have in recent years produced works which combine Jewish scholarship with secular learning, both acquired in America. The common ground on which they all meet despite their diverse philosophies is the recognition that the Jewish religion must respond to the needs of the contemporary Jew living in the freedom of American democracy.

The Individual and the Community

The third generation American Jew, unlike the spiritual leaders of all faiths, is not alarmed by the two-pronged process of religion going secular and secularism turning to religion. On the contrary, he is heartened by this process, in which he sees a reflection of his desire to turn his Jewishness into an aspect of his Americanism. He is becoming more and more conformist in his daily habits and in matters relating to his civic responsibilities, but he wants to retain his Jewish identification.

Earlier we alluded to the insignificant incidence of drunkenness among Jews and to the strong bonds that tie their families together as the foundation of Jewish group life. Both factors are still in evidence, but in a somewhat weakened state. Recent studies point to an increase in the consumption of intoxicating beverages among Jews and to a rise in the number of broken homes. Traditional Jewish rituals are not abandoned, but they are tailored to fit the rituals which the majority groups observe, and Jewish holidays are frequently celebrated as counterparts of non-Jewish festivals. Thus Hanukkah has become the Jewish Christmas and Bar Mitzvah the Jewish confirmation.

Summarizing all of the surveys recently conducted by chapters of the American Jewish Committee, Manheim Shapiro concludes:

The trend among American Jews seems to be to retain those customs and practices which are annual rather than daily or weekly, which are festive and which involve family gatherings and relationships.[34]

Even circumcision is veering away from its religious roots to become a hygienic operation, performed with growing frequency by doctors rather than *mohelim*. According to a study by Charles Weiss,[35] San Francisco with 50,000 Jews recently lost two of its three *mohelim*. Cities like Atlantic City, New Jersey, with 10,000

Jews, Jacksonville, Florida, with nearly 6,000 Jews, and Easton, Pennsylvania, with 1,700 Jews do not have a single *mohel*. Weiss cites cases of male infants circumcised a day or two after birth. The majority of the 36 boys born in San Francisco during the first five months of 1960 were circumcised at three to five days of age, and only 33 percent of the circumcisions were performed by a *mohel*. In only 22 percent of the cases was any kind of a religious ritual observed. Five percent of the respondents in the Miami survey said that they had Christmas trees in their homes, and 10 percent sent Christmas cards to their Jewish friends.[36] In the "Southville" survey, 22 percent of the respondents had Christmas trees in their homes, 49 percent exchanged family Christmas gifts, and 28 percent displayed in their homes the Christmas cards they received.[37]

Conformity, rooted in a desire to cut the distance to the non-Jewish community, penetrates all phases of Jewish life. This desire is enhanced as discrimination against Jews in employment and education is reduced. But conformity is not infrequently utilized to cement Jewish group cohesiveness, as the mounting membership lists of the synagogues demonstrate.

Sameness and Otherness

Sameness and otherness are intertwined in relation to American society as a whole; sameness and otherness are also intertwined in relation to world Jewry and to the state of Israel.

It is much too early for categorical assertions about the effects of the existence of the State of Israel on American Jews. The achievement of political independence by formerly subjugated peoples has invariably weakened ethnic ties among the descendants of these peoples in the United States; and such an effect, although different in form, may be discerned in limited circles of American Jewry. By overstressing the primary obligation of American Jews to strengthen Jewish life in this country, the leaders of these circles at times leave the impression that they regard Israel as of secondary importance in the creative survival of the Jewish people. It is a form of Jewish isolationism which is not unaffected by general American isolationism.

But infinitely greater thus far has been the ethnic impact of the emergence of Israel, as all surveys attest. Regarding the United States as their permanent home, over 90 percent of American Jewry feel that Israel has added a dimension of dignity to Jews the world over and has contributed toward their spiritual enrichment. In the studies of the American Jewish Committee, this feeling was also expressed in negative terms; i.e., the respondents stated that they would regard it as a personal tragedy were Israel to be destroyed.[38]

There are areas in which the American Jew would like to shed his separateness, but American society does not permit it; there are other areas in which American society presses him to give up his distinctiveness, but his membership in the Jewish people does not permit it. He has gone a long way in the effort to achieve an equilibrium between the two cultures in which he lives, but full and creative harmony between them is still beyond his reach.

The Jew feels secure, and with good reason, as our discussion of his attainments in acculturation has shown, and as the analysis of his economic progress given in another chapter demonstrates. To this should be added his success in the political field, where he has achieved a status of practical equality. He still has to contend with social inequality and with discrimination in various occupational and educational circles, but since these do not block his general progress, he is taking them in stride. He surmounts them by setting up his own social institutions and by entering the economic pursuits that are open to him, not infrequently as a pioneer. Nevertheless, he is socially and psychologically not at peace with himself. With all his accomplishments, he has not established a complete balance between the two parts of his personality. He is unsure of himself when reacting to situations which affect him as a Jew in the face of an unfavorable general public opinion. In such moments, he betrays the feeling that *as a Jew* he has to pay a higher price for the privilege of being an American than is expected of others, thus revealing traces of inner insecurity about his self-image as an American.

The aforementioned surveys of the American Jewish Committee shed considerable light on the significance many acculturated Jews attribute to the values of Judaism. "To them," states Henry T. Lipman, on the basis of a survey of White Plains Jewry, "the broad, general ethical and moral values which are basic to Judaism, but which by now have become part of the heritage of western civilization, rather than the unique practices and observances which traditionally distinguished Jew from Christian, are what is expressed as essential for being considered a good Jew."[39] It should, therefore, cause no surprise to find that three-quarters of the respondents in the surveys regard the gaining of respect of Christian neighbors as one of the primary essentials of being a good Jew, and to learn that this takes precedence over affiliation with a synagogue or marrying within the faith. This hardly expresses an appreciation of one's own intrinsic worth or a consuming devotion to the Jewish heritage.

Belief in God, loyalty to Jewish tradition, and activity in Jewish causes were also found to be subsidiary qualifications in a study made by Alfred Jospe (program director of the B'nai B'rith Hillel Foundations) of the attitudes of Jewish students in colleges and universities. However, as in the surveys of the American Jewish Committee, there is, as Jospe terms it, "an acceptance of the [Jewish] milieu"[40] on the part of the respondents. In other words, there is identification with the Jewish community, with little understanding of the values of this community.

We thus see that the contradiction between class and status has not been without psychological effect. Coupled with the demographic problems discussed in the first section, this effect makes it impossible to predict the course American Jewry will take in the future. One thing is certain: the disappearance of the Jews as a separate group is not in sight as long as prevailing social conditions in the United States and the present world situation of the Jewish people continue. They will carry on as a religio-ethnic community, within the limits which, despite the weaknesses and shortcomings, still allow for social and spiritual progress.

III

Economic Status

NATHAN REICH

INTRODUCTION

THE integration of newcomers into the economy of a receiving society depends largely on three factors: 1) the prevailing occupational trends, 2) the socio-economic potential of the newcomer, and 3) the degree of political and economic freedom accorded the newcomer in putting his abilities to the service of the economic needs of the country. A most favorable combination of all three factors resulted in the remarkably effective integration of the Jewish immigrant and his offspring into the American economy.

The waves of large-scale Jewish immigration into the United States—the German-Jewish influx during the period of 1820–80 and the much larger mass immigration of East European Jews following the 1880's—coincided with a vast economic expansion of this country. The opportunities offered by the rapid economic development beckoned to the millions of the Old World seeking a better life. While the country stood ready to absorb all kinds of labor, the accelerated development of commerce and industry, paralleled by an uninterrupted process of urbanization, offered special promise to the Jewish immigrant, who by tradition and historical experience was generously endowed with the kind of skills and aptitudes required by a growing commercial and industrial society. By and large, the Jew brought with him a tradition of urban living; a considerable reservoir of commercial and industrial experience; a marked degree of mental alertness and resourcefulness developed and tested in the hard school of survival in a hostile environment; a predisposition to rational and calculating thought processes; a highly developed sense of family responsibility and disciplined living; a capacity for hard and sustained effort; and a strong desire for economic security and advancement, whetted by deprivation and the insecurity of his life in the ghettos of the old country—all attributes which formed valuable vocational assets in the dynamics of a commercial and industrial society. And last but not least, the Jewish immigrant found himself in a highly favorable socio-political milieu. Although Jewish experience in the United States has not been wholly free from the restrictive effects of economic discrimination, the barriers of discrimination have been limited in scope and confined to selected areas of economic endeavor and have not significantly interfered with the successful integration of the American Jew into the economy of the country. It is perhaps the fortuitous but fortunate combination of the economic trends of the country, the socio-economic aptitudes of the Jew, and the climate of freedom which accounts for the remarkable economic career of the American Jew.

OCCUPATIONAL DISTRIBUTION

It has proven to be a successful career. Starting as a poor immigrant group a little more than a century ago, handicapped by a new language and the strangeness of a new environment, and not entirely spared the barriers of discrimination, American Jews have attained a high position in the economy of the country, as measured both by their place in the occupational structure and their share in the distribution of income. Indeed, the following tables (portraying the relative position of members of the major religious and denominational groups in the occupational and income hierarchy) show that the American Jews have come close to, and in some aspects have exceeded, the Episcopalians—the denominational group which has occupied the top rung of the socio-economic ladder.

However, before we proceed to a detailed analysis of the statistical material bearing on the subject, it is important to add a word of caution. As is generally known, the United States Census does not include a question on religious affiliation. The statistical material, therefore, is not derived from an actual census count but is based on representative sample studies conducted by reputable institutions and widely accepted as reflecting approximate economic trends.

An analysis of Table I reveals some extremely interesting information on the socio-economic structure of the members of the Jewish group as compared with that of the other major religious and denominational groups. A comparison of lines 1 and 2 discloses the marked deviations of the occupational composition of the Jewish group from that of the nation as a whole. The proportion of proprietors and managers among Jews is almost three times, and of sales workers a little more than three times, that of the national average. The percentage of professional, technical and clerical workers is substantially higher, but that of craftsmen, operatives and laborers is sharply below the national average.

Because the Protestants form the largest segment of the American population (over 65 percent), the occupational distribution of the Protestants as a whole comes close to that of the national average, as seen by comparing lines 1 and 3. But within the Protestant group there are marked variations among the various denominations. Thus lines 1, 4, and 5 show a marked degree of concentration in the higher rungs of the occupational ladder among the Episcopalians and Presbyterians, while line 7 indicates that the Baptists, largely because of the high proportion of Southerners and Negroes among them, are over-represented in the lower levels of the occupational structure. This occupational profile of members of the major religious denominations is, with minor differences, corroborated by a similar study which was conducted in 1957–58 by the Survey Research Center, University of Michigan.[1]

TABLE I

OCCUPATIONAL COMPOSITION OF HOUSEHOLD HEADS
BY RELIGIOUS AFFILIATION (IN %)

	Prof. Tech.*	Mgrs. Off. Prop.	Clerical Workers	Sales Workers	Crafts-men	Oper-atives	Service Workers	Laborers Non-farm	Farm Oper. or Mgrs.	Farm Laborers
1. Nation	10.0	12.6	6.4	4.8	19.4	20.3	7.6	6.1	10.8	2.0
2. Jews	17.6	36.0	9.6	15.0	7.2	12.0	—	1.3	1.3	—
3. Protestants (total)	9.5	11.8	6.3	4.5	19.2	19.7	7.4	7.0	12.9	1.6
a. Episcopalians	19.6	20.4	11.0	5.4	16.7	9.6	10.7	5.3	1.5	—
b. Presbyterians	15.3	16.1	8.2	10.6	16.7	15.8	4.8	3.6	8.0	1.2
c. Methodists	10.2	13.2	7.5	4.8	19.2	16.6	5.6	5.5	15.7	1.4
d. Baptists	6.0	7.6	4.1	3.0	18.2	25.3	10.0	10.0	13.3	2.4
e. Lutherans	8.0	15.4	5.4	4.4	24.0	15.1	6.2	5.2	15.6	.6
4. Roman Catholics	9.6	11.4	7.6	4.6	21.6	23.8	8.6	4.6	5.4	3.0
5. Other	17.7	15.2	2.2	3.0	18.0	16.9	14.4	6.8	4.6	1.2
6. No religion	11.7	13.0	0.8	4.2	20.2	19.6	10.8	3.0	13.0	3.7

Source: Special tabulations of survey data from the National Opinion Research Center, Jacob J. Feldman, senior study director. Adapted from Donald J. Bogue, *The Population of the United States* (Glencoe, Ill., 1959), p. 703.

* The term "Prop." also appears in this column heading in the Bogue volume. It has been deleted here upon advice of the Director of the National Opinion Research Center that its inclusion was an error.

INCOME STRUCTURE

The high concentration of Jews in the upper levels of the occupational distribution is reflected in the rather favorable position
of the Jews in the income pattern, as shown in Table II.

TABLE II

INCOME DISTRIBUTION OF HOUSEHOLD HEADS
BY RELIGIOUS AFFILIATION (IN %)

	less than $1,000	$1,000– 2,999	$3,000– 4,999	$5,000– 7,499	$7,500– 9,999	$10,000 and over
1. United States	7.3	23.8	35.1	21.3	7.0	5.6
2. Jews	1.3	13.5	23.4	31.5	11.4	18.9
3. Protestants	8.2	25.6	35.0	19.8	6.4	5.2
4. Roman Catholics	5.0	18.9	38.0	25.0	8.4	4.6

Source: Adapted from Bogue, *op. cit.*, p. 706.

A comparison of lines 1 and 2 discloses that while the percentages
of Jews in the income categories up to $5,000 are lower than those
for the nation as a whole, they are substantially higher in the income categories in excess of that amount. More specifically, the
national percentage of households receiving an income of less
than $1,000 was 7.3; among the Jews the percentage was only 1.3.
At the other extreme, in the income category of $10,000 or more,
the percentage for the nation was 5.6, but among Jews it reached
18.9 percent. Here again the income pattern among Protestants
in general approximates the national pattern, but there are sharp
differences among the various Protestant denominations, with the
Episcopalians and Presbyterians showing higher than average
proportions in the upper income groups, while the Baptists are
concentrated in the lower income categories. Except for the income category of $10,000 or more, the Roman Catholic group
also compares favorably with the national income pattern and
with the nation's Protestant population.

A study of the median incomes (the midpoint in the income
distribution above which and below which 50 percent of all
cases fall) in the various occupational categories also reveals the
favorable record of the Jewish group.

TABLE III

MEDIAN INCOMES OF HEADS OF HOUSEHOLDS BY OCCUPATION AND RELIGIOUS AFFILIATION (IN DOLLARS)

| | U.S. | Median Income by Occupation | | | | | | | | | |
		Prof. and Tech.	Mgrs. Off. Prop.	Clerical Workers	Sales Workers	Crafts-men	Oper-atives	Service Workers	Laborers Non-Farm	Farm-Oper. or Mgrs.	Farm Laborers
1. Total	4,094	5,876	5,936	4,032	4,882	4,462	3,762	2,610	2,852	2,838	1,779
2. Jews	5,954	7,333	6,924	4,775	4,300	5,000	3,792	—	—	—	—
3. Protes-tants	3,933	5,457	5,570	3,960	4,873	4,418	3,656	2,399	2,659	2,703	1,726
4. Roman Catholics	4,340	6,334	6,281	4,118	5,688	4,636	3,964	3,562	3,450	4,250	1,792

Source: Adapted from Bogue, *op. cit.*, p. 706.

A comparison of lines 1 and 2 reveals that, except for the category of sales workers, the median incomes of the Jewish groups are higher than the national average. The Roman Catholics on the whole show higher median incomes than the Protestants and the nation as a whole. But here again, the different Protestant denominations show sharply divergent income patterns, with the Episcopalians reaching median incomes higher than the incomes of Jews in some occupational categories and lower in other categories. The Baptists trail behind the median incomes of the nation and of all other religious groups.

The favorable income record of the Jewish group is confirmed by the above cited study of Bernard Lazrewitz,[2] as well as by a number of local studies. Thus a study of the Jewish community of Los Angeles disclosed that the median income for the Jewish group in 1959 was $6,465, while the urban average for the United States (in 1956) was $5,221. In 1951 the figures were $5,077 and $4,000, respectively.[3] Similarly, a study of the income pattern of New York City Jews established that in 1951 fully 12 percent of Jewish households had an income of more than $10,000, while the percentage among non-Jews was 5 percent; the percentage of Jewish households with an income of less than $4,000 was 29 percent, whereas that of the non-Jewish households was 49 percent.[4]

It should be noted that in all the studies the cut-off income amount was $10,000 or $15,000; we therefore have no information on what the pattern of distribution is in the income of categories in excess of these amounts. It is most likely that, in view of the high concentration of Episcopalians and Presbyterians in the upper echelons of business and corporate leadership, the relative position of Jews in income brackets in excess of $15,000 would compare less favorably with that of these two Protestant groups. It should also be noted that these cited figures pertain to distribution of income and not to the distribution of ownership of wealth in the country.

It is not surprising that there has been a close parallel between the relative levels of occupational and income stratification and the level of educational attainment. Thus while the national percentage of persons with four or more years of college education is 9.1, that among Jews is 21.8, topped only by the Episcopalians with a percentage of 23.8.[5]

There is little doubt that, as in the case of the Protestants, the overall Jewish figures conceal considerable occupational income and educational differentiation for the various religious sub-groups—Reform, Conservative and Orthodox Jews—as well as among Jews of the first, second and third generations. We do not have any information on these subjects. We do, however, have a breakdown of the occupational and income patterns of Jews in New York City and outside the metropolis. The Jews outside New York City have fared much better than New York City Jews. Thus, while among New York City Jews the percentage of business proprietors and managers is 23 percent, that of Jews outside New York City is 38 percent; the percentages of professionals are 17 percent and 21 percent, respectively. The percentages in the lower ranges of the occupational ladder are reversed: the percentages of clerical and sales workers are 18 and 15 percent, those of skilled workers 12 and 7 percent, and those of non-skilled workers 2 and 0 percent respectively.

The pattern of income distribution shows similar variations. New York City Jews have on the whole lower incomes than those outside of New York City. Thus the percentage of Jews earning less than $4,000 in New York City is 26 percent, while among non-New York City Jews it is only 12 percent; in the income category of more than $7,500, but less than $15,000, the respective percentages are 25 percent and 37 percent. The difference is even more striking in the top category of $15,000 or more, where the percentage of New York City Jews is 2 percent but that of non-New York City Jews is an impressive 17 percent. It is interesting to note that a similar differential pattern prevails between the Roman Catholics in New York City and those outside of New York City.[6] This differential pattern is explained as follows: "New York City Catholics and Jews have their relatively less desirable education, income and occupation distributions in large part because of in-migration of foreign born adults and out-migration of economically more successful adults who possess good education and are white collar workers."[7] In the case of Roman Catholics, the less favorable showing among the New

York City Catholics is without doubt due to the heavy influx of low-income Puerto Ricans into New York City.

DISTRIBUTION BY ECONOMIC SECTORS

While the preceding material gives us a fairly adequate occupational and income profile of American Jewry, we have no data of equal comprehensiveness and adequacy on the classification of American Jews by the major economic sectors such as trade, manufacturing, transportation, banking, and finance. Any generalization must, therefore, be based on local fragmentary studies made in different years and not strictly comparable.

Here again the pattern of New York City Jews differs from that characteristic of Jews outside of New York City. Thus, a study made in the late thirties claimed that in New York City a little over one fourth of the gainfully employed Jews derived their sustenance from trade, another fourth from industry, a little over 7 percent from professions, and the remainder scattered among construction, transportation, finance and other branches of economic activity.[8] But similar studies made in a series of other cities revealed that the proportion of Jews engaged in trade was over 50 percent (i.e., twice as high as that characteristic of New York City Jews), and that the proportion of professionals was substantially higher, while the percentage of Jews engaged in industrial pursuits was correspondingly lower. The study of Los Angeles Jewry mentioned earlier estimated that in 1959, 32.9 percent of the Jews were engaged in trade, 18.7 percent in manufacturing, 14.4 percent in the professions, 10.6 percent in personal services and 7.2 percent in construction.

It is clear that generalizations made on the basis of fragmentary studies compiled at different times must be accepted as rough estimates. It would not be wide of the mark, however, to conclude that of one hundred gainfully employed Jews, about 40 draw their sustenance from the commercial sector, about 20 from the manufacturing sector, 15–17 from professional work, and the remainder from personal services, transportation, construction trades and other occupations. Corresponding figures for the American economy as a whole in 1961 are 21 percent for the commercial and approximately 30 percent for the industrial sector.[9] A comparison of the two sets of figures confirms what has been obvious from general observation—that the trade group among Jews is proportionately about twice as large as it is among the total population, while the group attached to the industrial sector is about a third smaller among Jews than among the general population; the percentage of professionals is correspondingly higher.

PARTICIPATION IN ECONOMIC SECTORS

The preceding information dealt with the occupational and economic differentiation prevailing in the Jewish community. Another relevant facet of the economic position of the Jews is the extent of their participation within particular segments of the American economy. Unfortunately, information in this area is even less adequate than in the field of economic distribution.

The study of the economic characteristics of New York City Jews referred to earlier (see pp. 60–61) indicated that while Jews composed 27 percent of all gainfully employed persons, they constituted 41 percent of all New Yorkers engaged in trade; 39 percent of those engaged in the field of amusement; and 35 percent of those engaged in manufacturing industries; but only 14 percent of all construction workers; 13 percent of those in transportation; 12 percent of those engaged in finance; and 4 percent of the personnel in public utilities. A breakdown of the trade group, in which Jews formed 41 percent, revealed that Jews constituted 80 percent of the apparel group, 63 percent of the retail drug group, about 59 percent of the furniture and household group, 58 percent of the food group; but they formed only 21 percent of the drink dispensers and 12 percent of the automotive group. There was a similar pattern of concentration in the industrial sector. Thus, while the Jews formed 35 percent of all New Yorkers engaged in industry, they (including employers and employees) formed 82 percent of the fur industry, 56 percent of the clothing industry, 39 percent of the leather goods industry, but only 18 percent of the metal products industry and a mere 4 percent of the machine and machine shop industry.[10]

In 1936, the editors of *Fortune* magazine ventured a nation-wide estimate of Jewish participation in the American economy.[11] The conclusions of the *Fortune* editors confirmed what already had been known from general observation and fragmentary studies: Jews figured hardly at all in capital goods industries such as steel, coal, transportation equipment, electrical goods, oil, rubber and the manufacture of automobiles. But the Jews owned about 95 percent of ladies' wear factories, 85 percent of the men's garment shops, 95 percent of the fur industry, about 50 percent of the distilleries, and 30–40 percent of the boot and shoe industry. Jews owned three of the four leading cigar factories, controlled the tobacco buying business, but formed a small minority in the manufacturing of cigarettes. Jews played an important role in the moving picture industry. They loomed large in the independent retail trade, but were a decided minority in the chain-store field. The *Fortune* study dispelled some widely held exaggerated notions of the Jewish role in the financial institutions of the country. Jews played a decidedly minor role in commercial banking and constituted only 18 percent of the membership of the New York Stock Exchange.

These estimates were made over twenty-five years ago. The intervening years have undoubtedly seen considerable shifts in the relative Jewish participation in the American economy, but the lack of accurate data permits only very general observations. The years of prosperity which characterized World War II and the post-war period have undoubtedly witnessed a wider diversification of Jewish economic endeavor. Jews have been prominent in new fields of enterprise which were not pre-empted by old established interests, and in which a high level of technical knowledge and wide elbow room for individual initiative offered favorable opportunities to Jewish entrepreneurial talent.

Thus Jews have come to play fairly important roles in electronics, plastics, television, air-conditioning, frozen foods, and advertising. The growing demand for teachers, scientists, engineers and technicians has helped to break down the barriers of discrimination and opened new fields to ever-increasing numbers of Jews of the second and third generations. A study of a mid-western American city, probably typical of other cities outside a few metropolitan areas, has noted a remarkable shift, particularly among the third generation Jews, into the scientific, engineering and related professional occupations.[12] A study of the occupations of the parents of children attending the Yiddish schools, conducted by the Workmen's Circle (a fraternal order founded by Jewish workers and still regarded as an institution of the Jewish labor movement) has also noted a drastic shift into professions and other white-collar occupations. In 1954 almost one-half of the parents were skilled or unskilled workers and only 11 percent were professionals. Among the parents of 1962, about 30 percent were professionals, 30 percent were businessmen and only 25 percent were workers.[13]

Yet these shifts have not significantly affected the main pattern of Jewish participation in the American economy. Jews still tend to concentrate in merchandising, consumer goods' manufacturing, and professional and clerical work. They still hardly figure in the capital goods industries and are conspicuous by their absence in executive leadership of large corporate industry and business. Although, as indicated in the opening pages of this chapter, the Jewish occupational structure and income pattern has come close to that of the Episcopalians and has exceeded that of the other religious denominations, big business and corporate leadership has remained firmly in the hands of the Protestant group. Thus a study of the religious affiliation of business leadership in 1950 revealed that 30.3 percent of top executives were Episcopalians, although the latter constituted only 2.9 percent of the membership of religious bodies, while the Presbyterians, with 3.6 percent of membership, claimed 22.8 percent of top executive leadership. The Roman Catholics, with 32.9 percent of the membership of religious bodies, contributed only 8.9 percent of executive leadership. The Jewish percentage in the ranks of executive leadership was a modest 4.6 percent, concentrated primarily in merchandising, entertainment and mass communication media, thus confirming the essential pattern of Jewish participation in the American economy.[14]

GERMAN-JEWISH IMMIGRATION

The present economic status of American Jewry is the product of a long process of adjustment. The dry bones of statistics do

not reveal the harsh difficulties, the sweat and effort, the per-
severance and resourcefulness exhibited by the immigrant generation in planting their economic roots in the American soil. The
process of economic adjustment did not follow a uniform pattern.
It was different with each wave of immigration: the adjustment
of the German-Jewish immigrant differed sharply from that of the
later East European immigrant. Similarly, the economic integration of the smaller influx of Jewish immigrants during the Nazi
period of the thirties and during the post-World War II years
differed from that which characterized the earlier, East European
immigration. The differences were in part due to the character of
the immigration; but even more they were the result of the particular phase of economic development of the country in which the influx of immigrants occurred.

The mass immigration of German Jews during the period
1820–1880 coincided with the vast westward expansion of the
United States and the rapid formation of new towns and cities
which brought in its wake an increasing demand for traders to
serve the commercial needs of the new settlements. The German
Jews, most of whom had been traders in the old home country,
followed in the footsteps of the settlers. As a rule, they began as
peddlers; many soon became storekeepers, some department store
owners, and not a few laid the foundations for large and enduring
mercantile fortunes. Others stayed in the East seeking their
fortunes in commerce, finance and professional occupations.

A study made by John Billings in 1889 of 18,000 Jews gainfully
employed, four-fifths of whom hailed from German speaking
countries, found that 35 percent were retailers; 15 percent were
classified as bankers, brokers and wholesale merchants; 17 percent were accountants, bookkeepers, clerks and copyists; 12 percent were salesmen, commercial travellers and agents; 5 percent
were engaged in professions; 3 percent were tailors; and only 1
percent were peddlers.[15] Whatever reservations one may have as
to the representativeness of the study, there is no doubt that the
occupational structure of the German-Jewish immigration was
essentially of a middle-class character. The relatively small numbers of German Jewish immigrants, at a time of rapid economic
expansion in the United States, facilitated the absorption of the

immigrant and his offspring into commercial and other white-collar occupations congenial to the economic traditions and aspirations of the middle-class oriented Jewish immigrant.

Particularly noteworthy was the contribution of a small group of German Jews to the development of investment banking in the post-Civil War period. The rapidly expanding American economy looked to Europe for some of its capital requirements. At the same time, a small, closely knit group of prosperous German Jews tied by religious, cultural, and family bonds, and in close financial contact with their coreligionists in Germany, greatly facilitated the task of enlisting German capital in the development of the American economy. The economic historian Barry E. Supple ascribes the success of this group in the investment field to the following:

> . . . credit, confidence, security and reputation are so important that there has always been a need to formulate methods for testing credit and assuring confidence. Such a process is today institutionalized and given an impersonal, objective character, but in the formative years of the capital market there were few effective substitutes for personal acquaintanceship and private knowledge. It would, therefore, seem likely that the ethnic elite under consideration here would find its social structure eminently useful for its business activities.[16]

In assessing the role of the two main groups of investment bankers active in the capital market of the late nineteenth century, the New England and the German Jewish groups, Supple concludes that while it is difficult to evaluate their relative importance, ". . . it seems possible to say that the German Jewish group had a strategic role to play in the provision of capital from Germany for America's industrial development."[17] With the growing institutionalization of investment banking, the Jewish banks lost their strategic advantage and the Jewish role in investment banking receded into the background.

EAST EUROPEAN JEWISH IMMIGRATION

The process of economic integration of the second wave of Jewish immigration, that from East European countries, occurred under different circumstances and followed a different occupational pattern. The waves of immigration were more massive than the earlier immigration of German Jews. A substantial portion of East European Jews were craftsmen. The large cities, particularly New York City, were rapidly becoming centers for the manufacture of consumer goods and offered abundant employment opportunity to the semi-skilled and unskilled workers who formed the majority of Jewish immigrants.

A number of factors made the garment trades particularly attractive to the new Jewish immigrant: a) the concentration of industry in New York City, the port of arrival—a factor of importance in view of the severely limited resources of the immigrant; b) Jewish ownership in the industry which facilitated contact and job getting; c) the work, while exacting long hours and arduous effort, did not require the kind of hard physical strength necessary in heavy industry; d) the large proportion of immigrants who had had experience in tailoring and related skills in the old country; e) the skills required of the newcomer could be learned on the job within a relatively short time; f) a strong sense of kinship on the part of those already established in helping the newly arrived "landsman" to locate a job; and last but not least, g) the limited capital required in the garment and related trades which provided ample opportunity for graduating into self-employment and becoming an independent entrepreneur— a *balebos far zikh*. The latter was a particularly powerful motive in the aspirations of the Jewish immigrant.

A number of studies of the occupational structure of East European Jewish immigrants around the turn of the century document their concentration in manufacturing, particularly in the garment sector. A study of the occupations of "Russians" living in cities with a population of 250,000 and over, who are generally assumed to be identical with Russian Jews, revealed that three-fifths were employed in industry, over one-fifth in trade, 8 percent in domestic and personal services, 6.7 percent in clerical work, and 2.6 percent in professions. Of those employed in industry, by far the largest proportion were in the clothing industries. In the trade group, about one-half were proprietors of retail stores, and almost one-fifth were peddlers and hucksters. Among the professionals, about one-fifth were teachers, one-eighth physicians, and the remainder dentists, clergymen and lawyers.[18]

Another study, dealing with the occupational distribution of first and second generation immigrants from Russia, Austria (exclusive of Poland and Polish speaking areas) and Hungary residing in New York State in 1900 corroborated the findings mentioned above as applicable to the first generation immigrants, but already foreshadowed the transitory nature of the initial occupational adjustment. Among the first generation male immigrants from the three countries (i.e., Russia, Austria, and Hungary) 61.2, 59.5 and 60.2 percent were engaged in manufacturing and 27.5, 23.4 and 22.1 percent were in trade and transportation, respectively. For the second generation, however, the percentages were almost reversed: 32.6, 32.9 and 36.3 percent were in manufacturing and 57.8, 51.8 and 51.9 percent in trade and transportation. Somewhat similar shifts were registered by female workers.[19]

The shift from manufacturing into trade, clerical work and the professions, foreshadowed in 1900, continued apace. Local studies made in the twenties, thirties and forties,[20] while not strictly comparable as to scope and method, and reflecting local variations, all indicate a trend away from the factory bench to the trade counter, the office desk, and professional work. It is clear that, after a massive influx into industry in the period of mass immigration of the end of the nineteenth and the early years of the twentieth centuries, the occupational structure of American Jewry in the 1960's tends to approximate the characteristics of the 1880's before the mass immigration from Eastern Europe: high concentration in commerce, a decreasing participation in industry paralleled by a shift into professional and related services. The influx of German Jewish refugees during the thirties and of survivors of the holocaust of World War II in the forties did not change the occupational pattern of the Jewish community. Aided by the prosperity of the World War II and post-war periods, the newcomers were comfortably absorbed into the "conventional" Jewish occupations.

These broad conclusions are also corroborated by similar trends exhibited by Canadian Jewry, for which adequate census figures are available. The lower percentage of business, professional and clerical occupations and the higher percentage of industrial employment among Canadian Jews may be accounted for by the fact that Canadian Jewry, though substantially similar in ethnic background, is of more recent immigration origin than United States Jewry; it is the second and third generation Jews who move massively into white-collar occupations.[21]

The transitory nature of Jewish concentration in manufacturing should not obscure the great contribution of both Jewish entrepreneurs and the masses of workers to the development of consumers' goods industries, particularly in the garment trades. Apart from the purely economic aspects, the large-scale development of the garment trades was not without social impact on American society. The historian S. E. Morrison, in his *Oxford History of the United States,* pays tribute to the organizers and operators of the garment trades. In his words:

Human dignity owes much to the Hebrew organizers of the garment trades who wiped out class distinctions in dress. Jews may take credit for the fact that American women are the best dressed in the world and can do so on a slender purse.[22]

Of equal, if not greater, significance was the contribution of the Jewish industrial worker to the development of American trade unionism. The beginnings of Jewish trade unionism date back to the eighties of the last century, and some organizing effort continued through the opening years of the twentieth century. However, the firm establishment of the garment trade unions did not occur until 1909–1910, when two spectacular and superbly led mass strikes laid the foundation for the International Ladies' Garment Workers Union. This was followed a few years later by the Amalgamated Clothing Workers Union in the men's garment trades. Other smaller unions recruited primarily from the ranks of Jewish workers followed suit. It is estimated that by 1917 the United Hebrew Trades, the top federation of Jewish unions, numbered about 150,000 members.

Unlike the bulk of American unionism which professed a limited job-oriented approach to unionism—that is, limited to the task of improving wages and working conditions—Jewish unionism, as expressed by the articulate members and the union leaders, many of whom were imbued with a faith in socialism acquired in the revolutionary movement in Tsarist Russia, viewed the union as a vehicle to a just socialist order. The union was regarded not merely as an instrument for the increase of wages and the improvement of working conditions—important as these were—but also as a beacon to a new and better world. A strike was a "crusade," and the picket line was a rampart in the battle for human salvation.

Apart from their "socialist" faith, the Jewish immigrants had another reason for investing the union with more than usual significance. The Jewish immigrant found himself in a new world, torn from his traditional moorings. He was desperately in need of an anchorage. The Orthodox Jew transplanted his synagogue. Others tried to recreate some elements of the traditional environment in the *Landsmanschaft*. The Jewish "proletariat" sought and found a kind of security in the union. The union movement became to many a secularized version of that Messianic faith which had accompanied Jews throughout their history. The goal of unionism was salvation; the union hall with its lectures and concerts became the secular equivalent of the *Beth ha-Midrash*. Unionism was the blueprint for a better world.

In the course of time, under the sobering realities of American life, the goal of socialism receded into the background. The faith, the drive, the zeal and the resourcefulness, however, remained; but these qualities now became wedded to the tasks of trade unionism proper. The garment unions set out to improve and refine the traditional goals of American unionism. Within a relatively short time the ILGWU and the ACWU attained prominence and their activities attracted national attention. They widened the scope and refined the quality of the bargaining process. They pioneered in the development of sound methods in the administration of the terms of collective contracts, in the establishment of joint employer and union agencies in the adjustment of grievances, in the development of the now widely used institution of "Impartial Chairman"—that remarkable agency of a private judiciary for the settlement of disputes arising out of contested interpretations of the terms of the collective contract.

Jewish unions experimented with unemployment insurance long before public unemployment insurance was a plank in the platforms of political parties. They charted new paths in providing health services, union pension systems and many educational and recreational services. The garment unions were also among the pioneers in union-management cooperation in effecting improvements in efficiency and in translating the improvements into higher wages and better working conditions. It is significant that in his standard work, *Union Policies and Industrial Management* (Washington, D.C., 1941), the late Professor Sumner H. Slichter—perhaps the leading authority on the subject—selected four experiments in the growth of union-management cooperation in the United States: two of these pertained to the two garment unions. Finally, the garment unions pioneered successfully in the development of union-sponsored cooperative housing and union banking.

With the trade unions as a base, Jewish labor erected a comprehensive network of fraternal, political, cultural and educational institutions. It contributed mightily to the development of the Yiddish press, Yiddish literature and Yiddish schools. It extended aid to Jewish communities abroad and, after a hesitant start, contributed to the social and economic development of Palestine and Israel.

The record of Jewish unionism has not been free of the more seamy aspects of American unionism. It had sporadic encounters with the twin evils of gangsterism and racketeering, and for a time it had more than its share of communist penetration. Nor have Jewish unions escaped the vexing problems of bureaucratization, centralization of authority and many other problems which inhere in organizational bigness and are common to big government, big business and big unionism alike. These, however, do not diminish the significance of the record of achievements which is an eloquent testimony to the abilities and resourcefulness of the mass of newcomers, the remarkable organizing job of that group of dedicated and inspired leaders who presided over the birth and destiny of Jewish unionism and, notably, to the dynamic integrative quality of American civilization.

The exodus of Jewish workers from the factory has considerably thinned the ranks of Jewish membership. The Jews no longer form a majority of the rank and file. Italians, Negroes and Puerto Ricans have largely filled the places vacated by the Jewish members. The momentum of Jewish leadership still continues, but it is only a matter of time before the new ethnic complexion of the membership will be translated into a new leadership. Whatever the eventual complexion, the record and legacy of Jewish unionism will remain an indelible chapter both in the history of the American Jewish community and in the development of industrial and labor relations in the United States.

IS THE JEWISH OCCUPATIONAL STRUCTURE ABNORMAL?

No discussion of the economic status of American Jewry is complete without the ever-recurring question: is the economic structure abnormal? The heavy concentration of Jews in trade, the professions and other white-collar occupations, and their minimal participation in capital goods industries and in agriculture, has caused much concern. Only a few decades ago, lecture halls reverberated with the echoes of speeches bemoaning the "one-sided" occupational structure and predicting dire economic and social consequences unless Jews undertook a drastic occupational shift into agriculture and heavy goods industries and thus brought their occupational pattern into greater conformity with that of the average American. This concern was voiced by the intellectuals of the left, who, under the influence of Marxian doctrine, vested the industrial worker with special socio-ethnic significance and therefore deprecated the Jewish exodus from the workshop. Similar apprehension was expressed in Zionist circles, where, in recognition of the indispensability of a variegated occupational structure to the future Jewish homeland, they deplored the concentration in commerce and other white-collar occupations. Others were motivated by a vague feeling that some economic activities are more "socially" useful than others: that, for instance, agriculture is more productive than trade; that steel casting is more essential than the collection and supply of steel scrap; that coal digging is more useful than teeth-pulling, and ditch-digging more beneficial than office management. Finally, the whole argument was suffused with the feeling that the concentration of Jews in urban, economically more remunerative vocations, made for high "visibility" and acted as a contributing, if not causative factor, in feeding the fires of anti-Semitism.

Whatever the social and psychological motivation, these concerns have little economic relevance. In a highly interdependent economic society, *all* economic activities which are validated by the market—that is, supported by demand—are economically warranted and hence "useful." It is elementary economics that the functions involved in bringing an article from the factory gate to the doorstep of the consumer are as useful as the making of the article itself. It is also important to remember that the Jews are not the only group which exhibits an "abnormal" occupational structure. As indicated earlier, the occupational pattern of every denominational group has shown marked deviations from the "synthetic" national average. Occupational studies of the various *ethnic* groups in American society would also reveal "abnormalities" peculiar to each ethnic category. As the writer expressed it on an earlier occasion:

Every immigrant group brought with it certain traditions, skills and industrial arts peculiar to its home country. In arriving on American shores, the obvious tendency of the immigrant was to seek opportunities to utilize skills and experience acquired in the old home. For example, Norwegians turned to seafaring, and Welshmen to mining; Germans attained distinction in beer brewing; Italians became truck farmers and road construction workers; and Slav peasants filled the ranks of semi-skilled and unskilled workers, many of whom gradually filtered into agriculture. In like manner, when Jews arrived in the United States, they naturally gravitated toward occupations in which they were proficient. Most of the Jewish immigrants had resided in towns and cities, and the bulk of them were artisans, petty merchants, semi-professionals, or young people without any special training, but easily adaptable to any number of urban, industrial or commercial occupations. It was quite natural for the Warsaw tailor to become the dressmaker of lower Broadway, or for the Pinsk peddler to blossom forth as the storekeeper of New York, or for the talmudic scholar of Vilna to make his debut before the American bar.[23]

It is precisely the freedom with which the immigrants of variegated backgrounds were encouraged to fit their skills and vocational preferences to the requirements of the country that contributed so greatly to the spectacular rise of the United States to the position of industrial leadership in the twentieth century.

The dynamics of occupational integration of the Jewish group was especially favored by the fortunate circumstance that the social and vocational preferences of the Jewish immigrants and their descendants coincided with the general occupational dynamics of American and indeed of all modern societies. Students of the distribution of the labor force divide occupations into three broad categories: the primary industries producing agricultural and extractive products; the secondary or manufacturing industries which are engaged in the conversion of raw materials into finished goods; and the tertiary or servicing industries, such as commerce, transportation, the professions, personal services and public services. An examination of the decennial census figures reveals uninterrupted drastic decline of employment in the primary group; a rise in the proportion of those engaged in industry during the early phase of industrialization, with a gradual decrease in recent years due to displacement by automation; and a sharp rise in the proportion of gainfully employed in the service industries. Indeed, in the United States the number of persons engaged in services began in the late 1950's to exceed those employed in manufacturing industries.

In directing their economic efforts to commerce, the professions, and related white-collar occupations composing the tertiary or service industries, the Jews have simply responded to the basic occupational trends rooted in the economic realities of the modern world. Indeed, the drastic decline of agricultural employment from over 50 percent of all gainfully employed in 1870 to 8 percent in the 1960's, the gradual but constant displacement of industrial workers by automation, and the massive absolute and relative growth of employment in service industries, justifies the conclusion that the Jewish occupational structure, far from being "abnormal," actually foreshadows the occupational pattern of the future society.

IV

Inter-Group Relations

MILTON R. KONVITZ

IN the broad sweep of history, the relations of a dominant majority of people toward an exposed, weak minority group—or of the conqueror toward the defeated enemy—first took the form of total annihilation or of cannibalism; then the form of slavery or total subjection; then a milder yet still severe form of subjection into an inferior caste; then cooperation and equality.[1] Jewish historical development, however, does not always follow this progressively humanitarian course; e.g., in the biblical story, the Israelities in Egypt were first welcome guests, then they were subjected to slavery, and the last measure tried by the Egyptians before the Mosiac redemption was gradual genocide. In modern Germany, the Jewish position moved from caste to equality, and then a leap was made to the Nazi "final solution" of the "Jewish problem"; in the U.S.S.R., the Jewish community seems to be destined for religious and cultural, though not biological, destruction. Jewish history also records additional severe sanctions: compulsory assimilation (a form of religious and cultural, but not physical, cannibalism), and expulsion.

In the United States, Indians were first the victims of a policy of physical extermination; the remnant was subjected to slavery or caste system; then there was the policy of total separation, which still persists, moderated by measures that look to induced assimilation. The Negroes have gone through slavery, followed by ineffective inducements for their migration to Liberia, then a caste system, which only in our day has begun to give way to cooperation and equality.

ANTI-SEMITISM

Jews began to come to the shores of North America at least as early as 1654. They were oppressed, just as were Roman Catholics, Quakers, and other Christians who were not members of the established churches. By the time of the Revolution, there were perhaps two thousand Jews here, in a population of 2,500,000, and a significant number had probably been assimilated. Jews arrived from Germany after 1815 and especially following the failure of the liberal revolution in 1848; they reformed their religion and quickly became Americans of the Jewish faith. They were subject to some economic and social discrimination, but life for them was comfortably tolerable and promising. In 1880 there were about 250,000 Jews in the United States, and it was their experience, hope, and gratitude that were expressed by Emma Lazarus in the sonnet, written in 1886, that was placed inside the pedestal of the Statue of Liberty in October of that year.

By 1920 two million more Jews had come to the United States, most of them from Russia, Poland, and other East European countries. They differed from the earlier Jewish immigrants in speech, culture, and religious beliefs and practices, and because of their differences from the Jews and Christians who had preceded them, they tended to make their homes in large cities and cohesive settlements, where they would have their religious functionaries, be near their synagogues, be able to continue to speak their mother-tongue, establish newspapers and magazines in their own language, organize their *Landsmannschaften* (societies of compatriots) and their numerous social, welfare and mutual aid societies, and set up their religious and secular schools. Unlike the German Jews who had preceded them, these immigrants came not only with their religion, but with their own culture and styles of living. They did not want to become Americans of the Jewish faith; they wanted, surely, to become Americans, but they also wanted to remain Jews, which to them meant much more than merely to have their own places of worship.

They remained conspicuously Jewish, and thus became subject to two types of prejudice—that directed against foreigners generally, and anti-Semitism. While some employers or hotel operators were prejudiced against foreigners in general, many of them, while employing or even welcoming foreigners, rejected Jews. Thus Jews encountered the European anti-Semitism they had come here to escape.

The two revolutions in Russia in 1917 could not have made many Jews unhappy when they remembered the degradations, the sufferings, the miseries that they had undergone in the Russia of the Czars. They wanted to see their kinsmen, as well as all others in Russia, liberated from a despicable tyranny. But few of them were addicted to sweeping ideologies, such as anarchism or communism. Many Americans, however, partly responding to the anti-Semitic agitation stimulated by Russian *émigrés* who fled from the revolutions to Paris and New York, began to identify foreign ideologies with foreigners in general but particularly with foreign Jews—Jews in Russia, and American Jews, whom they continued to think of as foreigners. It was in this setting that Henry Ford in 1921 started to publish an anti-Semitic newspaper and to circularize the notorious *Protocols of the Elders of Zion.*

It was also in 1921 that Congress made a radical change in American immigration policy. Until then, almost any person in good physical and mental condition and of good moral character could enter the United States. In that year, that policy was abandoned. The Quota Act of 1921 limited the number of immigrants to be admitted annually to approximately 350,000. Each country was assigned a fixed quota. No overt national or religious distinctions were made in the law, but it was nonetheless discriminatory, for while it did not affect immigration from northern and western Europe, it effectively restricted immigration from southern and eastern Europe.[2] Congress did not consider this law sufficiently restrictive, so in 1924 it enacted a new statute, the substance of which was incorporated into the McCarran-Walter Act of 1952 and is still the law. The discussions and the debates centering around the adoption of the quota system and the "national origins" formula in 1924—it has been officially stated—

> leave little doubt that one of the motivating reasons behind the enactment of the law was the restriction of immigration from southern and eastern Europe in order to preserve a predominance of persons of northwestern European origin in the composition of our total population. The expressions of the proponents of the bill clearly indicate a belief in the necessity for the maintenance of a preponderance of strains of the early elements in our population if the fundamental institutions of the Nation were to be preserved and the superior position of the Nation maintained.[3]

The quota and national origins system incorporated into our immigration policy since the 1920's stands as testimony to the feelings of a majority of Americans that somehow certain peoples, including Jews, are not readily assimilable to American institutions and culture, and are perhaps even a weakening element in the nation. While these feelings do not always, or even often, exist on the level of consciousness, they may be assumed to be a latent force of anti-Semitism, against which American Jews, in both their personal and public relations, are on guard.

In the 1930's another group of foreign and domestic agents of anti-Semitism attempted, with a degree of success, to blame the Jews as the cause of all national and international problems. The Nazis, seeking to build up sympathy for themselves, their causes and criminal activities in Germany, Austria, and elsewhere in Europe, tried to get Americans to see the Jews as the basic cause of world unrest. The severe depression of the 1930's made this attempt easier than would otherwise have been the case. In 1932 there was only one anti-Semitic organization in the United States;[4] but in 1941 there were 121 openly anti-Semitic organizations.[5]

With the end of World War II and with the country enjoying economic prosperity, anti-Semitism slackened, and so by 1948 the number of anti-Semitic organizations had dropped to 45. Of these organizations, 27 collected and spent considerable sums of money, held well-attended meetings, distributed large quantities of anti-Semitic literature, and provided leadership and lines of propaganda for the anti-Semitic movement. In that year there were seven anti-Semitic newspapers and six magazines published by these organizations.[6]

A *Fortune* poll in 1946 found in a cross-section study of American adults that about 9 percent were anti-Semitic in the sense that they responded "the Jews" to one or both of the following questions: "Are there any organizations or groups of people in this country who you feel might be harmful to the future of the country unless they are curbed?" "Are there any groups of people you think are trying to get ahead at the expense of people like you?" A *Fortune* poll in 1947 listed the major religious groups and asked, "Do you think any of these groups are getting more economic power anywhere in the United States than is good for the country?" Over a third answered, "the Jews." Nearly a quarter gave the same answer to a similar question regarding political power.[7]

Interpreting such data, a study published in 1953 stated that they show that 10 percent of the American people "might be, under highly disorganized conditions, direct supporters of . . . [an anti-Semitic] movement; and perhaps half of the remainder would be sufficiently vulnerable to its appeal to give it some support or fail to resist it."[8] At the end of the 1950's and in the first years of the following decade there was relatively little *overt* anti-Semitism. Reviewing the situation in 1958, a reliable survey stated: "Today, anti-Semitism flows a quiet course, hidden, subtle and pervasive, just as harmful—and even harder to fight."[9] The survey pointed out that anti-Semitism had gone underground, because civil rights laws and educational campaigns had done their work by largely ending overt manifestations of anti-Semitism.

Yet two years later, we witnessed the "swastika epidemic." During the last week of 1959 and the first eight weeks of 1960, 643 incidents had occurred. Swastikas were smeared on synagogues, Jewish community centers, homes of Jews; anti-Semitic slogans appeared in schools and on store-fronts. Bricks were thrown through synagogue windows, there were bomb threats, some of which were carried out. In the investigations that followed, more than a score of neo-Nazi clubs of adolescents were uncovered in various parts of the country. A study of these incidents concluded that

[They were] intimately related to the level of anti-Jewish prejudice which exists in our present American culture. For let us remember that most of the incidents occurred in areas with large Jewish populations; that the swastika itself is an anti-Jewish symbol; and that Jewish buildings and institutions were singled out for the most violent desecrations . . . The desecration phenomena indicate that anti-Semitism is a more serious problem in the United States than is generally thought to be the case.[10]

Worse than the swastika epidemic was the epidemic of ultra-conservative or right-wing extremist organizations in the early 1960's, with about a thousand of them publishing propaganda. Although only few of them were anti-Semitic, the character of most of them made them suspect in Jewish quarters.[11] While many of their members are sincerely concerned with economic and social policies, and have no conscious feeling of religious or racial hatred, hate-mongers have infiltrated these organizations in their search for the appearance of respectability and in their eagerness to escape identification with the lunatic fringe. As a consequence, intended or otherwise, ultra-conservative groups tend to harbor anti-Semites, racists, and rabid nationalists.

Since very few Jews would subscribe to any of their policies or beliefs, and since the major Jewish organizations all stand for principles and policies that the right-wing extremists attack as "un-Christian" and "un-American," it is easy to see why the average American Jew suspects them as part of a hate movement that is latently dangerous to Jews, Judaism, and Jewish values and interests.

One ought not to be an alarmist; there is no cause for panic or despair. The United States, unlike European countries, has not subjected its Jewish citizens to the extremes of—to borrow a line from Wordsworth—"Tumult and peace, the darkness and the light." Nowhere have they enjoyed as much security, dignity, liberty, and equality. Yet we are aware that at the beginning we had the theocratic state in most of the American colonies; that the Protestant churches at one time had control of the public schools nearly everywhere; that there were at one time serious disabilities imposed upon Roman Catholics, Jews, Quakers, Unitarians, non-believers; that there have been bitter conflicts between Protestants and Roman Catholics, between the American-born and the new immigrants; that many Christians have never accepted the principle of separation of Church and State; that many, if not most Christians believe that this is, in some important senses, a Christian nation; that slavery could be brought to an end only by a civil war, and that white supremacy is still a dogma for millions of Americans; that nativism, isolationism, fundamentalism, and economic conservatism have millions of adherents; that Father Charles Edward Coughlin and Senator Joseph McCarthy at one time exercised a frightening measure of power over the opinions and liberties of Americans; that we have suffered from organizations like the Know-Nothings, the Ku Klux Klan, and the Christian Front; that almost every visitor who has written about America—from de Tocqueville to Denis Brogan—has seen conformism as a prominent feature of the American scene.

These and cognate facts of history affect the thoughts, feelings, and actions of American Jews and the programs of their leading organizations and communal agencies. American Jews are not preoccupied with defense; they go about their personal, religious, cultural, philanthropic, Zionist, educational, social, and political affairs with the conviction that here is their home, that America has provided them with more security and liberty than Jews have ever before known in the long history of the Diaspora, and that the basic values of a pluralistic, free and open society will prevail over the powers of ignorance, darkness, and bigotry. They meet the challenges and problems with optimism and faith, with loyalty to America as a reality and as an ideal, and support their national and communal agencies that do their work—which includes defense—with intelligence, self-respect, courage, and dignity.

The Jewish community in the United States does not stand alone when it defends the rights and liberties of American Jews. In fighting for these rights and liberties, it speaks for all Americans who value freedom and equality; so that vindication of the rights of Jews is, in fact, vindication of the ideals of the Declaration of Independence, the Constitution of the United States, and the Bill of Rights of each of the state constitutions. The Jewish community and its agencies thus have behind them the strength of principles, the power that comes from striving for ends that are universal, the interests which, as Emerson would say, "the divinities honor and promote—justice, love, freedom, knowledge, utility."

The efforts of the Jewish community have contributed substantially to giving the United States a solid civil rights base, such as does not exist anywhere else in the world. By 1963 there were enforceable fair employment practice laws in twenty states; ten states barred discrimination and segregation in private housing, fourteen barred such practices in public housing; twenty-eight states had statutes banning discrimination in public accommodations. There is an effective President's Committee on Equal Employment Opportunity to ban job discrimination in Federal Government employment and in private employment flowing from Government contracts. There is a Federal Civil Rights Commission, which has made reports that are models of political and moral courage.[12] These are cited only as selected symbolic instances of the implementation of the American ideal of equality by governmental action. The adoption of these and similar measures reflects the political strength won by religious and racial minorities; but it reflects, even more, the hold that American ideals have over the American people.

In the symbiotic relations between the Jewish minority and the rest of the nation, it is inevitable that problems should arise that will keep the groups in a state of tension. We can consider here only two such problems—the Sunday closing laws and compulsory school prayers. There are many other problems, but these two, considered in detail, will suffice to manifest the complexity, delicacy, gravity, and significance of the inter-group problems.

Within the framework of American constitutional government, many of the issues undergo translation from the language of life in the marketplace into the language of legal controversy, thus letting legislation or judicial adjudication settle the controversy; and the issues thereby get to be partially resolved, at least for the present, on a balancing of interests and values. All the issues in this area involve matters of policy and conflicts of values, which often cannot be estimated or even defined. It is a wholesome thing for all parties that such disputes can be mediated by agencies that try to be voices of reason and moderation. Awareness that the controversies will ultimately be resolved in such forums has a moderating effect on the feelings and on the demands. "Civilization involves subjection of force to reason," Roscoe Pound has said, "and the agency of this subjection is law."[13] While this is certainly true, it is well to keep in mind Justice Frankfurter's admonition.

Constant preoccupation with the constitutionality of legislation rather than with its wisdom tends to preoccupation of the American mind with a false value. The tendency of focussing attention on constitutionality is to make constitutionality synonymous with wisdom, to regard a law as all right if it is constitutional. Such an attitude is a great enemy of liberalism. . . . Reliance for the most precious interests of civilization, therefore, must be found outside of their vindication in courts of law. Only a persistent positive translation of the faith of a free society into the convictions and habits and actions of a community is the ultimate reliance against unabated temptations to fetter the human spirit.[14]

Jewish community leaders are aware of this, and so there is no neglect of educational, publication and other programs; but at the same time one should bear in mind that court litigation and efforts to achieve legislative goals have themselves educational values that are not to be underestimated, and that court decisions and legislative enactments make imponderable contributions to the translation of the faith of a people into community "convictions and habits and actions."

Sunday Closing Laws

In a case decided in 1902, Justice Holmes drily observed that the "Sunday laws, no doubt, would be sustained by a bench of judges, even if every one of them thought it superstitious to make any day holy."[15] Sixty years later the Supreme Court fulfilled this cynical prophecy.

Ten years after he had issued his Edict of Toleration in 311, the Emperor Constantine ordered that all "judges, city people and craftsmen shall rest on the venerable day of the Sun." He expressly exempted countrymen because of their dependence on the seasons.[16] From that day on, we may suppose, the Jews—and the

Christians who continued to observe the seventh day as the Sab-bath—had the problem of the Sunday closing laws.

In the United States such laws can easily be traced back to the "Lord's Day" laws of the colonies—their religious origin is clear and undeniable. Such laws, by failing to exempt Jews—and Seventh-Day Adventists and Seventh-Day Baptists, too—have cer-tainly weakened the Jewish Sabbath by making it difficult, if not impossible, for many Jews to observe the day in a religious spirit. For many years American Jews have asked for fair Sunday laws that would end the discrimination against them. In 1908 Louis Marshall called on the New York Legislature to adopt the follow-ing principle:

No person who observes the seventh day of the week as the Sabbath, and actually refrains from secular business and labor on that day, shall be liable to prosecution for carrying on secular business or perform-ing labor on Sunday, provided public worship is not thereby dis-turbed.[17]

This statement still serves as the position of American Jews, for whom the problem has become aggravated in the last few years by the injection of economic competition into what was mainly a religious issue.

The exodus to the suburbs following World War II and the rise of the highway discount houses and the shopping centers have made Sunday specially attractive for retail sales and shop-ping, and have brought the Sunday laws to the front pages of the newspapers. All this has had little to do with religious observance but a great deal with competition between the city merchants, who keep their shops closed on Sunday, and the roadside super-markets and cut-rate houses, which remain open for business seven days as well as six or seven nights a week. It was estimated that in 1962 discounters took in about $800,000,000 in Sunday sales. City merchants brought pressure on city and state officials to en-force dormant "blue laws" or to pass new and tougher legislation. Since 1959 the legislatures of Texas, Pennsylvania, New Jersey, North Carolina, Vermont, Virginia, South Carolina, Maine, Lou-isiana, Michigan, and Massachusetts have responded to these pressures, and vigorous campaigns have been conducted in other states. Participating in such campaigns for new or more stringent laws are some labor unions, retail businessmen, and church leaders, particularly those associated with the Lord's Day Alliance, leading Protestant defender of the Sunday laws, and the Roman Catholic Church, which historically was less concerned with Sunday observance (after attendance at Mass) than have been the churches that reflect a Puritan influence.

Now, obviously, the stakes in this contest are high; and besides the problem of unfair—or fair—competition between city and country merchants, and between conventional and unconventional methods of retailing, there are said to be other values at stake, such as an increase in highway traffic, possible affronts to religious sensibilities and traditional ways of life. In this tumult, who would pay much attention to the "still small voice" of religious conscience?

Since the state legislatures generally failed to respond to this voice, even when it was that of Louis Marshall, Jewish organizations defended in the courts the merchants who, keeping their places of business closed on the Jewish Sabbath, ventured to open them on Sunday; but generally the prosecution succeeded, even when the courts read the statutes as state enforcement of religious beliefs and observances.

In 1961 the United States Supreme Court had before it four cases, which it consolidated, as follows: (1) an attack on the new Pennsylvania law by a highway discount house; (2) a similar attack on the Maryland statute by the same discount house; (3) an attack on the Pennsylvania act by five Jewish merchants who kept their places of business closed on Saturday for religious reasons; and (4) an attack on the Massachusetts law by some *kosher* butchers of Springfield. The complexity of the issues and reasoning may be gauged from the fact that there were eight opinions in the cases, in about fifty thousand words.[18]

The laws were chiefly attacked as constituting an establishment of religion—Christianity—in violation of the First Amendment; as violations of the Equal Protection Clause of the Fourteenth Amendment, by reason of the arbitrary classifications that they make of the articles that may or may not be sold on Sundays; and, with respect to the Orthodox Jewish merchants, in that they prohibited the free exercise of religion, in violation of the First

Amendment. These lines of attack were taken in briefs filed by the major Jewish organizations, the General Conference of Seventh-Day Adventists, and the American Civil Liberties Union.

The Court upheld the constitutionality of the closing laws. In the two cases involving the discount house and its employees, the vote was 8 to 1, with Justice Douglas dissenting. In the other two cases—those involving the Orthodox Jewish storekeepers—the vote was 6 to 3, with Justices Douglas, Brennan, and Stewart dissenting. Chief Justice Warren wrote the majority opinion in each of the four cases. Justice Frankfurter wrote a long concurring opinion. One of the odd facts is that Justice Black, who generally takes an absolutist position in cases involving First Amendment freedoms, voted with the majority to uphold laws which three Associate Justices found to be infringements of religious liberty.

The majority held that, even though it was clear that originally the Sunday laws were intended to aid the Christian religion, "as presently written and administered, most of them, at least, are of a secular rather than a religious character." Their purpose is to provide a uniform day of rest. The fact that the day chosen by the legislature is a day that has special significance for the dominant Christian denominations "does not bar the State from achieving . . . [the law's] secular goals." The statutes do not, therefore, "establish" Sunday as a religious institution, but are, rather, an expression of the states' interest in the "health, safety, recreation and general well-being of our citizens."

As to the claims of the Jewish merchants, the majority observed that the statutes do not "make unlawful any [of their] religious practices," for they may close their shops in accordance with their religious beliefs. The six Justices recognized the economic burden involved in a compulsory two-day closing, but this is an indirect effect of a law that regulates a secular activity—this was not the purpose of the law. This indirect effect makes the practice of Orthodox Judaism more expensive, but is not, for this reason, a prohibition on the free exercise of religion.

Opponents of the laws showed that thirteen of the fifty states have no Sunday laws prohibiting work or sales; that thirty-one states restrict work or labor on Sunday, but twenty-one of these states grant exemptions to persons who observe another day as their Sabbath, as far as work or labor is concerned; that thirty-seven states restrict sales or commerce on Sunday, only few of which make provision for the seventh-day Sabbatarian. The contention was made that the secular ends of the Sunday laws in the thirty-seven states could be achieved even if they were to exempt the seventh-day observers.

The majority of the Court rejected this argument, saying, that while such an exemption may well be "the wiser solution to the problem," the Court's concern was not with the wisdom of the legislation but only with its constitutionality.

As to the point that the laws violated the Equal Protection Clause, the majority took the position that there were "valid reasons" for the variety of exemptions, exclusions and exceptions as to the articles covered by the laws, even though "in practice" the laws "result in some inequality."

In his dissenting opinion Justice Brennan said that the laws, as they affected the Jewish merchants in their two cases, were in fact a "clog upon the exercise of religion," and a "state-imposed burden on Orthodox Judaism," making that religion "economically disadvantageous"; and Justice Stewart added that these laws compel an Orthodox Jew "to choose between his religious faith and his economic survival. That is a cruel choice," one which no state may constitutionally demand. Justice Douglas shared this view that the laws violated the constitutional prohibition upon interference with the free exercise of religion, and argued that by them the states compelled minorities "to observe a second Sabbath, not their own" and thus preferred one religion over another, "contrary to the command of the Constitution." But he went further and said that the laws were also an establishment of religion by putting behind the practice of one religious group the sanction of the law. "No matter how much is written, no matter what is said," Justice Douglas wrote, "the parentage of these laws is the Fourth Commandment; and they serve and satisfy the religious dispositions of our Christian communities."

Perhaps the Jewish community was expecting too much, or the impossible; for a decision of the Court that Sunday closing laws are unconstitutional, as a violation of the prohibition on the establishment of religion, would probably have brought down on the

Court the wrath of the business, commercial, and industrial interests, of the labor unions, of churchmen—of almost everyone; for, rightly or wrongly, it would have been felt that an old and settled institution, rooted in religion and in folkways, and justifiable on welfare grounds, had been shaken, or even destroyed. A sense of revulsion—and even of panic—would have been felt, in some ways similar to what happened in the South in 1954 when the school desegregation decisions were announced.

The Sunday laws, then, are here to stay; and their validation as a civil institution ought to be seen by the Jewish community as a clear instance of the universal acceptance of an important part of the Torah—a part that has become one of the fixed habits of mankind, a habit that links all of mankind with Israel's heritage and spirit.[19]

But the plight of the seventh-day observers remains, and with respect to them the dissents of Justices Douglas, Brennan, and Stewart ought to carry weight in the state legislatures, where the statutes ought to be revised to allow such merchants to open their places of business on Sunday. In Kansas, Massachusetts, Missouri, New Jersey, New York,[20] North Dakota, Rhode Island, South Dakota, Texas, Washington, and probably in Connecticut and Maine, there is an exception that extends to labor but not to selling; in Indiana, Kentucky, Michigan, Nebraska, Ohio, Oklahoma, Virginia, and West Virginia the exception extends to selling.[21] But it is the states with the heaviest Jewish concentration where the exception in favor of selling does not exist, and the legislatures in these states should find instruction in the British statute, which permits Jewish traders to remain open until 2 P.M. on Sunday, provided that they are closed all day Saturday and from sundown on Friday. The act requires the shopkeeper to register, and to declare at the time of registration that he "conscientiously objects on religious grounds to carrying on trade or business on the Jewish Sabbath." False registration is a criminal offense.[22] We have the pattern of exemptions for religious scruples in Sec. 5(g) of the Selective Training and Service Act of 1940.

For the Jewish agencies, the decisions of the Supreme Court in the Sunday cases may perhaps have had the wholesome result of effectively separating the case of religious freedom and conscience from the case of those predatory business interests whose only concern is to be allowed to stay open seven days a week. The exigencies of constitutional litigation at times compel parties to assert a unity of interest that they really do not share.

Since often these days it is the Roman Catholic Church that assumes the position of defender of the Christian faith and institutions, a word about this Church's position on Sunday may be helpful as pointing up what the future may have in store.

Historically, the Church considered the Sabbath as part of the Jewish "ceremonial" law, and so the obligation to observe the Sabbath ceased with the abrogation of other Jewish rites and ceremonies at the death of Jesus. But while there was no binding biblical or natural law commandment about Sunday work, the Church held that there was a Christian tradition that made Sunday a day of worship and rest. Servile work was forbidden but liberal work was permitted, as well as common work where it was essential. The main required observance was attendance at Mass.[23]

It was the Puritans who, turning from tradition to the Bible, and not the Roman Catholics, instituted strict Sunday observance and punished desecration or profanation. But in our own day we see a tendency toward a reversal of roles. Perhaps as part of the ecumenical movement, Roman Catholics tend today to give a more prominent place to the Bible than was conceivable years ago; and perhaps it is in light of this fact that one should read the strong statements on Sunday observance in the encyclical letter, *Mater et Magistra*, issued by Pope John XXIII on May 15, 1961.

Since the decisions of the Supreme Court in 1961, several courts in New York have responded sympathetically to defendants who have shown that the closing laws are being misused—are being used, not to achieve humanitarian and social ends, but as a weapon in economic warfare among competitors. Perhaps these courts have been influenced by the dissenting opinions. Whatever may be the outcome in such cases in the future, they will contribute to the public awareness that the Sunday laws, as administered, are indefensible, and will help build up support for the efforts of the Jewish organizations to amend the laws in the interest of justice and equality.

THE REGENTS PRAYER CASE

Regarding the Sunday closing laws, it would not be difficult to find Jewish merchants who, keeping their shops open on Saturday, oppose moves to allow legislative exemption of competitors who close their shops for the Jewish Sabbath. Like their non-Jewish competitors, they think of business first. But this is not true of the Jewish organizations. Without exception, they stand firmly on the principle of religious liberty, and for justice and equality; and on the problem of the Sunday laws they continue to form a solid front for both attack and defense, and it is doubtful if the leadership or professional staffs of these organizations could be made to deviate from their principled position by the mercantile considerations of some of the members or supporters of their organizations.

But this is less true of the problems of religion in the public schools—released time, Bible-reading, the Lord's Prayer, Christmas celebrations, the use of school premises by religious groups, bus fares for parochial school pupils, government aid to education, and similar issues. The pros and cons of these questions agitate Jewish parents, rabbis, Jewish teachers in the public schools, Jewish merchants, local community relations agencies, and the national organizations; and while there is agreement on the principle of separation of Church and State, there is not always a consensus on whether or on how the principle applies to a set of facts; and even when there is agreement that the principle applies, there may be strong disagreement on whether principled action or temporizing might be the line to be followed. While the Sunday closing question may affect some merchants, and mainly their pocketbooks, public school questions affect thousands of children and their parents in their relations with other school children, their teachers, their neighbors; and thus an entire community can become agitated, and the aroused feelings may also affect the business interests. Thus, public school issues are considered potentially explosive, and the Jewish agencies deal with these issues with full awareness of the dangers involved. This awareness, however, does not paralyze them. They take calculated risks; but sometimes the public reaction, from both the Christian community and from a divided Jewish community, is more violent than could possibly have been foreseen. Fortunately, the problems are often local in character, affecting, e.g., Shaker Heights, Ohio, or Sierra Madre, California, or White Plains, New York, and in time matters get adjusted; but at times the experience is a traumatic one for the entire city or town, and one which leaves an aftermath of scars.

The Regents Prayer Case may be considered a more or less typical Church-State issue in the public schools, but written large as if it were the Platonic Form of such issues. An examination of the case in some detail will disclose—as did the discussion of the Sunday closing laws—the nature of Jewish inter-group relations and their consequences for American society as well as for the Jews themselves.

In 1951, at a time when McCarthyism was a powerful force and many persons tended to mix religion with politics in an effort to prove that they were anti-Communist, the New York State Board of Regents issued a "policy statement" that asserted that the American people have always been religious, and that a program of religious inspiration in the public schools will assure that the pupils will acquire "respect for lawful authority and obedience of law [and that] each of them will be properly prepared to follow the faith of his or her father, as he or she received the same at mother's knee or father's side and as such faith is expounded and strengthened by his or her religious leaders." The statement then said: "We believe that at the commencement of each school day the act of allegiance to the flag might well be joined with this act of reverence to God: 'Almighty God, we acknowledge our dependence upon Thee, and we beg Thy blessings upon us, our parents, our teachers and our country.' "

The prayer was only recommended to the local school boards in the state, and only a small minority of them acted to require the prayer in the local public schools. The school board of New Hyde Park was one of those that acted to accept the Regents' proposal; but the school board's order to the schools contained provisions to insure that no pupil need take part in or be present during the act of reverence. A group of parents of children in the public schools of New Hyde Park, assisted by the American Civil Liberties Union, brought suit in the state courts to declare the practice unconstitutional. In 1961 the New York Court of Appeals upheld the constitutionality of the practice, with Judges Dye and Fuld dissenting. The dissenters argued that the alleged "non-sectarian" character of the prayer did not save it from the charge that it was an establishment of religion. "The inculcation of religion is a matter for the family and the Church," the dissenting opinion said. "In sponsoring a religious program, the State enters a field which it has been thought best to leave to the Church alone."

The parents appealed to the United States Supreme Court where, by a vote of six to one, the judgment of the state court was reversed.[24] The Court held that the practice in New Hyde Park was a violation of the Establishment Clause of the First Amendment. "There can, of course," wrote Justice Black for the majority, "be no doubt that New York's program of daily classroom invocation of God's blessings as prescribed in the Regents' prayer is a religious activity. It is a solemn avowal of divine faith and supplication for the blessings of the Almighty." The Establishment Clause "must at least mean that in this country it is no part of the business of government to compose official prayers for any group of the American people to recite as part of a religious program carried on by the government."

Under the First Amendment, said the Court, government in this country is "without power to prescribe by law any particular form of prayer which is to be used as an official prayer in carrying on any program of governmentally-sponsored religious activity." The Court held that it made no difference that the prayer was "denominationally neutral" or that the recitation was voluntary; for the important fact is that the Establishment Clause was violated by the school board's order which established "an official religion."

The Court disavowed that its decision could be construed as in any way hostile toward religion or prayer. "It is," said Justice Black, "neither sacrilegious nor antireligious to say that each separate government in this country should stay out of the business of writing or sanctioning official prayers and leave that purely religious function to the people themselves and to those the people chose to look to for religious guidance."

The decision was important on the facts but perhaps even more for some of its implications: (1) The First Amendment bars not only governmental assistance to a denomination but also such assistance to religion in general. (2) It makes no difference whether the assistance is substantial or consists only of a "neutral" twenty-two-word prayer. (3) It makes no difference how "inoffensive" the religious act is, as long as it is intended by the officials as an act of religious reverence, devotion, or worship.

When the Regents first recommended the prayer to school boards, protests were made by the American Civil Liberties Union, the Synagogue Council of America, the New York Board of Rabbis, the American Jewish Congress, and the Citizens Union of New York. *The Christian Century,* leading Protestant weekly, opposed the prayer and said that it would likely "deteriorate quickly into an empty formality with little, if any, spiritual significance." Some conservative Protestant clergymen, notably Rev. Norman Vincent Peale, supported the action of the Regents.

The Roman Catholic Church historically had opposed any and all religious practices in the public schools, for the practices were Protestant in inspiration and character. Because Catholic children felt themselves to be discriminated against, and even persecuted, in the public schools, the Catholic Church was for a long time opposed to these schools. In more recent years, opposition has tended to become indifference; but now the Catholic Church shows a strong interest in public education. The change in attitude has been startling.

The public schools have moved from Calvinist sectarianism to a Protestant form of biblical non-denominationalism. Years ago this would not have been acceptable to Roman Catholics, but, as we have noted, Catholicism has moved toward a liberalization of its position respecting Bible-reading. This, strangely, has come about at a time when Protestants have begun to recognize the legitimate charge of the Roman Catholics that tax funds were used to support Protestant-oriented public schools, while they were being denied for the parochial schools, and Protestants—at least liberal Protestants—were willing to support a "secularization" of the public schools to meet the justice of the Catholic charge. But now the Catholic charge tends to concentrate on the claim that the public school is "secular" or "God-less," rather than that it is Protestant; and so the pressure to put Bible-reading, prayers, religious celebrations into the public schools is today strongly supported by Roman Catholics, as well as the conservative and fundamentalist elements in Protestantism, as a movement to put God into the schools. It is an interesting instance of the meeting of extremes.

Now, when the Regents announced their proposal, spokesmen for the Roman Catholic archdiocese of New York approved it. *The Tablet,* official organ of the Brooklyn diocese, became the strongest supporter of the prayer proposal.

When the Supreme Court announced its decision declaring the Regents prayer unconstitutional, a storm broke loose all over the nation. The Jewish organizations hailed the decision—briefs against the prayer had been filed with the Supreme Court by the American Jewish Committee, the Anti-Defamation League, the Synagogue Council, and the National Community Relations Advisory Council (on behalf of the American Jewish Congress, the Jewish Labor Committee, Jewish War Veterans and the sixty-one community relations organizations).

The Protestants, as was expected, were divided. The editor of *The Christian Century,* joined by a group of distinguished Protestant theologians, hailed the decision as one that "protects the integrity of the religious conscience and the proper function of religious and governmental institutions." Much louder, however, were the voices of Protestants who attacked the Court and the decision. James A. Pike, Protestant Episcopal Bishop of California, cried out that the Court had "deconsecrated the nation." The evangelist Billy Graham thundered: "God pity our country when we can no longer appeal to God for help." Reinhold Niebuhr, generally in the liberal corner, commented that the Constitution had not intended "a consistently secular education."[25]

Attacks on the decision came from prominent laymen. Former President Herbert Hoover called for an amendment to the Constitution which would establish the right to religious devotion in all government agencies—national, state or local. Former President Dwight D. Eisenhower expressed himself against the decision, saying: "I always thought that this nation was essentially a religious one." The General Federation of Women's Clubs adopted a resolution supporting a constitutional amendment.

Southern politicians exploited the occasion to vilify the Supreme Court. A southern congressman said: "They put the Negroes in the schools and now they've driven God out." A southern senator asked: "Can it be that we, too, are ready to embrace the foul concept of atheism? . . . Somebody is tampering with America's soul. I leave it to you who that somebody is." The Senate Judiciary Committee conducted hearings on proposals to amend the Constitution, and a substantial number of southern senators used the hearings as a forum from which to whip the Supreme Court; but some northern members of Congress joined in the attacks.[26] At the Governors' Conference, Governor Nelson Rockefeller was the only one who refused to vote for a resolution attacking the decision and calling for a constitutional amendment to overrule it.

The most violent attacks, however, came from Roman Catholics, led by Cardinal Spellman of New York, who stated that he was "shocked and frightened" and that the decision "strikes at the very heart of the Godly tradition in which America's children have for so long been raised." If the Regents prayer, he said, can be interpreted as violating the separation of Church and State, "then I, too, can only pray: 'God save the United States,' for America has surely traveled far from the ideals of her founding fathers when the prayerful mention of God's holy name in a public school breaks the law of this blessed land."[27]

Indicative of the change in the position of Roman Catholics was the view expressed by *The Pilot,* official paper of the Roman Catholic archdiocese of Boston:

We hear a good deal of talk about the rights of minorities in a democratic society—and this is as it should be. But we have come to the point where we must give some attention to the rights of the majorities as well and very few are prepared to raise their voices in this cause. As in the present situation concerning prayer in school, the long-standing traditions of the Republic are under continual assault.[28]

Cardinal McIntyre of Los Angeles called the decision "scandalizing to one of American blood and principles," and Bishop Fulton J. Sheen made this observation: "Our schools are now officially put on the same level as the Communist schools. In neither may one pray. . . ."[29]

Two days after the Court had decided the case, President Kennedy tried to introduce a word of reason and moderation. The Supreme Court, he said, has made its judgment, and a good many people obviously will disagree with it. Others will agree with it. "But I think it is important for us if we are going to maintain our constitutional principle that we support the Supreme Court decisions even when we may not agree with them. . . . I would hope that [the people] will support the Constitution and the responsibility of the Supreme Court in interpreting it, which is theirs, and given to them by the Constitution."[30]

But two months later, when it may have been assumed that the dust had settled, the influential Jesuit weekly magazine, *America,* released to the press its leading editorial scheduled for the issue of September 1, 1962, entitled "To Our Jewish Friends." The editorial began with the following apprehensive assertion:

Since June 25, date of the Supreme Court's decision on the Regents' prayer case, there have been disturbing hints of heightened anti-Semitic feeling. Responsible Jewish organizations were quick to sense this development. So were equally responsible Christian leaders, who share the concern of their Jewish brethren that this hateful thing should not arise to plague us both. In discussions together, Christians and Jews agree that all necessary steps should be taken to prevent an outbreak of anti-Semitism.

The editorial went on to say that anti-Semitic feelings have spread because Jews were among those who had petitioned the Court to bar the Regents prayer and because Jewish groups have been trying to promote a "climate of opinion" that will make it easy for the Court to continue to make decisions supporting an "absolutist" view of the separation of Church and State. The editorial singled out for special blame the American Jewish Congress and its counsel, Leo Pfeffer, and two Reform organizations, the Union of American Hebrew Congregations and the Central Conference of American Rabbis. These Jewish organizations, the editorial stated, are trying to stop legislation providing grants or loans to church-related colleges and universities, to get Congress to provide federal aid to public but not to parochial schools, and to have the Court declare the recitation of the Lord's Prayer and the reading of passages from the Bible in public schools unconstitutional. In the light of these facts, "We wonder, therefore," said the editorial,

whether it is not time for provident leaders of American Judaism to ask their more militant colleagues whether what is gained through the courts by such victories is worth the breakdown of community relations which will inevitably follow them. What will have been accomplished if our Jewish friends win all the legal immunities they seek, but thereby paint [sic] themselves into a corner of social and cultural alienation?

The time has come for these fellow citizens of ours to decide among themselves precisely what they conceive to be the final objective of the Jewish community in the United States—in a word, what bargain they are willing to strike as one of the minorities in a pluralistic society. When court victories produce only a harvest of fear and distrust, will it all have been worthwhile?

The American Jewish Congress responded at once in a statement by its president; and the chairman of the National Community Relations Advisory Council said, "Surely the editors of *America* do not want Jewish groups to stop asserting their beliefs in basic principles for reasons of 'security' or as a 'bargain purchase.' "[31]

The American Jewish Committee released a statement which *America* published in its issue of September 8, 1962, and which was widely noted in the American press. The statement asserted that *America*'s approach to the question of religious prejudice was disconcerting. If *America* was interested in combatting such prejudice, the statement pointed out, then its warning should not have been addressed to Jews but to its own Catholic readers. It reminded the magazine of the Catholic campaigns against reading the King James Version of the Bible in public schools, and its attack on attempts to outlaw or limit parochial schools. But now the magazine, forgetting history, took the tone of "an aggrieved majority admonishing an imprudent minority. . . ."

In the following week's issue *America* denied that it had intended to raise the spectre of anti-Semitism, but maintained its previous position on the entire controversy.[32]

An editorial in *The Commonweal*, liberal and lay Catholic weekly, joined the Jewish forces and said that if there is any real danger of anti-Semitism among Catholics, "then it is Catholics who ought to be warned. Indeed, 'warned' is too mild a word: they ought to be told as sharply as possible of the sin of any form of anti-Semitism." It is the function of our courts, it added, to interpret the Constitution, and "our whole system would become meaningless if the various minority groups were made to fear any resort to the courts to judge their claims. . . . If the result of the prayer decision is to break down community relations, the fault of this breakdown will lie with those Americans who single out particular groups to blame for the decision."[33] A few weeks later, this magazine issued a special sixteen-page edition devoted entirely to "The Jew in American Society," in which the managing editor, in "A Word to Catholics," asserted that "the Jew has to be perfectly free to argue for this or that constitutional or political position to his heart's content, whether we agree or not. . . . It is their right to argue for their convictions, and I can see no justification for suggesting that the Jews will thereby 'paint themselves into a corner of social and cultural alienation,' as *America* thought might be the case."[34]

The cardinals and their official organs were, however, silent— except for *The Pilot*, official organ of the see of Cardinal Cushing in Boston, which came out in support of *America* and its stand, and called on "other Jewish voices" to be raised "to make it plain that many Jews, like many Protestants and Catholics, are anxious about the increasing secularization of the American way and are seeking to find ways to reinforce the influence of religion in private and public life."[35]

An editorial in *The Christian Century* asked in its caption: "Is *America* Trying to Bully the Jews?" It called *America*'s stand a "thinly-veiled threat to the Jewish community of this country."[36] But few Protestant leaders felt the call to speak out for the Jewish side in the controversy.

CONCLUSION

In retrospect, the *America* episode disclosed a pattern in intergroup relations that is likely to have profound influence on the Jewish community. It may well be that, with respect to religious practices in the public schools, the Jews may find themselves standing alone on the principle of strict separation of Church and State, except for some help from Unitarians, humanists, and some liberal Protestants. The Roman Catholics—having in mind as their chief end government funds for their parochial schools—may continue to act militantly, as if engaged in a "crusade," to deny the separation principle in its applications to the public schools. The Protestants, not having their own parochial schools,[37] may, mainly by their silence, aid and abet the Roman Catholics. Some Orthodox Jewish groups, also seeking government assistance for their all-day schools,[38] will tend by their actions to split the Jewish organizational front. In June 1962 Young Israel withdrew its support from the American Jewish Congress on the Church-State issue, and Orthodox rabbis and lay leaders have openly attacked the decision in the Regents Prayer Case. Court decisions against religious practices in the public schools may be flagrantly violated or quietly circumvented. Jewish sensitivities will be aroused but there may be few open and rational outlets for them. Grievances may multiply and intensify; and the Jewish organizations may find it progressively more difficult to act *for* the Jewish community— more often than in the past, their actions may be *within* the Jewish community, to strengthen morale, to bring understanding of objective facts and circumstances, to maintain Jewish dignity and honor, to intensify joy, and to mitigate sadness.

The situation will be somewhat different on the issue of public funds for parochial schools; for on this question there is a common front of the leading Jewish organizations and the leading Protestant church groups. Typical of the latter is the policy statement of the National Council of the Churches of Christ in the United States, adopted by the General Board in 1961, in which the Council reaffirmed its support of the public school system, and stated its opposition to grants from federal, state or local tax funds for non-public elementary and secondary schools, directly or indirectly (through "scholarships," "tax credits," "tax forgiveness" or similar devices).

In the day-to-day encounters between Jews and non-Jews, there will be no dearth of inter-group problems—e.g., what to do about a proposed telecast of *The Merchant of Venice* in Central Park;

or a public announcement of an application by George Rockwell
and his American Nazi Party for a permit to hold an open meeting
at Union Square; or the menace of the special breed of anti-
Semitism fostered by the Black Muslims, with an estimated membership of about 250,000; or fraternity or social bias; or
anti-Semitic and anti-Israel activities by visiting Arab students;
or unfavorable references to Judaism in school textbooks; or
humane-slaughter bills in state legislatures;[39] or discrimination
against Jews in housing, employment, hotels and other recreational
facilities, and educational institutions;[40] or the relations between
Jews and Negroes, especially in the South; or the position of
Jewish organizations with respect to the abolition or continuance
of the House Committee on Un-American Activities.

Jews and the Jewish community, in their inter-group relations,
will continue to take the calculated risk that what they will claim
on the basis of justice and equality may become a power struggle,
and that rational argument may degenerate into group antagonism
or even bigotry. The tensions will require the intelligence, courage,
and skill of leaders—lay, rabbinic, and professional—and of the
national and community organizations, who will need to meet
problems with the awareness that Jewish history has been a series
of encounters—with the pagans of the Roman Empire; with the
Christian state; with Islam; with Nazism and terror and death;
with the secular state that is founded on the principle of political
and religious equality and liberty, and on the faith "that right
makes might." In these encounters, the Jews have a longer history
of experience than have any other people, a fact that stands as a
source for the tragic sense and the sense of trust and hope, two
senses that are inextricably intertwined in Jewish experience and
consciousness.

V

The American Jew and His Religion

ARTHUR HERTZBERG

THE evidence continues to mount in support of the fact that about three-fifths of all the Jews in America today, in 1964, are affiliated with a synagogue.[1] In close to two decades since the end of World War II, we have witnessed the greatest single synagogue-building boom in the whole of Jewish history in the Diaspora. This has taken place in the very same years during which the American Jewish community has been giving hundreds of millions of dollars towards strengthening the new state of Israel. The attendance of the Jewish young upon some form of Jewish education at some time during their early years has now reached the figure of over eighty percent.[2] It is unusual for a thirteen-year-old nowadays not to be Bar Mitzvah.

Atheism is no longer a recognizable force in the American Jewish community, though it was quite prevalent in the immigrant radical movements fifty years ago. The central institutions of the major religious denominations have flourished in recent years as never before. Among the Orthodox, the Yeshiva University has been transformed from the small struggling school of the 1930's to a major center of Jewish and secular learning. The Jewish

Theological Seminary, the central institution of Conservative Judaism, and its allied bodies have at least tripled in size in the last generation. More recently, the influence of Conservative Judaism has been spreading to countries overseas and even to Israel. Reform Judaism has benefited comparably: in the growing strength of its synagogue body, the Union of American Hebrew Congregations; in increases in staff and facilities at its rabbinical seminary, which now has major centers both in Cincinnati and New York; and in its spread, too, to other countries.

In this generation Jewish learning has been increasingly naturalized in many American universities, as a necessary and normal part of the scene, by the creation of chairs of Jewish studies. Though these academic posts are usually officially secular in nature, most of their incumbents have had rabbinic training, and it is tacitly assumed that their work is meant to contribute to a strengthening of the Jewish spirit at these various schools.

This brief sketch of the current scene evokes the image of a religious community which is mindful of and responsible to its Jewish heritage and clearly committed to continuing Judaism in its various contemporary forms. There is, however, a negative side to the picture. Jews do belong to synagogues at least to the degree to which Protestants and Catholics by birth identify with their churches, but it is notorious that, except for the High Holidays, synagogue attendance is radically lower than church attendance.[3] Various studies that have been made in recent years all point to the same conclusion: half of the enrolled Christians, with variations among the persuasions, go to church regularly on Sunday; no more than one, or at most two, in ten of Jews who belong to a synagogue, are there regularly at the Sabbath services.

Nowadays almost all of the Jewish young are attending college. What we are discovering about the religious views and observances of this generation is therefore of great importance. Various studies agree that almost all Catholic college students and most Protestants believe in God; a substantial number among the Jewish students classify themselves as atheists. Attendance at High Holiday worship on campus, in the years when college begins too early for the students to be at home with their parents, is known to be quite spotty. A growing number, perhaps a third, of the students at the

most intellectual schools have been declaring themselves as not
at all opposed to intermarriage; these views are indeed reflected in
a rate of marrying out that now approaches fifteen percent.[4]

The estate of Jewish observance in the American Jewish community must be added to the negative phenomena. To be sure,
everyone observes Hanukkah, but the same "everyone" knows that
this is a form of dealing with the problem of Christmas. Obedience
to the dietary laws, which are mandatory among both the Orthodox
and the Conservative, has declined disastrously. A study of the
most committed element of the Conservative laity, the members
of the boards of congregations, has demonstrated that even in
such circles no more than one in three keep completely *kosher*
homes. American Orthodoxy is substantially more obedient in this
area, but even among this element one-third does not observe
kashrut. Notoriously, only a small minority of American Jews,
mostly to be found among the Orthodox, observe the Sabbath
in their personal behavior.[5]

Thus, there is the image of growing numbers, economic prosperity of the religious institutions, and increasing power of the
denominational central bodies. Indeed, in relative terms this generation has witnessed the shift of influence within the American
Jewish community from the secular organizations which dominated
the scene in the 1930's to the religious bodies which, on every level,
are increasingly holding the foreground in the 1960's. On the
other hand, religion is ultimately not institutions and structures,
or even success in adapting to a changing scene. It is faith, and
the personal conduct which flows from it. In that deepest dimension
Jewish religion in America is failing amidst its great pragmatic
successes.

THE COLONIAL EXPERIENCE

This lack of faith is, however, not a new phenomenon; it is a
recurrent pattern of Judaism in America from its very beginning.
The Jews have been present on this continent for more than
three centuries, and upon arrival in New Amsterdam in 1654,
Jewish worship was immediately instituted. It has, therefore, been
said that there is a continuity to American Jewish history, and to

the history of Judaism in America that reaches back to these origins. This notion, as I shall try to demonstrate, is not true. The history of Judaism in America is the story of several fresh beginnings, after earlier thrusts and impulses created by earlier waves of immigration had worn themselves out. The earlier settlers disappeared either by marrying the newer arrivals or through assimilation and intermarriage. The newer immigrants inherited the institutions of the older community, wherever they did not create their own, thus giving the semblance of continuity, but not its reality. The continuing theme of Jewish religious experience in America has been the same: the creation of institutions in accord with the strength and the devotion of immigrants and their children, followed by their attenuation as these agencies are inherited or neglected by grandchildren and great-grandchildren.

Not all of the Jewish immigrants who arrived in America in colonial times were of Spanish-Portuguese origin; it is probable that half of the less than 3,000 Jews who were in America in the Revolutionary period were Ashkenazim.[6] Nonetheless, the Sephardi tradition was transplanted by the earliest founders of the first Jewish communities, and it dominated the American Jewish scene completely until the first quarter of the nineteenth century. All of the six Jewish congregations which existed in 1790 (New York, Newport, Savannah, Philadelphia, Charleston, and Richmond) were Sephardi. That tradition shared with the Ashkenazi the idea that every individual Jew in a community was subject to the discipline of a central body ruled by the Parnassim, i.e., the oligarchy of rich Jews. It goes without saying that all these early synagogues and communities were Orthodox.[7]

Each of the colonial communities tried to regulate the religious behavior of its individual members. One vital ingredient had changed however. From the beginning, Judaism in America was voluntaristic. In Europe governmental power usually enforced at least some of the decrees of the Jewish elders, because the Jewish community as such existed as a legal entity. In America this was not true. Individuals could therefore choose to behave in personalist terms, and excommunication or disapproval by fellow Jews was far less threatening. Beneath the surface of the Orthodoxy of the organized communities, individuals were drifting away; the congregations could only react by imposing sanctions. So, the mother congregation of the Sephardim in America, Shearith Israel in New York, warned transgressors in 1757:

Whoever . . . continues to act contrary to our Holy Law by breaking any of the principles commanded will not be deem'd a member of our Congregation, have none of the *Mitzvote* of the Sinagoge Conferred on him and when dead will not be buried according to the manner of our brethren.[8]

But there were transgressors beyond the control of this synagogue or any of the others. Even within the settled communities, intermarriage was a rising threat, which westward migration could only increase. In the eighteenth century and the early years of the nineteenth, the Jews in America, like the Catholics, were a small, respectable but exotic minority. Precisely like the Catholics, the earliest elements were drifting away into the life of the majority in the second and third generation. At least fifteen percent of the marriages contracted by Jews in America before 1840 were intermarriages. It is, for example, very revealing that only two American born clergymen, Gershom Mendes Seixas (during the Revolutionary War), and his nephew Isaac Seixas, ever served at Shearith Israel. After 1839, every one of the Sephardim to occupy that pulpit was born and trained abroad; the present American-born incumbent is an Ashkenazi of East European extraction.[9]

CURRENTS OF REFORM

At the beginning of the nineteenth century, the force of immigration from Central and even Eastern Europe was beginning to be felt on the American Jewish scene. These newer immigrants were coming in greater numbers, first as refugees from the Napoleonic Wars and later under pressure of political and economic changes in Germany. They soon began to organize their own synagogues. The first was Rodeph Sholom in Philadelphia, which was founded in 1802; the second was B'nai Jeshurun in New York, organized in 1825. American Jewish historians have remarked with approbation that these events, especially the second, met no real resistance from older Sephardi communities.[10] It is perhaps likely that the absence of resistance betokened a lessening of assurance in the older circles.

The wave of immigration after 1800 was in itself a mélange of people who came from various Central European countries, from Alsace to Posen, and it even included some Polish Jews. These differing elements were able to communicate with each other in what was then the *lingua franca* of this world, Yiddish. Their economic experience, unlike that of the earlier Sephardim, was not in international trade but in petty shopkeeping and trading. The ongoing American thrust to the West, beyond the Alleghenies, swept up quite a number of the newcomers to the budding towns in the Ohio Valley. There they kept many of the earliest stores and, using these as a base, they peddled in the hinterlands. In places like Cincinnati, Cleveland, and Louisville—indeed everywhere beyond the eastern seaboard—the first congregations to appear were all founded by this newer Ashkenazi immigration. On the frontier the influence of Europe counted for much less than in the seacoast cities of the earlier settlement. Even more than the Sephardim, who brought a few religious functionaries with them, these communities were entirely founded by laymen, and generally not learned ones. The facilities for Jewish observance often did not exist until a congregation was several decades old. The exigencies of life on the frontier, rather than theological change, thus created a predisposition towards religious reform which was soon to affect most of the new synagogues created by the Central European immigration.[11]

Between 1789 and 1882 American Jewish numbers grew from less than 3,000 to 250,000. In one crucial decade, from 1860 to 1870, the number of synagogues in America rose from 77 to 189.[12] This "boom" represented the thrust of the immigrants and of their children, who were raised in American homes within which the languages and memories of Europe were still strong. On the other hand, Jewish religious education throughout this period was of very low estate. This was the period in which education as a whole was being taken out of the hands of the religious bodies and made into a public concern of the state. At the end of the eighteenth century, the Sephardim in New York had been conducting their own schools for the young, in which instruction in English and in Hebrew was combined. In the second half of the nineteenth century these schools yielded to the public school. As a form of acculturation, Jewish instruction, regardless of the point of view of the individual synagogue, became largely an affair of Sunday morning, and it remained so in most places until the turn of the century, after the crucial battles out of which the several American Jewish denominations crystallized.[13] Catechisms were, however, not Hebrew, and certainly not the Talmud. Education more than ideology prejudged, within the nineteenth-century American Jewish community, the proposition that the American born were generally to be less loyal to the heritage than their parents, and that whatever loyalties they would have would be more sentiment than knowledge.

The centrifugal forces were many, and such a milieu was particularly hospitable to the influence of strong individuals. In American economic and social history as a whole this was the period of the making of large fortunes by strong-willed buccaneers. Untrammeled by a set structure, they could survive and flourish by the strength of their wills. Mid-nineteenth century American Jewish history can only be understood in a comparable manner. In actual expression, regardless of the radical nature of its theory, Reform Judaism in its cradle in Germany had been forced to be relatively conservative, for the arena within which the battle for change had to be fought was a legally organized Jewish community in which the State was the decisive power. So, some of Abraham Geiger's reforms failed to be allowed because the government was convinced by his enemies that his religious reforming masked a fervor for political revolution.[14] In America Isaac Mayer Wise, the greatest single figure in Reform Judaism, lost the battle from 1846 to 1850 to convert his first congregation in Albany to his views,[15] but he succeeded in Cincinnati. The same pattern occurred in other places, though often it was the pressure of the laity that created reforms, and not the leadership of the rabbi. Indeed, the very first attempt at religious reform in America had occurred earlier in Charleston, South Carolina, in 1824, when a group of laymen had seceded from the Sephardi congregation Beth Elohim in order to create a more dignified service accompanied by organ music. This soon disappeared, but it was a harbinger of the process of assimilation which was weakening the whole of the earliest Jewish population in America. Isaac

Harby, the moving spirit of this group had written, revealingly, in 1826, that not all who agreed with the founders had joined: "The Jews born in Carolina are mostly of our way of thinking on the subject of worship and act from a tender regard for the opinions and feelings of their parents in not joining the society."[16]

The European elements who were coming to the United States in the middle of the nineteenth century were venturesome and revolutionary. By the very fact that they emigrated, these people betokened their greater readiness to try the new, whatever it might be. Religious reform was, therefore, more likely to occur among these more revolutionary people, in the looser circumstances of American life. Nonetheless, the Jewish patterns from which they were emigrating all contained either the immediate reality or the very recent memory of a *kehillah,* i.e., of a centrally organized Jewish community, not only on the local and regional levels but even, in some places, as a legally recognized national body. The battle for Reform in Germany had begun not in the desire to create a separate party but in the hope of carrying the entire community, as it existed officially, into such modernity. The dream of Jewish rabbinic leadership in America in the middle years of the nineteenth century, regardless of shade of persuasion, tended to this image. The rabbis battled each other not for party advantage but for dominance in the total community. Isaac Mayer Wise hoped that a new liturgy which he edited would eventually be accepted by a rabbinic synod as the American way for all synagogues. He failed. In the same hope he founded a rabbinical seminary in Cincinnati in 1871, the Hebrew Union College. It did not remain a non-partisan school, however, because the more traditional elements soon left it. His synagogue body, the Union of American Hebrew Congregations, founded in 1873, was formed with the same dream, and it too could not hold on to those elements which were outraged by the ritual aberrations of the majority.[17]

Throughout the nineteenth century, since many were pressing for religious reform, a more conservative counter-theme was also present. More tradition-minded elements had also come over in the nineteenth-century immigration. Their leader in this period was Isaac Leeser, a German Jew by birth who served in the middle of the century as the minister of the Sephardi synagogue in Philadelphia. His consistent objective was the creation of an indigenous, American community on the lines of a modern traditionalism. Leeser was willing to cooperate with men of other shades of opinion, including Isaac Mayer Wise, but never to the degree of countenancing major reforms. Under Leeser's influence, the first seminary for the training of rabbis to be created in America, Maimonides College, was founded in 1867 and it lasted until 1873; but after his death religious Conservatism became an unorganized force, which had to find itself and create its tools under the pressure of its recoil from Reform. The men who could not find a place in the new Reform structure included a wide diversity of origins and opinion. They ran the gamut from Sabato Morais, an Orthodox Jew and a Sephardi from Italy, to Hungarian Jews of quite liberal persuasion such as Aaron Wise in New York and Benjamin Szold in Baltimore. In these circles the recoil from Reform represented attachment to the Sabbath, dietary laws, and, above all, to Hebrew as the language of prayer.[18] On the intellectual plane, this was a confrontation between rationalism and a historical romanticism. In human terms, it represented an argument about how far one needed to go from the Orthodoxy of the ghetto in order to be acceptably modern. Under the leadership of Morais, these circles created a rabbinic seminary of their own in 1887, the Jewish Theological Seminary of America.

East European Influences

By this time, East European Jewish immigration, which had been growing in America since the Civil War, had reached flood tide after the Russian pogroms of 1881. The newest wave of immigration was Orthodox; so, at least in inclination, were the earlier representatives of more traditional opinion. Nonetheless, the two streams did not really combine. Their crucial encounter occurred in the years before and after the turn of the century. It is in the understanding of what happened in American Jewish life in the twenty years between 1887 and 1906 that we can find the key to the most recent period of American Jewish history.

By the end of the nineteenth century, the German-Jewish immigration had reached its second generation. Economically,

it had participated in the great flowering of America that had occurred after the Civil War. Its most cherished self-image was
that it had become indigenous to the American scene. Reform
had swept the religious board, so that in 1881 only eight of some
two hundred major synagogues were still Orthodox.[19] Obviously
these Orthodox synagogue members could not be approached
through Reform, for they lacked both the language and the manners.[20] The bridge between the existing Jewish community led by
German Jews of Reform persuasion and the new immigrant
masses was the traditionalist element among the older settlers.
The great historical role played by Cyrus Adler was that he, more
than any other single individual, was the instrument through which
the circle headed by Jacob Schiff created a network of institutions
for the Americanization of the East European Jews.

Adler had grown up in Philadelphia, in the group which had
known Isaac Leeser; he was a disciple of Morais. Personally, he
was Orthodox in behavior, and he was in especial contact with the
traditionalists among the European Jewish scholars. He had taught
in the original Jewish Theological Seminary, and he became the
key person in creating the conditions for reorganizing it in 1902
and for calling Solomon Schechter to be its president. The reconstituted institution had on its board a group of laymen, headed
by Jacob Schiff and Louis Marshall, who were not traditionalists
but who regarded this venture as necessary for the East European
Jewish masses who were coming to America.

This venture began, like many an earlier one in the history of
the American Jewish religion, with the dream of being not a part
but of ultimately becoming the entire community. There is evidence
that it was presumed on all sides that Reform might remain a
separate group, the religion of the older settlers, but it was hoped
that all the rest would enroll under the banner of westernized traditionalism.[21] This failed in the first decade of the present century.
The lay and academic coalition which refounded the Seminary
could not agree, and the supposed clientele of the institutions found
it too remote in the early years. The division among the founders
came to a head in 1906 in a famous battle between Schechter and
Schiff over Zionism. The lay and academic leaders of the Seminary
fought each other openly in the columns of the newspapers, for

Schechter announced his adherence to Zionism and Schiff found such a notion to be abhorrent.[22]

Schechter was, of course, more authentically in touch with the sentiment of the people who would be attracted to the kind of Jewish spirituality which he and his faculty represented. But none of the intellectual leaders of this group, not even Schechter, could succeed in defining a non-fundamentalist theology of Judaism that was convincingly traditionalist. Their piety was related to the depth of their reverence for the past and to their sense of involvement in the living body of the international Jewish community. A Jewish high church, like the contemporary anti-Zionism of the rabbis of the various West European countries, simply did not speak for the sentiment of the new American Jewish masses. In stance and emotion the founders of this traditionalism in America belonged together with those of their contemporaries who were the makers of the renaissance of secular Hebrew letters in Russia and with the young pioneers who were then going out to Palestine. Had Schechter taken any other position, the school that he headed would have undoubtedly shriveled, for lack of students and faculty.

On the other hand, by the turn of the century, the flood of immigration from Russia and the lands nearby had brought with it a greater cross-section of that Jewish community. Rabbis and scholars of the East European kind had begun to make their appearance. In the various "East Sides" of the largest cities there were sufficient numbers of very new arrivals to create synagogues that reproduced unchanged the customs of the old world. The Yiddish press had begun earlier, in the 1880's, and some sections of it acted as a rallying point for the East European Orthodox sentiment. After 1881, the numerical changes in the numbers of Jewish synagogues in America were startling. In the census of 1880, 270 congregations of all sizes, the overwhelming majority of Reform persuasion, were to be found; by 1890 there were already 533 synagogues in America, and almost all of the new ones were created by the most recent immigrants.[23]

THE EMPHASIS ON TRADITION

Especially outside of New York City, the new arrivals felt the pressure of the then existing American Jewish establishment, which was overwhelmingly Reform. Men like H. Pereira Mendes, i.e., the most Orthodox elements in the relatively small circle of Americanized traditionalists, participated and even took the lead in trying to organize central bodies for Orthodox Judaism in America, in which they and the newer immigrants would belong together. The Union of Orthodox Jewish Congregations was founded under Mendes' presidency in 1898, and most of those who issued the original call for its creation were associated with the Jewish Theological Seminary of America. Nonetheless, this body was soon taken over by Yiddish-speaking recent immigrants, who regarded the Seminary as much too religiously liberal. The East European rabbis, who were fresh from the great *yeshivoth* of Lithuania, Russia and Poland, could not really imagine themselves as belonging together with Western, Seminary-educated rabbis whose lives were not entirely devoted to talmudic learning. These rabbis organized their own body in 1902, the Union of Orthodox Rabbis of America and Canada (the Agudath ha-Rabbanim). Those who belonged to this body were keenly aware that in their own persons they would have increasing difficulty in communicating with the American born young, who were beginning to appear in the families in their charge. Very early, they began to labor for the creation of *yeshivoth* in America of the old type, to produce not only learned laymen but also rabbis who would be as pious and as learned in the Talmud as their fathers, but who would also possess sufficient American education to be able to lead in the new land. The first kernels of the two existing major Orthodox institutions of rabbinic learning in America, the Yeshiva University in New York and the Hebrew Theological College in Chicago, appeared in the 1890's; despite many vicissitudes in the early years, they persisted. In 1915 two struggling *yeshivoth* in New York were combined, under the presidency of Dr. Bernard Revel, into the Rabbi Isaac Elchanan Theological Seminary, out of which has grown the present Yeshiva University, the largest Jewish academic institution in America. As the years have gone by, these schools have not remained alone, for, in every decade since its beginning, Orthodoxy in America has produced its *yeshivoth*. The tendency has indeed been for newer Orthodox groups arriving in America to produce institutions that are even more traditionalist than the older ones.

Two other problems confronted the leadership of Yiddish-speaking American Orthodoxy at its very beginnings. One was the setting of standards for Jewish observance, especially in the area of *kashrut*. This has been a consistent concern not only of the rabbinate but especially of the Union of Orthodox Jewish Congregations, which is today the major single agency in the field of *kashrut* supervision. Variations in degree of strictness even among the Orthodox and, more important, the failure to create real centralization in its organized ranks, have stood in the way of producing complete order in this field. Great Orthodox energies have gone into the field of Jewish education, and it is here that this community has scored its most notable successes. The movement for Jewish parochial education was initiated by these elements, often against violent opposition from their more religiously liberal, Americanized predecessors. The schools that now exist, with perhaps 50,000 students enrolled, are overwhelmingly to this day under Orthodox auspices, even though the Conservatives have entered this field within the last decade.

Within a generation, the East European Orthodox impulse produced its own version of Americanization. This was the notion that it was possible to participate fully in the life of America and yet to live in obedience to every prescription of the law. A second generation began to appear which was at once religiously separatistic and yet willing to cooperate with other bodies on a plane of equality. In 1922 the Young Israel Movement, which had begun in 1912 under the influence of younger leaders of Conservative Judaism, was taken away from them by Orthodox Jews, in the name of a completely Orthodox program and outlook. On the other hand, during this same decade comparable Orthodox elements were willing to join, as the Yiddish speaking Agudath ha-Rabbanim was not, in the formation of the Synagogue Council of America, which is the umbrella organization for all three of the religious denominations. Separatism and cooperation have, indeed, been the twin poles around which the career of Orthodoxy in America has revolved in organizational terms.

The post-1882 immigration not only changed the face of Orthodox Judaism in America; it has radically remade the other two movements. On the surface, the issue has been Zionism, but that has only been the symbol of a deeper movement. The great current represented by the children of the new immigrants can be characterized by three desires: the wish to upgrade themselves socially, either by joining congregations created by older waves of immigration or by establishing their own in an Americanized image; the need to affirm an unideological, often not even overtly religious commitment to the Jewish way; and the desire to continue strong emotions which bound them to the Jewish communities overseas, from which their parents had sprung. The travail of World War I, the continuing difficulties of the inter-war period, and the climactic horror of the Nazi years could only reinforce these feelings. These Jews were glad to be in America and deeply sensitive to what was going on outside this land of freedom. Except as a thin coating at the top, the descendants of the older Jewish community were evaporating from the Conservative congregations and even from those of Reform. The dramatic changes that have taken place in both groups in the last half century have been due not to a change of heart but to a change of population.

Until the death of Cyrus Adler in 1940, Conservative Judaism was headed at the top by a German Jew with Sephardi connections who was a non-Zionist, but in that period the largest single influence was probably that of Mordecai M. Kaplan. His Reconstructionism was religiously radical, almost a form of humanism, but it was unshakably committed to Zionism. Kaplan was the leader of many Jewish intellectuals who were the children of the most recent immigrants, regardless of their religious persuasion. The influence of this thinking was spreading in the 1930's among younger elements of Reform Judaism as well. In 1919, the Central Conference of American Rabbis, the organization of the Reform rabbinate, was still opposed to Zionism. Within two decades, by 1937, this body had moved to an official neutrality that was, in effect, a pro-Zionist position. The makers of the change were in largest numbers rabbis and their congregants who had come to Reform Judaism in recent decades from East European backgrounds. Those who soon organized the American Council for Judaism in opposition to this change quite validly claimed that they spoke for the authentic earlier Reform tradition. They were what remained in the organized Jewish community of the families of the immigrants of the nineteenth century, but the institutions created by their ancestors had been taken away from them.

RELIGIOUS DIVERSITY AND COORDINATION

In organizational terms, each of the three major groups within American Judaism today possesses well-developed, comparable structures. The earliest to be created were, as we have seen, those of Reform Judaism. It is probable that there are today about a million Jews affiliated with Reform congregations. There are 650 congregations identified with the Union of American Hebrew Congregations. More than 850 rabbis belong to the Central Conference of American Rabbis. From social action to education there is well developed programming at the two national headquarters of Reform in New York and Cincinnati. The Conservatives started later in the creation of their institutions. Their synagogue body was not organized until 1913, but the United Synagogue of America today numbers almost 800 congregations within its ranks. The enrolled strength of the Conservative movement is well over one million; moreover, because this is the middle-of-the-road group, the unaffiliated tend to look to it rather than to the other two as their own. All the recent studies of religious preference, as separate from formal affiliation, show almost unvaryingly that about half the Jews in America regard themselves as Conservative. The Rabbinical Assembly of America, the organization of Conservative rabbis, has a membership approaching 800. The Union of Orthodox Jewish Congregations claims all those synagogues which are not formally identified with the other two groups, some 2,500. Certainly nowhere near that number pay dues to that body. In all its varieties, from English-speaking liberal Orthodoxy to the most recent Yiddish-speaking Hasidic enclaves, Orthodoxy in America today commands the allegiance of perhaps one million Jews. In the Orthodox rabbinate, the Rabbinical Council of America numbers 800; the Agudath ha-Rabbanim perhaps 600; and there are many who are not affiliated with either body. To this day, despite some notable successes of the other two groups in producing their own religious leaders, the Orthodox remain the major suppliers of rabbis for all the divisions of American Jewry, since this group produces all of its own clergy and at least a substantial minority of those who serve the other two groups.[24]

The leadership of the major denominations, and of the various schools within them, have labored for decades to define theological differences among them. This has been particularly marked on the theological left, in the efforts of the Reconstructionists, and in the continuing ferment among the Orthodox, especially as they have battled against the inroads within their group of such Conservative practices as mixed seating. In theory, all the Orthdox groups agree on the revealed nature of all of Jewish law; for the Reform group the moral doctrine of Judaism is divine and its ritual law is man made; the Conservatives see Judaism as the working out in both areas of a divine revelation that is incarnate in a slowly changing and adjusting human history; the Reconstructionists view Judaism as the evolving civilization created by the Jewish people in the light of its highest conscience. But assent cannot be produced in each group for even these minimal definitions. What really marks the various bodies in the mind of the Jewish community is their differences in ritual practice. The Reform, in their overwhelming majority, disregard dietary laws; the Orthodox are committed formally to obey every jot and tittle of them. Even the leaders of Conservative Judaism are, in practice, usually sufficiently liberal about *kashrut* to permit themselves to dine out on food that is not in and of itself *trefah,* regardless of the dishes on which it is prepared. All but the Reform wear hats at divine service, and that custom is slowly returning to some Reform congregations. Only the Orthodox separate the sexes in the synagogue, but the practice is bit by bit becoming less prevalent in English-speaking Orthodox congregations. We are, in reality, on the religious scene confronted by a continuum, at least in native-born circles, in which the ritual variations shade from one group into the other. Each of the groups still has a distinctive character, based on the nature of the majority of its congregations, but the dissimilarities have clearly lessened. Predictions are dangerous but it is not unlikely that in fifty years the three denominational groups will continue to exist; this will, however, represent more the momentum of

their separate organizational strengths than any sharpening of theological and ritual differences.

That American Jewish religion is in many senses a continuum
is evident, in part, in the freedom with which many people change
denominational allegiance as they move. Their choice is very often
the nearest synagogue rather than the one that is denominationally
the same as the synagogue they just left. This phenomenon is
more evident still in the role of the rabbi in the American Jewish
religious community. It is substantially the same in all three groups.
Not even among the Orthodox, except for a few renowned authorities in the field of talmudic law, is the rabbi today much occupied
with rendering decisions on Jewish practice. He is everywhere a
preacher, chief executive officer of a congregation, pastor, and
moving spirit in the synagogue's educational program. With some
variations of emphasis, denominations expect their rabbis to be
communal leaders in Jewish affairs and representative figures in
the general community. Jewish scholarship, in either its classic or
modern forms, is rather low on the list of what congregations demand from their clergy. There are, indeed, a few notable scholars
in the practicing rabbinate in America today, but their learning is
more a matter of personal predilection than of communal demand.
In short, the rabbi in America today is a cross between a pastor or
parish priest and the leader of an ethnic group. The East European
Ashkenazi tradition produced, at its very end, two images of a
proper spiritual leader: either that of the Lithuanian tradition—
profound learning—or that of the Hasidic tradition—holiness. The
American rabbi today is rich in eloquence, organizational talent,
and practical achievement; the American scene has evoked neither
intellectual endeavor nor transcendant piety, but it has not done
so in American Christianity either. The most Jewish figure on the
American scene, the rabbi, is thus in many senses the most
American.[25]

In 1926, after the structure of the three denominations was well
developed, an initial attempt at co-operation was made in the creation of the Synagogue Council of America, the central body within
which both the lay and the rabbinic organizations of all the groups
sit together. For certain purposes, especially in the area of official
representation before the general community, this co-operation has

continued to work. It is nonetheless true that each of the major groups has by and large tried to behave, whenever possible, as if it were the total Jewish religious community. The real effort of organized Jewish religion in America continues to revolve around each individual synagogue and the denomination to which it belongs. There is a sense of belonging to *Klal Yisrael,* the entire Jewish community, but that feeling encompasses all Jews, regardless of their religion or lack of it. There is little sense of special relationship of the religionists with each other.

TRENDS AND PORTENTS

Several factors have operated to strengthen the institutions of American Judaism in the last quarter of a century. To deal first with the obvious ones, the travail of Jewry the world over recalled many American Jews to their moorings. In America as a whole, religious identification has increasingly become respectable, the "American thing to do," especially in the middle classes. As the mass of Jewry moved from its original economic station in the working class and in petty trade to economic affluence, it has conformed to the mores of the majority of that class by becoming "religious." The creation of the state of Israel has certainly served to raise the public dignity of Jewish identity, and that has expressed itself among some, in contemporary American terms, through joining the synagogue.

There was, in addition, perhaps a more fundamental factor: as before in the history of the American Jewish community, the second generation of the immigrants came to maturity by building a religious life in the image of its Jewish memories, tempered by the immediate reality of the America of its day. This had happened in the half century around 1800, through the agency of the small group then present in the country. Indeed, not only synagogues but both proto-Zionism, in the incident of Mordecai Manuel Noah's abortive attempt to found a Jewish territory near Buffalo, and proto-Reform, in Charleston in 1824, had occurred very early. The heyday of American Reform was in the last decades of the nineteenth century and the early years of the twentieth, when the human material which created the imposing synagogues built in that time was overwhelmingly first and second generation.

It can fairly be said that until the recent revival of Reform as one form of the Judaism of the descendants of East European immigrants, almost no Reform congregations, perhaps not even a single one, were founded in America by German Jews of the third generation. The second generation of East Europeans to some degree moved into Reform. Many more expressed themselves religiously by building new cathedral synagogues in the 1920's, during the brief years of prosperity which preceded the crash of 1929. Most of these institutions began as decorous, and therefore, "American," Orthodox congregations, with English sermons, and many were Conservative within two decades. It is not too much to say that the *Minhag America* of the East European second generation was Conservative Judaism, not necessarily always as part of the organized instruments of that group, but as an influence affecting the other two.

The third and fourth generations of previous waves of Jewish immigration were, at most, heirs and not builders or creators. We are now approaching the same point in the career of the last great wave. To be sure, American Jewry has been refreshed since the end of World War II by the arrival of some tens of thousands of deeply Orthodox Jews, those remnants of East European Jewry who survived Hitler. In places like Williamsburg in Brooklyn and a few other enclaves, some of these people, especially the Hasidim, have reproduced their old life. These newest immigrants have exerted a certain influence among older Orthodox elements, and it has been a revitalizing one. It is nonetheless true that the overwhelming majority of American Jews are not recent arrivals. Whatever may be the destiny of the newest Orthodox impulse, the future of the American Jewish community rests in the grandchildren and the great-grandchildren of older settlers. The mass of numbers and the strength of their institutions are positive factors, but it is probably true that, in relation to the size of their populations, the Jewish communities of 1800 and 1880 were equally well served by institutions as strong. The question remains: will that generation which is now the heir succeed where its predecessors, at a comparable point in their histories, failed? Will the account of American Jewish religious life to be written a generation hence be a tale of great historic success in enjoying religious freedom and coping with it, or will it be an elegy?

VI

Jewish Education

_____

1. *Achievements*

2. *Problems and Needs*
   OSCAR I. JANOWSKY

1. Achievements

Oscar I. Janowsky

Introduction

Education in the broadest sense is co-extensive with life, commencing in the cradle with habit formation, as distinct from reflexes and instincts, and ending only with the fading of consciousness. The subject matter of education is the limitless variety of living experience, and the agencies of education are the manifold influences which affect man as an individual and social being.

Jewish education, too, is a life-long process, involving the interaction of the individual and his environment—the immediate environment embracing the American Jewish community with its values and institutions, as well as the broader American milieu and world events, too, as they affect Jews and, notably, the people of Israel. In this process, the character, personality, intellect and loyalties of the Jew are affected by the home, the synagogue, Jewish organizations and institutions, general educational and cultural agencies, business associations, recreational media, individual contacts and other factors. All of these exert educational influence, which ranges from the direct and purposeful efforts of the school to the subtle and barely conscious effects of human contacts. This wide-ranging conception of Jewish education is obviously beyond the scope of a single chapter.

We are concerned here with the formal Jewish education of children and youth as evidenced by the Jewish school. We shall survey briefly the historical background of Jewish education in the United States, probe in some depth into the major developments and discernible trends, and analyze the basic problems and needs.[1]

The Background

Like all immigrants, the Jews brought to the New World their traditional customs and institutions, among which the school and the instruction of the young enjoyed special sanction. Education had through the centuries sunk deep roots in Jewish consciousness, and it transcended the visible forms of the learning process. To the Jew, education had become an ideal and a religious duty.

In biblical times, the instruction of children in Torah (law and lore for the guidance of man) was regarded as the duty of parents. Formal schools, according to a talmudic source, were established in Palestine, first for adolescents in the first century B.C.E., and then for children during the following century.[2]

During the Middle Ages, the school for boys became as indispensable as the synagogue in the Jewish communities of the far-flung Diaspora. While primary responsibility rested with the parents, the community afforded general supervision of education and made provision for orphaned and indigent children.[3] Study and learning were held in high esteem, and it was assumed that every male could at least read the Hebrew prayers and the Bible.

This pattern of devotion to Jewish education continued until the Enlightenment and the movement for Jewish Emancipation (during the eighteenth and nineteenth centuries) disrupted the Jewish communities in Western and Central Europe and occasioned wide-spread desertion of Jewish for general culture and of the Jewish for the state schools. What remained of Jewish education was attenuated religious instruction.

In Eastern Europe, however, the traditional forms and content of Jewish education persisted through the nineteenth century and well into the twentieth. In these areas of massed Jewish settlement, the sharp edge of the Enlightenment was blunted first by the Hebrew emphasis of *Haskalah* and later by Jewish nationalism. "Modernism," therefore, did not result in the disintegration and abandonment of Jewish education but in its partial reconstruction. The old schools for boys remained—the privately maintained *Heder,* the publicly supported *Talmud Torah* for the poor, and the talmudical academy or *Yeshivah.* But new educational ideas and agencies—the *Heder Metukan* (modernized school) and proposals for Yiddish schools—made their appearance toward the end of the nineteenth century. The *Heder Metukan* was truly modern in its physical facilities, teaching personnel, progressive methods of instruction and co-educational structure. The curriculum included Bible, the Hebrew language and literature, and Jewish history with strong Jewish nationalist overtones. The Yiddish school was the product of the Yiddish cultural movement and Jewish proletarian disaffection. Within the working class movement, opposition arose to the Hebraic and religious emphasis of the Jewish schools, and proposals were made for secular schools, with Yiddish, the vernacular of the masses, as the language of instruction. The organization of such schools, however, was delayed in Eastern Europe by Czarist regulations, and the Yiddish secular school took root first in New York City. But the influences which produced that school were East European.[4]

The Jewish immigrants to the New World brought with them the tradition of Jewish education, and, in varying degrees, the successive waves of newcomers transplanted the educational agencies and methods of their old homes. But these agencies did not produce Jewish learning, partly because of the fragmentation of American Jewry, more potently because of the environment and the rigors of economic and social adjustment.

JEWISH EDUCATION IN THE UNITED STATES PRIOR TO WORLD WAR I

Before the 1880's

Before the nineteenth century, the 2,500 Jews in the American colonies lived in the six seaboard towns where congregations had been established or were scattered in settlements without any organized Jewish life. There is no evidence of Jewish education in the unorganized settlements. Where synagogues did exist, a school was as a rule attached to the synagogue, but the majority of Jewish children who received some Jewish education apparently did so in private Jewish schools or from private tutors. The educational achievement was meager everywhere, even in the school of Shearith Israel of New York, perhaps the best of the Jewish schools of the time.

During the first three-quarters of the nineteenth century, the Jewish population of the United States increased markedly, as immigration mainly from the German states and from East-Central Europe mounted. New synagogues were established in the old seaboard towns and congregations were organized in the interior, and, like their prototypes, they usually sponsored some kind of Jewish education.

Dedicated persons like Isaac Leeser, Isaac Mayer Wise and Rebecca Gratz labored diligently to promote the instruction of the young, but they struggled vainly against unfavorable conditions. In the new settlements, especially those of the Middle West, the situation about the middle of the nineteenth century was deplorable. From the excellent collection of *Memoirs of American Jews, 1775–1865,* edited by Jacob R. Marcus,[5] we learn that "little [had been] done for religious instruction" in St. Louis; that there was no organized Jewish education in Chicago or Pittsburgh; and Leeser noted that "Jewish children do not attend, as a rule, Jewish schools, even where such are established"—a condition which apparently obtained in the East as well as the West.

In the larger eastern communities, especially New York and Philadelphia, Jewish education was provided in congregational day schools, where general and Jewish subjects were taught, or in congregational supplementary schools for Jewish subjects, in private boarding schools or by private tutors; and, in New York after 1865, in schools for the poor, established to counteract the influence of Christian missionaries. The day schools and Jewish boarding schools could provide a basic Jewish education, but these disintegrated as the movement for the public school gained momentum after the middle of the nineteenth century.

The afternoon supplementary Jewish schools continued to attract limited numbers of children, but the Sunday School soon became the prevailing agency for those who received some Jewish education. The first Sunday School was established by Rebecca Gratz in Philadelphia in 1838, and by the middle of the century it was spreading throughout the country. Although its limitations as an educational agency were evident, it was accepted as the best attainable. Even Leeser acquiesced: "The case may be deplorable," he wrote. "It in fact *is* so; but let us not reject the only remedy we have at hand. . . ." He pleaded for "more ample instruction" than "this fragment of religious education" could provide. The masses of the Jews, however, were either content or apathetic.[6]

This brief summary warrants the conclusion that Jewish educational endeavors prior to the 1880's mirrored the Jews and their American environment. Very few of the venturesome immigrants were men of Jewish learning, and the efforts of all were concentrated on striking roots in the new world and earning a livelihood. There were no norms by which to measure educational goals or the leisure and knowledge, and in many instances even the number of pupils, for planning or fashioning appropriate means to instruct the children in Judaism. Prevailing practice in the general community therefore largely determined the course of Jewish educational development.

When general education was under denominational control or furnished by private teachers, the synagogues maintained schools or, where the funds were inadequate or the number of Jews insufficient, they encouraged individuals to teach privately. When private boarding schools were the instrument of education for the wealthy of the general community, the Jews, too, founded a number of such schools—that of Max Lilienthal in New York City, for example, which was attended by boys from other cities as well as New York. Similarly, when Christian missionaries began to make inroads among the poor Jewish children of New York, special schools were established after the Civil War to counteract this influence. Finally, the rise of the Sunday School among the non-Jews of Philadelphia undoubtedly influenced the establishment of such a school as a Jewish educational agency. And when the public school drew the children away from the Jewish day schools, Sunday Schools grew as rapidly in the Jewish communities as they did in the Christian denominations. In a word, Jewish educational institutions were the result of improvisation rather than planning, and they were influenced by developments among non-Jews.

From the 1880's to World War I

The waves of immigration which swept over the shores of the United States between 1880 and 1920 brought two million Jews, the overwhelming majority from Eastern Europe. Like their predecessors, the newcomers were obliged to devote their best energies to the elementary needs of food, clothing and shelter. Comprehensive planning for Jewish education would have been difficult even if the immigrant masses had constituted a homogeneous people. In fact, they were fragments of a people differentiated by geographical origins, variations in religious loyalties, and ideological commitments involving especially socialism and Jewish nationalism. In providing for Jewish education, the new immigrants, again like their predecessors, resorted to improvisation. But a striking difference must be noted. Before the 1880's, the American environment exerted a powerful influence upon the trend of Jewish education. Among the East European immigrants, the major influence derived from the institutions of their old homes. Living in massed settlements, they were able for a time to ignore the new American environment.

The Jewish educational agencies of Eastern Europe—the *Heder,* the *Talmud Torah,* the Talmudical Academy or *Yeshivah,* the modernized national school and, in the twentieth century, the secular Yiddish school—were all transplanted to the United States. *Talmud Torahs* were generally established by special school associations for the education of the poor, but in time the better among them outgrew the stigma of charity and became "communal" schools for supplementary Jewish instruction in Hebrew, prayers, Bible, and religious observances.[7] Congregational schools, including weekday as well as Sunday schools, were maintained by congregations which admitted children of non-members, including a large percentage of the poor. Institutional schools were established by orphan asylums and by social work agencies. Four or five elementary talmudical *Yeshivoth* were organized as day schools. Several "national Hebrew Schools," with Hebrew as the language of instruction, took root early in the twentieth century.

The first of the secular Yiddish schools was established in 1910. And the numerous and generally incompetent proprietors of the *Hedarim* plied their trade freely in the chaotic conditions of the time and contributed to the alienation of a generation of Jewish youth from Jewish education.

The basic information is lacking for a full appraisal of the Jewish educational effort and achievement prior to World War I. Some children no doubt acquired a reasonably good Jewish education, but contemporary sources indicate that for the great majority the situation was deplorable.

The best sources on conditions immediately prior to and during World War I are two surveys of New York City: one directed in 1909 by Mordecai M. Kaplan and Bernard Cronson; the other, a comprehensive survey conducted by Alexander M. Dushkin and published in 1918. The former reported that school buildings, equipment and discipline were very poor, attendance irregular and qualified teachers scarce, and concluded as follows: "(1) The demand for Jewish education is comparatively small. (2) Small as the demand is, the means and equipment which we possess at present are far too inadequate to meet it. (3) Wherever that demand is met there is a lack either of system or of content."[8]

The Dushkin survey found that, of an estimated 275,000 Jewish children of school age, only about 65,000 (23.5 percent) received some Jewish instruction at the time of the survey; and 24,000 (37 percent) of the latter were in the *Heder* type of school or were taught in their homes. Moreover only one-eighth of the children were in school buildings "worthy of the name"; adequate records were wanting in most schools; teachers' salaries were low; and the "drop out" rate was staggering, most of the schools losing more than half of the children every year, and only 30 percent reaching the fourth grade and 3 percent the highest grade.[9]

Conditions outside of New York were certainly no better. A survey of Chicago revealed that perhaps 20 percent of the children of school age were in Jewish schools in 1919, that housing was inadequate, trained teachers scarce, and "about one-third of the registration was lost annually." For the country as a whole, the estimated number of children receiving Jewish instruction was no more than 100,000, and of these 37,000 attended the *Heder* and 26,000 the Sunday school.[10]

TURNING POINT IN JEWISH EDUCATION

In 1909, the Kehillah or organized Jewish Community of New York was established with Judah L. Magnes as executive head and Mordecai M. Kaplan as chairman of a Committee on Education. In the following year, the Kehillah established a Bureau of Jewish Education, with Samson Benderly as director. The Kehillah—a daring venture—soon fell apart, but the Bureau persisted.

Benderly was endowed with a keen intellect which quickly cut through to fundamental principles. He had broad vision and a luminous imagination, a charming and often devastating sense of humor, vigor, dynamism and daring, and a high sense of the dramatic. These qualities of leadership generated considerable progress, long before the community was ripe and ready, in lifting the amorphous mass of American Jewry out of the morass of educational disunity, confusion and neglect.

The Bureau of Jewish Education has been signalized as a turning point in Jewish education principally because of its emphasis on comprehensive planning. Previously improvisation, imitation and uncoordinated fragmentation had characterized Jewish schooling. It had been fashioned largely by American environmental influences before the 1880's and by memories of the old home after the East European masses had arrived. No sustained effort had been made to appraise the adequacy of borrowed American educational agencies like the Sunday School, or the suitability of transplanted East European institutions in the new environment. And the fragmentation of American Jewry had precluded coordinated educational planning and guidance.

The Bureau envisaged Jewish education as the means through which American Jewry might advance its unity and enhance individual and group living. Kaplan provided leadership in the reinterpretation of the heritage and in the clarification of the status of Jewry in America. Benderly evolved the comprehensive practical plans to advance Jewish education on a community-wide basis.

Fifty years ago, Benderly grasped the fundamental needs of Jewish education in America—needs and problems which, in large measure, still remain unresolved: the desperate need for trained and licensed teachers; professional dignity and status for the teacher; secondary and adolescent education; research and experimentation to evolve curricula for the masses as well as the gifted children; informal education; and educational summer camps. All of these needs, and the plans he devised to meet them, were envisaged in community terms, for Benderly regarded Jewish education as the responsibility of the Jewish community.

This great vision was balanced by a hard realism and courage. He recognized the irresistible attraction of the public school and conceded that for the great majority, Jewish education must be supplementary education. This involved a serious limitation on the time devoted to Jewish studies, but he did not yield to despair or to its equivalent, denunciatory preachments or cajoling. He sought solutions in improved methods of teaching and in curricular experimentation which reckoned with the steel frame of school time.

The efforts of the Bureau were wide-ranging but they were not improvisations, for they were segments of a comprehensive plan. Studies of the conditions and problems of Jewish education in New York and in other parts of the country were undertaken. The work of the New York schools was stimulated and coordinated through the organization of a Hebrew Principals Association, a Jewish Teachers Association and a board of the lay leaders, the directors and trustees of schools. Conferences were held on the aims, methods and content of Jewish education. Assistance was rendered in the publication of *The Jewish Teacher,* a professional journal. Methods were devised for the collection of tuition fees and for subsidies to schools in the form of scholarships for poor children. A Board of License was established for the certification of teachers. Modern textbooks and teaching aids were prepared, and magazines were issued for children and older pupils. Experiments were conducted in the teaching of Jewish art and dramatics, in club work and festival celebrations. Special elementary and high school classes for girls were conducted by the Bureau, with the view of preparing them for training as teachers. Schools were encouraged to organize parents associations.

The unschooled children and adolescents received special attention through extension education. A Circle of Jewish children and a League of Jewish Youth reached some 20,000 of the unschooled in 1917 through the celebration of festivals, Bible stories, singing, and the explanation of customs and ceremonies. And visual aids in the form of stereopticon slides were employed in that early period.

Perhaps the greatest achievement of the Bureau was its success in attracting to Jewish education a group of able and dedicated American university-trained young men and women—I. B. Berkson, Alexander M. Dushkin, Leo L. Honor, Israel S. Chipkin, Emanuel Gamoran, Jacob S. Golub, Ben Rosen, Mordecai Soltes, Samuel Dinin and others. These men were later called to important posts in various parts of the country, and even in Israel, and they exerted a powerful influence on Jewish education throughout the land.[11]

TRENDS IN JEWISH EDUCATION SINCE WORLD WAR I

The immediate effects of the Bureau were less impressive than its far-sighted plans and creative programs. Opposition was encountered, but that was far less serious than the general apathy and disunion in the Jewish community and the consequent lack of financial support. The comprehensive plans of the Bureau required the support of a unified community which was then unattainable. We have dwelt on the plans and programs of the Bureau because they indicated the direction for sound educational policy and because they did influence the development of Jewish education in America when more favorable forces became operative.

The forces which affected Jewish education are discussed elsewhere in this book: the end of immigration; the internal mobility of American Jews which led to the desertion of the congested immigrant centers and produced suburban communities; the achievements in general education; the occupational transformation and the growing prosperity of the second and third generations which revolutionized social status and advanced homogeneity. These forces began to operate after World War I but their effects did not become fully evident until the period following World War II. Moreover, the Nazi holocaust and the rise of Israel stirred American Jewry from its apathy, and the return to the Synagogue, lacking in depth as it may be, underscored the need of filling the void in Jewish content and values. Parents in increasing numbers began to seek for their children something more than the formal Jewish identification which was their response to a heightened consciousness of kind. They turned to the Jewish school for rootage and anchorage.

Increase in Jewish School Enrollments

Figures set in neat tables often convey a deceptive impression of reliability. In Jewish education one must be especially cautious because the basic data are lacking. Until recently, there were no census figures whatever on the total number of Jews in the country or on the number of children of school age; and the recording of Jewish school enrollments was fragmentary and inadequate. Statistical entries for the period prior to World War II are, therefore, little more than knowledgeable guesses, at least for the country as a whole. Even today, with improved methods of gathering school data, the figures are estimates based on reports received from schools or from central community agencies. And while the reports cover the overwhelming majority of American Jews, they do not include many of the smaller communities. However, trends may be discerned even from the incomplete data.

Table I indicates trends in enrollments:

Thus Jewish school enrollments increased during the past 60 years from 45,000 to 589,000. And this assumes even greater significance when the ratio of enrollments to the estimated Jewish child populations is examined. Before World War II, the increase barely kept pace with the growth in the Jewish child population: in 1908, perhaps 25 to 30 percent of the school-age children were receiving instruction, while in 1935, the proportion was about 25 percent. Since World War II, however, the rate of growth has been accelerated. The National Study estimated that 40–45 percent of the children (5–14 years of age) were receiving instruction

TABLE I

ESTIMATES OF JEWISH SCHOOL ENROLLMENTS (in round numbers)

Year	Total Enrollments	Enrollments in Weekday Schools (Yiddish and Day schools included)	Enrollments in One Day Sunday Schools	Numbers in Hadarim or receiving private instruction
1901	45,000	(11,000 in Talmud Torahs and 25,000 in congregational schools)		9,000
1908	100,000	36,000	26,500	37,000
1935	200,000	113,000	75,000	12,000
1950	268,000	133,000	135,000	
1952	336,000	160,000	176,000	
1954	400,000	192,000	208,000	
1956	488,000	248,000	240,000	
1958	554,000	304,000	250,000	
1962	589,000	291,600	297,400	

Sources: *Jewish Education Register and Directory*, 1951, p. 27, for the years 1901, 1908, 1935; A. M. Dushkin and U. Z. Engelman, *Jewish Education in the United States* (New York, 1959), p. 45, for the years 1950–1958; and U. Z. Engelman "Jewish Education," *American Jewish Yearbook, 1963*, vol. 64 (Philadelphia, 1963), p. 151, for 1962.

in 1958. And Engelman estimated that Jewish school enrollment in 1962 reached about 53 percent of Jewish children and youth 5–17 years of age.[12]

This trend is confirmed by information for New York City, as indicated in Table II.

The absolute increase in enrollments in New York from 41,000 in 1909 to 154,000 in 1962–63 conforms to the pattern of the country as a whole. And equally noteworthy is the increase in the proportion of Jewish children of school age who received Jewish instruction during a given year. Until World War II, the ratio was little better than one out of five (21 percent in 1909, 23.5 percent in 1917, 23 percent in 1935). After World War II, however, the proportion rose to 25.7 percent in 1951–52, and to 29 percent in 1958–59. Moreover, if account is taken only of elementary school-age children (omitting pre-school and high-school units in which

TABLE II[13]

ESTIMATES OF JEWISH SCHOOL ENROLLMENTS IN THE FIVE
BOROUGHS OF NEW YORK CITY AND AFTER 1950 IN GREATER
NEW YORK (in round numbers)

Year	Total Enrollments	Enrollments in Weekday Schools (including Yiddish and Day Schools)	Enrollments in One-Day Sunday Schools	Numbers in Hedarim or receiving private instruction
1909	41,000	22,000	5,000	14,000
1917	65,000	41,000 in Weekday & Sunday Schools (88%)	12%	24,000
1935–36	75,000	49,200	13,300	10,000–15,000
1951–52	98,000	65,000	23,000	8,000 Released Time c. 2,000 Private Instruction
1953–54	110,000	71,000	29,000	8,000 Released Time c. 2,000 Private Instruction
1955–56	132,000	81,000	41,000	8,000 Released Time c. 2,000 Private Instruction
1957–58	144,000	92,000	42,000	8,000 Released Time c. 2,000 Private Instruction
1960–61	152,000	100,000	42,000	8,000 Released Time c. 2,000 Private Instruction
1962–63	154,000	102,000	42,000	8,000 Released Time c. 2,000 Private Instruction

Sources: "Report of Committee on Jewish Education of the *Kehillah*," *Jewish Education* (Summer, 1949), p. 115 (for 1909); Dushkin, *op. cit.*, pp. 155–58 (for 1917); I. B. Berkson, *1936 Jewish Education Study* (New York, 1936), unpublished (for 1935–36); statistical tables in *JEC Bulletin*, January, 1960 pp. 10–11 (for 1951–52); December, 1954, p. 7 (for 1953–54); February, 1957, pp. 8–9 (for 1955–56); September, 1958, pp. 8–9 (for 1957–58); September, 1961, pp. 10–11 (for 1960–61); September, 1963, pp. 10–11 (for 1962–63).

enrollments were relatively few) the proportion was still higher—
31.2 percent in 1951–52 and 37 percent in 1958–59.[14]

It is thus clear that enrollments have increased markedly. In
part this may be explained by the rising birth rate which began
in the middle 1940's. But the National Study estimated that enrollments increased 131.2 percent during the decade 1948–58—
a figure unquestionably far greater than the increase in the Jewish
child population. Even if allowances are made for exaggerated reporting by the schools, the mounting enrollments signify a new
interest in Jewish education by elements formerly hostile or unconcerned.

Modernization and Liberalization

This quickened interest in Jewish education was undoubtedly
affected by the very considerable progress made in the modernization and liberalization of Jewish education. The *Heder* and the
old-fashioned and generally unqualified *melamed* apparently have
disappeared. The estimates are that these unwholesome educational
agencies accounted for 20 percent of enrollments in 1901, and for
no less than 37 percent (estimated) in 1908.[15] In New York City,
about 34 percent of the children receiving instruction were taught
in *Hedarim* or at home by *melamdim* in 1909, and about 37 percent in 1917. In 1935, only about six percent of the children
throughout the country received such instruction, and these institutions are presumed to have disappeared entirely since World
War II.

A liberal trend frequently underscored relates to the Jewish
education of girls. It has been assumed that at the beginning of
the twentieth century girl pupils were rare in the afternoon Hebrew
schools and that even a Sunday school education did not reach
many. The evidence does not support these assumptions, but it is
true that the proportion of girls in Jewish schools has increased
considerably since World War I.

The New York Survey of 1909 found that more than one-
quarter of total enrollments were girls.[16] In 1935, the estimated
proportion of girls was about one-third: they constituted a majority
of Sunday School enrollments and about one-fourth those of

Weekday Afternoon Schools. The National Study (1958) estimated that girls composed about one-half of the students of the Sunday Schools, about 29 percent of the Weekday Afternoon Schools and 38.4 percent of the Day Schools. And the estimates for 1962 showed an even more striking increase in the proportion of girls: 43.2 percent of total enrollments.

Especially noteworthy has been the increasing involvement of girls in the more intensive forms of Jewish education. They had long composed a large proportion of Sunday School pupils, but the Weekday Afternoon School had attracted them in smaller numbers. In 1962, more than one-third (34.1 percent) of the registration of Weekday Afternoon Schools was female, and in the Day Schools the proportion of girls stood at 43.2 percent.[17]

School buildings and facilities were primitive before World War I, especially in the congested areas of recent immigrants. Teaching was done in rented rooms, remodeled dwellings, underground vestry rooms of synagogues, the homes of pupils.[18] The intervening years have seen striking advances in the number and character of school buildings and in their equipment. To be sure, increased enrollments have taxed existing facilities, but, as a rule, the Jewish school has the appearance of a modern educational institution.

School management has improved. The importance of a planned and graded course of study has been recognized. Greater attention has been given to the classification of students by age and knowledge; record keeping has become more widespread; and most schools employ principals.

Teaching staffs and teaching methods have likewise changed. Men and women of modern education have been attracted to Jewish teaching and they have encouraged wholesome pupil-teacher relationships. New text books, pedagogically sound and appealing in format, have been produced, and audio-visual aids and dramatizations are utilized. Finally some effort has been made to modify the rigid curriculum transplanted from Eastern Europe. In addition to the traditional subjects of Hebrew, prayers and Bible, schools have introduced Jewish history, current events, news of Israel, music, arts and crafts. Moreover, attention has been given to extra-curricular activities, including clubs, and to holiday celebrations which have emphasized dramatic presentations.

Types of Schools

The types of schools in Jewish education are distinguished by (1) the level of studies—primary, elementary and secondary; (2) Hebrew or Yiddish emphasis; (3) congregational or non-congregational auspices; and (4) the time and relative intensity of Jewish studies.

Levels of Jewish Education: The level of Jewish education in the United States has been and remains elementary. There is very little information on secondary Jewish education prior to the past decade, and that which may be gleaned from community studies cannot be used for comparative purposes because the level of Jewish "high schools" has varied widely. This condition still obtains, and even today we do not know the number or nature of Jewish elementary-school graduates.

The National Study (1958) estimated that 82 percent of total enrollments were in the elementary grades, and the same proportion (82.1 percent) was recorded for 1962. The high school student body has remained small: a rough estimate placed it at "about 5% of that in the elementary schools" in 1950; the National Study (1958) found 42,606 pupils or 7.7 percent of total enrollments; and in 1962 a decline was registered—38,058 or 6.5 percent. The remainder of the school enrollment (10.3 percent in 1958 and 11.4 percent in 1962) was in the primary grades, that is the kindergarten and grades 1–2.

The past two decades have witnessed the development of the Foundation School, modeled after the Beth Hayeled of New York, which aims to integrate general and Jewish studies on the primary level. The Beth Hayeled includes the pre-school and the first grades of the elementary school, but the general tendency has been to limit the Foundation School to the nursey and kindergarten. The hope of providing through these schools an intensive and integrated foundation for Jewish education lends special significance to this experiment. But the pace of development of the Foundation School appears to have slackened and, at this writing, the Beth Hayeled of New York is being discontinued.[19]

Rise and Decline of Yiddish Schools: We have noted above that proletarian and Yiddish cultural influences produced a movement for secular Jewish education with emphais upon the Yiddish language and literature. This movement gained a following in the United States, but it was divided by the issues of Zionism and Jewish nationalism, by attitudes toward the Hebrew language and Jewish tradition, and by leftist party affiliations. As a result, three or four splinter school systems arose.

The first enduring Yiddish secular school was established by the Labor Zionists in New York in 1910, and similar schools were soon founded in New York and in a number of other cities. Total enrollments in these Yiddish *Folk Shulen* were about 750 in 1935 and about 1,000 in New York in 1957. Another type of school which came to be known as *Sholem Aleichem Folk Shulen,* made its appearance in New York in 1913 and spread to several other cities. In 1935, they enrolled some 1,200 children and in 1957 about 1,000. The largest segment of Yiddish schools was sponsored by the Workmen's Circle. These were first organized in 1919 and spread rapidly. In 1928, enrollments reached about 6,500, but by 1954 they had declined to less than 6,000. Finally, a split on the issue of Communism in 1926 led to the secession of many Workmen's Circle schools which came under the influence of the Communist-Oriented International Workers Order.

All of these schools concentrated on the Yiddish language and literature, Jewish history, current events and the folk arts. Toward the Hebrew language, Jewish traditions, and the ideals of labor in Palestine, the Labor Zionist schools were the most positive in attitude and the Workmen's Circle schools the most hostile.[20] However, since World War II, even the *Sholem Aleichem Folk Shulen* and the Workmen's Circle schools have drawn closer to traditional Jewish customs and values. Jewish holidays are celebrated, Hebrew and the achievements of Israel are taught, and Bar Mitzvah too, has penetrated the Yiddish schools.

Through the years, the Yiddish schools have functioned in an atmosphere of enthusiasm, zeal and dedication characteristic of a "cause." The American environment, however, has been less than kind, and the influence of the Yiddish schools has waned. In New York City, the center of Yiddish education, the Yiddish schools claimed 9.2 percent of total enrollments in 1935; by 1951–52, the proportion had fallen to a little over 5 percent, and in 1962–63, it was 2.8 percent in the five city boroughs, and 2.2 percent in Greater New York. For the entire country, the estimate in 1950 was that Yiddish school pupils composed 5 percent of total enrollments. In 1958, the estimate was 1.3 percent, and in 1962, it was 1.2 percent. Even in absolute numbers, the student body of the Yiddish schools has declined: in 1950, some 13,265 students were reported in attendance; by 1958, the number had fallen to 7,254; and in 1962, it was 5,065 (3,187 in Greater New York and 1,878 in the rest of the country).[21]

Predominance of Congregational Schools: At the end of World War I, the Jewish schools (with a few exceptions) were either under congregational auspices or they were "community" schools. The latter were sponsored and maintained by school committees unrelated to congregations, and they sought to attract the children of a neighborhood irrespective of Jewish religious orientation. Although reliable information for the country as a whole is lacking, it is safe to assume that the great majority of Sunday schools were maintained by congregations, but that in the more intensive type of education the "Communal" School predominated.

The best Jewish educational thought then envisaged a further growth of the "Communal" schools and their coordination into community systems of Jewish education. This growth continued during the early 1920's, but sociological forces soon reversed the trend. As the Jewish population moved to new neighborhoods and later to the suburbs, the large "Communal" schools of the old neighborhoods declined, and the individual congregations in the new neighborhoods made provision for the education of their members' children. By 1950, estimates indicated that nearly 83 percent of total enrollments had been concentrated in congregational schools and only 17 percent in "Communal" schools. In 1958, the congregational schools accounted for 88.5 percent of total enrollments. This included 95.6 percent of Sunday School pupils and, what is especially significant, nearly 83 percent of those attending Weekday Afternoon Schools.[22] Jewish education in this country has become congregationally controlled and synagogue oriented.

Intensity of Jewish Education: The time devoted to Jewish education is a primary factor in determining the range and depth of studies. The growing enrollments which we have noted have been distributed among three types of schools: The Weekday Afternoon School, the Sunday School (one-day-a-week), and the Day School. The latter will be discussed below, and the trend of enrollment in the Sunday Schools and the more intensive types is indicated in Table I (page 134).

The relative concentration in Weekday Afternoon Schools (Yiddish and Day Schools included) and Sunday Schools is best perceived in percentages. In 1908, over 26 percent of the children receiving a Jewish education were in Sunday Schools, and over 37 percent in Weekday Afternoon Schools. During the 1920's, the Weekday Afternoon School grew more rapidly than the Sunday School, and in 1935, the proportion was over 56 percent of enrollments in the former and about 37 percent in the latter. However, this trend was reversed in the following years, and during 1948–54, the Sunday Schools claimed 50 to 52 percent of the children. The National Study recorded a progressive decline after 1954 in the proportion of children in Sunday Schools to about 45 percent in 1958, and a significant rise in Weekday Afternoon, Yiddish and Day Schools to nearly 55 percent of total enrollments. But the latest study by Engelman (1962) found 50.5 percent of enrollments in Sunday Schools, 41 percent in Weekday Afternoon Schools, and 8.5 percent in Day Schools.[23] The significant conclusion is that more than half the children now in Jewish schools receive the limited education provided by the Sunday School.

The Problem of Time: This analysis may leave the impression that the Weekday Afternoon School provides *intensive* Jewish education. But the latter too, must be related to school time, and the trend has been to reduce the hours of study in the Weekday Afternoon Schools.

During the 1920's and early 1930's, the Afternoon Weekday Schools generally required attendance five days a week. In 1950, only about one-third (32.9 percent) of these schools maintained a five-day-a-week schedule; and by 1958, three days a week had become the norm of the Weekday Afternoon Schools.[24] This progressive attenuation of the Weekday Afternoon School—the agency of "intensive" Jewish education—was undoubtedly a compelling reason for the dramatic rise of the Day School.

The Day School

The Day School provides instruction under Jewish auspices in the general subjects of the public school as well as Jewish studies. It is not necessarily a parochial school in the strict sense of the term, because more than three-quarters of the Day Schools are not under congregational control. It is a private school with strong religious orientation.

We have noted above that American Jews maintained a small number of Day Schools until the 1870's, when the last of them succumbed to the effects of the improved and secular public schools. The massive East-European immigration following 1880 produced a new type of Day School, the talmudical *yeshivah,* but few of these were established and only five were in existence in 1917. After World War I, increased concern with Jewish education added a new motivation for the Day School—the desire for an intensive Hebraic education—and stimulated a moderate growth. In 1935, there were sixteen Day Schools in New York and one in Baltimore, with total enrollments of less than 5,000.

The phenomenal increase in Day Schools began in the 1940's as a consequence of Nazi persecution, the holocaust and the rise of Israel. Among the refugees who found asylum in the United States were substantial Orthodox elements zealously devoted to traditional learning and determined to transmit it to their children through intensive Jewish education. They served as the spearhead in the drive for the Day School,[25] and conditions in the Jewish community helped win them a following. The quickened sense of identification with things Jewish induced parents to seek for their children a more effective Jewish education than the minimum offered in the supplementary Jewish schools. Furthermore, emphasis on habits of study in the best Day Schools made their general (non-Jewish) education an attractive alternative to the public school, especially in New York City. These factors contributed to the rapid growth of Day Schools. By 1945, 78 schools were functioning with an enrollment of close to 10,000. In 1948, the numbers were 123 schools and over 18,000 children; ten years later, there were 214 schools and close to 43,000 pupils; and in 1962, the Day Schools numbered about 252 (145 in New York

City and 107 outside New York) with total enrollments of over 50,000.

During the past two decades, the Day School has aroused considerable controversy among Jews. Some have attacked it as a threat to the public school, as a sectarian influence which isolated Jewish children, and as an obstacle to future adjustment as American citizens. For these and other reasons (e.g., the high cost of Day Schools, lack of funds, the preponderance of Orthodox control), Federations at first refused to allocate central community funds for their support: in 1948, only six Federations granted subsidies to eleven schools, and all grants were earmarked exclusively for the Hebraic segment of the school program.

In recent years, the opposition to the Day School has mellowed, in part because of the realization of its potential for the education of Jewish leadership and because of the growing support of the Day School by the leaders of Conservative Jewry.[26] The argument that the removal of 40,000 or 50,000 Jewish children to the Day School weakened the public school appeared specious, when some five million American children were drawn off to private and Christian parochial schools.[27] If the democratic public school could abide the exclusive "prep school" and the parochial schools, it had nothing to fear from the Jewish Day School, especially since the latter followed the curriculum of the public school and used its textbooks. As a result, prevailing opinion in Jewish circles now accepts the Day School as a legitimate agency for Jewish education.

What of the future? Has the Day School reached its full growth potential or is further expansion to be expected? In the first place, the increase in the *number* of schools may be discounted because many of those outside of New York are school fragments—a few classes, a kindergarten, the beginnings of a high school, etc. Even in New York City, where the average enrollment per Day School exceeds that of the other types of schools, the number of units reported for 1962 varied from 145 to 179. It is enrollments that are most significant, and these suggest that the rate of growth of the Day Schools may be leveling off. Day School enrollments for the entire country, estimated in 1942 at 4.6 percent of total enrollments, increased by 1948 to 7.7 percent. However, in 1958 the relative figure was still 7.8 percent of total enrollments, indicating that the Day School did no more than attract its relative share of increased enrollments. For 1962, a relative increase was again recorded—8.5 percent of total enrollments. But the dramatic growth of the 1940's appears to have abated.

Moreover, the Day School is predominantly a feature of New York City. In 1948, over two-thirds (68 percent) of Day School enrollments were concentrated in New York City; and in 1962, despite the increase to 107 in the number of Day Schools outside New York City, the proportion remained the same.

The Day School likewise has been and remains predominantly an Orthodox educational agency. In 1958, about 95 percent of Day School children studied under Orthodox auspices, and in 1962, the proportion apparently remained about 90 percent.

A number of conclusions appear to be warranted.

(1) The Day School affects only a small proportion of children receiving a Jewish education. The overwhelming majority attend the public schools and come to Jewish schools for supplementary education. Since this situation is likely to continue, more effective Jewish education for the large majority can be achieved only through the improvement of the supplementary school, especially the Weekday Afternoon School.

(2) The Day School has a legitimate place in American democracy, no less than any other type of private school. The fears of its harmful effects on the public school are groundless, and the apparent ease with which Day School graduates adjust to the general high school and college should dispose of the presumed ill effects of this type of segregated education.

(3) The dangers of the Day School are internal, and they relate to standards. Many are fragment schools (at least outside of New York), and such units are not viable educational agencies. Moreover, the cost of Day School education is high and the schools are under continuous financial strain. This results in low teacher salaries and not infrequently in sub-standard facilities. Subventions from central community funds are likely to increase but not in sufficient amounts to cover costs. Federations are not willing to subsidize the general, non-Jewish educational budget; and so long as the Day School is predominantly under Orthodox (that is

"partisan") auspices, there will be opposition to substantial allocations.

(4) Under proper community auspices, the Day School might become an agency for the education of future leaders, and it would be of incalculable value if it could be helped to fulfill this function.

Very little basic research has as yet been done on the achievements of the Day School. Some pioneer achievement tests, recently administered, confirm the general impression that Day School pupils learn considerably more than those of Weekday Afternoon Schools. It is also established that more of the former reach the higher grades of the elementary school and continue their studies in Jewish high schools. A significant pioneer study of the graduates of six Day Schools, recently completed by George Pollak, revealed that a majority did not continue their Jewish education beyond the elementary Day School, but that study habits and interest in Jewish learning did persist. This interest, however, did not result in Jewish scholarship or a preference for Jewish books in their home libraries, or in subscribing to Jewish periodicals. Some were active in Jewish communal organizations and assumed positions of leadership. And, while 90 percent of the respondents came from Orthodox homes, only a small proportion remained strictly Orthodox. This would suggest that the Day School has failed to achieve its religious aims, but Pollak is careful to emphasize the limitations of his study. A full appraisal of Day School graduates in adult life must await further research of the type done by Pollak.[28]

Jewish Education As a Profession

The process of modernizing the Jewish school was accompanied by a trend toward professional standards and practices in Jewish education. Before World War I, only two Hebrew teachers' colleges had been established—Gratz College in Philadelphia in 1895–97, and the Teachers Institute of the Jewish Theological Seminary in New York in 1909. The ferment generated by the New York Bureau of Jewish Education, the desire for American Jewish teachers, the realization that the qualifications of teachers involved more than Jewish learning, and the heightened Jewish

consciousness of the war and post-war years underscored the need
for teacher education. By 1928, seven more teachers colleges had
been founded in New York, Baltimore, Boston and Chicago.
Subsequently, Los Angeles achieved a flourishing Teachers Institute, several rabbinical seminaries organized teacher-training departments, and a number of schools arose for the preparation of
Sunday-school teachers. Especially noteworthy was the development of graduate studies in Jewish education at the Dropsie College and at several of the Hebrew teachers colleges.

In-service courses and workshops have grown extensively since
World War I. They have been provided locally and regionally
and at times even nationally. Recently several of the teachers' colleges have begun to sponsor off-campus in-service courses in
neighboring communities to help teachers achieve certification.[29]

Professional standards in education require the certification of
teachers, and this, too, has been pursued with some success. The
New York Board of License has been mentioned, and other large
communities established similar bodies. In 1941, the National
Board of License was established as "a coordinating and standard-
setting body" to deal with the individual teacher only where no
local board of license existed. Otherwise it was to help organize
local boards and function through them. The National Board has
provided for examinations and licenses. It has also exerted a
salutary influence on teachers colleges by means of accreditation;
the graduates of approved institutions have been exempted from
the qualifying examinations.[30]

Professional associations have been formed—the National Council for Jewish Education (1926), the National Federation of
Hebrew Teachers and Principals (1944), and several denominational associations—for the promotion of professional standards
in Jewish education and for the improvement of the status of the
teacher. These bodies have held numerous conferences on educational problems, and they have issued a number of professional
journals, among them *Jewish Education* (published by the NCJE),
which represents all major orientations in the field.

Efforts have also been made, especially since the shortage of
teachers became acute, to promote salary scales, tenure, paid
vacations, retirement, pension and group insurance plans; and

recently the principles governing these and other aspects of teacher-school relationships have been incorporated into "A Model Code of Practice" which, it is hoped, will be adopted locally on a community-wide basis.[31]

Research in the form of surveys and studies has become a widely used tool for the clarification of problems in Jewish education and for the determination or evaluation of policies. We have records of occasional studies in Jewish education after the 1860's, and we have referred to the New York surveys of 1909 and 1917. It was after World War I, however, that this method of purposeful and analytical stock-taking became accepted practice in local Jewish communities. The most ambitious effort in educational surveys was the comprehensive Study of Jewish Education in the United States, conducted during 1952–59.[32]

Advances in Community Coordination of Jewish Education

The progress achieved in Jewish education during the past four or five decades has been due in no small measure to central agencies organized in local communities or established by denominational groupings. The pioneer efforts of Benderly and the New York Bureau sought to promote Jewish education on a coordinated, community-wide basis. The emphasis placed on the role of the community by Benderly and his disciples, and the development of community organization especially in unified fund raising, contributed to the rapid growth of community agencies for Jewish education. These were variously named, but the usual designation was "Bureau of Jewish education." Some 35 or 40 Bureaus were organized: one (in New York) prior to World War I; three during the course of the European War; 12 between 1919 and 1928. The depression temporarily halted this trend, but at least 24 agencies have been established since 1937. Several have been discontinued, and a few have been consolidated with related bodies.

The Bureaus, especially the more effective ones, have performed a variety of functions which will be discussed subsequently. Their central objective has been to coordinate the educational work in the community through inter-school cooperation.[33]

Parallel with the work of the Bureaus have been the coordinating efforts of denominational or ideological organizations. The Commissions on Jewish Education of the Reform and Conservative movements (organized respectively in 1923 and 1940) have issued statements of objectives and standards, encouraged intensive Jewish education, developed curricula, published textbooks and teaching aids, convoked conferences, organized in-service training courses, and otherwise sought to improve the effectiveness of the congregational schools.[34] The Yiddish schools have had their central bodies for many years, and the Orthodox groups have more recently established national agencies like the National Council for Torah Education and *Torah u-Mesorah,* which furnish curricula, texts and other school materials for their following. All these agencies have attempted to bring the individual school into the stream of Jewish educational thinking and planning and they have, no doubt, improved its effectiveness. However, the efforts of the ideological congregational bodies and those of the community Bureaus which seek to include schools of all ideological leanings have not as yet been coordinated in most communities. This is one of the current unresolved problems in Jewish education.

Coordination on a nation-wide level, which seeks also to bridge the gap between the community Bureaus and the national ideological agencies, has been attempted by the American Association for Jewish Education, established in its present form in New York in 1939. The primary objective of the American Association has been to advance Jewish education by enhancing its image in the community, by reaffirming its indispensability for Jewish survival, by promoting community responsibility and local organization for the betterment of the schools, by fostering cooperation among all elements involved in Jewish education and, in general, by serving as exponent of the cause. The American Association has promoted the establishment of Bureaus and helped them in their functioning. It has become a center of Jewish educational information and an instrument for surveys and studies. It has convoked national conferences for the consideration of crucial problems like the shortage of teachers, the relationship of the Jewish center to the school, and the respective roles of community Bureaus and national ideological Commissions. It has sponsored coordinating or cooperating committees on teacher education and welfare, on adult Jewish education, on Jewish audio-visual materials, and on other matters in which various Jewish organizations are involved. It has concerned itself with recruitment and placement, especially of management personnel in Jewish education, arranged conferences and workshops on educational questions and published materials on educational developments. Recently, it organized a National Curriculum Institute for the study of this vital aspect of the educative process. In a word, the American Association has sought to provide leadership in a Jewish education "movement" and to coax the diverse elements in American Jewry into cooperative community efforts for the advancement of Jewish education.

Acceptance and Support of Jewish Education

One of the most notable trends in Jewish education has been its increasing acceptance by children, parents and community leaders. The National Study devoted much attention to attitude probing, and it discovered that over 93 percent of a sample of Jewish school children regarded Jewish education as desirable. A large majority of the children liked the Jewish school: only about 14 percent registered dislike; the remainder liked the school very much or at least "a little." Nearly three-quarters (72.9 percent) found that the Jewish school interfered with other interests and activities; and yet, close to 60 of every 100 (61.5 percent of the Weekday School and 56.9 percent of the Sunday School) said that they would attend of their own free choice.

The reactions of the parents are especially revealing. As many as 62.1 percent stated that their attitudes to Jewish education had undergone change during the preceding 15–20 years; and of this number, nearly 90 percent had developed a greater interest in Jewish education. It is most significant that, in the view of these parents, anti-Semitism and the rise of Israel played secondary roles in this changed climate of opinion. For the majority, the heightened interest in Jewish education was the result of personal evaluation and appreciation of need. That these responses were not idle musings to humor opinion testers is attested by another finding, namely, that about half of the estimated $60,000,000 spent annually on Jewish education in the United States is provided by parents in tuition fees and other charges. This is firm evidence of parental acceptance of Jewish education.[35]

The increasing acceptance of Jewish education is strikingly revealed by the changed attitude of the leadership of central Jewish community organizations. Prior to World War I, Federations did not regard Jewish education as their responsibility, and during that war and the following decade, heated controversy raged in many cities over the question of "diverting funds" from the primary needs of the poor to educational and cultural purposes. When a pittance was then allotted for education, it was often justified as "philanthropic religious endeavor," that is, as charity for the poor. Even this rationalization was seriously challenged during the depression years of the 1930's. In fact, the issue was not resolved in some communities until the years following World War II.

During the past two decades, Jewish education has been generally recognized as a proper concern of Federations, and today grants are made in practically every city with a Jewish population in excess of 15,000, in three-quarters of the cities with 5,000 to 15,000 Jews, and in about half of the cities with less than 5,000 Jews. The allocations—total as well as proportionate—have increased during the past two decades, despite the pressing demands of Israel, overseas aid, and mounting local needs. However, the amounts allotted to education have neither met basic requirements nor kept pace with the rising enrollments.

In 1936, Federation and Welfare Fund allocations for Jewish education (in 29 reporting cities) amounted to some $524,000, which constituted 6.1 percent of total allocations for local purposes. In 1947, the total in 53 cities reached about $2,181,000 or 8.8 percent of local allocations. Ten years later, 97 communities reported total grants of $3,508,000 or 11.8 percent of local allocations. And in 1961, the same 97 communities allotted to Jewish education $4,280,000—12.6 percent of total local allocations.[36]

Jewish education has won recognition as an important communal function worthy of Federation support. The unresolved question is: how important? The pattern of local allocations reveals a scale of priorities on which education is outranked by health services and by family and child services, each of which received in 1961 about 22 percent of all local allocations. The issue of the relative claims to Jewish communal support of these services and of Jewish education has become especially relevant since the government has entered the field of social welfare and granted increasing financial support to "non-sectarian" social services.

Teaching of Hebrew in High Schools, Colleges and Universities[37]

The acceptance of Jewish studies in the general American community is graphically illustrated by the introduction of courses in Hebrew and Jewish culture in public high schools, colleges and universities. Classical Hebrew had long been offered in departments of Semitic studies, especially in graduate schools and theological seminaries. The emphasis here is upon the more recent interest in modern Hebrew as a living language and as the key to current as well as classical literature and to the cultural life first of Jewish Palestine and then of Israel.

Modern Hebrew as a secular language was introduced into New York City high schools in September, 1930, through the combined efforts of eminent Jewish leaders and the Bureau of Jewish Education. Enrollments increased gradually to a total of 3,173 in 1940. After World War II, enrollments rose, reaching a high of 5,543 in 1950 and continuing to average more than 5,000 a year until 1958. Since then the numbers have declined to some 3,502 in 1963. The decline has been due chiefly to the increasing emphasis upon the study of science and to the complications resulting from the rise of the Junior High School.

Many of the pupils who have studied the Hebrew language and selections from secular Hebrew literature in the public high schools have received supplementary instruction in Jewish history and literature and coaching in dancing, dramatics and music provided by a Jewish Culture Council. These Jewish cultural influences have reached a wider audience through high school assemblies, radio broadcasts and art exhibits.

The 3,502 students enrolled in 1963 in Hebrew classes in New York public high schools were, of course, a small fraction of Jewish youth. But this number attains significance when we note that the total high-school enrollment in all New York Jewish schools (exclusive of the Day Schools) in 1962 was only 3,745. In other words, the number of high-school youth enrolled in supplementary

Jewish high schools exceeded only by 243 the segment involved in Hebrew studies in New York public high schools.

The movement to introduce Hebrew in the public high schools has made some headway outside of New York City. At this writing (1963), Hebrew is taught to some 1,100 students in 23 high schools situated in 16 cities and towns, including Los Angeles, Chicago, Cleveland, Detroit and Philadelphia.

Many colleges and universities have likewise introduced Hebrew studies, especially since the independence of Israel. Whereas in 1940, only 10 institutions of higher education offered modern Hebrew courses, by 1958, the number had reached 48. And the enrollments totalled about 7,000 students in 1950 (half of them in *modern* Hebrew courses), and some 14,000 in 1958.[38]

This survey of trends has outlined areas in which considerable progress has been made in Jewish education. Enrollments have multiplied; school facilities and methods have been modernized; efforts have been made to advance the professional status of Jewish teachers; and community-wide coordinating services have been furnished to many of the schools. Especially noteworthy has been the increasing acceptance of Jewish education by parents, children and the general community. However, Jewish education is beset by serious problems which hamper the realization of the school's objectives. The efforts of Jewish educators have not yielded commensurate pupil achievement.

2. Problems and Needs[39]

Oscar I. Janowsky

THE Jewish educator is aware of the progress and quickened interest in Jewish education, and yet he remains depressed by frustrations and dashed hopes. The uninformed faith of the parents in the Jewish school and the large enrollments present challenges which he cannot meet under present conditions. His thoughts must be on achievement, on the effects of the educative process on the child, and the effects do not appear impressive.

Achievement in education is extremely difficult to measure, especially when loyalties, attitudes and cultural influences are involved. In Jewish education, the difficulties are multipled, because aims frequently remain embedded in sweeping generalizations, objectives are often unformulated, and loyalty to the time-honored curriculum rests on the faith that somehow the results will justify the process. Moreover, the indispensable instruments are still in the experimental stage in Jewish education, so that even what is measurable—progress in the Hebrew language, for example—cannot be evaluated with precision.

Occasionally we are afforded a glimpse of the results attained.

[153

In 1953, a survey was made of synagogue *leadership*—officers and board members—in the congregations affiliated with the United Synagogue of America, the Conservative wing of American Jewry. The survey revealed that 54 percent of the respondents had attended Weekday Afternoon Schools or had had private tutors for four years or more; that another 24 percent had attended less than four years; and that 7 percent had attended Day Schools. In other words, 85 percent had had what we call "intensive" Jewish education. Moreover, 37 percent had continued formal Jewish education after Bar Mitzvah!

The results? Only 27 percent of the respondents could follow the Hebrew text in Synagogue service and could understand "quite a lot of it"; 51 percent could follow the text but understood "very little of it"; and 13 percent could not even follow the text.[40]

This is an indication of the results of "intensive" Jewish education among synagogue officers and board members, men and women who occupy positions of leadership in the central Jewish religious institution. What the situation is among the rank and file, especially among the products of the Sunday School, may be left to the imagination of the reader. The situation was grasped in a telling sentence by a solid citizen in a good community, who remarked to the present writer: "We want our people to be good Jews, even if ignorant ones."

Space will permit analysis of only five major problems which affect achievement—(1) the time factor; (2) the fragment (small) school; (3) the congregational school; (4) the curriculum; and (5) the status of the teacher.

THE TIME FACTOR: INTENSITY OF JEWISH EDUCATION

In the first place, we must reiterate that Jewish education is predominantly part-time education, supplementary to that of the public school. Only 8.5 percent of the enrollments are in the Day School. The overwhelming majority who are affected by Jewish education attend the Weekday Afternoon and Sunday Schools which enjoy neither the sanction of law nor effective social pressure to enforce attendance. The children come after a day's work in the public school, and Jewish education must compete with the multifarious and intriguing recreational and social interests of the middle-class environment in which American Jews live.

The enrollment figures show that a large proportion of the children do come. But for how long? More than half of them attend the Sunday school, with or without an additional session during the week; and 41 percent attend Weekday Afternoon Schools, two to five sessions a week. In terms of time, this means that at least nine-tenths of the enrolled children receive instruction two to six hours a week. How much achievement can one expect from such schooling?

If the children remained in school long enough, something might be accomplished. But they do not. Large numbers drop out before they reach the higher grades of the elementary school, and Bar Mitzvah marks the terminal point in the Jewish education of the great majority. The National Study hesitantly concluded "that probably the average American Jewish child attends *about three years of his childhood in a Weekday Afternoon school, or about four years in a Sunday school.*" Even this may be an optimistic overstatement; Samuel Dinin estimated in 1954 that the average child received about two-and-a-half years of schooling, and that the effects were minimal.[41]

Close analysis of the grade distribution of the school enrollments warrants little optimism about achievement. A sample study made by U. Z. Engelman of pupils in 22 communities indicated that in 1958 nearly 87 percent of the children in the Weekday Afternoon Schools had not reached the fifth grade; 75 percent had not reached the fourth grade; and nearly 57 percent were in the first two grades or the kindergarten. And the detailed and unpublished community studies were even more discouraging.[42]

We often deplore the fact that Jewish education is elementary education, that relatively few children reach the high-school level —7.7 percent of enrollments (including those of the Day School) in 1958, and 6.5 percent in 1962. The problem of Jewish secondary education is complicated by factors external to the Jewish school, but it is true that Jewish education fails to meet the spiritual needs of adolescents. It is also an understatement to say that Jewish schooling is elementary education; relatively few reach beyond the fourth grade! In the sample of the National Study, less than 11 in 100 children of the Weekday Afternoon Schools were in grades 5 to 8.[43] This is *intensive* Jewish education for the large majority who do not attend the Day School. In effect, it consists of about two-and-a-half or three years of instruction, perhaps four to six hours a week. Can one help concluding that the *intensive* Jewish school is a revolving door? The mistaken assumption is still widespread that if the children could be corralled into the schools education would take care of itself. The major problem is not recruitment but retention.

We are comforted by the rationalization that over 80 percent of all Jewish children receive *some* Jewish instruction at *some* time during their elementary school age. It is not education they receive, but exposure. There is high correlation between exposure and infection; but Jewish education is not infectious.

Important efforts have recently been initiated to cope with this situation. Conservative congregations are attempting to increase the hours of the Weekday Afternoon Schools to a minimum of six; they are setting attendance requirements prior to Bar Mitzvah; and they are striving to limit their Sunday Schools to the younger age-group, so that more children will attend the Weekday Afternoon Schools. Reform congregations, too, are trying to establish more weekday classes. The problem of time, however, remains crucial.

THE FRAGMENT SCHOOL

Another problem is that blight on Jewish education, the small or fragment school. It is impossible in that type of school to maintain a well-rounded curriculum or to grade children properly by age or knowledge of subject matter. Staff is too small for effective supervision, for teaching of special subjects, or for extra-curricular activities. And a fragment school provides neither the warmth of a school atmosphere nor the intimacy of private instruction.

It is generally agreed that, for effective functioning, a school should have at least 150 to 200 pupils. Yet, a sample study of 30 communities other than New York showed that in 1958 less than 12 percent of the Weekday Afternoon Schools and less than 30 percent of the Sunday Schools enrolled more than 200 children. As many as 62.3 percent (28.1 percent of the enrollments) of the Weekday Schools had each 100 pupils or less; 81.1 percent (50 percent of enrollments) had less than 150 students. The unpublished community studies added a touch of realism to this fragmentation. Rochester had 10 Weekday Afternoon Schools, of which nine had enrollments under 100, five under 50. Savannah had two such schools, each with an enrollment under 100. Akron had 272 pupils distributed among four Weekday Afternoon Schools. In Los Angeles, 68.1 percent of the Weekday Schools affiliated with the Bureau (37.4 percent of enrollments) had each 100 pupils or less; over one-fifth of the schools (5 percent of enrollments) had each less than 25 pupils. The extremes of fragmentation were revealed by the finding that 14.7 percent (2.2 percent of enrollments) of the Weekday Schools in the sample mentioned above each enrolled less than 26 pupils.

The figures for the high schools are even more startling. The National Study sample showed that 52.9 percent of the Weekday High Schools (19.8 percent of enrollments) and 60.5 percent of the Sunday High Schools (20.4 percent of enrollments) had each less than 26 students![44]

CONGREGATIONAL VERSUS COMMUNAL SCHOOLS

We noted above the trend toward congregational auspices of Jewish education. By 1962, over 91 percent of all enrollments were in congregational schools, as shown in Table III.

At one time, there was considerable controversy over the merits of the "communal" as against the congregational school, and echoes of partisanship are still heard in the literature of Jewish education. Many "communal" schools did indeed grow into large, well-staffed and competently administered neighborhood agencies of Jewish education. In time, too, local federations and welfare funds began to appropriate community funds for the support of "communal" schools. And in some cities, like Detroit, genuine community systems of Jewish education developed.[45] However, the issue is no longer "communal" *versus* congregational school, because the latter has attained the commanding role in Jewish education.

TABLE III

DISTRIBUTION OF ENROLLMENTS (a) BY TYPE OF SCHOOL AND CONGREGATIONAL ORIENTATION (1962)

Orientation	Type of School							
	Day		Sunday		Weekday Afternoon		All Types[a]	
	Number	Per Cent	Number	Per Cent	Number	Per Cent	Number[a]	Per Cent
Orthodox	42,936	85.3	25,694	8.6	55,765	23.1	124,395	21.1
Conservative	1,510	3.0	79,252	26.6	121,150	50.2	201,912	34.3
Reform	503	1.0	181,603	61.1	30,698	12.7	212,804	36.1
Intercongregational and noncongregational			10,858	3.7	33,601	14.0	44,459	7.6
Yiddish	201	0.4					201	b
Not indicated	5,184	10.3					5,184	0.9
TOTAL	50,334	100.0	297,407	100.0	241,214	100.0	588,955	100.0

a Jewish school-students in 299 reporting communities.
b Less than one-tenth of one per cent.
Source: U. Z. Engelman, "Jewish Education," *American Jewish Year Book, 1963,* p. 154. Reproduced with permission of the publisher.

Congregational auspices need not necessarily constitute a problem; indeed, they offer some distinct advantages. The child is prepared for participation in the synagogue, which is the vital center of Jewish activities. The Hebrew and prayers taught in the school are utilized in religious services. History, customs and ceremonies have relevance to holiday celebrations, and the religio-social functions, like Bar Mitzvah, provide motivation. Moreover, the synagogue serves in some measure as a surrogate for the Jewish environment which the home no longer furnishes. The idea of *Klal Israel* (loyalty to the total Jewish community) is an abstraction unless symbolized by institutions which affect the life of the child; and the synagogue visibly represents Jewish life.

However, the division of congregational schools into Orthodox, Conservative and Reform segments has raised difficulties. Some of the serious defects in Jewish education have been laid at the door of the congregational schools. While many admit children of non-members, they tend to emphasize denominational partisanship in Jewish education and they promote competitive fragment schools in Jewish neighborhoods. The New York Survey, for example, showed that the average number of weekly teaching hours per teacher was smaller in the congregational than in the non-congregational Weekday Afternoon Schools; teacher turnover was higher; and the proportion of licensed teachers was sharply lower —81 percent for the non-congregational and 50.5 percent for the congregational schools.[46] Certainly the factors of teacher turnover and unlicensed teachers are indicative of a lower quality of instruction.

The congregational schools do constitute a problem, but the solution can no longer be sought in the alternative of the "communal" school. The issue is: how can inter-congregational cooperation be achieved so that community-wide efforts might be made to remedy the defects?

THE CURRICULUM

This analysis of the curriculum will be limited to the supplementary Jewish schools which affect over 90 percent of the enrollments.

But it is extremely difficult to discuss the studies of the Weekday Afternoon and Sunday Schools because of the discrepancy between stated principles and actual practice, and because of the variation in time allotment to the various subjects. Even the functioning definitions of the subjects differ: for example, Jewish history and Bible-and-Prophets often mean Bible stories. The best analysis of the curriculum was made in the Greater New York Survey of 1951–52.[47]

The subject matter of the curriculum has remained virtually unchanged since the modernization of the Jewish schools after World War I. It consists of the Hebrew Language, Prayer and Worship, Jewish Holidays and Observances, Bible (Humash-Pentateuch and Prophets), Jewish History, Talmud, Israel and Current Events. School time, however, has been reduced in the Weekday Afternoon Schools, and the attempt to teach too many subjects in the few hours of instruction has fragmentized available time and lowered achievement.

In fact, not all of the subjects named are really taught in the Weekday Afternoon and Sunday Schools. Current events and Israel are minor subjects, Talmud is rarely taught outside of the Day School, and Bible-Prophets only by the best of the Weekday Afternoon Schools. Even Bible-Humash in the original Hebrew is not a major subject for most of the children: in the Sunday Schools it consists of Bible stories in the lower grades and selected readings in the higher grades; in the Weekday Afternoon Schools it is taught mainly in the upper grades, which the majority of the children do not reach. Jewish History is taught at most an hour a week in all types of schools. Very little is taught about the American Jewish community and its institutions.

The principal difficulty with the curriculum of the Weekday Afternoon School appears to be the emphasis on the study of Hebrew as a spoken language or for the ready comprehension of classical and modern Hebrew literature. The motivation is justifiable, for language is the expression of a people's genius. Hebrew is the language of prayer. It is the key to the spiritual and cultural heritage of the Jews. It provides rootage in the Jewish past and serves as a powerful link to the people of Israel and to Jews throughout the world. The problem is that the supplementary school does not accomplish the purpose. On the average, children attend the Weekday Afternoon School perhaps three years, during which period about two hours a week are devoted to the study of Hebrew. Proficiency in the language cannot be acquired under such circumstances. Pilot achievement tests have recorded progress in Hebrew in the early grades, but lower scores for children beyond the age of ten. When Hebrew is the main subject of the curriculum, a large portion of school time is consumed in learning a limited vocabulary which is quickly forgotten, and the effects of Jewish education are thereby minimized.

The solution does not lie in the abandonment of Hebrew, for Jewish education without Hebrew would be truncated and shallow. Hebrew must remain an important part of the curriculum, but we must be mindful of the fact that limited school time renders impossible effective achievement in language study. The solution must be sought in the clarification of the goals for the study of Hebrew.

The objective appears to have been proficiency in Hebrew for communication, for the study of Hebrew literature, and for reading. This has not been achieved, and the conversational Hebrew to which the children have been exposed has proved insufficient for communication or the reading of the Bible and other literature. Nor have they learned to understand the synagogue prayers.

A small number has indeed learned to converse in Hebrew and to read it with understanding,[48] and some have continued their studies to become Hebrew teachers. This achievement is significant, but it cannot justify the exposure of all children of the Weekday Afternoon School to the present course of studies. The latter produces a small "élite," but thousands of students emerge from the schools with little to show for their efforts. The "élite" is important, but it should be the product of conscious selection.

Not all children have the aptitude or inclination for serious and sustained language study. The first two years of the Hebrew school should be adequate for identifying these children, who may then be given special attention by skilled teachers and advanced methods of instruction. The cooperation of parents should be enlisted to increase the school time of such pupils. For those wanting in aptitude, or in sustained effort, the goal of Hebrew study should be a more modest one—to learn, perhaps through the translation method, to understand selected prayers, and to acquire a limited vocabulary embracing the symbols, rituals and phrases which characterize Jewish life. This would free much time for other subjects in which the children might experience a sense of accomplishment. What we need is not one course of studies in Hebrew but several, which should be evolved through continuous experimentation and evaluation. We may add that the entire curriculum in Jewish education calls for extensive research and experimentation.[49]

THE CRUCIAL PROBLEM OF TEACHERS

The problem of teachers in Jewish education is truly alarming. The teacher is the heart of all education, even of disciplined, state-supported and state-enforced school systems. In Jewish education, the teacher must be a model of all the pedagogic virtues, a conjuror who can achieve the impossible. He must grapple with an insurmountable time-handicap and create a Jewish environment lacking in the child's home. His school is voluntary, supplementary, fragmentized and isolated. His curriculum is in many schools rudimentary, teaching aids a luxury, supervision intermittent, and administrative direction tenuous, when not ornamental.

Does the reality approximate this need? The National Study estimated the total Jewish teaching force in 1958 at 17,483—7,924 in the Weekday and Day Schools, and 9,559 in the Sunday Schools, a ratio for the Weekday Schools of one teacher to 38 pupils. Since many of the schools are small and many of the teachers do part-time teaching, the shortage is obviously critical. Outside of Greater New York the shortage must be staggering.

How qualified are the teachers? Well over one-half of the total teaching force is in the Sunday Schools, teaching two or three hours a week. These are hardly qualified, for over 9 percent have had no Jewish schooling at all, and another 58 percent no more than a Jewish elementary school education. Many have had no pedagogic training, and they apparently do not miss it. The teaching experience of a great many is limited, and nearly 60 percent have been in their present positions less than three years. More than three-quarters (77.1 percent) of all Sunday School teachers have no Jewish teaching license and have not been urged to qualify for one. Clearly, about half of our children, those in the Sunday Schools, are taught mainly by unqualified teachers.

What of the teachers in the Weekday Afternoon School? Their training is better than those of the Sunday Schools. However, 10.4 percent have had no more than an elementary Jewish education; and an additional 9.4 percent no more than a high school Jewish education in the United States. Nearly 40 percent have no Jewish teaching license. The general education of this group is likewise unimpressive: over 30 percent have not completed college, and nearly 6 percent of these are still in high school.

Even more somber is the status of the Jewish teaching profession. The evidence here is not conclusive, but it appears that less than half of the teachers in "intensive" Jewish schools devote their time and energy *entirely* to Jewish education. Nearly 38 percent do not consider Jewish education their main occupation—a startling discovery, for it can mean only that their best energies are employed elsewhere. This and the fact that more than one-half (51.6 percent) of the Weekday School teachers have been in their present positions less than three years—a staggering turnover—must inevitably depress standards of instruction and hamper student achievement.

If salaries symbolize the status of a profession, the pay of the Jewish teacher is an index as well as a cause of the depressed state of his calling. In 1951–52, the Code of Practice in Greater New York proposed a scale ranging from $2,200 to $4,800 a year, when teaching in the public schools commanded an annual minimum of $4,000 and a maximum of $8,000. The average annual salary paid in the Weekday Afternoon Schools was $2,795. For the country as a whole, the National Study (1958) estimated a range for most Weekday Afternoon (not Sunday School) teachers of $1,500 to $4,500 a year. Apparently the Jewish community does not consider Jewish teaching a vital function which calls for adequate remuneration.

The failure of the wealthiest Jewish community in the world to provide adequately for the education of its young is further illustrated by the fact that over three-fifths of present teachers in the

Weekday Afternoon Schools were born abroad. This is not necessarily a deficiency, but it affords proof that American Jewry has not produced the qualified teachers necessary for its schools. Indeed, a careful survey in 1949 revealed that all the existing Hebrew teachers colleges could at best provide 25 percent of the necessary annual replacements. Little wonder that the dedicated teacher feels isolated and forgotten, like a sentry without hope of being relieved.

A large proportion of the teachers of the Weekday Afternoon Schools regard Jewish education as a temporary occupation to be suffered or exploited until something better turns up. And our youth shuns the profession, as indeed it should, under prevailing conditions. Why should promising young people, even those who prefer Jewish communal service, choose Jewish education as a career, when they can enter the rabbinate, fund-raising, community relations, or social work? Salaries are higher, social acceptance more assured, status better and, in many instances, they do not need to study as long or as much.

The basic elements of the teacher problem—unqualified teachers, the depressed state of the profession, high turnover, and the shortage—all derive largely from low salaries and economic insecurity. One can endorse all that has been said about idealism, dedication, the spiritual rewards of teaching, but the economic factor remains paramount. The best human material shuns a profession that does not yield a livelihood, and once the recruitment potential is reduced shortage becomes inevitable. Increased enrollments only aggravate the situation, for the schools must fall back upon inadequately trained and less competent teachers. Furthermore, competent teachers who persevere cannot devote all of their energies to the enhancement of their calling. The result is deterioration of standards and loss of status for the teacher and his profession. The problem will not be resolved until salaries, tenure, retirement, group insurance and other fringe benefits become competitive with similar occupations.[50] Only then will schools be able to command licensed teachers, in-service training and professional growth.

A realistic solution, however, must reckon with another factor. Adequate salaries will not be paid unless the teacher performs a full-time function, for a profession cannot be subsidized. If a school can offer a teacher no more than a ten- or twelve-hour schedule per week, it will not be able to pay a full salary. It is, therefore, imperative to direct attention to the limited conception of the function of the teacher.

The vogue of over-specialization in Jewish communal service has reduced a number of important functions to part-time professions. Space will not permit a full analysis of this matter. But certainly adult education and informal education or group work can and should be the domain of the teacher. The latter should be trained to perform these functions which, together with formal education, can restore Jewish teaching to a full-time profession. This can be dealt with only on a community-wide basis.

Aspirations versus Realizable Goals

It is not difficult to identify numerous needs in Jewish education. We have been told that "the stream of Jewish education" must be deepened; that children must devote more time to Jewish studies; that the community federations must allocate more funds to Jewish education. Parents have been exhorted to have their children attend the Jewish school more hours per week for a greater number of years and to continue their schooling after Bar Mitzvah; to insist that the children be taught by full-time, and well-trained teachers; to provide "in the homes and in the community an atmosphere of respect and desire for Jewish culture and learning." It has been urged that unified "community schools" would be better than congregational schools. And there are people who have insisted that the Jewish school must develop the total personality of the child.

These are worthy aspirations, but it is imperative to distinguish between realistic goals and noble sentiments. The desirable must not be confused with the possible. A "community school" may be preferred, but rabbis and congregations will not yield the education of their children to the community. Full-time and well-trained teachers are a necessity, but it will not be met by demands of parents, even if they could be induced "to insist." And teachers will not be paid full salaries if schools provide only part-time teaching schedules. Respect for learning will not issue from public appeals. The total personality of the child cannot be developed in a part-time school which enlists the attendance and loyalty of the students two to six hours a week for a few years at the elementary level.

Zeal for the optimum should be restrained, and the time element must, above all, be viewed realistically. It should be possible to induce a larger proportion of the children to attend the Jewish school more than one day a week. The lever of Bar Mitzvah, the "compulsory school law" in Jewish education, should likewise enable the schools to increase the years of schooling. For increasing numbers, summer camping might provide additional time for Jewish study. But for the large majority, six hours a week are likely to remain the norm of the Weekday Afternoon School. This is the time-element with which we must reckon. It is a steel frame confining Jewish education, and curricular research and experimentation would do well to concentrate on the development of courses of study appropriate to it.

The long-range desiderata can remain guiding principles, but we must be reconciled to the thought that they will not be realized for a long time; that progress will be governed by the inevitable process of gradualness. It is necessary to begin with what we have, with the schools as they exist and function today. The agencies which can lead the way to improvement must be identified, for the individual school cannot alone cope with the multifarious problems.

TOWARD A SOLUTION: COMMUNITY AGENCIES AND STANDARDS

The most promising instruments for progress are the central agencies for Jewish education: the ideological Commissions on Jewish education (Conservative, Orthodox, Reform, etc.); the Bureaus of Jewish education or Jewish education committees which attempt to coordinate the work in individual cities or regions; and the American Association for Jewish Education.

Each of these bodies performs a vital function, and its operations merit extended treatment. But we must confine ourselves here to an analysis of the role which the Bureau of Jewish Education or Jewish Education Committee of the local community can play in attacking the problems which beset Jewish education. The emphasis is placed upon the central agency of the *local community* because of the conviction that standards of performance and achievement must be dealt with primarily on the local level. The national bodies can formulate principles, propose codes of practice or retirement and insurance schemes, and furnish educational media, such as publications, texts, school-aids, achievement tests, etc. The application of principles, the utilization of techniques, and the advancement of standards through supervision can best be furthered in the local community under the aegis of its central agency for Jewish education.

We have noted above that Bureaus of Jewish education function under various names in some 35 or 40 communities. During the past two or three decades, the best of these agencies, like the Jewish Education Committee of New York, have evolved a variety of truly significant services directed to the improvement of standards and the promotion of co-operation among the independent and ideologically discordant schools of the local communities. They have provided facilities and personnel for supervision and guidance of school activities, for consultation, for the stimulation of the arts in the schools. They have furnished reference libraries, organized in-service training courses for teachers, encouraged research and experimentation, and begun to fashion instruments for testing pupil achievement. The publication services of some of the Bureaus are prize assets for the conscientious teacher. The Junior Hebrew Library of the Jewish Education Committee of New York, for example, is an invaluable educational medium, and its children's magazine, *World Over,* which reaches into 1,300 schools and over 100,000 homes throughout the country, merits high praise. Bureaus have organized Boards of Review for the adjustment of disputes and conditions of employment. They have promoted Codes of Practice governing teacher welfare, group insurance, retirement and other benefits. The Jewish Education Committee of New York initiated in 1957 an imaginative School Accreditation Program which furnishes a publicly recognizable measure of adequacy.[51] These services of the best Bureaus constitute a model of what is needed and can be supplied by community agencies for Jewish education. If fully utilized and conscientiously applied by the autonomous schools, this reservoir of knowledge, skill and experience could lift Jewish education out of the present morass of confusion and frustration.

Far more haltingly and less successfully, Bureaus have attempted to draw the schools out of their individual isolation and to bridge the chasm of ideological disunity. This is the area of weakness in the central community agencies for Jewish education. They are, as a rule, service agencies. Their policy is to offer services to *all* of the Jewish schools of a city which will ask for or accept a service. The emphasis is on the principle that service must be rendered to all schools, irrespective of ideological orientation. But in reality, this neutralism must inevitably reach beyond respect for ideological differences. Some Bureaus will provide service whether or not the school authorities have the capacity to conduct an educational institution; whether or not they appreciate the importance of standards; whether or not the proferred advice will be heeded; whether or not the operation of the school is harmful to the children. If a group, with or without a sense of responsibility, will establish a school even in a well-served area, corral some children, run up a deficit, and appeal for aid, the Bureau will offer its services. The principle of all-inclusiveness sounds democratic; but if the area is well served, and the school duplicates work done better by others, fragmentation and waste are thus encouraged.

Similarly, the notion that a central agency in Jewish education can help all schools, even the bad ones, do better, is unrealistic. It has not the means to serve adequately all of the schools, especially in the large city. And every hour spent on a school which cannot or will not profit from the service involves a waste of money and, more important, a waste of human resources. When a central agency spreads thin the time and energy of its limited staff, it weakens the total effort to raise standards.

Some of the central agencies in Jewish education operate entirely without any principle of affiliation with the individual school. Where affiliation exists, it is often a mere formality—the schools serviced are designated "affiliated schools." Affiliation involves no commitment to adopt proposed reforms, even when flagrantly necessary. A school can select a service or discard it; it can disregard expert advice; it may come again to waste the staff's time; and it may announce to its clientele that it is affiliated with the Bureau of Jewish Education.

The justification of this practice is a cliché which passes as a principle. The slogan "Unity in Diversity" or "Cultural Pluralism in Jewish Life" is popular in Jewish education circles. But there is little unity in Jewish education and not much diversity.

There is, of course, some diversity. The Yiddish schools—a small fragment—do have a distinctive orientation. The extreme Orthodox elements likewise have a clear position. But many of the so-called Orthodox synagogues do not really differ from others designated Conservative, because Orthodoxy, too, has in large measure made its peace with non-observance. In many of the Weekday Afternoon Schools, Orthodox or Conservative, one finds substantially the same curriculum. And are the Reform and Conservative Sunday Schools basically different?

A sample study of community leaders made by the National Study indicated that in selecting a school for their children, the schools' ideological orientation *per se* was the factor of choice for only 9.7 percent. The remainder chose the school because of family background and synagogue affiliation (26.9 percent), the school's reputation and program (25.1 percent), general educational goals (19.8 percent), convenience (13.0 percent), or social considerations, that is, snob appeal (5.5 percent).[52]

We must repeat that there is some diversity. Where it exists, it should be respected. But it need not become a fetish. Much of what passes as diversity is no more than vested institutional interests.

What, then, can a Bureau of Jewish Education do to cope with the problems of disunity and fragmentation and to render more effective its services for the improvement of Jewish education?

Obviously, it cannot and should not espouse one viewpoint in Judaism. If it did, it would cease to be a central community agency. But it can champion a viewpoint as to what are essential *standards* in Jewish education; and it can adopt the policy of directing its services to those schools which cooperate in promoting acceptable standards.

A central community agency in Jewish education cannot evade or avoid the basic issues of voluntarism and discipline, of autonomy and unity. Autonomy without a commitment to the larger unit is isolation, and voluntarism without disciplined cooperation is anarchy. To continue to give service, especially service of high quality, to isolated and undisciplined schools in the hope that some of it will be utilized or that some improvement might result is not a policy, but an accommodation to a troublesome situation. Such a community service agency cannot cope effectively with the problem of standards.

To be truly effective, a central community agency must do at least three things: (1) it must take a position on standards, and its services should be governed by affiliation involving a commitment; (2) it should exercise genuine leadership; and (3) it should fashion some sanctions to guarantee cooperation.

Affiliation is essential, and it need not be a mere formality. But, we must repeat that the commitment should relate to standards and not ideology. Affiliation should require commitment on at least three basic standards: to achieve accreditation for the school, or at least to strive to qualify for accreditation; to employ licensed teachers, or at least to make sustained efforts to have the teachers qualify for licenses; to accept the salary scale proposed by the Code of Practice. Service should then be accorded only to affiliated schools which honor these commitments.

Such a policy may well reduce the number of schools served by the central agency, but it would render possible service in depth. Moreover, even without affiliation, the central agency does not actually serve all the schools of a large community. It serves a self-selected portion determined largely by chance. Affiliation and commitment on standards would provide a more meaningful basis of selection; it would set concrete goals for the central agency and the schools.

The central agencies do supply leadership in Jewish education through their services. But that is not enough. Leadership in Jewish education requires planning and zealous pursuit of principles governing *not ideology* but *standards*.

Two areas calling for leadership may be mentioned by way of illustration. The removal of a large part of the Jewish population to suburban communities has contributed to the difficulties in Jewish education. This offers a challenge to a central community agency to plan and stimulate the new settlements to concern themselves with Jewish education, and this must be done before the divisive influences become intrenched interests. With early planning, it might be possible to forestall congregational fragmentation and to achieve inter-congregational neighborhood schools, where such are feasible.

The problem of existing fragment schools likewise calls for leadership of a high order. A central agency should not remain reconciled to fragmentation in the name of ideological neutralism. It should condemn school fragments on principle, proclaim their deficiencies, and strive to effect consolidation. Where real ideological differences prevail, the situation must be accepted. But there is a wide field of possible coordination within ideological groupings and even across such divisions. The way must be found to consolidate schools without separating the children from the rabbi and the congregation. That this is not a hopeless task is attested by what the Jewish Education Committee of New York has achieved on the Junior High School level.[53]

Finally, a central community agency must concern itself with sanctions. Effective unity without sanctions exists only in the optimistic theories of philosophical anarchism. In the voluntaristic Jewish community, coercion is out of the question. But money can serve as a powerful stimulant.

The wealth of a school or the size of its budget is not in itself a measure of excellence. But without adequate funds the problems in Jewish education will not be resolved. While poverty may furnish a mantle of zeal and dedication, gross deficiencies will fester underneath. Effective education requires money, which not many individual schools, not even large congregational schools, can raise in sufficient amounts. At least a portion of the funds must be supplied by the organized community fund-raising agencies.

Community allocations for Jewish education have increased in recent years both in total amounts and in the proportionate share of allotments for local needs. However, the increase in federation support has not kept pace with the growth in school enrollments. The National Study estimated that the combined sums received from federations and welfare funds cover no more than seven to eight percent of the money spent annually on Jewish education. That this is insufficient is evident from what has been said about the low salaries paid the teachers and the sub-standard conditions in many of the schools. The need must be pressed upon federations and welfare funds to find additional moneys for the schools. This can be done only through the central community agency. Chaos and inevitable failure would result if the schools were to press their individual claims upon the community allocation committees.

Two further and obvious needs must be met, if the Bureau is to function effectively. First, its leadership, lay and professional, must be representative of the affiliated schools as well as of the total local Jewish community. The Bureau will not have the confidence and cooperation of the schools if it is superimposed upon them or if its lay leadership is distantly related to Jewish education. A representative Bureau will, of course, suffer the handicap of divided loyalties; the clashing ideological and institutional rivalries will trouble the board and committees of the Bureau. But the issues cannot be side-stepped. Cooperation or accommodation will not be achieved if these issues are ignored.

A great responsibility rests upon the top leaders of the community who are concerned with the allocation of funds. They are pressed to divide the educational allocations among the ideological groupings, and in some communities they have shown a tendency to yield to this pressure. If this prevails, community-wide standards in education will not be achieved. It is essential that the top leadership recognize only one central agency for Jewish education in the local community.

This community agency should have a determining voice in the distribution of educational allocations. Both the former and the top leadership of the community should insist that community funds be applied to the improvement of standards rather than to cover such deficits as are due to waste, duplication or incompetence. If community funds are applied to increase the salaries of licensed teachers and to enable schools to achieve accreditation and affiliation with the central agency, and if the schools are held acccountable for the proper use of the funds, a powerful instrument will be forged for the betterment of Jewish education.

VII

The Cultural Scene

---

1. Development and Decline of Hebrew Letters in the United States

EISIG SILBERSCHLAG

SLOW GROWTH OF HEBREW LETTERS

AMERICAN Jewry is numerically and economically stronger than any Jewry in the world. Its contributions to the growth of the United States and its share in the building of the young State of Israel are too well-known to need documentation or elaboration. But that which has been the glory of Jewry in past ages, the excellent achievements through Hebrew letters in the domain of the spirit and the intellect—that is still to come. And our historical experience indicates that this twin aspect of Jewish life—the spiritual and the intellectual—has a tradition of slow maturation. Though history moves at an accelerated pace in the age of the jet and the atom, it is rash to predict a Golden Age of Jewry in America, as optimists hasten to do. Two factors militate against quick and great Hebraic achievements in this country. In previous centuries, Jews who were compelled to leave their old homes carried their Hebrew learning with them to new places. But the Jews who settled in North America often brought neither material nor intellectual possessions. Their knowledge of the Bible was limited, their understanding of post-biblical literature less than adequate. And, with the rise of scientific learning and the corresponding deterioration of humanistic disciplines in the last century, the study of Hebrew and the two other classical languages, Greek and Latin, suffered a serious decline. These factors do not augur well for the future of Hebrew literature in this country.

The First Two Centuries: 1654–1860

Jews in colonial, and later in independent, America had an elementary Hebrew education: they recited their prayers in the synagogues which were established along the eastern seaboard as early as the middle of the seventeenth century, and they read the Pentateuch in the original.

The ancestral language—Hebrew—was respected by the clergy and the populace. It was studied arduously and reverentially at such institutions as Harvard College. The Puritans, especially, loved the Old Testament to such an extent that they referred to Boston as the "Jerusalem of this land" and to New England as the "New English Canaan." But the Jews, with rare exceptions, did not share the intense passion of the Puritans for Hebrew study. The great historic movements of Sabbataism and Hasidism, the rationalist revolution of Spinoza and Mendelssohn, left few traces on their thinking and writing. For two hundred years, from the middle of the seventeenth to the middle of the nineteenth century, Hebrew literature in this country perpetuated documentary curiosities which survived in manuscript or in print or in stone— such as the unpublished nomenclator of Judah Monis, preserved in the Library of Harvard University, or the circular letter of Congregation B'nai Jeshurun, printed in 1826, or the rhymed epitaph in double acrostic on the tomb of Samuel Zanvill Levy.[1]

It is a sad reflection on Hebrew literature in this country that, especially in the eighteenth century, epitaphs are among the best and most skillful efforts of the Hebrew muse. At a time when Moses Hayyim Luzzatto (1707–1746) invigorated Hebrew letters with remarkable plays and idyllic poems, with a genuine mysticism and a personal piety, anonymous Hebrew poets in America were courting the families of eminent merchants with tombstone poetry. Among the epitaphs, collected by David de Sola Pool in *Portraits Etched in Stone,* there is perhaps one inspired poem—on the death of Walter J. Judah, who died in 1798 at the tender age of twenty. In rhythmic, partially rhymed prose, the anonymous epitaphist extols the healing virtues of the deceased, who was a medical student and contracted yellow fever in his ministrations to a stricken community. He even coined a Hebrew equivalent for yellow fever: *Eshta Zehubta*—a rare occurrence of a neologism on a tombstone. The first two centuries of Jewish settlement in America are distinguished by a paucity of Jews, a rarity of learned Jews, and a sparseness of literary documents in Hebrew.

First Flowering: 1860–1914

The year 1860 is an important date in the history of Hebrew literature in America: the first original Hebrew work appeared in that year in New York City. It was a commentary on the *Sayings of the Fathers* and it was entitled *Sefer Abne Yehoshua* (Book of the Stones of Joshua). In form, in content and even in the title the book conforms to medieval miscellanies of homiletics. The author, Joshua Falk, wavers between optimism and despair: he is aware of the receptivity of Jews to learning, but he realistically stresses the milieu of the New World as non-spiritual and non-intellectual in its deepest drives. This polarity was to characterize Hebrew literature in America for the next hundred years.

An even more important date than 1860 is 1871: the first Hebrew periodical in this country, *Ha-Zofeh be-Erez ha-Hadashah,* appeared under the editorship of Zevi Hirsch Bernstein. It is unfortunate that no complete set has been preserved in the libraries of the United States or abroad. But the extant issues show lack of talent and slavish imitations of Hebrew periodicals in Russia. This can also be said of other Hebrew periodicals which appeared in the last decades of the nineteenth century and which mushroomed before World War I: *Ner ha-Ma'aravi; Ha-Pisgah,* and *Ha-Tehiyah,* which was a continuation of *Ha-Pisgah.* Wolf Schur, who edited *Ha-Pisgah* and *Ha-Tehiyah,* and Gershon Rosenzweig, who edited *Ha-'Ivri* and *Ha-Deborah,* strove to maintain their periodicals against enormous odds. Both experienced humiliation and poverty, both inculcated love for Hebrew and love for Zion in the unreceptive hearts of their contemporaries. Financial stress prevented immigrants from subscribing to periodicals, and struggle for mere subsistence robbed them of the time to read or the leisure to think. Editors lacked not only readers but literary contributors.

It is surprising that the Hebrew writers had the leisure to write at all in the land of unlimited opportunities. "Their lot," writes an author in 1887, "was like the lot of the majority of Hebrew writers from time immemorial: some of them were teachers, some store attendants, some peddlers, some merchants. But the majority were merely poor . . ."[2] But Ephraim Deinard, bibliophile and bibliographer, was wrong when he stated that in 1888, in the year of his arrival in the United States, there were no Hebrew writers and no libraries of Hebrew books. The great libraries of Harvard and Yale, to mention only two, had Hebrew books. And Hebrew writers were scattered throughout the land.[3] But it is true that Hebrew books were uncommon and Hebrew writers were scarce in the eighties of the previous century. While America was groping toward a renaissance of letters under the aegis of transcendentalism, Hebrew writers compensated their lack of originality with an intense patriotism.

Heading the list of American patriots in Hebrew literature is Judah David Eisenstein (1854–1956), who translated into Hebrew the two basic charters of liberty in America: the Declaration of Independence and the Constitution of the United States. For the centennial of American independence in 1876, Moses Aaron Schreiber, cantor of the congregation Shaaray Tefila in New York, wrote a long and graceful poem, "Minḥat Yehudah" (Gift of Judah). In its passionate love of liberty and loyalty to America, Schreiber's poem sets the tone for many similar compositions:

> Unto these coasts
> Migrated hosts.
> Jew and Gentile . . .
> Braved the sea
> To be here free.[4]

The theme of immigration also inspired Emma Lazarus, who wrote in English, and Sabato Morais (1823–1897), the first president of

the Jewish Theological Seminary, who dedicated an admiring tribute to her in Hebrew.

Early Hebrew writers in this country were not uncritical of the
American milieu, of its vulgarism, optimism and shallow panaceism.
They were particularly keen in denunciation of internal squabbles
and ills. They were conscious of the democratization of society
and the attendant ills of the leveling process: "the tanners" (an
obvious term of opprobrium) have usurped the place of the erudite
and the learned, the arrogant have ousted the knowledgeable.[5]
They even deplored the chaos in the organization of Jewish life.
They could not reconcile themselves to the fact that stature and
status were no longer coincidental.

The entire fabric of traditional life changed under the impact
of America. Even the literature of responsa, which dates back to
the Gaonic period in seventh-century Babylonia, was flooded with
American place-names like Kalamazoo and Leavenworth. The
Jewish *Kulturkampf* was fought out with an intense bitterness in
the United States. Reform was branded as an ally of ignorance, and
the Golden Calf as an ally of Reform. An early author complains:
"The basis of all things in America is the dollar . . . it's the
method, it's the aim, it's the glory, it's the power, it's the one true
document according to which most people evaluate their deeds in
this city and in this country."[6]

Yet in those days writers discussed the merits of Hebrew style
with an appositeness that lost nothing of its actuality. How should
Hebrew writers write? Should they imitate the Bible or the so-
called neo-Hebraic style of the Mishnah and Midrash? Hillel
Malachovsky, a perceptive essayist at the turn of the century, contended that the talented writer always created a style of his own:
Gordon wrote à la Gordon and not like a prophet of old, Smolenskin in the language of Smolenskin, and Frischmann wrote in
Frischmann's style.[7] But he, too, viewed the future of the language
and its practitioners in America with unqualified pessimism.

This estimate stands in remarkable contrast to the indigenous
appraisal which was done almost a decade earlier. Bernard Drachman, rabbi of the congregation Zichron Ephraim and dean of the
Jewish Theological Seminary at the turn of the century, wrote in
the year 1900 that "with the exception of the physical and techni-

cal sciences, every brand of literature is today represented by He-
brew works of importance written and published in America."[8]
This was enthusiasm carried to exaggerated lengths. The works of
Hebrew authors at the turn of the century do not substantiate
Drachman's assertion: they refute it.

On the basis of his travels in America, Benjamin II predicted
a hundred years ago "that men of great learning will never arise
among the Jews in America."[9] And a generation later Hillel Mal-
achovsky predicted in 1895 that "in a little while the name of the
Jew—would that I were a false prophet—will be nonexistent in
America . . . Instead, a new generation will arise calling itself
Americans of Mosaic Faith. . . ."[10] This pessimism, voiced by
the enlightened in the nineteenth century—from Shalom Cohen to
Abraham Mapu to Judah Leb Gordon—was a persistent theme.
That it proved unjustified was a freak of history or an act of
Providence.

In such a climate of opinion, humor appeared in the guise of
mordant wit or scathing satire. It was somewhat heavy-gaited in
the nineties, but it achieved artistic merit in the writings of Gershon
Rosenzweig (1861–1914). His *Talmud Yankai* (Yankee Talmud),
which appeared in book form in 1907, was an important contribution to the treasury of Hebrew satire. His barbs were sharp,
pointed, poisoned like Indian arrows, and they drove into the
heart of the greenhorn, the peddler, the teacher, the rabbi.

In his summation of American Judaism, Rosenzweig repeated
the perennial dirge on neglected learning: "By two things is
America sustained: by worship and by deeds of loving-
kindness . . . but not by Torah for it is written (Deut. 30.13)
'And it is not beyond the sea.' "[11]

While Rosenzweig castigated his people in prose, Naphtali Herz
Imber (1856–1909), who made his reputation as author of "Hatik-
vah" before he reached the shores of America in 1892, deplored
his own lot in verse. But his addiction to alcohol lessened his sensitivity and his output. Small wonder that he was attracted to Omar
Khayyam whose poem, "The Rubaiyat," he translated from Fitz-
gerald's English version into Hebrew under the significant title
"Ha-Kos" (The Cup).

Two tracts of Imber—*Education and the Talmud,* and *The*

Letters of Rabbi Akibah, or the *Jewish Primer as It Was Used in the Public Schools Two Thousand Years Ago*—were incorporated by the U.S. Commissioner of Education into his reports for the year 1894–95 and 1895–96 (not 1898, as his brother asserted). They were irresponsible ventures into the arcana of post-biblical literature. But Imber redeemed his failures with his successes in humor. His last will and testament was a Rabelaisian attack on real and imaginary enemies.[12]

Hebrew humor in America lacked the genius of a Shalom Aleichem or a Mendele Mokher Sefarim who wrote their best books in Yiddish. But it had a long line of talented practitioners between the two world wars: Daniel Persky (1887–1962), who steered the feuilleton into kind-hearted witticism, Abraham Regelson (b. 1897), who indulged in delicately humorous silhouettes in prose between massive poems, and Isaac Dov Berkowitz (b. 1885), who not only translated the work of his father-in-law, Shalom Aleichem, into immaculate Hebrew, but wrote original comedies on the frailties of Jewish life in America.

Zenith: 1914–1960

It was World War I which effected a change in the development of Hebrew literature in general, and in the development of Hebrew literature in this country in particular. Till 1917 Palestine and America were minor foci of Hebrew literature. But after the Communist Revolution in Russia, Hebrew literature began to languish in that country. The formerly insignificant centers in Palestine and in the United States assumed a new importance. In Palestine there was an overwhelming concern for the immediate and the ephemeral; in America there was a leisurely yearning for the remote and the eternal. A "realistic," soil-bound literature developed in Israel; a "romantic," soul-bound literature matured in America.

Poets predominate—as they always have—in the Hebrew literatures of Israel and America. Even the foremost novelists in Israel—Hazaz (b. 1898) and Agnon (b. 1888)—lapse into a poetic lilt. This can also be said of such Hebrew prose writers as Yohanan Twersky, who spent his formative years in this country and developed a staccato style for romanticized biographies à la

Maurois and Ludwig; Samuel L. Blank, who in his novels prefers the idyllic life of the Bessarabian Jews to the hectic drive of American Jews; and Harry Sackler, whose recreation of the past imparts poetic overtones to his style. Even the philosophical disquisitions of Maisels, the critical essays of Brainin, Ribalow, Epstein and Isaiah Rabinowitz, the educational essays of Touroff and Scharfstein, the discerning essays of Maximon and Ovsay, Mikliszanski and Steiner, the light-hearted essays of Persky and Goldberg, the well-documented essays of Rivkind and Malachi, and the scholarly essays of Tchernowitz, Mirsky, Feigin, Federbusch, Waxman, Churgin and Bernstein, are charged with poetic overtones.

Hebrew writers in America made important thematic innovations. They mined native ores in poetry and prose: they introduced the Indian and the Negro into their works. Their sympathies were stirred, their emotions were aroused: the poor and downtrodden races of America fortified their analagous status in the world.

One of the first writers to become acutely aware of new thematic potentialities in America was B. N. Silkiner (1882–1933). In the year 1909, which will be remembered as a turning point in the history of Hebrew literature in this country, he presented the Hebrew reading public with the first important and native Hebrew poem, *Mul Ohel Timmurah* (Before the Tent of Timmurah). It was cast in the form of a poetic story told to an Indian girl by her father, Timmurah—hence the name of the poem. With a fine sensitivity to the early injustices of the white man and with an excellent command of the Hebrew language, he succeeded in portraying the noble savage against the paradoxes of primitive religion, and, above all, the American landscape:

High mountains of flint to the east—these are for eagles,
The hoary sea to the west—for the whales, the spawn of the deep,
The ancient woods in the south—for the lions, the roaring leopards,
The desert of awe to the north—for the storms and the whirlwinds.[13]

Neither Longfellow's "Hiawatha," thematic kinsman of Silkiner's narrative poem, nor the noble savage of Chateaubriand, is the latest fashion in contemporary literature. Still, "Before the Tent of Timmurah" is a milestone in Hebrew literature: it is the first native epic which a Hebrew poet fashioned out of Indian folklore, the Spanish conquest of America, veiled allusions to early Jewish history, and the inevitable ingredient of every poem—personal vicissitudes.

The direction Silkiner gave to Hebrew letters in America was eagerly followed by his younger contemporaries, Ephraim Lisitzky (1885–1962) and Israel Efros (b. 1890). Thus Lisitzky achieved the best integration of his poetic gifts in *Medurot Doakot* (Dying Campfires). This book of Indian legends, carefully paraphrased and woven into an epic poem, shows the undoubted influence of Silkiner. Both tell the story of the destruction of Indian civilization, out of love and sympathy for the Indian rather than the white man. Both tend to idealize the way of life of the Indian and overlook the unsavory aspects of his barbarous cruelties. And Israel Efros, in his narrative poem, *Wigwamim Shoteḳim* (Silent Wigwams), created against an early American background a tender love story of a white man and a half-Indian girl. It was not startlingly new or original, but it effectively repeated what so many Hebrew publicists and essayists had been preaching since the second half of the nineteenth century: man must strike roots in the soil and possess it with the sweat of his brow.

Efros made another discovery: primitive culture does not imply a primitive mind. And while his Indian girl Lalari shares simple tastes and simple ways with tribal brethren, she is a refined and even sophisticated lover. From her surrender to Tom till her suicide, she articulates her love experience with a complicated ardor worthy of as civilized and corrupt a woman as Lawrence Durrell's Justine.*

It was the Negro, in particular, who attracted the attention of Hebrew writers in America. Hillel Bavli (1893–1961) was among the first to interpret their rich folk-songs and folk-poetry. Other Hebrew poets followed and even improved on his example. Some of them translated Negro spirituals, some imitated Negro folk-

* The author of this essay, an outstanding Hebrew poet, modestly refrains from alluding to his own works. In one of his poems, "Mexico," a modern Mexican broods on the vicissitudes of the ancient Aztec civilization and arrives at the startling metaphor: "Man is all: Snake and eagle and god." The American landscape, too, is limned in all three collections of Silberschlag's poetry. See: *Bi-Shebilim Bodedim* (In Lonely Paths), *'Aleh, 'Olam, be-Shir* (Arise, World, to Song) and *Ḳimron Yamai* (Arch of Days) (editor).

songs, some depicted the Negro. While Reuben Grossman-Avinoam, who settled in Israel more than thirty years ago, contented himself with renditions of Negro spirituals, Simon Ginsburg and Ephraim Lisitzky paraphrased Negro poetry and portrayed Negroes in their original poems.*

Lisitzky has even woven a long series of poems around Negro themes in his book *Be-Ohole Kush* (In Negro Tents). In contradistinction to other Hebrew poets, he let the Negro speak for himself and he let the reader draw an implicit analogy to his own fate. Thus he achieved a subtler integration of the Negro into Hebrew poetry. What is perhaps disconcerting in his Negro poems is his constant preoccupation with the theme of death. The humor and the joy which are such prominent and winning characteristics of the Negro have almost no place in his poetry. They had no place in his life: "All my life I bore a crown of thorns upon my head"—he wrote in his autobiography.[14] This consanguinity of sorrow was to be a major obstacle in Lisitzky's achievement. His book of Negro poetry hovers on the brink of greatness but never quite achieves it.

The Hebrew writer in America conquered new ground for modern Hebrew literature: to the German, Russian and Polish influences which dominated Hebrew literature for the past two hundred years, he added a new factor—the literature of the English-speaking countries in translation, in critical appraisal, in subtle absorption. It was he who rendered Shelley and Tennyson, Yeats and Eliot, Frost and Amy Lowell, Melville and Walt Whitman into Hebrew. It was he who first apprized the Hebrew reader of the existence of the new poetry, the avant-garde criticism, the stream-of-consciousness fiction. And Hebrew poets, especially Simon Halkin and Abraham Regelson, Moses Feinstein and Hayyim Abraham Friedland, Reuben Grossman-Avinoam and Gabriel Preil, cannot be properly evaluated without constant reference to English and American literature. Even older poets like Abraham Samuel Schwartz and Simon Ginsburg, who had not received their formal education in this country, were not untouched by Anglo-

---

* In a cycle of Negro poems, the author, Eisig Silberschlag, depicted the myths of creation, in the main, as felt and seen by the unsophisticated Negro. See his "Mi-Pi Kushim" (Out of the Mouth of Negroes), in *'Aleh, 'Olam, be-Shir* (New York, 1946), pp. 107–122 (editor).

American influences. Robert Browning guided Regelson toward a poetic form which was most congenial to his considerable talents: the dramatic monologue. John Milton taught him the use of pathos and the use of the long phrase, and John Keats lured him into the world of mythologies. Yet, not only in subject matter but in form, he remained essentially a Hebrew poet whose technique is poetic midrash, whose habitat is the empyrean. His heroes like Ahijah the Shilonite and Israel Baal Shem Tob converse in incorporeal bliss. His most ambitious poem, "Cain and Abel," does not depict a struggle of two primitive men; it is a struggle of two opposing forces. Cain is the blind will in the Schopenhauerian sense or the Dionysian impulse in the Nietzschean sense, the builder and architect who knows no respite in his untiring work. Abel, on the other hand, represents the thinker, the critic, the skeptic whose impotence in action is matched by a sovereign consciousness of the vanity of all things. When Cain kills Abel, it is will itself which kills thought.

For Halkin (b. 1898) intellectual poetry is a creed: "Only cerebral poetry will sustain man in our time."[15] But the philosophical and metaphysical foundations of his poetry do not harmonize with his strong talent for lyricism which is tinged with an ancient, almost pre-human anxiety and yearning. That disharmony of poetical antinomies is a source of tension in his poetry. He is the first Hebrew poet to adopt the techniques of the Shakespearean sonnet and use them in a cycle of thirty-six poems which make up his volume, *Be-Yamim Shishshah u-be-Leylot Shivah* (In Six Days and Seven Nights). They are the best documents of abortive love in modern Hebrew literature. In them and in his ambitious poem, "Tarshishah" (To Tarshish), he expresses the conviction that an exterior life presses on our lives, disrupts relationships, and welds disparate entities. Memories of thousands of years are taken for granted as they were taken for granted by Baudelaire in his sonnet, "La Vie Antérieure," and by William Butler Yeats in his *Essays*.

In this preference for the abstract and the metaphysical, Aaron Zeitlin (b. 1898) resembles Regelson and Halkin. As the son of the mystic Hillel Zeitlin, he was predisposed to a weird symbolism and allegorism. Almost untouched by the American landscape and the American way of life—he came to this country in his forties—he may be considered the most abstract poet in modern Hebrew literature. His reality is the world of Kabbalah. In his massive poetic book, *Ben ha-Esh we-ha-Yesha'* (Between Fire and Salvation), he has revived and recreated obscure symbols and matched them into a vivid antithesis: Judaism on the one hand, the non-Jewish world on the other.

Zeitlin is a Hebrew poet *in* rather than of America. A Regelson and a Halkin, who have spent the latter decades of their lives in Israel, are still very much American in the poetical texture of their work. So is Moses Feinstein, who learned a great deal from Victorian poetry and who attacked the theme of redemption in two narrative poems, "Halom we-Goral" (Dream and Destiny) and "Abraham Abulafia." The former is indirectly concerned with the Land of Israel, the latter is a poetic biography of the thirteenth-century mystic who sought to convert Pope Nicholas III to Judaism.

While Regelson, Halkin and Feinstein are indebted to English literature, Gabriel Preil (b. 1911) has drawn on the resources of American literature. He translated Sandburg's "Prairie"[16] and echoed Whitman's verse in numerous poems. He is especially drawn to the latter's technique: blank verse is his exclusive form. As an introspective lyricist in pursuit of the poetic fact rather than the artifact, he is unique in Hebrew literature. In an idiom which is dangerously close to prose, he seeks to establish the inner identity of the small and petty things which are the raw stuff of man's associative powers: a map, a mailbox, a picture of Vincent van Gogh. It is no mere chance that he is attracted to the landscape of New Hampshire and Vermont: the cool sobriety of the northern regions corresponds to his temperament, which never ventures into the grand flights of pathos.

Not only the American landscape but the native American appeals to the imagination of the Hebrew writer in this country. Thus, in the lengthy poem "Mrs. Woods," Hillel Bavli has created the charming portrait of a woman who is an American version of the idealized characters of Moses Hayyim Luzzatto and Abraham Mapu. Efros, on the other hand, has delved into American history and reproduced, around the adventurous career of an imaginary hero, the feverish days of the gold rush in his narrative poem, "Zahav" (Gold).

It was not only the poet who was attracted to the native American. The Hebrew novelists and short-story writers in this country took a cursory glance, sometimes, at the gentile American. Usually, their hero was the Jewish immigrant in the early stages of Americanization: the greenhorn or at best the first-generation American. He was bewildered by the unaccustomed ways in his new home; in a later stage he enjoyed his success in business but he was not compensated for the absence of spiritual elevation; his holidays were almost ordinary workdays; his temples resembled social clubs rather than religious meeting places; his children, when they came of age, were guided by untutored rabbis whose inadequate knowledge of Judaism was matched by empty rhetoric and harmless ideas. This mélange of baffled fascination and repulsion was, incidentally, the chief characteristic of immigrants, as Oscar Handlin showed in an excellent historical study, *The Uprooted.*

While the theme of the Hebrew novelist was monotonously repetitious, the variations were endless. And the talent expanded on the theme ranged from sensitive to senseless, from first-rate to tenth-rate. The Hebrew short story which had a century-long European tradition predominated, while the novels depicting American Jewry were few and far between.

Isaac Dov Berkowitz (b. 1885) is perhaps the most sensitive portraitist of the immigrant. In an exemplary Hebrew style, he depicts the confusion of the newcomer in this country and his longing for "the other side." Sometimes, in imitation of his father-in-law, he writes a monologue which is pathetic and witty at the same time: e.g., *Yaroḳ* (Greenhorn). Sometimes he composes a comedy, *Ba-Arazot ha-Reḥoḳot* (In Distant Lands), which is full of love for the older and unadjustable type of Jewish and gentile immigrant. Sometimes he indulges in a tour de force: *Yemot ha-Mashiaḥ* (Days of the Messiah) reflects the inner turmoil of an un-Americanized Jew from Russia, who foresees wild possibilities of freedom when Czarist Russia suddenly changes into a free republic. But America is no more than a station or a stopover on the way to the ancestral home of the Jew. Berkowitz himself left it at the end of the twenties. And so do his heroes: they simply cannot adjust to the American environment. The title of his story, "America 'Olah le-Erez Yisrael" (America Leaves for the Land of Israel), is emblematic and ironic: American Jewry is on the way to its ancestral homeland.

Though Berkowitz never struck roots in America, he had a profound influence on its Hebrew literature. His addiction to refined, almost precious Hebrew, his choice of subject matter, his editorial imprint on the monthly, *Miklat* (Refuge), which appeared briefly after World War I—all these educated a generation of Hebrew writers during their formative years. Reuben Brainin (1862–1939) may have championed a wider range of literary predilections in the influential periodical, *Ha-Toren* (The Mast), and he may have been responsible for that catholicity of interests which is so characteristic of the generation of Hebrew writers between the two world wars. But Berkowitz's was an influence in depth. If Rosenzweig, Imber and Silkiner may be regarded as progenitors of Hebrew literature before World War I, Berkowitz will emerge as the father of Hebrew literature in this country after World War I. In one decade he created the few masterly stories which overshadowed the literary bric-à-brac of a previous epoch. But he was a stranger in transit.

It was Harry Sackler (b. 1883) who struck deep roots in America. Like Berkowitz, he was addicted to the immigrant. In a long novel, *Ben Erez we-Shamayim* (Between Earth and Heaven), he traced the history of an immigrant family from its departure from Europe through its expectant voyage to its painful years of adjustment. And he had a gift which no other writer in this country possessed in such abundance and maturity: a historical imagination. It was this gift which served him in his plays, in his novels, in his stories. On a vast historical canvas, he boldly recreated the Canaanite civilization and early America, rabbinic and especially Hasidic Jewry, and attempted to fathom the eternal mystery of his people.*

* Historicism, which is the general domain of the Hebrew novel, occurs in the poetry of Silberschlag: Yehudah Halevi and the disciple of Rabbi Nahman of Brazlav are represented by monologues in his book, *'Aleh, 'Olam, be-Shir,* pp. 67–85; Solomon ibn Gabirol is represented in *Bi-Shebilim Bodedim,* pp. 88–91 (editor).

The most characteristically American artifact of Sackler is un-doubtedly *Mashiaḥ Nosaḥ America* (Messiah American Style). The hero is the famed Mordecai Manuel Noah (1785–1851), journalist, politician, playwright, diplomat, adventurer.[17] In a mix-ture of shrewd real estate dealing and misplaced idealism, he ac-quired Grand Island in the Niagara river and renamed it Ararat—the penultimate resort of the Jews. In Sackler's play, Noah is characterized as a man who lives simultaneously in the land of dreams and in the land of reality. He is partly a charlatan who manipulates current events to his advantage, partly a dreamer who outruns reality and misleads his followers. And that is why an-other messiah, the half-legendary Joseph della Reyna in the play *Ketoret be-Af ha-Satan* (Incense for Satan), fails in his mis-sion: he is conquered by the very symbol of evil and his helpmate Lilith because he lacks the sacral fire and the childlike innocence of the truly religious leader. It was not an arid historicism that im-pelled Sackler to seek his heroes—real and imaginary—in the past. It was a personal need which happened to coincide with a literary trend in Europe and in America.

This was also the inner need of Yohanan Twersky (b. 1900). Though settled in Israel since 1947, he wrote most of his books in this country: a prodigious output of historical stories and novels. He was the first Hebrew writer who explored and exploited depth-psychology to the hilt. Freud and Adler were not only his masters: they guided and still guide his pen. This addiction to psychologism, coupled with an insatiable historicism, made Twersky what he is: a writer who holds the interest of his reader through an endless repetition of a successful formula.

What Sackler and Twersky have in common is a pre-occupation with the inner rather than with the outer life. To use a Riesmanism: both are inner-directed and tradition-directed.

That inner-directedness is also characteristic of Halkin's two novels, *Yeḥiel ha-Hagri* (Yehiel the Hagrite) and *'Ad Mashber* (To the Edge of Crisis). They are different in scope, in concept, in execution. But they bear the unmistakable stamp of their crea-tor, who sought to project himself in both novels. The first novel, *Yehiel the Hagrite,*[18] is the work of a youthful writer whose hero strives after a living God. Hence the name Yehiel (God Lives).

This pursuit of God is the preoccupation of Halkin in prose and poetry. In technique, *To the Edge of Crisis* resembles *Yehiel the Hagrite:* it is also an interior monologue on the whole, only lengthier and wittier. And the hero is a vastly different type of person: Professor Reuben G. Fowler, rabbi of an important congregation in New York, a member of the faculty of the Jewish Theological Seminary, author of a number of books on Judaism, reformer and philosopher. He is as far removed from Yehiel as a mature and successful intellectual can be from an immature, poetical, God-intoxicated youth.

Two other Hebrew poets have made important contributions in prose: Regelson and Friedland. Regelson seems to have reserved metaphysical flights for his poetry, and the more common experiences of life for his prose. A sense of humor informs his sketches, which read like autobiographical accounts. Friedland, an expert sonneteer, has written a few conventional stories which show a fine understanding of Jewish life in this country.

The stories and novels of Reuben Wallenrod (b. 1901) present a different type of Jew: an individual in the tradition of Berkowitz, suffering, unadjusted and frequently unadjustable. He starts at the bottom and he never reaches the top. He listens to advice but it comes from people who have not benefited by it: "In America you have to begin from the ground up, you have to suffer a bit and to wait for an opportunity."[19] Thus begins the story, "Hizdamnut" (Opportunity). And Wallenrod sympathizes with the petty lives of his heroes—with the lives which ebb away in colorless monotony. The element of sex predominates in his stories. But the dialogue between man and woman is on the appetitive rather than on the psychological plane. Like many Hebrew writers in this country, Wallenrod is less preoccupied with the ancestral home of the Jews and more with the adjustments of the greenhorn to the New World. And the search for a new identity is the central theme of Hebrew literature in America.

What about the future? Hebrew literary efflorescence in this country is a thing of the immediate past—the last fifty years. The writers who have brought about this minor renaissance are dead. The few who survive here and in Israel are old and past their literary prime. And the young are yet to come. The rigorous logic of events would necessitate a prognosis of demise. But Jewish history is replete with miraculous resurgences of the spirit. And a miraculous resurgence of Hebrew letters in this country is not an impossibility.

2. Yiddish Literature in the United States

HASYE COOPERMAN

YIDDISH literature in the United States reflects a unique cultural experience. No minority group has so well represented itself on American soil, in its own tongue and with indigenous values, as has the Yiddish group through its authors in the United States. The rich fabric of prose and poetry, so varied and of such high quality, is Jewish in theme and in attitude, but also American in that it describes the American experience. And the American environment has engendered a distinctive and independent growth, one quite different from its European counterpart, although both European and American Yiddish literature acknowledge their roots in the classics of Mendele, Peretz and Shalom Aleichem.

The Yiddish language was brought to the American colonies by the Ashkenazi Jews as early as the seventeenth century, and it was used in speech, correspondence and business letters during and after the eighteenth century.[1] But American Yiddish literature emerged in the 1870's, when creative writers as well as journalists began to reach their public through the periodical press. Even in those early formative years, the struggling journals printed poems, stories and critical essays, along with lighter feuilletons and editorials. Journalism and literature thus exerted a strong influence upon one another.

In 1870, two weeklies were launched and soon abandoned. Another periodical, *Di Yiddishe Tzaitung,* appeared sporadically from 1870 to 1873. Its publisher, K. H. Sarasohn, established *Di Yiddishe Gazetten* in 1874, the weekly out of which the first Yiddish daily, the *Tageblatt* or *Jewish Daily News,* subsequently developed.[2]

During the early period, Yiddish literature reflected social motivation and an awareness of the Jews' problems in the new milieu. But the quality was unimpressive. In the main, attempts were made to satirize current events, such as a conference of Reform Rabbis and the elections of 1872; or to portray the prevailing ignorance and unconcern with cultural values, and to mirror the plight of the learned. An illustration is afforded by "The Polish Scholar in America," a poem of some significance by Y. Z. Sobel, himself a former rabbi and university student in Russia. The poem describes a scholar who became a peddler and improved his lot, only to decry the callous disregard of spiritual ideals among the immigrants.

Sobel's collection of verse, published in brochure form in 1877 under the title *Yisroel der Alte* (Old Israel) is said to be the first Yiddish book printed in the United States.[3] Its dedicatory poem rather naively and zealously tells the reader that "these golden songs" are meant to persuade him "how lofty and significant" is Yiddish verse.

THE HEYDAY OF AMERICAN YIDDISH LITERATURE

While a handful of zealots were struggling with these initial literary and journalistic efforts, Russian-Jewish immigration reached mass proportions after the pogroms of 1881. Among the newcomers were working men, petty traders and intellectuals. Accustomed to the serenity of the small town, they were overwhelmed by the chaos of the big city, and an agonizing process of adjustment set in. The upheaval, the nostalgia for the traditional and integrated life, rent the soul of the immigrant, as the struggle for existence under sweatshop conditions racked his body and spirit.

These conditions nourished a literature of protest. Yiddish authors and journalists rallied their fellow-immigrants to the cause of justice and brotherhood, appealing to the teachings of the Jewish prophets and to the principles of modern socialism. In essays and in fiction, in poetry and in drama, the intolerable conditions were portrayed and a better life envisaged. The flourishing press maintained close contact between writers and thinkers and the avid public.

The Press

Mass immigration provided rootage for a press which grew to startling proportions. Between the 1880's and World War I, no less than twenty dailies appeared for varying periods of time in New York, Chicago, Cleveland, Philadelphia, Pittsburgh, Los Angeles, and other large cities. The *Tageblatt,* mentioned above, was launched in 1885 and continued until 1928. The *Forverts* was established in New York City in 1897 as the mouthpiece of the laboring masses, and it soon achieved considerable influence among the Yiddish readers. The first editor was the dynamic Abraham Cahan, who remained at the helm for half a century, guiding the daily's policies, among which Americanization ranked high. The *Forverts* was and remains pro-labor and socialist in orientation, but violently anti-communist. For many years anti-Zionist, it assumed a friendly attitude to Israel during the days of the Nazi holocaust and more especially when the state of Israel was established.

Of the other leading dailies, *Der Yiddisher Morgn Zhurnal* was founded in 1901 as the organ of the Orthodox, Conservative and pro-Zionist elements. *Der Tog* was founded in 1914 and reflected the liberal-intellectual and Zionist viewpoints. In 1953 these two dailies were consolidated into *Der Tog-Morgn-Zhurnal,* which continues publication.[4]

By 1927 the Yiddish dailies attained a peak circulation of 598,-347 of which over 200,000 represented readers of the *Forverts*.

These newspapers served as powerful media of opinion and literary expression, and they attained a special position as primary sources of Jewish news deriving from all over the world.

A periodical press—weeklies, monthlies, annuals—also flourished. Practically all of these included literary and cultural matter, but some were also politically oriented, pressing upon the public the precepts and programs of the ideological factions. Thus *Die Freie Arbeiter Shtimme,* founded in 1899, represented the "socialist-anarchist" elements, and *Der Yiddisher Kempfer,* established in 1905, was the organ of the Labor Zionists. Humorous magazines, like *Der Groiser Kundes* (published from 1909 to 1927), were especially popular.

The oldest monthly, and in many respects the best of the Yiddish periodicals, the *Zukunft* (Future), was established in 1892 as the vehicle for serious literary and cultural expression. One of its earliest editors was Abraham Cahan, but, in a large measure, the character of this journal was molded by the poet A. Liessin (1872–1938), who served as editor from 1913 to 1938. Some of the best Yiddish poetry appeared in this magazine, and it still attracts the foremost in current Yiddish literature.

At the height of Jewish immigration to the United States, the Yiddish newspapers also deemed it of major importance to instruct their readers, to educate and to elevate; hence, translations from the best of world literature were printed in serial or abridged form, as were articles on a great variety of subjects, among them civic duties, Americanization, the home, the school. And the Yiddish press was enlivened by readers' forums, debates, and controversies of a political, social, cultural and literary nature. The most abstruse philosophical arguments were elucidated, and they sparked an unusual intellectual exuberance among the readers. Indeed, the Yiddish press has been a unique kind of lively journalism.

Poetry

The Jewish labor movement regarded poetry as a forceful social weapon. Verse was recited on every possible occasion, especially at shop and union meetings. A good deal of the poetry was set to music and became part of the folk repertoire. Thus an uprooted people, stunned by exploitation, siphoned off its perplexities and anguish in songs of self-pity, social sentimentalism, satire, or revolutionary fervor. There were more than forty poets writing then, but only a few can be mentioned in this brief essay.[5]

Morris Winchevsky (1856–1932) was fondly dubbed "the grandfather of Jewish socialism." He was a publicist of some significance and a dramatist, but above all a poet of compassion. Such poems as "In Regn, in Vint, un in Kelt" (In the Rain, the Wind, and the Cold) which describes the bleak street as the home of two huddling orphans, or "Drai Shvester" (Three Sisters), one of whom sells flowers, the second, laces, and the third—her body, became symbols of protest because their imagery was direct and uncluttered. His songs of struggle, such as the oft-quoted "A Bezim un a Ker" (A Broom and How I Sweep) were poignant and dramatic.

Morris Rosenfeld (1862–1923) was the most dynamic and the most versatile of the early poets. He wrote songs of labor, poems describing the Jewish holidays, expressing yearnings for Zion, glorifying Jewish history and its heroes. He also wrote miscellaneous lyrics, and sometimes bitter satire. When Professor Leo Wiener of Harvard discovered him in 1897, his famous poems, "Main Yingele" (My Little Son), "Die Svet Shop" (The Sweat Shop), "Der Yiddisher Mai" (The Jewish May), and "Der Kanarik" (The Canary), were already recited and sung at meetings and in homes. In 1898 Professor Wiener published *Songs from the Ghetto* in English transliteration, accompanied by prose translations. Other translations followed into Russian, French, Czech, Roumanian, Hungarian, German, Polish, and even Japanese. Rosenfeld read his poetry at Harvard University, at Chicago, Wellesley and Radcliffe. Edwin Markham, whose "Man With the Hoe" Rosenfeld translated into Yiddish, addressed him as "a comrade in arms." Leo Wiener wrote: "Rosenfeld's poetry will survive as a witness of that lowermost hell which political persecutions, religious and racial hatred, industrial oppression have created for the Jew at the end of this our enlightened century."[6] Characteristic of Rosenfeld's poetry of exploitation is his "In the Factory":

Oh here in the shop the machines roar so wildly,
That oft, unawares that I am, or have been,
I sink and am lost in the terrible tumult;
And void is my soul . . . I am but a machine.

The face of the clock has the eyes of a foe;
The clock—oh I shudder—dost hear how it drives me?
It calls me, "Machine" and it cries to me, "Sew."

I sink in the slime of the stagnant routine;
There's tumult, there's struggle, oh lost is my ego—
I know not, I care not, I am a machine![7]

Morris Rosenfeld's songs of Jewish nationalism were tinged
with melancholy descriptions of nature, but they were not without hope. "Hannukkah Likht," "Golus Marsh" (March of the
Diaspora), "Oifn Buzim fun Yam" (On the Bosom of the Ocean)
or "Der Yiddisher Mai" (The Jewish May) are still sung in the
Yiddish schools.

Hero-hearts shall throb with gladness
'Neath Moriah's silent hill.
Nevermore of dread afflictions
Or oppressions need ye tell;
Filled with joy and benedictions
In the old home shall ye dwell.[8]

David Edelstadt (1866–1892), who died of tuberculosis at the
age of twenty-six, wrote Yiddish verse during the last four years
of his life. In his youth he had regarded himself as a Russian
revolutionary poet, for his parents had been Russianized and he
had had no contact with Jews in the old country. He learned to read
and write Yiddish among the Jewish proletariat in the United
States, and it was of proletarian freedom that he sang. His poem,
"In Kampf," spoke of "creating a free and joyous world for all hu-
manity." In "Main Tzavaa'h" (My Testament) he wrote:

And even in my grave I'll hear
My freedom song, the battle's cue.
And even there, I'll shed a tear
For all the slaves, Christian or Jew.

Joseph Bovshover's (1872–1915) earliest verse was clamorous
and challenging, in the tradition of Winchevsky, Rosenfeld and

Edelstadt. He came to this country at the age of seventeen, soon became steeped in American and English literature, and wrote English verse under the name of Basil Dahl. "To the Toilers" attracted much attention. Under the influence of Whitman's cosmic consciousness and Emerson's transcendentalism, Bovshover's Yiddish poetry assumed grandeur; its universal concepts of nature, its very style, became classical. "I come like a comet ablaze, like the sun when the dawn is awaking," he wrote. He wrote essays on the meaning of poetry, on form and style, on Emerson's concepts of nature, on Whitman and Markham, on the Muse. His esthetic approach was unique at a time when poetry was regarded as utilitarian.

Interest in the immediate present was uppermost; yet Rosenfeld had already demonstrated that the Jewish past had symbolic significance. A. Liessin wrote majestic poetry describing the martyrs and the heroes—"Yehudah Hamakhbi," "Bar Kokhbah," "Reb Akibah"—the Jewish holidays, the Bible. And Yehoash (S. Bloomgarden, 1871–1927) wrote songs to David, to the tomb of "Mother Rachel," to Jephtha's daughter. In "The Feet of the Messenger" he described a journey to Palestine. And Yehoash went on to write verse steeped in symbolism of individual and universal import, with startling imagery and pantheistic overtones:

> Have you cut your ears of grain,
> Have your sheaves been harvested?
> The night draws near.

or,

> From the bough of a tree
> Sways a sun of pure gold in a dewdrop immured;
> A vast forest aquiver with song has been lured
> Into a cage that is wee.[9]

Of prime significance was Yehoash's translation of the Bible into Yiddish, a collossal undertaking, painstaking and scholarly, with especial regard for the nuances of modern Yiddish.

Abraham Reisin (1876–1953), whose deceptively simple verse was often more impressionistic than realistic, was perhaps the best-loved of the Yiddish writers in America. Many of his songs, among them "Mai-Ko-Mashma-Lon" (The Raindrops) were set to music, and are still popular. He was a prolific versifier, with a sense of delicacy and gentle pathos, and an intense identification with the people, whom he perceived as individuals, not as masses.

Individual lyricism, personal motifs, self-expression—these represented a reaction against the social poetry and the traditionally Jewish concerns of the 1880's and 1890's. At the turn of the century, particularly when the new wave of immigration after 1905 brought a better-educated immigrant, new voices were heard. A movement known as "Die Yunge" demanded art, not propaganda; esthetics rather than ethics. "Die Yunge" had intensified individualism and introduced impressionism by the end of the first decade of the twentieth century. The poets (M. L. Halpern, J. Rolnik, Mani Leib, Ruvin Iceland, Z. Landau, I. J. Schwartz and H. Leivick) reacted to the melancholy anonymity of the big city. A sense of resignation, of escape into a private world, often made their poetry seem ethereal, grey, even weary. Twilight was their favorite theme. Mani Leib (1884–1953) wrote of "dark wounds that are my crimson roses"; M. L. Halpern of "the sweet earth wasted into desert," and of the prophet turned to stone. Yet they rhapsodized the land too: I. J. Schwartz, for example, wrote about the blue grass and the hills of Kentucky.

H. Leivick (1888–1962), who began as one of "Die Yunge," remained somewhat apart. Best known for his *Golem,* a dramatic poem in eight scenes, his images and symbols were related to man's ethical dilemmas and his striving for redemption from evil. Leivick's work was deeply Jewish as well as human in its outlook. He was the poet of supplication, of mysticism and of determination. "The world embraces me with thorny hands," he wrote. "It lifts me on to the fire and carries me to the stake. I burn and I burn, though I am not consumed. I rise once again, and I stride further off." Most of his verse is rhymed, and the style is terse. Those poems which have been set to music are sad and moody, and are often sung at gatherings.

When "Die Yunge" rebelled in 1907 against the nostalgia for the *Shtetl* and assumed the attitudes of esthetes and individualists, they set the stage for diversity. A score of individualistic and romantic poets appeared, each contributing his lyrical note, each with his own variation of content and style. Among them was

Menakhem Boraisha (1888–1949), who combined realism with mysticism and whose five-hundred-page epic poem, *Der Geier* (The Pilgrim), portrayed the Jewish intellectual groping for self-realization. The climax of individualism was reached in "Insichism" (Introspection), a movement launched by a manifesto in 1920. This was undisguised expressionism, a defiance of all pre-determined values.

The "Insichism" school of imagism proclaimed each poet to be a kaleidoscope of visions, dreams, realities, fantasies. Free associations, allusions, deformations of the outer world, views turned inward, distortions, incongruities—these were the Insichist terms of reference. For the Yiddish readers and critics, these new attitudes were shocking in the extreme, for Yiddish literature had always expressed a strong folk tendency. The readers accepted idyllic or romantic deviations, but expected the author to relate himself to his people in "reasonable" imagery.

A. Glanz-Leyeles, N. B. Minkoff and J. Glatshtein who signed the manifesto and edited the Insichist magazine were also writers of prose criticism. These poets approached Yiddish literature as a universal and esthetic experience, but they did not deny the poet his privilege to react to socially significant episodes or to specifically Jewish themes. As the years passed, their position won acceptance and their influence upon Yiddish literature was considerable. Glanz continued his preoccupation with the big city, and wrote an eloquent poetic drama on *Shlomo Molkho;* Glatshtein remains a versatile poet and critic; and for many years Minkoff was the managing editor of the *Zukunft* and wrote scholarly essays as a literary historian and critic.

The years that followed "Insichism" were marked by lesser schools and movements and by individual experimentation. Some poets delighted their readers with jazz effects, others were scintillating and humorous, using the language as an instrument for word-play; and still others were influenced by left-wing ideology. And there were always the traditional balladists, like B. I. Bialostotsky and E. Auerbach, who were steeped in folklore and Jewish romanticism. The period before the Nazi holocaust has aptly been called the "halcyon period in Yiddish literature. A feverish productivity characterized many of the writers."[10]

Fiction

Short stories and novels came into being along with the social poetry at the height of Jewish immigration. Despair was translated into vivid prose realism by Z. Libin, Leon Kobrin and S. Levin. Libin said of himself: "My muse was born in the dreary sweatshop, beside the Singer machine where I first heard her anguished outcry; my muse was nurtured in the dark tenement graves." It was Libin who caught the moments of quiet pathos which overtook "the superfluous one." It was Kobrin who dramatically described the baser passions, the crowded rooms, the secret loves, the coarser moments. "Whether the sun shines, or the rain pours, or the snow falls—it never matters; the large ungainly tenement house never changes its frozen, unfriendly, grey, stone-blind expression." And he went on to tell how "behind each door there is a special little world." Levin wrote simpler sketches of immigrant life and aspirations; less dramatic, but touching. And all three authors later wrote plays for the Yiddish theater on the same theme: Jewish life in America and its conflicts.

Abraham Reisin, the poet, was a superb craftsman of the short story; he wrote over a thousand stories. Their sense of delicacy, their fragile humor and muted descriptions suggest a rare combination of deep compassion and imagination. His stories about children are especially touching. And his insights into each individual as a unique being might best be summed up by "Abraham the Orchard-Keeper," who creeps into a tumbledown hut and curls himself up into a ball. "But to remain hidden from the world is not so easy," writes Reisin.

The fiction writers among the Yunge, especially J. Opatoshu, A. Raboy and David Ignatoff, wrote impressionistically about the new land. Raboy described life on the prairies, or in the Dakotas in such works as *Der Yiddisher Cowboy* or *Herr Goldenbarg.* Ignatoff pictured the lovely scenes in and around New York City. Joseph Opatoshu, who vacillated between impressionism and realism, described life in various parts of the country, but more especially the stark ugliness of poverty and gangsterism in New York City. Ignatoff and Opatoshu also turned to the mystique of Hasidism, to miracle tales of old Prague and Regensburg, to biblical settings and to Jewish history generally. Opatoshu's *In Poilishe Velder* (In Polish Woods) has become a classic.

Many writers of fiction, like Lamed Shapiro and Jonah Rosenfeld, veered from impressionism to extreme naturalism in exotic stories of the abnormal and the excessive. Some resorted to psychological symbolism of an erotic nature. Experimentation with form and concern with craftsmanship account for the wide range of theme and the great variety of output.

Shalom Asch (1880–1957) achieved fame as a creative writer before he came to the United States. His writing was epic in scope, panoramic in sweep, and he portrayed the world of the unlettered with its passion and brute force. A prolific writer, he had an especial flair for grandeur and for intricacy of plot, but his Yiddish often lacked polish. His christological novels (*The Nazarene, Mary, The Prophet*) were never accepted by Yiddish readers or critics, and his best historical novels, like *Kiddush Hashem* (Sanctification) and *Shabse Tzvi,* are hardly known to English readers. However, *Three Cities,* and *Salvation (Der Tehillim Yid)* were on the best seller lists.

David Pinski (1872–1960), who came to the United States in 1899 via Poland and Germany, was a disciple of Peretz. His first stories were of working-class people; his style was robust and his interests psychological. Several of his novels have been rendered into English: *The Generations of Noah Eden* and *Arnold Levenberg* are best known. He is perhaps more famous as a playwright.

The Drama

The Yiddish theater, like the press, was a vital part of Jewish immigrant life. It provided relief from an otherwise drab existence, but it must be emphasized that it was *not* an escape. When Shalom Aleichem first visited this country, he referred to a "new way of life," a cultural exuberance, which had to be seen to be believed.

There were Yiddish theaters in New York, Boston, Philadelphia, Baltimore, Chicago, and Los Angeles, and acting troupes visited many other cities. In New York City great actors like Boris Thomashefsky, J. P. Adler and David Kessler established themselves in their own theaters and played to enthusiastic audiences, which often included many who did not understand the language. For half a century the Yiddish theater in the United States was the center which attracted actors from Jewish settlements overseas.

In 1918, Maurice Schwartz organized his troupe, which three years later became known as the Yiddish Art Theater. For a quarter of a century he produced a variety of plays of merit and distinction and contributed to the advancement of the Yiddish drama. This actor-director-producer raised the standard of the theater and drew large audiences. To his colorful performances he added a sense of timing and grouping that were quite remarkable. He himself dramatized many Yiddish novels, and his theater inspired the writing of some excellent plays.

The father of the modern Yiddish theater, Abraham Goldfaden (1840–1908), had begun his performances in the taverns of Roumania in 1876. He brought part of his troupe to this country in 1882 on the initiative of Boris Thomashefsky, and his musical, *Kolddunya,* launched the first professional Yiddish theater in New York City. Goldfaden's operettas left much to be desired in theme and plot, but his melodies were lilting and intriguing. The intellectuals and critics chided him for his rollicking humor and bad taste, the excessive glamor and the melodrama of his song-and-dance entertainment. But he was popular, and his songs, like "Rozhinkes Mit Mandlen" (Raisins and Almonds), became folk songs. Goldfaden also wrote plays and librettos on historical and biblical themes, like *Uriel Akosta* and *Bar Kokhbah.*

Jacob Gordin (1853–1909), who was also a superb story writer, incorporated into his otherwise serious drama the comic interlude and the musical tidbit which he had found so enchanting in Goldfaden. But he took his cue from the intellectuals, and imbued the stage with lofty principles and moral earnestness. He belonged to the period of social realism and his central characters were flesh-and-blood people, dignified and tragic in stature. *Mirele Efros,* which he wrote for the actress Kenny Lipzin, depicted a proud Jewish mother enmeshed in the drama of rich and poor and in the strife between the generations. *Gott, Mentsh un Taivl* (God, Man and Satan), modeled on the theme of Job, was written for David Kessler; it was a realistic study of exploitation. *Sapho,* on the theme of womanhood, was written for the majestic Bertha Kalich. Gordin left some seventy dramas and provided translations and adaptations from Shakespeare, Molière, Ibsen, Shaw, Strindberg, Chekhov, Goethe and Schiller.

The Yiddish Theater enlisted the talents of poets and novelists. David Pinski, whose works had been produced by Max Rheinhardt in Germany, made use of a variety of themes in his dramas, among them Jewish historical incidents (*The Eternal Jew, Family Zvi, Shlomo Molkho*) and social and psychological conflicts. The treatment was naturalistic, with marked poetic overtones. Some of his plays were produced in English translation: *Der Oitzer* (The Treasure) by the Theatre Guild, and *Der Letzter Sakh Hakol* (The Final Balance) by the Provincetown Players.

Other gifted writers found in legend and folkways the source materials for their plays. S. Ansky's *The Dybbuk* was a tragedy with strong Hasidic overtones, blending the natural with the supernatural. Peretz Hirshbein, a poet of folkways who combined impressionism with allegory, wrote *Die Puste Kretshme* (The Haunted Inn) and *Dem Shmidt's Tekhter* (The Blacksmith's Daughters). And Leivick, who viewed his plays as dramatic poems in scenes, based his play, *Der Golem,* on the legend of a sixteenth-century sage who fashioned a being out of clay and dared to breathe life into it.

Many of the plays portrayed or caricatured Jewish life in America. Leon Kobrin and Z. Libin exploited these themes, as did Ossip Dimov, author of *Bronx Express* and *The Eternal Wanderer. Shmates* (Rags) by Leivik was a compassionate portrayal of the factory.

Maurice Schwartz's The Yiddish Art Theater produced many of the plays mentioned above, and also the ever popular dramatizations of the stories of Shalom Aleichem ("Tevye—the Dairyman," "Sweepstakes," and others) as well as those of Shalom Asch ("Kiddush Hashem" and "Three Cities," "Salvation," "The Witch of Castile"). Asch's own dramatizations of his novels, like *Got Fun Nekamah* (God of Vengeance) and *Mottke Ganev* (The Vagabond) were enthusiastically received, as were *Yoshe Kalb* and *The Brothers Ashkenazi,* plays based on novels by I. J. Singer.

In the 1920's, there were also experimental groups like Undzer Teatr (Our Theater), the Rudolph Shildkraut Theater in New York, and independent productions like those of Jacob Ben Ami.

The Artef, a left-wing troupe, produced propaganda plays of some merit.

The professional Yiddish theater has vanished, but semi-professional and amateur groups persist. Recently, the Folksbiene, associated with the Arbeiter Ring, presented *A Khasene in Fernvald* (A Wedding in Fernwoods), a new play by Leivick, and lately it has played *The Eleventh Inheritor,* a realistic depiction of the contemporary New York scene by the very talented M. Dluzhnovsky.

The Essay

Chaim Zhitlowsky (1865–1943) and Chaim Greenberg (1889–1953) employed the essay to expound philosophic themes and as a tool for social propaganda. The former championed Jewish cultural rebirth in the countries of dispersion (socialism and territorialism), while the latter was the eloquent exponent of labor Zionism. In the 1920's their debates and polemics in the journals stimulated much agitation and study. Greenberg wrote for *The Kempfer* from 1914 until his death in 1953, and Dr. Zhitlowsky was a staff member of *The Day* and a prolific essayist. Zhitlowsky's *Die Filosofye* was the first of its kind in Yiddish.

Literary criticism and analysis have been a feature of the Yiddish press from its early days. In 1887, Getzil Zelikowitch published his first critical essay on the theater, and thereafter most poets and novelists wrote essays or reviews on the style and content of the numerous works produced. Professional literary and drama critics like J. Entin, A. Mukdoni, B. Rivkin and A. Coralnik (known for his great lucidity and charm) each had a coterie of followers who espoused various points of view. The foremost literary critic was S. Niger (1883–1955), who came here in 1919 after eighteen years as editor and publicist in Poland and Russia. An historian of Yiddish letters, conservative in his tastes, he wrote on virtually every Yiddish writer. Among his dozen volumes was *Die Tzveishprakhikeit Fun Undzer Literatur* (1941), where he argued that the Jews were creating one literature in the two languages, Yiddish and Hebrew.

N. B. Minkoff wrote formal essays on the classical poets, books on the early Yiddish critics and on old Yiddish literature, and a definitive work on the earliest Yiddish poets in the United States.

S. Bickel, who came to these shores in 1939, writes informal and lively literary criticism for the press. And I. J. Trunk, who arrived in 1941, was the author of many literary-philosophic volumes; his psychological insights and philosophical perception made him an essayist of special merit.

THE HOLOCAUST AND AFTER

The restriction of immigration and the mass murders by the Nazis have contributed to the decline of the Yiddish press. The number of Yiddish readers has diminished. But there still are three dailies, five weeklies, one bi-weekly, fifteen monthlies, and about thirty other periodicals. One may still read in the Yiddish press articles on early and present-day Israel by Ben Gurion, interviews with Jews from all over the world, essays on European existentialists, on world-wide books and authors, and there are always the memoirs, the original short stories and the poetry.

The mood of the writing has become traditional and neo-classical. Religious symbols, old Yiddish literature, the roots of the past —these have all taken on new meaning. And, of course, the new state of Israel is a source of pride and inspiration.

Post-war immigrants like H. L. Fuks, M. Shtrigler, and R. Bryks, whose grim tale *A Cat in the Ghetto* has been translated into English, have introduced a new kind of realism. Dovid Einhorn, the impressionist, came to this country in 1940, although he had been writing for the *Forverts* since 1920. A. Tzeitlin writes poetry of a religious nature. And Itzik Manger effects a self-conscious and stylized folk quality in his verse. The poet and novelist Chaim Grade, outstanding among the new immigrants, is versatile in theme and concerns himself with ethical and spiritual values. Lately he has published a series of poems describing the natural wonders of the land—Yosemite, the Grand Canyon, California.

I. Bashevis (Singer) is perhaps best known to English readers because of his novella *Satan in Goray* and his story of *Gimpel the Fool*. His style is terse, his satire dramatic, and the pathos of his plots derives from the incongruities of the outer world pitted against the interior of the mind and the imagination. In 1960 the

American Academy of Arts and Letters awarded him a grant, the first grant given to an American author not writing in English. Bashevis describes his Hasidic background in Poland as well as the Jewish-Khurbn American milieu.

The post-war period has also introduced a new kind of writing: *Khurbn Literatur* (holocaust literature). Besides poetry, short stories and diaries (among which the most moving, *Finf Yor in Varshever Ghetto* by Bernard Goldshtein, 1947, was translated as *The Stars Bear Witness*), there are several hundred *Yizkor,* or commemorative volumes. These describe, each in its own fashion, the people, places, buildings, cultural life, folkways and religion, as well as the leading figures of the towns and cities destroyed by the Germans.

Many of these books have been published by branches of fraternal organizations like the *Natzionale Arbeter Farband* (Jewish Workers Alliance) or the *Arbeter Ring* (Workmen's Circle). These are nation-wide organizations which conduct their business in Yiddish, as do the chapters of the Yiddish Cultural Congress and the YIVO Institute for Jewish Research. Originally founded in 1925 in Vilna, Poland, as the Yiddish Scientific Institute, YIVO established branches in many countries, and in 1939 its American branch in New York City became the center. Its various sections (history, economics, folklore, linguistics, education) are devoted to documentation, research and the training of young scholars. Its Yiddish library and its archives are extensive; its exhibitions give evidence of painstaking scholarship.

In 1950 N. Stutchkoff compiled the monumental thesaurus of the Yiddish language (*Oitzer Fun der Yiddisher Shprakh*). Somewhat later the Encylopaedia Britannica included Yiddish as one of the seven languages of its polyglot dictionary, the Yiddish section edited by D. Graubart. The most significant project under way is the comprehensive Yiddish dictionary (sponsored by YIVO) which is expected to comprise about 200,000 words in ten volumes. Volume I has been published.

Yiddish is now taught at the New School for Social Research, at City, Brooklyn and Queens Colleges and at Columbia University in New York City, and at the University of California. Perhaps

Yiddish in the United States will find its future in the seats of higher learning.

Yiddish has attained a new dimension: it has become a *loshon kodesh,* a language of the martyrs. And it must be noted that not only does Yiddish have strong roots in centers of Yiddish culture in Europe, South America, South Africa, Australia, and of course Israel (where one Yiddish daily, six weeklies, six monthlies and an excellent quarterly are published), but also that Yiddish is indispensable for the study of recent Jewish history.

Yiddish has thrived in a variety of centers. Once it was Poland; later, the United States; and at present, Argentina appears to be a close second to the United States. There are some three hundred Yiddish writers in the United States today (for lack of space, some important names have had to be omitted from this study), one hundred and fifty in Israel and the same number in Argentina. In the United States such authors as Maurice Samuel, Saul Bellow, Isaac Rosenfeld, Irving Howe, Alfred Kazin, have by their appraisals and translations been presenting Yiddish literature to an ever-widening public. Who can say what the next decades will bring?

3. *Jewish Awareness in American Literature*

Marie Syrkin

Beginnings

In 1852 Henry Wadsworth Longfellow visited the Jewish cemetery in Newport. The occasion inspired him to write a poem in which he exclaimed: "How strange it seems! these Hebrews in their graves. . . . Closed are the portals of their synagogue/No psalms of David now the silence break." After describing the vanished piety and grandeur, he concluded: "But ah! what once has been shall be no more,/The groaning earth in travail and in pain/Brings forth its races, but does not restore,/ And the dead nations never rise again."

Longfellow proved to be even less successful as a prophet than as a bard. Anyone surveying the American scene a hundred years later would probably be tempted to comment not on how silent but on how vocal "these Hebrews" were. By mid-century American Jewish writers were winning recognition in the forefront of American letters in impressive numbers. They were not exactly chanting psalms of David, however; they dealt in their peculiar fashion with Jewish themes and the Jewish background from which they sprang. What distinguished the American Jewish writer of the 1950's and 1960's from his predecessors was not so much his choice of subject matter as the status he now held as an American writer. Any enumeration of leading American writers of the sixties would include a striking proportion of second and third generation American Jews high on the list. This represented a marked departure from previous decades, when American Jewish writers, while numerous and articulate, enjoyed no such general acclaim. The progress from the immigrant ghetto to a commanding place in the literary life of the United States had been achieved.

Another change worth noting is that discussion as to who was a "Jewish" writer now appeared dated. The coincidence of ethnic origin and its literary manifestation in the work of serious American writers who were Jews had been sufficiently frequent so as to make such a distinction superfluous. Nevertheless, Ludwig Lewisohn's dictum, "A Jewish book is a book written by a man who knows he is a Jew," remained useful.

To a large degree the American Jewish novelist, in particular, reflects the historical experience of the Jew in America. Stage by stage, the successive alterations in the social structure of American Jewry are depicted by the writers who are the products of these changes. From the immigrant Abe Cahan to American-born Saul Bellow or Philip Roth, we perceive the processes of taking root and alienation, of adaptation and recoil which mark the inner biography of the American Jewish community. Within the general framework of American experience and attitudes, the specific problems of the immigrants and later of their sons and grandsons are crystallized and expressed in fiction. The picture of American Jewish life created is equally likely to be a vulgar cartoon or an idealized portrait; but whatever the distortions, enough realistic contour remains to make an examination of the American Jewish novel instructive for a discussion of Jewish literary expression in the United States.

Before the twentieth century there are only occasional fictional works by Jews. After the Civil War a few novels appeared, but the Jewish community in the United States was still too small numerically and too peripheral to its environment to offer fertile ground for the creative writer as distinct from the reporter. By the first decade of the twentieth century, the impact of the large-scale Russian Jewish immigration streaming into the country since 1880 began to make itself felt. The immigrant newcomer, learning English in the night-schools and sweatshops, became articulate. The encounter with the new world was evaluated in accents of enthusiasm or disillusionment. Mary Antin's autobiography entitled *The Promised Land* is an example of the former.

The Promised Land (1912) epitomized purely and uncritically the immigrant's grateful delight in the new world of freedom and opportunity. "I must not fail to testify that in America a child of the slums owns the land and all that is good in it," rhapsodized Mary Antin in a vein which no later immigrant generation was to recapture. But she adds, significantly, "I think I have thoroughly assimilated my past. . . . I want now to be of today. It is painful to be conscious of two worlds. The Wandering Jew in me seeks forgetfulness." The American dream emerges here as the vision of the great melting pot. Assimilation for Mary Antin is not tired escape, but an exultant affirmation of the American promise in which the immigrant girl believes with a naive optimism.

Abraham Cahan's *The Rise of David Levinsky* (1917) shows us the other side of the coin. Cahan's account of the "success story" of the Talmud student, who becomes a rich clothing manufacturer, has become a classic of its kind. Success has its personal defeats, however; the transformation brings losses as well as gains which are not confined to the ledger. The chief merit of the novel is a sturdy, honest outlook which depicts the New York East Side neither vulgarly nor sentimentally. The encounter with America is evaluated objectively: the new world receives as well as gives. Levinsky meditates with pride on the productive role of the Jewish immigrant in the clothing industry: "Foreigners ourselves, and mostly unable to write English, we had Americanized the system of providing clothes for the American woman of moderate or humble means. . . . Indeed, the Russian Jew had made the average American girl a tailor-made girl."

THE TWENTIES AND THE THIRTIES—TAKING STOCK

Inevitably, the East Side remained a source of literary inspiration not only for the first-generation immigrant but for his descendants, as novels appearing in the sixties testify. Norman Fruchter's *Coat Upon a Stick* (1963) indicated the continuing vitality of the theme. But while the writer of the sixties was to recreate the past with characteristic acerbity, the popular novelists of the twenties dealt with their more immediate material nostalgically and sentimentally. Anzia Yezierska, for instance, herself an immigrant, has a heavy streak of pathos despite a realistic core. Fannie Hurst, born in Ohio, milks the emotional aspects of her material with formidable energy. "A laugh on life with a tear behind it" is her own characterization of one of her works. In extenuation, one should mention the genuine sympathy and tenderness these writers bring to their ghetto tales.

The depiction of the ghetto may be humorous as well as lachrymose. Montague Glass, in his Potash and Perlmutter series, succeeded in adding to the gallery of American comic types. Abe Potash and Mauruss Perlmutter are genial and light-hearted caricatures drawn with affection by a skilled cartoonist. One need merely compare them with the creations of the later "sick" comics who exploit the same subjects to appreciate the profound difference in attitude that would take place in the course of two generations. Perlmutter is amusing, but never offensive. We laugh with him when he comments on the troubles of the cloak and suit trade: "Real-estaters ain't got no such trouble like we got it, Abe. . . . They ain't wearing stripes in tenement houses one year, Abe, and solid colors the next."

With the spread of Jewish communities to various parts of the United States away from the Eastern seaboard, and with the entrance of first-generation Jews born or brought up in the United States into a more varied economic and social life than that of their parents, the themes of the novelists change. Not the encounter with the new world, but the process of taking root is described. The locale may be Montana (*Singermann* by Myron Brinig), California (*Roots in the Sky* by Sidney Miller) or Chicago (*The Old Bunch* by Meyer Levin and *On the Shore* by Albert Halper). Many more names could be mentioned here, but whatever the region, the central subject of these novelists becomes growing up in America.

Meyer Levin was to wait for years till the publication of *Com-*

pulsion, a narrative based on the sensational crime of Leopold and Loeb, for a duplication of the success which met the publication of *The Old Bunch,* a sharp study of young Jews becoming "Americanized" at the expense of their Jewish past. The deep Jewish passion only implicit in the early writing of Levin was to become polemically explicit, sometimes at the cost of his literary stature, in his subsequent work. In fiction, drama and essay, Meyer Levin became one of the few American writers wholly dedicated to the portrayal of the central experience of the Jewish people in the twentieth century: the Nazi holocaust and its consequences.

Albert Halper, whose novels of working-class life (*Union Square* and *The Foundry*) ally him to the "Proletarian" school of the thirties, is, despite the ideological classification, at his best in character portrayal and in the evocation of mood. His most successful work is to be found in sketches such as those in *On the Shore,* in which the individual rather than the plot is primary, and in the authentic tenderness of some of his portraits of Jewish life.

The depression of the thirties was to spawn a host of "proletarian" writers, revolving around the *New Masses,* many Jews among them, whose work was to prove ephemeral. Perhaps the most vocal of the "social consciousness" school who wrote specifically of Jews was Michael Gold. His *Jews Without Money* (1930) was a fair sample of a reaction to social conditions not anticipated by the lyric Mary Antin of a generation earlier. For Gold, the promised land consisted of "the sweatshops, the bawdy houses, and Tammany Hall." The land of opportunity has grown "so rich and fat because it has eaten the tragedy of millions of immigrants." As in the work of other proletarian writers, all perplexities receive a dogmatically simple answer: there is no Jewish problem; there is only class struggle. Jewish bankers are fascists; Jewish workers are radicals. What is the solution? Gold is beset by no anemic doubts: "O Workers' Revolution, you brought hope to me, a lonely suicidal boy. You are the true Messiah." Gold's faith was to prove strong enough to withstand the disintegration of the pro-communist nucleus among intellectuals, a process which began after the Moscow trials and gathered momentum after the Nazi-Soviet Pact. The apparently flourishing proletarian school was to prove short-lived. The impact of Stalinism and a rebellion against the sternly administered precepts of "socialist realism" were to cause mass desertions among Jewish and non-Jewish writers who had been drawn to the communist cause. Practically nothing remains in the United States of the originally influential *New Masses* and its circle.

The most striking Jewish novel of the thirties evades ready classification. *Call It Sleep* by Henry Roth won extraordinary critical acclaim in 1934 when the author was twenty-eight years old. It has been periodically rediscovered since then and was again hailed upon its republication in 1960. The work remains unique in a literal as well as literary sense; for despite his striking talent, Henry Roth wrote no subsequent novel in the intervening years.

Call It Sleep deals with immigrant life on the East Side of New York as seen through the sensibility of a child. The entire action is concentrated in two years of the life of David Schearl, from the age of six to eight. The characters and environment, at once grossly palpable and elusively mysterious, are perceived through the anguished awareness of the child. With immense skill the dark entanglements of the adult world are unravelled through David's intuitions and confusions. We can see and smell the dingy streets and tenements, we can hear the marvellously reconstructed Yiddish-English speech, just as we know the full-bodied characters in all their emotional complexity. Here is no childhood, wistful, cute, or tragic, remembered in anger or nostalgia by the adult intelligence. The impact of the book's unfolding domestic drama is not weakened by the hindsight of adult comprehension. Experience presents itself raw, frightening, radiant, unsullied by understanding.

Part of the force of the novel lies in its transcendence of the fashionable realism of the thirties. *Call It Sleep* cannot be pigeonholed as a social document or a slice of life in the slums of Brownsville. The frequent comparison of Henry Roth with James Farrell is misleading, because nowhere does Farrell evince the poetic vitality of Roth. In Roth, fidelity to the depiction of environment is always complemented by an imaginative capacity to weld the drab details of the outer world into the transport of the child's vision. In this fusion of the realistic and the poetic Roth is far closer to Joyce, whose influence is sometimes too apparent, than to the social realists of the thirties. In its union of symbolism and realism, *Call It Sleep* belongs more to the era of Bernard Malamud than to that of Farrell and Dos Passos. Perhaps one clue to Roth's silence lies in his anticipation of a style more characteristic of the fifties than of the thirties, at a time when "social realism" was almost mandatory.

Concomitant with the reaction against the ghetto another trend may be detected. The emancipated Jewish writer, who in breaking away from his traditional moorings often bespatters his past, begins to examine his presumed emancipation more critically. The pluses and minuses are not all one-sided. The most significant figure in this re-evaluation was Ludwig Lewisohn, whose career started brilliantly in the twenties when his general literary influence was at its peak. As critic, essayist, pamphleteer, translator and novelist, Lewisohn was enormously productive, and he became the leading exponent of Zionism in the United States in fiction and essay. As an explicitly "committed" Jewish writer, his development is of particular interest for this survey.

Lewisohn's two dominant themes—sexual revolt against the repressions of Puritanism and Jewish revolt against the effacement of assimilation—each conceived in deeply personal terms, appear early in his writing. *Upstream,* the autobiography composed in his youth which rang as a kind of *J'accuse* in the twenties, exposed the shock of his realization that though his "psychical life was Aryan through and through," his Jewish birth kept him from complete acceptance by the world he sought to enter—he could not teach English literature in an American university. This discovery led to his outcry, "So long as there is discrimination, there is exile." He bids "the German and the Jew, the Latin and the Slav [to] preserve his cultural tradition and beware of the encroachment of Neo-Puritan barbarism—beware of becoming merely another dweller on an endless Main Street."

In direct exposition and didactic narrative, Lewisohn was to hammer at these theses for the remainder of his life. Though *The Case of Mr. Crump* is the most powerful of his novels and offers the fairest estimate of Lewisohn's talent, one must go to *The Island Within* (1928) for the next step in his treatment of the Jewish prob-

lem. The pain of rejection apparent in *Upstream* has been subli-
mated into a proud acceptance of his Jewish heritage. The hero of
the novel, an American Jewish intellectual alienated from his Jewish origins, meditates after the failure of his marriage to the daughter of a Protestant clergyman: "He must try to save his son's
heritage for him, his incomparable spiritual heritage. His son should
not stand before a Gentile friend as he had stood beside Charles
Dawson, and wish that he, too, could boast as ancestors tartaned
clansmen who had fought at Flodden Field. . . . His son should
be incapable of feeling excluded; he must possess the knowledge
that he stood by birth at the human center of things."

The twenties and thirties can be viewed as a period of stock-
taking for the American Jewish writer. The successful emergence
from the ghetto may be remembered nostalgically or pictured with
the repelling grossness of Jerome Weidman in *I Can Get It for You
Wholesale*. The febrile energy of a young Jew on the make may be
depicted by Bud Schulberg in *What Makes Sammy Run?* The
proletarian novel may turn the success story upside down, but by
and large, with the already noted exception of Ludwig Lewisohn,
the position of the Jew in America is not seriously questioned.
While American Jewish life may be presented critically or satiri-
cally, as a Sinclair Lewis satirizes the American businessman in
Babbit, the basic assumption is that of the viability of the Jewish
minority in America. The Jews pictured may be vulgar go-getters
or starving proletarians, middle-class Philistines or frustrated
artists; they may suffer insult or disability because they are Jews;
nevertheless, they are an abiding part of the American society.
Such is the fundamental premise until the forties.

THE FORTIES—REACTION TO CATASTROPHE

In the forties there is a marked change. The Hitler terror in Europe, accompanied by such manifestations in the United States as
the Christian Front and Father Coughlin, shake this assurance. For
the first time, there appears a group of novels which deal exclusively
rather than incidentally with the problem of American anti-Semitism. The native-born Jewish writer begins to voice the spoken and
unspoken fears of the American Jewish community.

The popularity of *Gentleman's Agreement* (1946) by Laura Hobson is an indication of this growing concern. A far more probing and effective study of the same theme is *Focus,* a novel by Arthur Miller which appeared a year earlier. Miller, like Hobson, uses an artificial device. In each case anti-Semitism is viewed through its impact on a Christian who is mistaken for a Jew. However, in *Gentleman's Agreement* the pretense of Jewishness by the journalist hero is voluntary, while in *Focus* the leading character, an "average American," suddenly begins to look like a Jew when he is obliged to wear glasses. From then on he is mistaken for a Jew. Though the literary trick is unconvincing—the eyeglasses are almost magical in their potency—the unwilling protagonist is forced to participate in the experience of being a Jew in an increasingly hostile environment. The forms of anti-Semitism described are far more brutal than the social discrimination exposed in *Gentleman's Agreement.* Arthur Miller, in depicting the activities of the Christian Front gangs, plainly poses the question of the physical safety of the American Jewish community. It could happen here. The book ends on a note of programmatic optimism. "Mr. Average American" has his eyes opened through his disfiguring glasses and joins in fighting the reactionary forces. Whether or not one accepts the happy ending, the problem of anti-Semitism in America has been boldly raised.

Another novel of the period, which might be mentioned not because of literary merit but because of its subject matter, is *Wasteland,* by Jo Sinclair, winner of the Harper Prize in 1946. Here there is a shift of emphasis. The American Jew's trouble is inner, not outer. The hero, who has changed his name, discovers the cause of his affliction on the psychoanalyst's couch: he is sick because he has rejected himself and his past. A psychic need has been denied. Only when Jake-John accepts his people will he escape the wasteland of negation and be healed. The question of Jewish identity has been introduced, to be pursued with growing insistence by subsequent writers.

Towards the end of the forties the impact of World War II begins to be felt. Three of the most popular war novels of the period are by Jewish writers: *The Young Lions* by Irwin Shaw, *The Naked and the Dead* by Norman Mailer, and *The Caine Mutiny* by Herman Wouk. Though the most erratically gifted of these writers is Norman Mailer, Irwin Shaw's *The Young Lions* must be considered here since its subject is the experience of an American Jew in the American army. While anti-Semitism in the army has been dealt with peripherally by various writers, Shaw makes it his central theme. Noah Ackerman, the small Jewish soldier, is tormented by his platoon and wins acceptance only after he has fought an impressive collection of bullies. The counterpart to fiery little Noah is big 200-pound Fein, who is not bothered by the platoon and who offers this classic advice on Jewish survival: "The best equipment a Jew can have is a deaf ear . . . if all the Jews had been like you, we'd all have been wiped out 2,000 years ago." Noah answers: "I want every Jew to be treated as though he weighed 200 pounds."

Despite the savagery of the army experience depicted, Shaw, like Miller in *Focus,* ends on a note of hope. Noah is finally accepted as a buddy; American officers are horrified by the concentration camps and, though Noah is killed by a Nazi bullet, we are left with the assurance that in the final encounter the good people will win over bigotry. The same note is sounded in *Act of Faith,* a much anthologized short story by Shaw. Here an American Jewish soldier who gets a disquieting letter about anti-Semitism in the United States is tempted for a moment to keep his German revolver. But the wavering is momentary; he sells the pistol. "What could I use it for in America?"

One sees that the Jewish writer in America in the forties has become deeply disturbed—sufficiently disturbed to ask fundamental, frightening questions. In each instance mentioned a reassuring answer is given that does not flow naturally from the situation as stated; the consolation is too pat. The conversion of the meek little man in *Focus* into an outraged battler for justice does not ring true. If life in the American army was really as nightmarish for a Jewish soldier as the experiences of Noah Ackerman indicate, there is small reason for trust in the triumph of the forces of light. The weakness of these works lies not only in their optimistic finales, but in the dichotomy between the author's presentation and his conclusion. The alarm is genuine, but the moment of panic is followed by a whistling in the dark of which the depressing *Act of Faith* is the ultimate example. The *deus ex machina* salvation derives from the author's preconceived ideology rather than from the view of character and society that he has given.

It is an indication of the superficiality of the approach of these authors that the interest in the status of the Jew fluctuates with the current scene in the United States. Organized anti-Semitism recedes, the memory of the crematoria fades, and the wound which gaped for a moment closes. By the fifties another phase in the integration of the American Jew with his world becomes apparent.

INTEGRATION OR ASSIMILATION

The extraordinary success of *Marjorie Morningstar* by Herman Wouk (1954) indicates the change of mood. The novel, a mildly satirical portrait of the American Jewish middle-class, is a kind of Jewish *Main Street* and Marjorie is not too far removed from Carroll Kennicott. While the characterization lacks depth and the style is undistinguished, one cannot deny the book a surface realism: "the mean, sensual man," his mores and his limitations, have been shown. But the significance of the book lies in the closeness of Jewish Central Park West to its Gentile equivalent. The heroine, in her struggles and desires, is a typical American middle-class girl. The novel is something of a landmark in that it presents one of the first Jewish heroines to be accepted widely by the general reading public as a representative American character rather than as a quaint, sinister or romantic alien figure. Here is no Jessica, or Rebecca of *Ivanhoe*. Marjorie might be any young matron with dreams of a career, and hundreds of thousands of non-Jewish women readers bought the book because they could identify themselves completely with the problems of the main character; and these were not Jewish problems. Despite a generous sprinkling of Jewish atmosphere, the novel depicts a complete acceptance of the American social pattern with an almost total absence of specific Jewish values. Without physical assimilation the psychic assimilation of the American Jew has become so far-reaching that the "gilded ghettos" have become indistinguishable replicas of the non-Jewish world. The paradoxical physical cohesiveness and cultural assimilation of the American Jew appear clearly in Wouk's book.

Remember Me to God by Myron S. Kaufmann (1956), a novel

which inherited the mantle of *Marjorie Morningstar* as a best-seller study of contemporary American Jewry, takes the process a step further. The author has managed to avoid some of the clichés which afflict the American Jewish novel: the stereotype of the slick, rapacious Jewish "operator," as routine as the medieval stereotype of the ritual killer; the stereotype of the vulgarian whose apotheosis is generally celebrated at a *seder* whose supposed grossness has become a set piece in many American Jewish novels; and the stereotype of the East Side dreamer whose goodness presumably acts as an antidote to stereotypes one and two. Instead, the novel makes an honest attempt to present the doubts and discontents of a third generation American Jew. The scene is Boston. The hero, a Harvard undergraduate, suffers from no dramatic disabilities. His trouble is deeper: he wants to know why he should remain a Jew. The fact that Richard is a particularly feeble specimen makes his predicament plausible without weakening the force of his question. Through his confusion he manages to voice the dilemma of a generation. Without either religious faith or national attachment, what is there to keep him Jewish? Richard's perplexity in trying to define the nature of his bond is authentic. That the author contrives a mechanical solution for his hero's difficulties is a defect of the narrative; that no satisfactory answer is offered strengthens the reality of the dilemma.

While the fifties pose the question of Jewish ethnic and religious survival more pointedly than before, this is ironically also the decade when American Jewish writers begin to receive general critical acclaim as major figures in the contemporary literary scene. Saul Bellow, Bernard Malamud, J. D. Salinger, Philip Roth and others move to the forefront of critical consideration among the American writers of their period, and though none achieves the stature of a Hemingway or a Faulkner, they are taken seriously as American writers. Previously an occasional figure had been hailed by an avant-garde clique as, for instance, Nathaniel West, whose sardonic *The Day of the Locust* and *Miss Lonelyhearts,* originally appearing in the thirties, are being rediscovered. But West is singular, like Daniel Fuchs or Henry Roth. It is not till mid-century that the second and third generation American Jewish novelist comes into his own.

The critical accolade which greeted the appearance of Saul Bellow's *The Adventures of Augie March* proclaimed him to be the first American Jewish writer of authentic literary rather than journalistic importance. And Augie was described by as brilliant if willful a critic as Leslie Fiedler as the most interesting character ever created by a Jewish writer in the United States.

As the title indicates, *The Adventures of Augie March* is a picaresque novel. Augie, a poor Chicago boy growing up during the depression, and most of the other characters are Jewish. While there are few explicit references to Jewish problems as such, Augie's background, family and friends come magnificently alive. Instead of the usual naturalistic debunking, the characters are depicted with a poetic verve which testifies to Bellow's creative energy. Augie is presented as an integral part of American life. His first words are: "I am an American, Chicago-born." There are almost no overt references to Augie's experiences as a Jew. Of his slum childhood Augie remarks cheerily: "Sometimes we were chased, stoned and bitten and beat up for Christ killers . . . but I never had any special pain from it or brooded, being by and large too larky and boisterous to take it to heart, and looked at it as needing no more special explanation than the stone-and-bat wars of the street gangs."

Yet Augie is as authentically Jewish in his eagerness, ability and imagination as he is American. One need merely compare him with the go-getter caricatures of lesser writers to perceive his vitality. A bold creation, he is already on the way to complete assimilation. Absorbed in the tempo of American life, he has left the Jewish community in more ways than through intermarriage. (Augie's wives are Gentile but no word is wasted on this aspect—it is no problem for Augie.) Bellow appends no formula in conclusion. Whatever truths emerge are the truths of life as it is lived, palatable or unpalatable.

In *Seize the Day,* an intensive character study, the weakling antihero, as depressed as Augie is ebullient, answers curtly when asked if he has suffered from anti-Semitism, "I can't afford to notice." Like Augie he can't be bothered by the subject, no matter how much else may bother him.

In view of this development it is worth noting that in the forties, Saul Bellow contributed one of the most sensitive studies of anti-

Semitism to appear among the large number of novels on the subject at the time. *The Victim* (1947) raised the question of moral responsibility. The ambiguity of the title appears to leave unresolved the identity of the victim—the nervous tormented Jew or his Gentile persecutor who hounds him with irrational accusations. The process of self-examination and self-accusation triggered in the hyper-sensitive Jew brilliantly anticipates the probings into guilt and innocence subsequently to become fashionable on a larger scale in relation to the extermination of European Jewry.

Bernard Malamud, on the other hand, consistently uses Jewish themes. In *The Assistant* (1956), we can already observe the mingling of realism and symbolism in which Malamud is most effective. With the beguiling simplicity of a folk tale, Malamud develops his story of the mutual redemption of a poor Jewish grocer and his thieving Italian clerk who assist each other in the profoundest sense. The symbiosis of saint and sinner, Christian and Jew, reaches its climax in a startling conclusion. The clerk, who adores St. Francis, the True Assistant, is moved by the grocer's moral values to a paradoxical act of Christian fulfillment—he becomes a Jew.

Whether or not one finds the finale convincing, the emotional statement transcends the plot. The same holds true for Malamud's collection of short stories, *The Magic Barrel* (1958). Nowhere has the American writer used Jewish tradition and folkways to better advantage. Sometimes the whimsy may sound like a cross between Kafka and S. J. Perelman, but in most of the stories the drab streets and their semi-pathetic, semi-humorous inhabitants, while presented with realistic fidelity, are haunted by the memory of spiritual grace or illumined by its hope. Such muted stories as "Take Pity" or "The Mourners" indicate Malamud's power of evocation. In his purely realistic novel, *A New Life* (1961), he is less successful.

If Malamud represents the possibilities inherent in an imaginative utilization of Jewish subjects, the reverse may be seen in so gifted a writer as Philip Roth. The pathology of Jewish self-hatred has been a steady component of American Jewish writing, as the productions of Jerome Weidman and the offensive caricatures in Ben Hecht's *A Jew in Love* indicate. The art of making *matzoh* balls of mud has had zealous practitioners since the thirties.

Though Philip Roth is too richly endowed a writer to be relegated to this category, his rebellion against the Jewish world from which he springs is so extreme that the characters he describes are frequently unconvincing and revolting. In his much-applauded collection of short stories, *Goodbye, Columbus* (1959), or his ambitious first novel, *Letting Go* (1961), whether he is describing upper or lower middle class Jews, the Fifth Avenue success or the Brooklyn failure, the college-bred matron or the self-made man, his characters are vulgar, stupid or cruel. The grossness of family encounters may be smudged with sentimentality or shrivelled by a narrow bigotry; they remain unrelieved. Despite Roth's marvellous ear for dialogue and his brilliant satiric touches, the totality is false. The umbilical cord which ties the author to his Jewish past is torn with such violence that the clinical details of the rupture obscure every other element.

In *Letting Go* the two chief characters are Jewish intellectuals, both instructors of English literature at the University of Chicago—the post of which Lewisohn dreamed in the twenties. Though their backgrounds and destinies are different, both are deracinated as well as emancipated. Through the melodrama of the plot, what emerges most forcefully is the arid unhappiness of the protagonists. All of the significant erotic relationships involve intermarriage. Gentile and Jew seek in each other something that each has lost. But in this world of the lost, the disoriented young Jews tap most hopelessly for a non-existent light.

From the Jewish point of view, Philip Roth is a disturbing writer because the image of Jewish life that he sees has registered on a vision wonderfully acute in many respects. The fact that he has been hailed by leading Jewish literary critics like Alfred Kazin and Irving Howe as an accurate portrayer of the Jewish "bourgeoisie" is equally revealing.

We cannot assume, however, that only young intellectuals like Roth's pair of anti-heroes find Jewish life a wasteland. We need merely look at *Stern* (1962), a remarkably effective first novel by Bruce Jay Friedman, another addition to the growing galaxy of highly accomplished American Jewish novelists. The book is described on its jacket as "A novel about being Jewish." With humor, poignance and narrative felicity, the author develops his theme. For

Stern, a moderately successful copy-writer who moves into a Gentile suburb where he is the only Jew, the experience of "being Jewish" has been reduced to neurotic misery because of a suffered insult. Stern's vision of his family, "all three of them, his wife, his son, himself, sitting on the lawn, sucking blankets, and trying to rock themselves to sleep" becomes a contemporary apocalypse of emptiness and impotence.

What has happened to the young Jewish writer's awareness of Jewish idealism, Jewish ardor, of the abiding Jewish spiritual quest? J. D. Salinger, the darling of America's collegians since the publication of *The Catcher in the Rye,* offers the quest in a new guise. His chronicle of the half-Jewish Glass family, the former Quiz Kids, is among other things a search for answers. These are found characteristically in Zen Buddhism and the "Jesus prayer." Little of the author's background or that of his characters appears overtly.

We can hardly view the popular success of *Exodus* (1958) by Leon Uris as an antidote. The grandeur of Uris' subjects—the Nazi holocaust and the struggle for Israel—is a welcome change from the self-defeating triviality of the novels mentioned above; but the style is mawkish and the character portrayals are wooden. One must conclude a survey of the American Jewish novel with the unhappy reflection that for many of the ablest of its sons, "being Jewish" has become a dry well.

THE DRAMA

Since the novel affords the most explicit portrait of the American Jew, its examination has been most directly fruitful for this study. But fiction is only one of the forms in which the American Jewish writer has been productive. Before the emergence of the novelists of the last decade, a survey of American Jewish writing would probably have revealed the drama as the literary field in which the American Jew had won greatest distinction. Such names as Elmer Rice, John Howard Lawson, George S. Kaufman, Moss Hart, Sidney Kingsley, Clifford Odets, Irwin Shaw, Lillian Hellman, S. N. Behrman and Arthur Miller suggest the variety of talents.

If we include television and the motion picture, the catalogue of Jewish writers would defy any attempt at evaluation. Many Jews have been prominent in Hollywood and Broadway successes as well as in the non-commercial experimental theater beginning with the Washington Square Players, the Neighborhood Playhouse, and the Theatre Guild up to the most recent off-Broadway productions. However, it is more difficult to trace a pattern of development of specific Jewish relevance in the drama than in the novel. On the stage there is no dearth of Jewish characters, ranging from the mildly endearing vehicles for Gertrude Berg to the usual stereotypes of East Side dreamers, smart-alecks, go-getters and idealistic scientists. But despite the cloying abundance of Jewish family comedies, the presentation of Jewish life is not a major dramatic theme. Such hits as the froth of *Milk and Honey,* a comedy about American tourists in Israel, or the travesty of Jewish tradition to be found in Paddy Chayefsky's *The Tenth Man,* do not represent serious literary contributions by the American Jewish dramatist.

The most significant of these playwrights—Lillian Hellman and Arthur Miller—show in the main body of their work a social awareness, sometimes a revolutionary protest, which might obliquely be viewed as Jewish. The earlier work of Clifford Odets, one of the chief figures in the "social consciousness" school of dramatists during the thirties, was in the same tradition. His *Awake and Sing,* a title taken from Isaiah, provided an antithesis to the *Having a Wonderful Time* Bronx Jews of Arthur Kober, merrily popular at the same time. We should add that when Lillian Hellman directly considers Jewish life as in *My Mother, My Father and Me* (1963), she presents the same unconvincing image of vulgarity and corruption characteristic of the depiction of Jewish life in the sixties.

However the locale shifts—the East Side, the Bronx, Central Park West or Hollywood—the stage provides fertile grounds for the exploitation of superficial characteristics such as idiom or accent; and the temptation to degrade or sentimentalize the more obvious possibilities of the subject matter is rarely resisted. The satiric wit of George S. Kaufman, for instance, leavens his characterizations even when he burlesques them; but all too often we are left with treacle or slops.

Jews are also prominent among the "sick comedians" of the sixties. Though they reflect the disenchantment of their time rather than a particular segment of the population, their exploitation of so-called Jewish humor testifies to a sick Jewish awareness. The Jewish world they evoke in their monologues is not, for example, the mildly gross or innocuous one of Arthur Kober's Bronx. Trivial vulgarity has given way to a savage depiction of human motives and relationships. The stereotypes remain—the Jewish mother, the Jewish businessman, the boy on the make—but depicted with a baleful nastiness. The original *shmalz* of Al Jolson's *Mein Yiddishe Mame* has been rendered to a distillate of pure malice. While it is a manifestation of our age, this genre is tagged as Jewish by virtue of what it mimics.

POETRY

In poetry we find something of the same situation that obtains in the drama: the practitioners are numerous but there are few American Jewish poets of serious quality whose writing on Jewish themes is other than incidental and peripheral. At the same time, the Jewish motif is early heard in American poetry. In the nineteenth century a Sephardi Jewess of Charleston, South Carolina, Penina Moise (1797–1880) composed *Hymns Written for the Use of Hebrew Congregations,* and the dramatic Adah Isaacs Menken (*La Belle Menken,* 1835–1868) interspersed a sensational career as an actress with passionate verses written on such occasions as the kidnapping of Edgar Mortara by the Holy Inquisition. She made enough of an impression to be characterized by the New York *Sunday Mercury* in 1860 as "a lady who is a Jewess, and almost insane in her eagerness to behold her people restored once more to their ancient power and glory."

Emma Lazarus (1849–1887), whose famous sonnet, "The New Colossus," is inscribed on the Statue of Liberty, belongs to the same period. Precocious and cultivated, she won attention early with poetry on classical subjects such as "Admetus" and "Agamemnon's Tomb." When a well-known American writer—not a Jew—urged her to use Jewish as well as classical themes, she is supposed to have answered that "although proud of her blood and lineage, the Hebrew ideals did not appeal to her." The Russian pogroms of 1881 changed this indifference. She dedicated "Songs of a Semite" to George Eliot, and announced her conversion to Zionism in a series of articles on "The Jewish Problem" in *The Century Maga-*

zine. Her poetry, too, began to reflect her change of heart. She industriously translated Ibn Gabirol, Halevy and Heine, and her poetic dramas and lyrics shifted their emphasis. A verse drama, *The Dance of Death,* dealt eloquently with the fourteenth-century accusation that Jews were causing the Black Death. While a minor poet writing in the literary fashion of her period, she is by no means negligible.

In the twentieth century American Jewish poets have become increasingly numerous, and more representative of various fashionable literary trends. From early imagist to mid-century "beat," American Jews are in the choir. While no Robert Frost, T. S. Eliot or Robert Lowell appears in the roster, the level of competence is so high that any listing of names would degenerate into a catalogue. One need merely mention an indefatigable anthologist like Louis Untermeyer, an imagist like Maxwell Bodenheim, an objectivist like Louis Zukofsky, a word fetishist like Gertrude Stein or a "proletarian" poet like Kenneth Fearing to suggest the variety of talents in the 1920's and 1930's. By the 1960's enumeration becomes pointless. For the purpose of this survey, therefore, only those poets will be considered who deal with Jewish experience not in an occasional poem but as a central theme. By this criterion few remain.

Among those who, in addition to a major body of work on general themes have written with power and originality about "being Jewish," Delmore Schwartz should be counted. His collection of verse, *In Dreams Begin Responsibilities,* which includes the much-anthologized, "In the Naked Bed, in Plato's Cave," made an immediate impact in the late 1930's. His subsequent long verse narrative, *Genesis,* and his verse play, *Shenandoah,* whose subject is a circumcision ceremony in the Bronx, deal directly with the growth of a poet's mind as shaped by the circumstances of American Jewish life.

Karl Shapiro, too, for a number of years editor of *Poetry* and a poet of general reputation—no local bard of the Anglo-Jewish press —has devoted a volume to what he describes as "documents of an obsession" in *Poems of a Jew* (1958). The demonstrative title indicates that the theme rankles even though the poet himself demotes his poems to "documents."

In his introduction, Shapiro elaborately explains in what sense he considers himself a Jew: "Being a Jew is the consciousness of being a Jew, and the Jewish identity, with or without religion, with or without history, is the significant fact." The Jew appears in *Poems of a Jew* primarily in the poet's uneasiness—in the raw nerve, the sense of alienation. We need only compare such Jewish poetry with the Irish poetry of Yeats to perceive the difference between a passion to which the poet is committed and an obsession from which, by definition, he seeks to escape.

Among the committed poets one should mention the Canadian Abraham Klein, who avoiding current fads of style and diction, writes with skill and grace. His *Hath Not a Jew* indicates his quality. Charles Reznikoff, whose delicate free verse stems from the imagists, has been described by C. P. Snow, in his introduction to Reznikoff's verse in *By The Waters Of Manhattan,* as a poet in whom are found "the Jewish loneliness, the Jewish delight in God's gifts, and the Jewish triumph."

A comparison of Reznikoff's moving *Kaddish* written during the Hitler era with Allen Ginsberg's *Kaddish* (for his mother) indicates the range of style and interpretation found in the adaptation of traditional material by American Jewish poets. Ginsberg, chief figure among the "beat" school, writes with a Whitmanesque passion and a contemporary ferocity which gives his *yisgadal* a quality not dreamed of in the prayer book. Though Ginsberg is often diffusely rhetorical and too frequently descends to shocking the bourgeois, he has a new and individual voice.

The eminence of Jews as "wits," already noted in connection with the drama, is also observed in their high percentage among the writers of so-called "light verse." Dorothy Parker, whose mordant comments and epigrams have become part of the modern American idiom, may be viewed as *prima inter pares* among her many fellow practitioners, among whom F.P.A., Arthur Guiterman and Samuel Hoffenstein early made their mark. That such grass-roots American successes as *Oklahoma* and *South Pacific* resulted from the collaboration of Rodgers and Hammerstein is also worth noting. All America sings light-heartedly, "Oh what a beautiful morning" and joins in the paean, "There is nothing like a dame." The "wits" may be innocently gay as well as caustic.

Non-Fiction

The literary field in which Jews are without qualification in the front rank is that of the essay, be it column or book-length exposition. As social analyst, political commentator or literary critic, the American Jewish writer occupies a major role. In journalism every shade of political opinion has Jews among its ablest exponents. The gamut runs from the conservative Arthur Krock through the less predictable Walter Lippmann to the liberal Max Lerner on to extreme radical pundits. In literary criticism the same variety and excellence are present. From the academic Lionel Trilling to the capricious Leslie Fiedler, all trends and attitudes are represented. One need merely mention Alfred Kazin, Philip Rahv, editor of the influential *Partisan Review,* and Irving Howe, editor of the socialist *Dissent,* to get a notion both of the concentration and dispersion of Jewish minds in the United States.

Yet despite the dazzling number of Jewish essayists and the range of their intellectual concerns, there is a noticeable dearth of first-rate writers whose primary interests are directly relevant to Jewish life and problems. Among the most gifted of these few is Maurice Samuel. A brilliant polemical writer, Samuel has dealt with questions of anti-Semitism, Jewish nationalism and Zionism in many trenchant books. In addition, his studies of Yiddish writers, among them Peretz and Shalom Aleichem, have served to bring the vanished world of the *shetl* to an English speaking audience. In essay, novels, verse and prose translations, Maurice Samuel has devoted his talents with indefatigable energy to the study and illumination of contemporary Jewish life.

The rise of Israel has elicited many single sallies on the part of journalists and observers. Among those who have written consistently on Zionist and nationalist themes are Ben Halpern, Arthur Herzberg and Judd Teller.* But while Israel and Zionism continue to be subjects which precipitate journalistic debate and a steady stream of travelogues, the resultant writing is largely ephemeral.

* Marie Syrkin should be included among those who have devoted themselves effectively to writing primarily on themes of Jewish concern— political and literary (editor).

In addition to the handful of consciously nationalist writers, the last decade has seen the emergence of a group of Jewish intellectuals who may be classed as representatives of a philosophic neo-Orthodox trend. With Will Herberg as dean, such younger writers as Arthur Cohen indicate the search for a religious orientation among some sectors of the Jewish intelligentsia.

While one can hardly overstate the profusion of publicists and essayists of Jewish origin whose names appear in every serious American magazine and newspaper as regular contributors, the Anglo-Jewish press shows no such equivalent richness. Though almost every sizable Jewish community in the United States boasts some kind of periodical, these journals are primarily of local interest garnished with syndicated columns. Paradoxically, the events surrounding the establishment of the state of Israel and the consequent "breakthrough" of Jewish affairs to the front pages of the great American dailies have served to deprive Jewish periodicals of what formerly had been a prime function—adequate reporting of happenings affecting world Jewry. The few Jewish journals which attempt an ideological or literary evaluation of the Jewish scene are limited in circulation and influence. An exception should be noted in the case of *Commentary,* which, while equivocally cast in the role of a "Jewish" magazine, has won general recognition. Among the serious magazines with a "positive" Jewish orientation are (in alphabetical order)—the *Congress Bi-Weekly,* the Labor Zionist *Jewish Frontier,* the *Jewish Spectator, Judaism,* the Zionist quarterly *Midstream,* and the *Reconstructionist.*

THE QUESTION

The Jewish contribution to the cultural life of America is striking both in quantity and quality. The creative abundance observed in literature appears in greater or lesser measure in all the arts. In the sciences, too, Jewish achievement is considerable. For the objectives of this survey, however, the self-portrait of Jewish life in the United States offered by the Jewish writer has been the most useful. Even within this circumscribed field, the material is so abundant that it has only been possible to suggest lines of development. Particular writers have been chosen by way of illustration, since any comprehensive attempt would result in a self-defeating catalogue.

As we consider Jewish cultural life in the United States from the vantage point of the second half of the twentieth century, we can see that the sons and grandsons of immigrants are midstream in the full current of American life. They represent every intellectual and artistic trend not only as followers but as initiators. At the same time, their general involvement in American life has not been accompanied by a deepening awareness of Jewish identity. While disenchantment and "alienation" are characteristic of the modern intellectual, many of the most gifted of the younger Jewish intellectuals have added a specific belligerent estrangement from their origin to the general sense of alienation. In this respect they give added point to a frequently debated question: "Which way American Jewry?" A superficially optimistic conclusion hardly seems warranted. The very liveliness of Jewish contemporary performance in every field wryly raises the problem of the continued survival of American Jewry as a cultural entity.

4. Art and the American Jew

ALFRED WERNER

It is not surprising that *The American Jew,* published in 1942, contained no chapter on the space arts: painting, sculpture and architecture. Two decades ago there was no longer a dearth of American Jews in all the realms of art. Among artists were men of the stature of Max Weber, already past sixty and nationally known for his paintings, as well as gifted young men like Jack Levine, only twenty-seven, but already famous for his "String Quartet" and other remarkable oils. Among patrons of modern art, American Jewry had produced a Solomon R. Guggenheim, who had endowed in 1939 a museum devoted mainly to non-objective art. Still alive and active was Alfred Stieglitz, a pioneer photographer, who had also made important contributions by acquainting the American public with modern European artists and by sponsoring many struggling American artists, including Max Weber.

But the Jewish community, as such, like the larger American community, was not yet "art conscious." Jewish leaders, well read in philosophy or belles lettres, rarely used their eyes for the enjoyment of the plastic arts. They owned many books, but few pictures, and the latter were far below the level of their libraries. For them, buildings, secular or religious, existed only to serve utilitarian functions. Altogether, the situation prior to World War II was nearly as lamentable as were the conditions about which, decades earlier, John Ruskin had complained in England: "Hundreds of people can talk for one who can think, but thousands can think for one who can see."

During the great Depression, a large number of artists would have starved without the commissions provided by the WPA. The Museum of Modern Art first secured adequate premises in 1939. The treasures of ritual art owned by The Jewish Theological Seminary of America were shown most inadequately until 1947, when the Jewish Museum opened its doors. To American readers, no book was available on Jewish ritual art, or on the contributions of Jews to general art until 1946, when *A History of Jewish Art* by Franz Landsberger was published. Between January 1930, when the large and costly Temple Emanu-El was dedicated on Fifth Avenue, and V-J Day in 1945, very few synagogues were erected, and they were of little interest artistically.

Art in Suburbia

By 1946, however, the scene had altered radically. The exodus of Jews from the congested large cities to the semi-rural outskirts brought to the fore young native-born, college-educated Jews of the middle income group whose esthetic standards departed sharply from those of their parents. The lead in acquiring paintings, prints and even small pieces of sculpture was usually taken by the suburban housewife who may have had a course or two in art appreciation. And the husbands offered little objection to the wives' efforts to beautify the home, to excursions to museums, art classes, bazaars, amateur shows and the like, often arranged on the premises of, and in cooperation with, the local synagogue or Jewish Center.

These efforts may have been inspired more by "status-seeking" than by lofty esthetic motives. But art was "discovered" about the time when Jews began to show greater interest in religion, and one may, at least, assume that preoccupation with art and religion reflected the realization that in a mechanized and standardized society there was an ever-increasing need for bridges to span the rapidly widening gulf between matter and mind.

The Temple Boom

The major beneficiaries of this new art consciousness were the scores of synagogues—Reform, Conservative and, to a lesser degree, Orthodox—that sprang up, after 1946, in areas twenty to thirty miles away from the city's downtown section. In the 1920's, the trend favored huge, mosaic-inlaid domes, heavy marble columns, dramatic arches, bronze chandeliers, and walnut furniture.[1] To the Jew of today, however, the notion that a house of God must be richly decorated, and the corollary notion that simplicity is synonymous with poverty, are quite alien. The modern Jew needs no mystifying darkness à la medieval cathedrals. He does not need to impress with bigness his Gentile neighbor (whose new church also hugs the ground) or himself.

Suburbia provided beautiful locales along brooks, surrounded by groves, lawns and gardens. The great advance was in the use of majestic trees which, instead of being uprooted as in the past, were incorporated into the plan. Stained-glass windows, formerly used to shield the congregation from the ugliness of a city street, were no longer necessary; modern architects availed themselves of tinted glass, and even of clear glass, to let God's nature—sun, sky, clouds and green foliage—make their contributions to the religious service.

As a violent reaction to the "gingerbread" façades, to the pretentious showpieces of the past, architects tended to replace the over-decorated stone boxes with cement and glass structures that, in some instances, were a bit too "naked." For buildings entirely devoid of ornament are somewhat tedious; taken in at a glance, they do not call for a second look. The more imaginative builders of this era realized, of course, that quiet elegance, achieved through the omission of detail, and through the beauty of unbroken, unencumbered flowing line was not enough. They used imagination, since there was no Jewish style of architecture to follow, not even a tradition of synagogue building.[2]

Deviating from what might be called the pattern of the typical new American synagogue is a work of the late Eric Mendelsohn, the B'nai Amoona Synagogue in St. Louis, distinguished for a parabolic roof which reaches to the sky like an outstretched hand.

When the octogenarian Frank Lloyd Wright received his first and only commission to do a synagogue, he boldly conceived Beth Sholom Synagogue (in Elkins Park just outside Philadelphia) as a tentlike arrangement formed by two giant-sized Tablets of the Law. (The completed building resembles a craggy mountain.) Percival Goodman, now perhaps the most active among synagogue builders, gave to the Beth Sholom Temple in Miami (Florida) the shape of an eggshell's upper half. He felt that a round form would be of conspicuous significance in this world of sky-scraping hotels, and would blend well with the semi-tropical vegetation.

It would appear that Mr. Goodman's work for the B'nai Israel congregation at Millburn, New Jersey, is more in keeping with what young America likes and needs. A small building of brick, wood, and glass, with a walled garden, it should be a welcome relief from the huge structures in which the professional and business men spend their working hours. The entire hall can be used for services, or divided for other functions by two movable partitions. This austere structure blends into the suburban trees and lawns, and is distinguished only by Herbert Ferber's abstract "Burning Bush" sculpture and a simple *Magen David* window. The interior decorations are understated: a mural for the foyer by Robert Motherwell (a Gentile); and, hanging before the Ark, a velvet curtain designed by Adolph Gottlieb. Both artists have used Jewish symbols in a near-abstract manner, with the idea that Judaism is basically averse to figurative representation. The view has been expressed that abstract art provides an atmosphere of austere sacredness, while realistic art distracts the worshipper, which, of course, is a moot point.

Other architects have done even less to distinguish their temple façades from secular structures, limiting themselves to showing one symbol such as a *Menorah* or a *Magen David* accompanied perhaps by Hebrew writing somewhere on the wall. This is in reaction against the unduly rich ornamentation of older synagogue façades. American architects are acting on the belief that the modern Jew does not need a profusion of symbols to remind him that he is about to enter a synagogue.

He does need, and he usually gets from the architect, daylight from large apertures, so that the prayer books can be read without eye strain, and good acoustics so that the sermon can be heard. The pews are comfortable, the seating arrangements so constructed that the ceremonies at the *Aron Kodesh* can be observed by every congregant. In addition to the main auditorium—the synagogue proper—the well-lighted premises include lecture halls, libraries, the rabbi's study, staff offices, gymnasiums, workshops, playrooms, and storage rooms. For synagogues have become social centers and schools to an extent that would startle many a European Jew even in the 1960's!

In the late 'forties, and even in the 'fifties, the invective "eyesore" was frequently hurled at the new temples. Undoubtedly, some of them were failures. Often they were built in too great haste. In the 'fifties, a novelty was introduced: "prefabricated" synagogues that could be shipped, erected, and made ready in less than six weeks— the latest infiltration of standardization and mechanization into America's cultural and spiritual sphere. While some of the synagogues were, indeed, uninteresting, others were, perhaps, too interesting—the products of sensationalism, the striving for originality, or the desire to gain acclaim at any cost. But these were the exceptions. Most of the new synagogues were above reproach, except that they did not look the way old-timers expected temples to look. But did not the Bible say that each generation must sing a new song unto the Lord? And is it not in keeping with the American tradition that "houses should be built fresh for every generation?"

Ritual Art

Significant, too, is the modern synagogue's fostering of the fine arts and the crafts. Few American synagogues possess ritual objects predating 1850. Yet most of the objects that were shaped in the late nineteenth century or in the early decades of our century are esthetically unsatisfying. They were coldly mass-produced imitations of older work, totally devoid of the subtleties achieved by the individual craftsman with his hand tools. Immediately after the building boom began, it was not unusual to enter a steel-framed synagogue of simple brick and concrete, and to observe, in this modern building, in and around the Ark, pseudo-baroque monstrosities in silver and bronze that should have been discarded and replaced by new, modern work.

Gradually, the new congregations came to understand that, if the glass used in the home at social gatherings was an elegant product of unobtrusive twentieth-century craftsmanship, the *Kiddush* cup did not have to be an over-decorated imitation of an eighteenth-century piece. It was also in the 1940's that silversmiths and other master craftsmen began to infuse new ideas into their work. The new emphasis on elegant functionalism, on simplicity without coldness, could be seen in the work of many young artist-craftsmen who exhibited in 1958 and 1960 at the Jewish Museum's "Contemporary Ceremonial and Synagogue Art" shows. While the bleakness characteristic of earlier pioneering functionalism has passed, ornament is still used sparingly, or at least in an abstract, sophisticated manner. To these craftsmen, who produce Torah pointers, spice boxes, wine goblets, *seder* plates, *tefillin* cases, *mezuzzoth* and other small objects for use in synagogue or home, quality is not inextricably bound up with luxury; clarity, order, harmony and functional integrity are preferred.

Larger objects, such as *menoroth* and Eternal Lights, are often the work of distinguished sculptors such as Arnold Bergier, Herbert Ferber, Nathaniel Kaz, Ibram Lassaw, Seymour Lipton and Ludwig Wolpert. These works, in steel, bronze and other materials, are usually poetically free, while retaining all the required characteristics of the objects traditionally in use for many centuries. Often the Hebrew script, in a terse and somewhat archaic form, is the only decoration the artist permits himself to use.

New and often exciting are also some of the Torah curtains, wall hangings, tapestries and other textiles designed for the present-day temples. In the past, Torah curtains were often heavy with embroidered decoration, sometimes commemorating the donor in elaborate script. Modern weavers, however, generally avoid pearls, precious brocade, gold and silver threads, and attempt to please the onlooker by subtle color combinations, unobtrusive reference to biblical events, and textural variations. As a rule, weavers and other craftsmen know that the cultured Jew of today does not require every pictorial idea to be spelled out in obvious graphic language.[3] The craftsman has learned to maintain a healthy balance between the free flow of imagination and the restraint necessary for the object's quick identification and untrammeled usefulness. He has discussed his sketches with the architect, members of the building committee, and especially with the rabbi, and there is a constant exchange of suggestions and ideas.

The Rabbi's Role

The rabbis of 1963, especially the younger men, are less likely to make a sharp distinction between "ethics" and "esthetics," and to maintain that the two are opposed to each other (which is false both philosophically and historically), or that esthetics is a realm for Gentiles only. The modern rabbi knows that the plastic arts are as necessary as the spoken or written word, or as music, to help the public formulate the ultimate questions which are to be answered by religion. He is aware that what makes art is—to quote the French painter and writer, Fromentin—the faculty of expressing "the invisible by means of the visible." If he is uneasy about the sudden flowering of the visual arts within a community whose links with them were rather tenuous in the past, he can find encouragement in Mordecai M. Kaplan's *The Future of the American Jew,* where the founder of Reconstructionism stresses "the value of giving esthetic expression to emotional experience." Rare, indeed, now is the American rabbi who is totally unfamiliar with the latest trends in architecture, has no eyes to distinguish sound from insincere architectural solutions and interior decoration, and who can fall prey to hucksters peddling hieroglyphic atrocities and other gimmicks in the name of "Jewish Art."

MODERN ART AND THE JEW

The term "Jewish art" is the subject of much controversy. Some have attempted to concoct something called "Jewish art" as a carrier of values historically identified with Jewish tradition. Others have warned against the effort to define, within the plastic arts, that elusive quality called "Jewishness" which is always intermingled and blended with numerous other general values, nonrational and non-sectarian. We do not know what is going on in the artist's mind beneath the level of consciousness; why, for instance, in an otherwise abstract canvas by Seymour Drumlevitch, a *Magen David* turns up unexpectedly. This writer knows of no American artist who has claimed to produce "Jewish art" in the manner of the late composer, Ernest Bloch, who insisted that he aspired to write "Jewish music." Even Ben-Zion, who began as a Hebrew writer and turned to painting to express, preferably, Jewish and biblical motifs, would not agree with Bloch as to the necessity of "racial consciousness." Basically, the American Jewish artist is first an artist, and secondly, an American or a Jew or both.

It would be futile to pursue this controversy here, but it is necessary to determine what may properly be included in an essay relating to art and the Jew. To do so, we must distinguish between the plastic arts in general and their application in synagogue construction and decoration and Jewish ritual objects. The latter are clearly within the scope of our subject, but the former call for a word of elucidation.

American Jews, making a real contribution to art since the early years of the twentieth century engaged in Expressionism (Bloom, Kopman, Weber), Social Realism (Gropper, Harkavy, Levine, Shahn), Surrealism (Blume), or Non-Figurative Art (Gottlieb, Rothko), no more and no less than their Gentile colleagues. The Jewish motif was dominant, though far from excluding other interests, in men born around 1880 such as Abraham Walkowitz, Jacob Epstein (prior to his departure for Europe) and Max Weber, who were fascinated by the East Side which lent a particular Yiddish-Russian character to certain New York streets at the peak of mass immigration. In the past twenty years, Jewish subject matter has not been ignored, either. Jewish motifs turn up in the early work of Hyman Bloom and, less frequently, throughout the oeuvres of the four social-realists listed above. Astonishingly, neither the decimation of European Jewry nor the emergence of Israel has led to the creation of many impressive works on a high esthetic level. Notable exceptions are sculptures by Jacques Lipchitz, himself a refugee from Nazi Europe, such as "The Prayer," the *kapparot* ritual, meant as a grim reminder of the slaughter of Jews, and "The Miracle," an exultant figure facing the Tablets of the Law, out of which grows the seven-branched candelabrum.

Among American Jews, the self-taught Ben-Zion is possibly

the only artist to whom Jewish childhood memories and Hebrew mean as much as they do to Marc Chagall. Among artists born after 1920, the sculptor Elbert Weinberg, the sculptor and print-maker Leonard Baskin, and the painters David Aronson and Marvin Cherney might be singled out among those few figure artists who have been fascinated by Jewish legend or reality. Whereas Cherney is a realist who, with a muted palette, treats with sympathy and understanding the "beauty" and dignity of a bygone generation of Jews, Aronson's work has surrealist overtones. Figures and faces inspired by the Old Testament are endowed with a haunting intensity of expression. He portrayed Jesus as a "typical" Jew wearing *tefillin* and a prayer shawl.

Among Americans, these four are in a minority, as today more than three-quarters of the artists move in the realm of non-figurative painting which rarely permits, or warrants, identifications along national, religious or ethnic lines. Albert Alcalay, Helen Franken-thaler, Sidney Geist, Michael Goldberg, Sidney Gordin, Reuben Kadish, Milton Resnick, Bernard Rosenthal—these are a few names of abstract painters and sculptors who exhibit frequently, and several dozen more might be added. The vast majority contribute to the arts, not as Americans, and not as Jews, but as human beings. Inevitably, their work is colored by aspects of American life, just as the tenets of Judaism, the lessons from Jewish history, and perhaps psychological traits of a minority group may have entered, silently and unconsciously, into their work to give it a slightly different flavor. But this cannot be proven empirically. They do not wish to say, through their work, "I am a Jew," or, as a matter of fact, to demonstrate anything non-artistic. The realm of the arts has, happily, remained free of the ugly aspects of chauvinism.

At the same time, those who do display an interest in the Jewish present or past are in a position to show it without any belligerency, without the need to prove a point, echoing the sentiments of John Sloan, who categorically denied that it was necessary to paint the American flag to be an American painter. The very fact that a Jew can produce a convincing work on a Christian theme, while a non-Jew can find esthetic inspiration in a Jewish religious subject and give it the proper expression, has discouraged many who might be tempted to succumb to self-flattery, or to anti-Semitic definitions of what constitutes Jewishness and what makes a man a Jew.

It would be misleading to imply that this view has not been challenged. But one thing is above doubt—that there is a great deal of artistic talent among American Jews, and that few, if any, have complained of racial or religious bias on the part of the numerous public institutions in the United States, from the American Federation of Arts to the museums in the remotest corners of the country. As a Jew, the American Jewish artist no doubt has hopes and anxieties, memories and dreams which he does not share with his Gentile confrère. Yet he shares with him the ability to develop his talents without any artificial hindrances, within the framework of a free, democratic society.

5. *Music and the Jew*

JUDITH K. EISENSTEIN

MANY individual Jews have made significant contributions to the musical life of America in the role of composers, performers and patrons, but their efforts and achievements are beyond the scope of this essay. Here we are concerned with musical activity among Jews in their specific role as Jews, within their homes and communities. The substance of this activity cannot be defined in musical terms; that is, no characteristic style, no set of rhythmic or melodic patterns, and no all-pervading mood can be identified. It can, however, be described in terms of function, in relation to the needs of Jewish life which it serves, or the aspect of Jewish life which it reflects.

Three stages may be identified in the musical activities of American Jewish life. Roughly, and with allowances for overlapping, these are: (1) the Immigrant Stage, embracing the successive waves of Jewish immigration until World War I; (2) the Nationalist Stage, under the impact of Zionism and the Hebrew Renaissance, and the Yiddish and Yiddish Labor Movements; and (3) the period since World War II, and particularly since the independence of Israel. The last stage is difficult to characterize, because we cannot as yet see it in full perspective.

THE IMMIGRANT STAGE

In the immigrant stage, each successive group brought with it a heritage of religious music and some folk song in its vernacular, (i.e., Ladino or Yiddish). The earlier immigrants shed the folk song along with the vernacular, but synagogue music persisted.[1] The synagogues of the Spanish and Portuguese Jews have maintained their Sephardi chant by oral tradition almost intact in its fifteenth century form.[2] German Jews who were Orthodox retained their characteristic Ashkenazi tradition, which had developed beyond the chant to include choral music based on nineteenth-century West European forms.[3] In their homes, they continued to sing their Sabbath *Zemirot* and festival songs which for generations had been set to typical German tunes. German Jews of the Reform movement brought with them hymns in the German language, modeled closely on the German Protestant chorale, or derived from the melodies of Mozart, Beethoven, Mendelssohn and others.

During this period, only the Reform Jews made any deliberate effort to develop their religious music. They substituted English hymns for the German,[4] organized temple choirs, and engaged professional organists who directed the choirs and composed new anthems for them. These organists were generally non-Jewish, and their music conformed to the style of the current American Protestant churches. They published hymnals[5] and choral music, and attained a degree of uniformity in many communities.

However, it was the East European Jewish immigrants who established the tastes and nostalgias of subsequent generations. Their cantors and male choirs transmitted the florid Eastern version of the Ashkenazi synagogue chant.[6] They also sang in their homes *Zemirot* and holiday songs, some of which had been borrowed from their German brethren, while others were tinged with the Slavicism of the "old country," or with the mystic strains of Hasidic tunes. They brought with them their *badchanim,* those minstrels and entertainers who wailed or made merry at weddings and other joyous gatherings, and whose sentimental ballads and humorous songs found their way into that tin pan alley of the Jewish "ghetto," Second Avenue, with its center in the Yiddish Theater. In the popular mind these melodies are still identified as the essence of Jewish music.

THE NATIONALIST STAGE

The second stage came in the wake of a nationalism which had already made its impact on European Jewry. Yiddish songs, sought out and written down for the first time by folklorists in Russia and Poland, Zionist songs in Yiddish, German, Russian, and Hebrew, and the new songs of the *Halutzim* of the second and third *Aliyot* to Palestine were brought here and published in American editions.[7] Community choral groups were organized in the Yiddish Labor Movement and among Zionist groups.[8] Singing was introduced into the curricula of the Jewish schools, and books of songs were compiled by the teachers. These books were planned also for community singing by youth and adult groups in national organizations. They contained selections from the worship service, folk songs, a few from the repertoires of the *badchanim,* and songs created especially for children in English, Yiddish and Hebrew.[9]

During this period the first musicologists in the Jewish field began to migrate from Europe, and the first scholarly writings on Jewish music in English were published. Most important of these was the first definitive history of Jewish Music by the pioneer in the field, Abraham Zevi Idelsohn.[10] Among the immigrants were also representatives of the school of nationalist Jewish composers and musicians, who came from the conservatories of St. Petersburg and Moscow, and who had also been influenced by the burgeoning nationalism of their Russian environment. Uprooted by the Russian revolution, they made heroic efforts to continue their work here.[11] In the 1930's particularly, when the American music world was seeking a national idiom, this movement attracted a limited audience of enthusiasts devoted to both music and the Jewish people. They formed organizations, and sponsored research and community concerts.[12]

The concert programs consisted of art songs and choral pieces based on contemporary Yiddish and Hebrew poetry, and some solo instrumental and chamber music. On rare occasions, even in those depression days, there was financial backing for performances with full chorus and orchestra, such as the giant pageants of "The Romance of a People" and "The Eternal Road," and a complete presentation of J. Weinberg's opera, *Hechalutz*. Almost all of the music in these programs, it must be noted, had been composed and published abroad. Stylistically, it was for the most part "turn of the century" modernist, utilizing melodic material taken from folk songs of Eastern Europe, fragments of biblical cantillation, and Europeanized versions of Yemenite song which had become popular in Jewish Palestine. Sometimes large audiences came to listen, but chiefly for extra-musical reasons; they were motivated by national feeling or nostalgia, or even by strictly organizational loyalty expressed in fund-raising activity. No permanent audience of any size was developed.[13]

It remained for the Reform Movement to corral the wasting talents of the nationalist composers, as well as the Jewish musical scholars, for its own purposes; to write new hymns; to teach, pursue research and publish scholarly articles; but most important, to create a new type of unified worship service for soloist (cantor), choir and organ, based on the *Union Prayer Book*. Perhaps the most significant single event was the première performance in Carnegie Hall of Ernest Bloch's "Sacred Service" in 1934, under the sponsorship of Temple Emanu-El of New York. But on a less resplendent scale this service and others were performed within the Temple itself, and in other Reform synagogues. By the 1940's, publication of such complete services had grown considerably. New composers from Western Europe had fled to America, and among them were some who had had a thorough grounding in the liturgical tradition, as well as a highly developed musical training. These, too, were recruited for the work of creating and directing religious music.[14]

Recordings of music of Jewish interest were still very sparse, outside of the strictly "Second Avenue" trade. A few of the great virtuoso cantors still had a strong enough appeal to the older, immigrant generation to fill halls, and to sell recordings. Their music was, of course, entirely traditional in character. A few recordings of Palestine folk songs, one or two albums of liturgical music from the Reform movement, and some children's songs rounded out the meager catalogues.

THE CONTEMPORARY PERIOD

Since the end of World War II and Israel's War of Independence, the character of Jewish musical activity has changed. In some respects the change is a development, but it also reflects a retracing of steps, even a rejection of the motivations of the previous decades.

Development has been most marked in the music of the synagogue. The standards set by the Reform movement were adopted to a great extent by the rapidly growing and prospering Conservative movement.[15] Cantors of Conservative synagogues have introduced into their services both music and musical practices from the Reform group, and they have stimulated the composition of new musical settings of passages from the traditional prayer book.[16] On the other hand, many Reform temples have re-introduced the cantor into their ritual. Music directors and cantors now move across denominational boundaries, enriching the performance repertories, and enhancing the quality of rendition in both. While the large majority of congregations throughout the country still are served by vocal quartets of professional singers, or amateur choirs, most large cities have at least one full-sized professional choir functioning in at least one place of Jewish worship.

These developments accentuated the need of providing musical personnel. With the drying up of European sources of Jewish musical talent and tradition, it became necessary to train cantors and musical directors in this country. A new generation had to be equipped not only with the techniques and materials of religious music, but with the knowledge of the Hebrew language, liturgy and Jewish life, which are essential for meaningful performance or composition. The immediate answer to this need was the founding of schools for the training of cantors within the leading rabbinical seminaries.[17] These quickly expanded to allow for study and research, and even for the republication of valuable out-of-print collections of traditional source materials. Apart from the schools, books and articles dealing with various phases of Jewish music have increased in number, and they have ranged from the most scholarly to the most popular.[18] Also, the area of scholarship has come to include the comparatively new discipline of ethnomusicology, which is beginning to interest younger workers, particularly since the ingathering in Israel has provided a highly concentrated and convenient field for the study of the music of Oriental Jews. In the United States, too, Hasidic and Ladino-speaking communities offer opportunities for the study of ethnic music.[19]

In a sense, it is this very development and expansion which has produced the retracing of steps mentioned above. In the process of eliciting new music from a generation of young composers, many of them born in this country, it became apparent that the fine thread of continuity with the past was wearing thin. Musical skill alone could not effect the quality of depth in time and memory which might stir or release religious feeling in the masses of worshippers. Nor could the purely passive role of the congregation arouse a religious experience. In response to some newly felt dissatisfaction, there has been a trend to simplify the music, to return to the clean line of chant, to omit extraneous matter, to reintroduce congregational singing, and to compose complete services in Hasidic style. The aim has been to make the new music so melodious and uncomplicated harmonically as to invite audience participation.[20]

Coincidental with this process has been the narrowing of the range of musical activity to the limits of the individual synagogue or community center. This has weakened the incentive to the young composer, who may not be interested in archaizing or simplifying, or who may wish to write large works requiring chorus and orchestra, or music not based on specifically liturgical texts. Consequently, this latest era has seen almost a complete abandonment of serious national art music. Occasional works based on the Bible or medieval Hebrew poetry are still being composed, with very little chance of performance under Jewish auspices. A small repertory of four or five chamber operas, ranging from the most serious to the most trivial, has developed as a result of the establishment of the Westchester Opera Theater, and a few commissions to composers have been provided by a group of interested laymen in that county in New York.[21] Works of a purely secular character and purely instrumental works are scarcely being produced. This is no doubt partly a reflection of general musical trends of the day, both in America and in Europe, away from national idiom and in search of an international, experimental style. Jewish musical organizations outside of the cantorial groups have just about disappeared, and the large secular Jewish choral groups have dwindled. The National Jewish Music Council, sponsored by the National Jewish Welfare Board, continues to foster an annual month of Jewish Music Festival, by promoting broadcasts on radio and television, and by offering resource materials and program advice. Examination of the resulting programs reveals that they consist of brief liturgical pieces, or of folk songs. On rare occasions a selection of art music from Israel is performed.

It is in the area of folk and popular music that the positive impact of Israel is being made. In tune with the great vogue for folk-singers and folk-singing, many of Israel's young entertainers have visited the United States, their repertoires have been recorded, and local performers have borrowed from them extensively. Groups of guitar-playing youth are singing semi-Oriental settings of the Song of Songs, Isaiah, talmudic passages, and poetry of Yehuda Halevi in Hebrew, by rote or from English transliterations. In the search for new and more exotic material, they have created a demand for recordings of native singers of the numerous Oriental and North African settlements in Israel.[22] These "ethnic" records have brought a new type of instrumental sound, a new melodic and rhythmic pattern into the musical vocabulary of young Americans. Whether this will be identified in their minds as "Jewish music" remains to be seen. Whether it will affect the writing of new art or religious music in this country is equally uncertain.

Jewish Communal Services: Health, Welfare, Recreational and Social

Charles S. Levy

Introductory: Jewish Communal Services Defined

In its broadest meaning, the term "Jewish communal services" would embrace all activities—religious, educational and cultural, philanthropic, health and welfare, protective and others—performed by Jews for the well-being of the group and its individual members. Such inclusive scope, however, would both duplicate content contained in other chapters of this book and render meaningful analysis impossible. A sound delimitation of the range of this chapter is indicated by the recent tendency to regard community services as functions requiring professional education, and not as just "righteous deeds" devolving upon all Jews.

For the purposes of this discussion, therefore, Jewish communal services are defined as those philanthropic, social planning, health, welfare, residential care, counseling and group services to which the social work disciplines of social casework, social group work and community organization work are primarily related. This definition is limited also to the services which are organized, financed and rendered under Jewish auspices, whether they are intended exclusively for Jews or not. Other and related services may be touched upon, but attention will be centered on those which are primarily based on the social work disciplines.

JEWISH COMMUNAL SERVICES BEFORE WORLD WAR I

Emphasis on Relief of Jews in Need

Peter Stuyvesant's concern that any of the group of Jews who came to settle in New Amsterdam in 1654 might become public charges was quite unfounded. In the first place, the Jews, motivated by religious tradition, were accustomed to providing for those among themselves who were in need. In the second place, it was the colonial custom for various religious sects to minister to their own. As far as communal services are concerned, therefore, the culture of the American colonies accorded with the culture of the first Jewish settlers.

The Jews who migrated to the colonies gave prompt attention to the communal services for which there was immediate need. The first recorded capital investment was made for a cemetery. However, a congregation was equally indispensable, and the synagogue which served as the congregation's center of activity became the focus of a wide variety of charitable functions.

Consistent with the emphasis in the sacred literature of the Jews, the chief beneficiaries of the communal services of the colonial period were widows and orphans, and aged and disabled persons. To protect themselves and their families from debilitating adversities, Jews organized themselves into mutual aid societies of various kinds. Provision was made for members and their families who might be in need of funds, medical attention or burial. In this respect, again, the Jewish immigrants were in tune with the surrounding culture, for tradesmen and artisans in the colonies had formed many mutual aid societies for similar purposes.

Such societies were generally founded under synagogue auspices. In fact, some synagogues continued for some time to provide, out of their own funds, direct assistance to the needy. Gradually, however, these services, and organizations through which they were implemented, became independent of synagogues. Until they did, public and non-Jewish services had to be resorted to when a Jew experienced a condition for which a Jewish-sponsored service was not available—a mental or medical condition, for example.

Benevolent and relief societies proliferated in the middle of the nineteenth century and served as a significant instrument for the administration of aid to the poor and disadvantaged. The approach to financial assistance for the needy was rather personal and quite direct. Investigations and records were sparse and decisions were individual and subjective, based on personal acquaintance rather than eligibility criteria.[1]

Leisure-Time Programs and Associations

The Young Men's Hebrew Literary Associations which made their appearance in some of the larger cities of the United States around the middle of the nineteenth century proved to be the precursors of a movement indigenous to the new world, and specifically designed to provide leisure-time programs and activities for Jews of all convictions and orientations.[2] Although initiated to serve the leisure-time needs of Jewish young men, as these associations evolved into Young Men's and Young Women's Hebrew Associations and into Jewish Community Centers, the age range and composition of their clientele broadened. On the other hand, although established to serve as a meeting ground for Jewish people, the program of the "Y" was principally secular in nature.

Impact of Immigration on Communal Services

When the masses of East European Jews migrated to the United States before World War I, they had to cope with the problem of survival in a strange land and with the pressure, not only from native non-Jews, but also from native and acculturated Jews, to accommodate to its customs and language. To meet financial and social crises they had to resort at first to the communal services founded and supported by representatives of the earlier migrations, who were often viewed as "assimilationists" and oppressive employers.[3] Soon, however, immigrants were resorting extensively to self-help and mutual aid organizations. Fraternal orders, sick and death benefit and burial societies were organized in great numbers.

In spite of the emergence of these protective devices, immigrants escaping from pogroms and other old country harassments continued to require assistance either in finding a haven or in being nurtured for a reasonable interval after a haven was found. Immigration laws which required the assumption of responsibility for immigrants, and the hazards of migration, made imperative the availability of funds and services for immigrants. A number of organizations concentrated their efforts on these tasks; noteworthy among them were The Hebrew Sheltering and Immigrant Aid Society (HIAS) which was created in 1884, and the National Council of Jewish Women, founded in 1893. The range of the services rendered on behalf of immigrants included payment for transportation, representation at ports of entry, prevention of unjust deportation, and protection from exploitation.[4]

The heavy urban concentration of Jews inevitably led to a great need for a variety of communal services, since conditions of employment (physical and financial) as well as unemployment resulted in poverty, misery, disease, and family tribulations. The sharp increase in the intensity of these needs, and the increasing mass of people facing them, presented a considerable challenge to the sponsors and administrators of American Jewish charities and to contributors to American Jewish philanthropies. The new demands made necessary a much too sudden transition from personal but prompt and considerate administration of assistance to more impersonal and controlled dispensation of relief.

In response to the expanded social needs, the leadership of relief agencies introduced controls in the administration of relief which required investigation of petitions for financial assistance and often encouraged the substitution of advice for aid, ostensibly as a means for reducing dependency, but more often as a means for preserving funds by discouraging fraud and duplication.

Beneficiaries of Jewish communal services soon expressed their indignation, and their advocates established additional services of their own or fought until their interests were more effectively represented in the administrative councils of existing services. Thus, for example, the United Hebrew Charities (which later became the Jewish Family Service) of New York City opened district offices in the stronghold of Eastern European immigrants, the lower East

Side of New York. This provided for administrative representation from that area on the central board of the agency.

Child Care Services

The concern for orphaned children which was so integral to Jewish tradition was early manifest in Jewish communal services in the United States. Early in the 1800's children's institutions were established in Charleston, South Carolina, and in New York City. By 1916 facilities in various parts of the country could accommodate as many as 6,000 children.[5] However, as emphasis on the American social welfare scene began to be placed on foster home placement and on adoption, as well as on small group institutional care, the Jewish orphan asylum ceased to be the predominant medium of help for dependent and neglected children. Increasing effort went into providing resources to make possible the care of children in their own homes or in foster homes.

Although relatively few Jewish children could be classified as delinquents, provision had to be made for those who came to the attention of the courts. The Hawthorne School for Boys, which began operations in 1906 as a correctional school, was a noteworthy example of a cottage plan institution for boys who had had encounters with the law. The Cedar-Knolls School was established in 1913 to provide for girls who had experienced similar difficulties. Other institutions and services were also established to serve such children, including child guidance centers and personal supervision by interested volunteers through Jewish "Big Brothers" and "Big Sisters" associations.

JEWISH COMMUNAL SERVICES SINCE WORLD WAR I

Jewish communal services experienced many changes after World War I, and particularly after World War II, in emphasis, in scope, in clientele, and in purpose. As responsibility for financial assistance to dependent families shifted gradually to public tax-supported agencies as a result of mothers' pensions, for example, and as community chests developed to provide for community-wide support of sectarian as well as non-sectarian services, Jewish agencies concentrated on services other than those which primarily characterized Jewish efforts before World War I. Increasingly, attention was centered on personality and social development. Such services were the particular province of YM and YWHA's and similar institutions and programs, but they were emphasized also in casework and residential care programs for children, aged persons, families and various other indigent, dependent and troubled persons and groups.

Legislative restrictions on immigration to the United States and the growth of a native-born Jewish population also effected a change in the welfare needs of Jews, which consequently led to gradual revision in the services and sources of support of Jewish agencies.

Changes in Emphasis in Jewish Family Services and Child Care

During the depression years of the 1930's, financial assistance became once again the modal form of agency service for Jews as for others in the United States. However, the burden was too great for the voluntary agencies, sectarian and non-sectarian, and the depreciation of the fund-raising capacity of voluntary agencies made their resources all the more inadequate to meet existing needs. The New Deal of 1933 and the Social Security Act of 1935 gave the federal government a larger share of the responsibility to cope with the effects of unemployment. The government began to fulfill this responsibility with social security, public assistance and unemployment insurance.

A corresponding change occurred in the functions of Jewish family agencies. The emphasis on financial assistance to economically deprived Jews was gradually replaced by preoccupation with counseling, vocational guidance and other qualitative services. This trend became especially marked after World War II, when attention was directed to the social and psychological needs of a swelling population of financially self-sufficient Jews. Emphasis was placed on preventive, counseling and therapeutic services designed to help Jewish individuals and families to avoid or cope with disturbances in personal, family and social relationships, and other problems which led to personal and family breakdown. The impulse of agency leadership to render charity to the needy was thus increasingly converted to the effort to provide services to those willing to pay for them.

As Isidore Sobeloff observed at the National Conference of

Jewish Communal Service in 1956, "The nature of the need for Jewish services is changing and with it the conception of our clientele and our function is also being modified." Acknowledging the fact that two-thirds of the Jews in America were native-born, he went on to say:

There has been a tremendous economic advance in the Jewish population. The Jews are basically a middle-class group . . . . There has been a great deal of talk about services being increasingly available to all Jewish groups. This new interest may be due to the fact that our services have been disowned by the poor who are now able to find help—financial help—from the government agencies at one level or another. The change of function on the part of our agencies and the awareness of the service needs of other than the poor are often motivated by a loss of the old clientele.[6]

To deal with the assumed reluctance of middle and upper income Jews to resort to the casework and counseling services, Jewish family agencies established fee schedules. "Family agencies hoped to persuade these groups to look upon such service as professional help similar to that received from doctors and lawyers."[7] Despite the inconsequential budgetary impact of fee charges in family service agencies in the United States (although the proportionate income from payments for service did increase from less than two percent to nearly seven percent of the total between 1950 and 1960),[8] the practice evidently succeeded in attracting economically self-sufficient Jews.

Mr. Sobeloff provided the following estimate of the situation he anticipated as a result of increased recourse of middle-class Jews to services under non-sectarian auspices including industry, unions, and private agencies:

Relieved of the responsiblity for a volume of casework service by other private and public agencies, the Jewish casework agency will be free to provide individual service more heavily weighted in the direction of intensive treatment for children and adults to fill the gap between private psychiatry and present-day casework. This development, while expensive, will be encouraged by the stimulation of fees more closely approximating costs.[9]

Child care services, which had manifested a preference for services to children in their own or in foster homes, and were further encouraged by the federal program of Aid to Dependent Children (now Aid to Families with Dependent Children), de-emphasized institutional custody as a treatment of choice and allocated reduced priority to the construction of bulky facilities. When building was undertaken or arranged, the tendency was to provide residences for relatively small living units. Moreover, custody gave way to a multi-disciplined approach to individual and family treatment in the interest of the psychological and social welfare of the children.

At present, most cities with populations of over 5,000 Jews have specialized casework agencies which provide family or child care services. As a rule, these are local services, although several are regional or national institutions; for example, Bellefaire in Cleveland and the National Home for Asthmatic Children in Denver. Eighty-three family agencies reported a total of 59,809 open cases on their rolls in 1961, a negligible proportion of which were receiving financial assistance. A total of 7,213 children were under the care of fifty-two reporting child care agencies in 1961, 38 percent in foster homes and 26 percent in institutions at the end of the year.

Central communal allocations by Jewish federations and general community chests accounted for some 79 percent of the total receipts of family agencies, and 31 percent of the receipts of child-care agencies. Forty-three percent of the receipts of the child care agencies were provided by public tax funds. Chest allocations for family and child care services were six times as high as federation allocations.[10]

Medical Services

Jewish hospitals have been a distinctive feature of the American Jewish community. First established about the middle of the nineteenth century, the number of hospitals and the scope of their services increased during the period of mass immigration. Poverty and congestion bred disease, but Jews avoided the public hospitals because of the lack of *kosher* food, the difficulties with language, and fear of abuse and discrimination. In later years, a further justification was found in the need of internships and residencies for Jewish medical students. As a result, virtually all communities in the United States with a Jewish population of over 30,000 have had hospitals under Jewish auspices. In 1963 there were sixty-six general and special Jewish hospitals, and local health allocations accounted for nearly 30 percent of total local allocations in cities with a population of over 40,000 Jews.[11]

Noteworthy qualitative changes have taken place in hospitals under Jewish auspices. Between 1950 and 1960, the proportion of ward beds in the general hospitals dropped from two-fifths to one-fourth of all beds. Similarly, during the same period, the proportion of "free days' care" (that is, the number of days' care for which hospitals received no payment from any source) declined from one-third to one-fourth in hospitals of all types, and from one-fifth to one-eighth in general hospitals. These changes were, of course, related to the expanding health insurance programs.

Of special interest was the decline in Jewish hospitals of Jewish patients served, from one-half of all in-patients to less than two-fifths in hospitals of all types. The proportion of Jewish patients served by out-patient departments and clinics under Jewish auspices dropped in the decade from 1950–1960 from two-fifths to one-third. These changes were undoubtedly all influenced by changes in population density and neighborhood composition. Radical changes also took place in the patterns of hospital financing. The proportion of support from Jewish central funds dropped as sharply as the proportion of public tax fund payments for the care of the patients rose.[12]

Services to the Aged

The rapidly increasing population of Jewish aged and the sensitivity in Jewish communities to their needs have led to greater concentrations of services to the aged in Jewish communal agencies. These services have included counseling, rehabilitation, homemaking, nursing care, recreation, social casework, social group work, occupational therapy and friendly visiting. In 1954, one client out of every four served by Jewish family agencies was an aged person.[13] Moreover, seventy-five Jewish homes for the aged reported to the Council of Jewish Federations and Welfare Funds in 1960, as compared with fifty-five homes in 1950. More than three-fourths of the residents of the homes reporting in 1960 were 75 and over, as compared with two-thirds of those reporting in 1950.

Recently, Jewish communal agencies have given some priority to the development and strengthening of services designed to promote opportunities for independent living for the aged, reserving institutional services for persons with excessively limited capacities for self-care. The means employed have included casework and counseling services, specially designed housing projects with on-site social service facilities, foster home and boarding home placement, homemaker services and home medical and nursing care, day center and group service and recreation programs, sheltered workshops and job counseling and placement. Increasingly close relationships have also been maintained between non-residential community services and institutional services to facilitate transition from one to the other as indicated by the emerging needs of aged persons.[14]

The trends in financing the homes for the aged reveal greater emphasis upon payment for services and greater reliance upon public funds. Thus Jewish federations and general chests provided one-fifth of the aggregate income of the homes reporting in 1950, and one-sixth of the income of those reporting in 1960, and the contribution of Jewish federations declined from one-sixth to one-tenth during the ten-year period. Actual dollar contributions rose, of course, since budgets increased rapidly. About three-fourths of the income of Jewish homes for the aged was secured as payments for service in 1960, as compared with one-half in 1950. And the increasing role of public funds should be especially noted.

Whereas one-twentieth of the residents of Jewish homes for the aged were beneficiaries of Old Age and Survivors' Insurance in 1950, one-third were beneficiaries in 1960. Old Age Assistance provided for half of all residents in 1960, as compared with one-third in 1950.[15]

Emphasis on Cultural Resources in Jewish Communal Services: The Jewish Community Center and Youth Services

A noteworthy trend since World War II has been an increased emphasis on cultural resources, which has reflected a mounting concern with the welfare of the Jewish community as a whole rather than merely with the distressed and disadvantaged, and with the preservation and enrichment of the cultural heritage of the Jewish people. This trend is evidenced by the Jewish Center.

Between 1945 and 1960, the membership of Jewish Community Centers rose from 427,000 to 646,000. Although there was not an appreciable change from 1950 to 1960 in the percentage of Center members under seventeen years of age, there was a sharp decline from 19.2 to 5.4 in the percentage of total membership of the 18 to 24 age group, and an increase from 34.9 to 43.7 of total membership of those between 25 and 59 years of age. Members under fourteen continued to constitute approximately one-third of the total membership. Members over the age of sixty, on the other hand, began to be a quantitatively significant segment of the Center population.[16]

Between 1945 and 1960, annual expenditures by Jewish Community Centers rose from $7,171,000 to $25,051,000, an increase of 249%.[17] And a major shift was evident in the primary source of Centers' financial support. Increasingly greater reliance was placed on income from membership dues and activity fees. Between 1950 and 1960, income from these sources increased at a rate of 160 percent as compared with the 66 percent increase in income from Community Chests and Jewish Federations and Welfare Funds. Whereas in 1950 these central funds provided 51 percent of the income of Centers and dues and fees 49 percent, in 1960 the central funds furnished 40 percent of Center income and dues and fees furnished 60 percent.[18]

The original emphasis of centers, YM and YWHA's, Jewish settlement houses and neighborhood centers had been on the "Americanization" of immigrants, and hence on programs designed to increase mastery of English and general acculturation. After World War II, however, the emphasis at least in administrative and professional deliberations, if not consistently and universally in actual program practices, turned to what has loosely been labeled "Jewish content" and "Jewish values."

The Janowsky Report, or the JWB Survey,[19] devoted primary attention to the question of the fundamental purposes of the Jewish community center. A large majority of the participants in the survey favored a Jewish purpose and "Jewish content" programming for the Jewish center. Janowsky summarized his conclusions as follows:

The most important conclusion of the Survey is that the Jewish center should have a Jewish purpose—that it should be an agency with which the Jew might identify himself in order to satisfy his specialized Jewish needs. From this premise, it follows logically that the program of the Jewish center should devote primary attention to Jewish content, without, of course, excluding or ignoring the general activities which are essential for a well-rounded center program.

This position further implies that Jewish centers cannot be non-sectarian agencies. I maintain that non-sectarian neighborhood centers are highly desirable. But, if special *Jewish* centers are established, they must have a Jewish purpose. They cannot be Jewish and non-sectarian at the same time. If Jewish centers are truly non-sectarian, they have no reason for existence *as Jewish agencies*.[20]

He recommended that the JWB take the initiative in formulating a tentative statement of principles, in which the Jewish center should be identified as an agency for the satisfaction of specialized Jewish needs, and that the principles should include the following: that the program of the Jewish center should devote primary attention to Jewish content ("Jewish content" was characterized as embracing "the totality of Jewish spiritual and cultural interests and needs");[21] that participation in the Jewish center be open to all inhabitants of the local community, Jews and non-Jews; and that the establishment or maintenance of non-sectarian Jewish centers was not the responsibility of the Jewish center movement. He recommended further that the tentative statement of principles be submitted to the Jewish centers for consideration and that, after thorough discussion, the JWB adopt the statement of principles as its policy. This was subsequently done. The statement of principles which was adopted became the subject of considerable debate among Jewish community center leaders.

In 1956 Isidore Sobeloff expressed the view that:

In the increased emphasis on cultural programs the importance of the community center is expanded in the Jewish communal picture. It meets the requirements of the middle class Jewish population and its potential as a flexible cultural institution has an appeal for the broadest group. . . . Where the Jewish community affords a center that is a well-equipped city club for its middle class population, it will be more successful in developing an integrated package of recreation with a Jewish cultural component for large segments of Jews who continue to desire such a program under our auspices.[22]

In addition to the Jewish cultural factor in Jewish center programming, the issue of "religious" influence likewise arose. The *synagogue* center developed, offering informal education and recreation activities under congregational auspices, and attempts were made to distinguish its purposes and functions from those of the *community* center, which sought to serve Jews of varying religious predispositions or none at all.[23] Moreover, community centers were recently subjected to an attack, based on charges of inadequate religious emphasis in programming.[24] The situation in Jewish center work remains fluid, and center personnel are seeking a balance between the professional principles which presumably guide their practices and the concern for cultural and religious survival which is emphatically represented in the Jewish community. As this book goes to press, a national Commission on Jewish Community Center Purposes, created by the National Association of Jewish Center Workers, chaired by the writer, is actively engaged in a carefully planned and deliberate attempt to define, clarify, and refine the purposes of the Jewish Community Center.

These issues have also been of interest to the youth agencies and movements sponsored by B'nai B'rith and various Zionist and fraternal organizations. Youth organizations which operate through local, regional and national groups, clubs, chapters or councils, and which have conducted programs with a Jewish emphasis, include the B'nai B'rith Youth Organization and the Hillel Foundations, the Inter-Collegiate Zionist Federation, the National Council of Young Israel, and the junior divisions of the National Council of Jewish Women, Hadassah and the Workmen's Circle.

Issues similar to those which have faced Jewish community centers and youth organizations have been posed to the leadership of casework agencies and community organizations under Jewish auspices. However, aside from some sensitivity about the proportion of Jews they serve, and about the characteristics which are deemed peculiar to Jews and which require, if not a personal identity with them on the part of the social worker, then at least considerable understanding of them, there is relatively little evidence of the distinctiveness of social work practice with Jews in Jewish community services as compared with practice in non-sectarian settings. Some case material has indeed been proposed as affording evidence of distinctiveness but it is far from conclusive.[25]

Camp Programs Symptomatic of Shifts in Emphases in Jewish Communal Services

The character of camping services has likewise changed since World War II. Jewish agency camps are no longer primarily health-centered as they were during the 1930's and before. Emphasis in agency camping programs has been placed on social adjustment and personality development. Moreover, the camps have become increasingly available to middle and upper income groups and not almost exclusively to children of lower income groups as they once were. In addition, the clientele of Jewish agency camps has become much more inclusive, and service is provided for families as well as individuals, for aged persons and adults as well as children and young adults. Herman Stein has observed that:

Today camps under the auspices of community centers and other social agencies characteristically charge fees—though the fees are modest in comparison with private camps. . . . (Poor Jewish children no longer have difficulty in securing at least a few weeks of summer camp.) The problem has rather become one of justifying communally subsidized camps for children whose families might be able to afford to pay the higher fee of private camping. The general feeling is that such camps, like other Jewish social services . . . should become increasingly available to the entire community. . . .[26]

EXPANSION OF FACILITIES

The building boom in Jewish communal institutions since World War II expanded the facilities of community services. Indicative of this development is the increase in the estimated value of Jewish community center buildings in existence and under construction, from forty million dollars in 1946 to seventy-five million dollars in 1955. In 1961, Harry A. Schatz summarized the trend in center construction as follows:

The Center movement during the years of 1945–1960 was characterized by a phenomenal rate of construction of new Center buildings and expanded indoor and outdoor facilities. Intermediate sized communities led the field in this development with the large and metropolitan cities following in their wake in more recent years. Out of fifty-two intermediate size communities . . . twenty-five have already operated new facilities for more than one year, eight more are in their first year of operation, and fourteen are in various stages of planning and construction.[27]

In a listing of twenty-five center buildings which had been in operation for more than one year, and which had been completed between 1950 and 1959, Schatz provided estimates of cost of individual structures which totaled over twenty-one million dollars.[28]

Much of the acceleration in construction and the attending development of communal services has been occasioned by the movement of middle-class Jews to the suburbs of metropolitan centers. This has required the provision of new facilities and new approaches to old services in order to accommodate the needs of prosperous Jews.[29]

Summer resident and day camps were similarly affected by a rapid rate of expansion. The number of resident camps operated by Jewish community centers rose from thirty-six in 1951 to fifty-two in 1955, and has continued to increase since then. An estimate was ventured that 120 resident camps with a bed capacity of 24,700 were sponsored under Jewish community auspices in 1961. In addition, it was estimated that 275 summer day camps accommodating 70,000 children were operated by Jewish community centers in 1961. The growth of day camps since 1945 is suggested by the datum that of 113 day camps reporting to the National Jewish Welfare Board in 1961, 70 percent were organized after 1945. Not all of these involved the acquisition or the construction of new sites. However, many of them made extensive use of outdoor sites away from the city, whether under a rental arrangement or through outright purchase. Whether owned or rented, both residential and day camp sites have been extensively improved by the addition of buildings, swimming pools and artificial lakes.[30]

Symptomatic of the spirited increase in capital investment in Jewish communal services is the current building fund program in New York City. Elaborate plans have been made for the construction of facilities for local Jewish communal services, with a campaign goal of $104,365,000. This building program provides for the construction of facilities for the following: Hospitals and

Medical Care—$60,700,000; Care of the Aged—$18,100,000; Community Centers and Religious Education—$15,200,000; Family Welfare, Child Care and Vocational Guidance—$8,600,-000; and Camps—$1,800,000.[31]

THE JEWISH FEDERATION MOVEMENT

Although the Jewish Federation movement began before World War I, it has experienced its greatest growth since then. It is undoubtedly one of the most significant of the developments experienced by Jewish communal services in America. It began with the organization in 1895 of the Federated Jewish Charities of Boston—a federation in the specific sense of the term, for it was an organization of local agencies, societies and institutions. Cincinnati, however, conducted its first federated campaign in 1896, and is therefore regarded as "the first city to assume full responsibility for agency programs and for eliminating separate agency appeals."[32]

The federation movement demonstrated that Jewish communities "had the capacity to organize and to maintain a central instrument concerned with all types of Jewish welfare services and agencies," and "to organize Jews on a communal basis."[33] The implication of control, both of solicitations and disbursements for welfare services which emerged out of successful federation experience, was especially attractive to Jewish communal leaders in various parts of the United States. Within ten years after the organization of the first federation, such bodies were established in Chicago, Philadelphia, Cleveland, St. Louis, Kansas City, Milwaukee and Detroit. New York did not establish a federation until 1917, because of the resistance of a number of the city's large Jewish agencies, which feared that a central community agency might undermine autonomy and result in deterioration of services. The experience in federation communities, which indicated marked reduction in campaign costs and increased efficiency in campaign procedures, finally led to the agreement of New York City's agencies to federate.

By the time the New York Federation was established, some forty-five cities had become federated, including cities with small Jewish populations like Des Moines, Iowa; Dayton, Ohio; Dallas,

Texas; and Hot Springs, Arkansas. However, the six or seven million dollars in expenditures which federations reported in 1918 were primarily for local services, very little of the campaign collections being allocated for the support of national programs.[34]

Since World War I, federations have continued to grow and multiply and to exercise increasing influence on the nature and standards of local Jewish communal services. Changes in emphasis and in planning have been especially marked since World War II, and federations have come to have the following characteristics:[35]

1. They are organized on a city-wide or other geographic basis to collect funds primarily from Jewish contributors.

2. They raise funds for the support of Jewish communal services.

3. They plan local Jewish communal services.

4. They represent the interests of the local Jewish population in relation to the planning, support and coordination of Jewish communal services, and to the social welfare structure of the local community as a whole including its public and private, sectarian and non-sectarian services.

5. They generally combine in a single agency Jewish responsibility for local, national and overseas services, although in a few of the largest cities this responsibility may be divided between an organization concerned with the support of local services and one concerned with the support of national and overseas services.

6. They are administered by a governing body which includes representation from their contributors and their constituent agencies.

PROFESSIONALIZATION AND PROFESSIONAL EDUCATION FOR JEWISH COMMUNAL SERVICES

The impact of mass immigration and the overwhelming need for social services resulted in national meetings of leaders of Jewish communal agencies in 1885 and in subsequent years. One such meeting of delegates of welfare societies in Cincinnati, in 1899, resulted in the organization of the National Conference of Jewish Charities, which became a forum for deliberations on the current social service issues and served as the enabling vehicle for a variety of inquiries, investigations and analyses. Its interests included

"Standards and Qualifications for Jewish Social Workers," an indicator of the extent to which charity workers were becoming "professional." The Conference underwent several changes in name (National Conference of Jewish Social Services in 1919, National Conference of Jewish Social Welfare in 1937), and has been known since 1952 as the National Conference of Jewish Communal Service. It publishes a quarterly professional journal—the *Journal of Jewish Communal Service.* One of the constituent bodies of the National Conference is the National Association of Jewish Center Workers which was founded in 1918 by a group of YMHA executives.[36]

Jewish communal workers were especially influenced in their professional attitudes by the development of social work as a profession in the larger American community. A body of knowledge and principles specific to social work practice accumulated rapidly. Schools of social work were established, and the role of the social worker was clarified.[37]

Professional education for Jewish communal workers was affected by these professional and educational currents. It became increasingly apparent that Jewish communal service required special preparation and competence.[38] The National Conference of Jewish Charities, which had been formed in 1899, began a scholarship program in 1902 for the professional education of Jewish social workers, but the candidates were scarce. Charitable work was not in high vocational repute and the rewards were unimpressive. A School of Jewish Social Service was established in 1913 in Cincinnati, offering an educational program which consisted of six months of academic study at Hebrew Union College and the University of Cincinnati, and six months of field experience in a local agency. This attempt, too, was unsuccessful. In 1915, the New York Kehillah created the School for Jewish Communal Work as one of seven functional bureaus designed to help fulfill the Kehillah's purpose as a community council. The purpose of the School was to provide professional training for prospective employees of the philanthropic, recreational, educational, cultural and vocational agencies represented in the Kehillah. Both the School and the Kehillah had collapsed by the time the United States entered World War I.

The concern about the large proportion of untrained personnel in Jewish communal service continued to be expressed in professional associations and community organizations until the Training School for Jewish Social Work was founded in 1925. As the Graduate School for Jewish Social Work (as it came to be known), it offered a fifteen month graduate curriculum, including Jewish background courses and intensive study of Jewish social services. The general principles, methods and techniques of social work were studied at the New York School of Social Work, with concurrent field work under the direction of the Graduate School. The period of study was extended to two years in 1929. The funds for the support of the school, optimistically anticipated from federations, foundations and individual contributors did not materialize, and the School was closed in 1940.

The need, however, remained evident to the leadership of Jewish communal services, and it was underscored in the JWB Survey.[39] A Committee on Training for Jewish Social Work was created to ascertain the extent and validity of this need, and the study which it sponsored[40] called for supplementary preparation for social workers practicing in Jewish communal services. To fulfill this purpose, the Training Bureau for Jewish Communal Service was initiated in 1947. The curriculum of the Training Bureau emphasized understanding of the American Jewish community and Jewish communal services. A fourteen-month course of study provided orientation to Jewish life and Jewish history, and principles of community organization as well as field practice and its evaluation. Although intended exclusively for full-time students on leave from their agencies, the program was modified to accommodate part-time students, since practitioners in a position to take extended leaves were not available; nor were scholarships provided. Again, operating funds were not forthcoming and the Training Bureau was closed in 1951.

The first graduate school of social work under Jewish auspices and in a university setting, with the express purpose of preparing social workers for Jewish communal services was established by Yeshiva University. The Wurzweiler School of Social Work (as it is currently known) was an outgrowth of the School of Education and Community Administration which was established by Yeshiva

University in 1948 to provide a program of classroom and field instruction. The Wurzweiler School began operating as a graduate school of social work in 1957, and was accredited by the Council on Social Work Education in 1959. Another significant development was the introduction of a doctoral program in social work at Brandeis University in 1959 when the Florence Heller School for Advanced Studies in Social Welfare was established.

The stress on the professional preparation of social workers for Jewish communal services has been impelled particularly by the shortage of personnel, which has been acute in all the social services in the United States. Recruitment has become a dominant concern of the professional and lay leadership of Jewish agencies.

ISSUES FOR THE JEWISH COMMUNAL SERVICES

Jewish communal services in the United States have been faced by a number of questions affecting the premises for their administration, their support and even their existence: Should Jewish communal services rely on public tax-support? Should they serve non-Jews? Should they be run exclusively by Jews? Should they charge high fees? Should they serve the rich and the poor alike? Should they even exist if the kinds of services they offer are already available under governmental or private non-sectarian auspices? Should they provide services to their clientele which are fundamentally different from the services provided by non-sectarian agencies?

These are dilemmas! For the moment public support is rebuffed, the fiscal foundations of many Jewish agencies are shaken. The moment that the clientele of Jewish agencies is narrowed to Jews, the democratic ethos which lines the sinews of many third generation American Jews is offended. But, then, if the clientele of Jewish agencies is broadened to include a disproportionate number of non-Jews, the case for a correlation between clientele and auspices, between beneficiaries and sources of support is weakened.

What is and should be Jewish about agencies under Jewish auspices has been and continues to be difficult to determine. With the growth of a native Jewish population, an increasingly "adjusted" or "integrated" community, and preponderantly tax-financed support of the poor, many Jewish agencies have faced the challenge of producing a rationale for social services consistent with Jewish financial support, or justifying a rationale for Jewish-supported social services not founded on sectarian premises.

Some facts have been embarrassing for some Jewish community leaders. For example, either through direct payments to Jewish agencies for projects or services, or through support of agency clients, government funds have increasingly been made available to medical institutions, to agencies for the aged and chronically ill, to child placement and vocational guidance agencies and, to a lesser extent, to family service and child guidance agencies, to community centers, camps, and other services.[41] Proportions of non-Jewish clients of many Jewish institutions have risen. Many of the services of Jewish family or child care agencies are not programmatically distinguishable from the services of non-Jewish or nonsectarian services. And Jewish community centers, which have emphatically declared their Jewish purposes, have been charged in some quarters with not being "Jewish" enough.[42] Even the assumption that Jewish agencies, by virtue of voluntary auspices and selected clientele, could sustain a better quality of service than public agencies, is rapidly becoming specious as public agencies move toward the professionalization of qualitative services and the extension of the scope of public assistance services.

Jewish agency objectives have always been responsive to economic, political and social changes. When legislation put the brake on Jewish immigration, social coaching on "the American way" gave way to reinforcements to the second generation American. When Jews were ground under the Nazi boot, and the State of Israel became an imminent reality, Americanization gave way to survival. When the Social Security Act paved the way to government responsibility for the unemployed, the aged, the disabled, the blind and other dependents, relief gave way to counseling. When psychiatric enlightenment accelerated understanding of the complexities and the needs of the human personality, asylum custody gave way to residential treatment, and institutions gave way to foster-care.

The question now is whether fundamental changes in the objectives of Jewish agencies must follow because unprecedented numbers of Jews are native-born, and are either economically self-sufficient or are otherwise provided for without the need to resort to Jewish agency resources.

The phenomenal growth of the fund-raising capacity of the American-Jewish community has been used to validate the maintenance of Jewish agencies. The very fund-raising process, with its emphasis on leadership development, has been viewed as essential for the kind of identification which is prerequisite for the survival of the Jewish group. From this viewpoint, the sponsorship by Jews of agencies is more significant than the nature of the agencies sponsored or the services offered.

This rationale has become unsatisfactory, as the so-called religious revival has led to increasing emphasis on the substance of Jewish experience. Mere association with Jews is considered by many to be insufficient for the perpetuation of both the Jewish group and its traditions. To be effective, social association must be built on content appropriate and peculiar to Jews, and content derived from Jewish precepts. The more extreme view of the Jewish purposes of Jewish agency service holds that Jewish financial support should be applied to professional services primarily for Jews; that the services should be rendered only by professionally competent Jews, and administratively governed by Jewish leadership; and that the services should reflect sensitivity to the needs not only of individual Jews, but the Jewish group as a whole, and to knowledge about Jewish beliefs, values, and traditions.[43] This position may be justified by the argument that, since social welfare services are designed to meet the needs of people, and since some needs are readily definable in sectarian terms, Jews, like other sectarian groups, have the right to enjoy sectarian services.

In consideration of the American creed, Jewish agencies generally make their services available to non-Jews. In doing so, they usually assert their right—no doubt also in accord with the American creed—to maintain their Jewish purposes, implying, therefore, that non-Jews are welcome to avail themselves of the services but must accept them on the agencies' sectarian terms. Although this seems a plausible condition for the agencies' services, it can hardly be gainsaid that the needs of the non-Jews are not being met unless their own sectarian requirements are also provided for. On the other hand, the argument may be advanced that non-Jews are free to use services offered under other auspices.

Does this mean that only Jews can serve Jews, even if the agency's purposes are avowedly Jewish in a specifically sectarian sense? The reality is that non-Jews *are* serving Jews in many Jewish communal agencies, and many are serving Jews—*well*. However, there are Jewish community leaders who are convinced that this is not possible, and if possible, undesirable. This conviction is based on concepts not yet carefully defined, like Jewish commitment, identification, and so on.[44]

Perhaps a resolution of some of the issues related to the Jewish purposes of Jewish agencies may be found in the premise that there need be no uniformity of approach among the various professional disciplines which share responsibility for the effectuation of the purposes which Jews assign to their institutions and services. Some are concerned with the valid purpose of group survival. Others, like social work and psychiatry, rest on understanding of human needs, problems, growth and behavior. The latter may be rendered effectively by professionally skilled and personally well-equipped individuals, even if they are not of the same faith, color or class as the clients.

Jewish educators and rabbis are obliged directly to communicate to—nay, perhaps even to urge upon—agency clients the beliefs and behaviors represented by the institutions through which they function. Social workers, on the other hand, guided by knowledge and understanding of Jewish clients, Jewish agency and the Jewish community, *help* agency clients in the way *they* need to be helped— whether that be through increased self-understanding, environmental change, application of various resources, and so on. The Jewish educator and the rabbi necessarily have a pre-determined end. The social worker does not, unless it be the social well-being of the client; bases for choice are afforded the Jewish client, but the choice is the client's. Even if, as in Jewish community centers, program opportunities and services are afforded which are in tune with Jewish traditions and goals, they are still opportunities and not dicta. They still allow ample room for choice, with recognition of the differences among people as well as their similarities and common concerns. The social worker in the Jewish social service agency is not *a minister* of religious services. He is employed by a religious group *to minister* to the social needs of those who are, in a significant way, linked to that religious group by birth or by personal perception and acknowledgement. The social worker concentrates on the Jewish *person* and not on Jewish *material* to be transmitted to him. While the social worker does transmit, his action is based on the readiness and need of the client to receive. The chief consideration is that there is room for both approaches, in their appropriate times and places.

The Jewish community has validated its support of Jewish agencies if it has insured provision for Jews in the manner their needs can best be served. This very perspective of service should be a stimulus to survival. It should be a source for collective pride and collective reassurance. Moreover, it should provide channels for ego-reinforcement which is a key to self-acceptance, another requisite for Jewish survival.

But the same is owed to others who may come, and the stranger has always been welcome at the Jewish gate. Just as it is a compelling argument for the financing of Jewish agencies when it can be said that Jews prefer to go to them, it is no argument against such financing when it can be said that non-Jews prefer to go to them. The ability of Jews to pay for services is the least convincing reason for having or for not having agencies under Jewish auspices. The important thing to insure is that no Jew goes without needed service for lack of ability to pay or for any other reason.

IX

Overseas Aid

JOSEPH J. SCHWARTZ and
BEATRICE I. VULCAN

EMERGENCY AID BEFORE WORLD WAR I

As recently as fifty years ago, the Jewish community of Frankfurt, Germany, raised more money in an appeal for the relief of Balkan Jews than was contributed at that time by all the Jewish communities of the United States. World War I initiated a shift in leadership and responsibility for international Jewish welfare from Europe to the United States, and this change reached its climax after World War II. Since 1946, American Jews have raised over $100 million annually for the relief, reconstruction, and rehabilitation of Jews in other countries.

Before the Civil War, the small Jewish population of the United States was primarily oriented to local communal problems, except for occasional modest contributions to Palestine. But reports of disasters or persecution of Jews abroad resulted in the formation of temporary committees which disbanded after organizing a protest meeting and collection. The first sustained and unified effort to deal with the needs of Jews overseas was the Board of Delegates of American Israelites, "organized in 1859, almost simultaneously with the (French) Alliance Israélite Universelle, and the immediate occasion for the creation of both societies was the abduction by papal authorities of Edgar Mortara."[1] Shortly after its creation, the Board raised nearly $20,000 for the relief of Jewish refugees from Morocco—one-third of the total amount raised for this purpose throughout the world. Later it sent lesser sums to Jews in Persia, Italy, Roumania, Tunis, Russia, Turkey, and Palestine before it was absorbed by the newly formed Union of American Hebrew Congregations in 1878.

The half-century following the Civil War witnessed a tremendous increase in the Jewish population of the United States, where masses of East European Jews sought physical safety and better living conditions. The shocked reaction of American Jewry to the Kishinev[2] and other pogroms resulted in the organization of relief committees to aid the victims, and the Central Relief Committee in Kishinev received close to $100,000 from the United States. This sum represented about one-half the amount contributed in Russia and one-fourth of the total received from all the countries of the world. It was the European Jewish organizations which carried the principal burden of mass relief and migration assistance during this period, notably the Jewish Colonization Association (ICA) of London, the French Alliance Israélite Universelle, and the German Hilfsverein der deutschen Juden in Berlin.

JDC AND WAR RELIEF

The outbreak of war in 1914 caught millions of East European Jews in the area of active hostilities, and the unprecedented need for aid overwhelmed the European Jewish relief organizations. They sent appeals to the United States, where numerous drives for relief funds had already been started by Jewish communities and organizations. It quickly became apparent that the pressing needs could not be met without planned coordination. The American Jewish Committee therefore called a conference in New York in October 1914, at which representatives of Jewish organizations with hundreds of thousands of members resolved to form the American Jewish Relief Committee. One month later this Committee, together with the Central Relief Committee (formed by the

Orthodox groups) established the Joint Distribution Committee of the American Funds for Jewish War Sufferers (JDC) under the chairmanship of Felix M. Warburg. In August 1915, the base of JDC was further broadened to include the People's Relief Committee, representing Jewish labor groups. JDC was destined to become one of the world's greatest voluntary welfare agencies.

Initially, JDC was a disbursing agency, allocating to responsible bodies in the receiving countries the funds raised in the United States by the cooperating committees. By December 1915, the end of their first year, the three committees had succeeded in raising $1,500,000, but intensified fund-raising efforts were required to cope with the incredible destitution of the hundreds of thousands of Jews evacuated from the military zones. JDC therefore turned to raising its own funds, and the methods developed to collect millions of dollars during the war years had a marked influence on subsequent fund-raising campaigns of JDC and other organizations. In addition to the fund-raising activities of committees representing the various currents of Jewish opinion, a national humanitarian and non-political appeal was organized on a geographic basis and the cooperation of almost two thousand communities throughout the United States was enlisted to make over $16,500,000 available during the war years.[3]

Except in a few special instances, JDC was not itself an operational agency. It channeled its contributions through the well-organized local Jewish community bodies, and as a result was able to reach Jews in the war areas regardless of which army was in control. In unoccupied Russia, the local JDC affiliates were the local committees and correspondents of EKOPO, an organization which had been supported by Russian Jews before the war and had received subsidies from the Czarist Government. The funds transmitted by JDC to EKOPO were used to evacuate, transport, and assist the hundreds of thousands of Jewish refugees. For the evacuees, EKOPO built new settlements in the interior where it created many of the necessary community facilities—schools, orphanages, hospitals, and manual workshops for training artisans and mechanics—before it was dissolved by the Soviet Government in 1917.

In German-occupied Russia, JDC funds sent through the Berlin

Committee and the American Consul in Warsaw enabled the Jüdisches Hilfskomite für Polen und Litauen to operate kitchens where bread, potatoes, clothing, and wood for fuel were distributed to Jewish war victims in several hundred cities and towns. The Hilfskomite repaired and equipped hospitals, kindergartens, and orphanages and made loans to artisans and merchants through credit associations. Herbert Hoover, active in relief programs in Europe at the time, called JDC "a major lifeline to Jews in Poland," and estimated that in February 1916, 700,000 Jews in Poland, Lithuania, and the Baltic States were entirely dependent on JDC aid for their continued existence.[4]

In Austro-Hungary, the Israelitische Allianz zu Wien supported 400,000 refugees through cooperating committees in such major cities as Budapest, Lemberg, and Cracow, where JDC funds supplemented government aid. Schools and other public buildings were recruited for emergency shelters and barracks were built for the overflow. Rabbis, teachers, and students received financial aid; public kitchens distributed food; fuel and clothing were provided for the needy. The final appropriation was made in February 1917, shortly before the entry of the United States into the war made further direct communication impossible.

When American relations with Germany were broken off, JDC could not have continued its life-saving task had it not been for State Department approval to transmit money to Jews in territories controlled by the Central Powers through a Dutch committee established in neutral Holland in August 1917. This committee forwarded JDC funds to local Jewish communities in Eastern Europe through Dutch ambassadors in Berlin and Warsaw.[5]

THE AFTERMATH OF WAR AND REVOLUTION

The cessation of hostilities in 1918 seemed to be the signal for intensified attacks upon Jews in Eastern Europe. In the month in which the Armistice was signed, there were pogroms and anti-Semitic incidents in one hundred and ten towns and villages in Poland. Nearly 200,000 Jews perished in the Ukraine during its civil wars, and in Roumania, Hungary, and Lithuania, the number of victims of anti-Jewish riots mounted steadily. News of these disasters reached the United States together with a desperate cry for help from starving victims of the famine, which was widespread throughout Eastern Europe. The American Jewish response to these catastrophes was multi-faceted: emergency aid to preserve lives, economic reconstruction for those whom the war had ruined, and assistance for those who wished to emigrate and start anew elsewhere.

JDC was entrusted with the task of emergency aid and reconstruction, and for these purposes American Jews doubled their war-time contributions during the first two post-war years: over $27,000,000 were raised to alleviate the stupendous misery of war-seared Jewish communities. Wherever JDC was prevented from dispensing its funds directly, distributions were made through governmental, quasi-governmental, and voluntary agencies, such as the American Relief Administration, the U.S. Food Administration Grain Corporation, the YMCA, the Siberian Prisoners' Repatriation Fund, the Near East Relief Commission, the American and British Friends Societies, the American Red Cross, and the Polish Relief Committee of America.

Relief Programs

In 1919 and 1920, JDC sent its first two teams of child care, welfare, and sanitation experts to organize relief work in Eastern Europe. These missions were backed by the American Government and the workers were in American uniform; yet the personal risk was great, for Eastern Europe was in turmoil, and Professor Israel Friedlaender and Rabbi Bernard Cantor were killed by marauding guerillas. The first team set up 12 regional offices in Poland, and in the ensuing years such offices were established in every city in Europe where the need was manifest. JDC policy, which has remained unchanged throughout its almost fifty years of service, was to allot funds to Jewish communities to enable them to maintain existing community services and develop new ones under the professional guidance of JDC workers.

The teams helped set up emergency life-saving distributions of food, shelter, clothing, and medicines for hundreds of thousands of adults and children—transients, refugees, and repatriates—driven out of their homes and countries by war, pogroms, and hunger.

ORT, a Russian Jewish organization which trained artisans and unskilled workers, cooperated with JDC in establishing and promoting trade schools to provide vocational training for thousands of boys and girls. Primary and religious schools, teachers' seminaries, and institutions of higher learning were restored and maintained. Medical services were regenerated by an American medical unit of physicians and sanitary personnel. With the help of OSE (Russian initials for Jewish Health Society, founded in Russia before the war), the medical unit revived, transformed, and installed hundreds of medical and sanitation institutions—public baths, dispensaries, hospitals, sanitariums, X-ray stations, nurses' training schools, and other institutions such as milk centers and pediatrics clinics. Thousands owed their recovery from war injuries and disease to the existence of these services.[6]

In Soviet Russia, JDC was prohibited from engaging in relief activities until the great famine of 1921, when the Government authorized the American Relief Administration (ARA), directed by Herbert Hoover, to set up feeding programs in the famine areas. Under the aegis of ARA, JDC was able to make arrangements for joint ARA-JDC feeding operations in the Ukraine. On-the-spot reports[7] indicated that soup kitchens had been set up in almost every one of the cities, towns, and villages where Jews lived, and during one period over one million adults were fed daily. Most of the hundreds of thousands of children who came to the soup kitchens could count on no other source of food. Anticipating the withdrawal of ARA from Soviet Russia, JDC negotiated an independent agreement with the Soviet Government in 1922, which authorized the continuation of the relief programs. In his book on the ARA, *The American Epic,* Mr. Hoover paid tribute to the enormous role played by JDC in making possible the survival of the Eastern European Jewish community after World War I.[8]

Reconstruction

One of the most important undertakings of the post-war era was the creation of the American Reconstruction Foundation to carry on the JDC program of restoring and expanding credit cooperatives, producers' cooperatives, and loan societies which provided credit for the economically disfranchised Jewish shopkeepers, artisans, and farmers of Eastern Europe. These programs, initiated by JDC and carried out in partnership with ICA, typified the American Jewish concept of philanthropy as "social action" which encouraged self-help. At their peak, the credit cooperatives granted over $60,-000,000 in loans to several hundred thousand members in all the countries of Eastern and Central Europe.[9]

Agro-Joint (American Jewish Agricultural Association)

The relief programs in Russia were similar to those introduced elsewhere in Eastern Europe, but the reconstruction programs were much broader in scope. The Revolution had liquidated middle-class occupations, and the Jews were expected to work in industry and agriculture, for which most of them were untrained. Seventy percent of the approximately three million Jews in Russia were thus affected. In 1924, JDC was asked by the Soviet Government to assist in the economic reconstruction of Jews. For agricultural resettlement the Government supplied free land, seeds, machinery, cash credits, and reduced transportation rates. Agro-Joint (American Jewish Agricultural Association), the JDC operating agency in Russia, established a network of economic, medical, and social institutions which helped settle 300,000 people in agricultural colonies in the Crimea and the Ukraine. For those who were not suitable for farming, vocational training was provided either in trade schools or in cooperative workshops. In cooperation with ICA, loan societies financed these projects, and with the help of ORT thousands were trained for industry. Through the ORT Cooperative Tool Supply Company, Americans could prepay the cost of tools, machines, and equipment for recipients in Russia.

At various stages the Agro-Joint projects were taken over by local government agencies, and in 1938 all outside aid was withdrawn at the request of the Soviet Government. Betwen 1924 and 1938 American Jews contributed approximately $16,000,000 to Agro-Joint. Less than half was allocated by JDC; the balance was raised through private subscription by the American Society of Farm Settlements which transmitted the funds to Agro-Joint. Joseph C. Hyman, executive director of JDC during this period, concluded his graphic report on Agro-Joint with these words:

In less than a decade and a half, the work of the Agro-Joint helped to transform Russian Jewry from a downtrodden, almost helpless ghetto population into self-reliant and productive workers of the field and factory. It had liquidated the problem of the Jewish *lishentzy* or declassed group. Former President Herbert Hoover, who as director of the American Relief Administration had an opportunity to know the problem facing the Agro-Joint, called the Agro-Joint achievement, long before its conclusion, one of the most amazing feats of "human engineering" in modern history.[10]

Emigration

Over 1,500,000 European Jews seeking work and living space on the American continent arrived in the United States between 1899 and the outbreak of World War I. The end of the war saw the resumption of the mass migrations, and during 1921 about 1,000 Jewish persons arrived at American ports each month. JDC was active in facilitating emigration from Eastern Europe during this period and HIAS (Hebrew–Immigrants Aid Society) established to deal with the problems of pre-war immigration to the United States, greatly expanded its European services. HIAS and ICA joined forces and, subsidized by JDC, expedited emigration from Eastern Europe through the aid of American relatives who sponsored and financed the transportation of the prospective immigrants. *Landsmannschaften* were also active in immigration and welfare: a study of about 3,000 such societies estimated that they raised over $7,000,000 during the post-war period to aid those in the old country.[11]

The restrictive laws of 1921 and 1924 so drastically reduced immigration from Eastern Europe that fewer Jews were admitted in the decade 1927–1936 than had arrived in almost any single year between 1904 and 1914. Emigration to the United States thus ceased to be a factor of importance in planning for the solution of the pressing problems of European Jews.

PALESTINE AND THE JEWISH NATIONAL HOME

In 1901, the Jewish National Fund (JNF) was established to raise money throughout the world for the acquisition, development, and afforestation of land in Palestine. The amount collected by the JNF from American Jews during the first thirty-five years of its existence was $6,000,000 or 25 percent of the total sum raised throughout the world. The JNF appealed particularly to the Jewish masses, relying on small contributions for about half the funds and on the familiar "blue boxes" in homes and public places for almost one-fourth. The balance came from inscriptions in the "Golden Book," tree planting, Flower and Flag Days, and revenue stamps.

At the outbreak of World War I, a plea for help for Jews of Palestine came from Henry Morgenthau, United States Ambassador to Turkey, and $50,000 was forwarded to him by the American Jewish Committee. Shortly afterwards JDC arranged for the shipment to Palestine of vitally needed food and medical supplies. Through a committee established in Jerusalem under the chairmanship of the American Consul-General, it provided financial assistance particularly to rabbis and religious leaders. Soup kitchens which also dispensed bread and flour were set up, and bread was distributed to schools. Several thousand orphaned and needy children were cared for in orphanages and training schools.

During the war, all the American Zionist groups had united in a Provisional Zionist Committee to raise and distribute funds to Zionist institutions in Palestine. Through its Transfer Department (patterned after those of JDC and HIAS), individual American Jews were able to transmit money to their relatives in Palestine and other parts of the Middle East. Medical, health, and sanitation programs were provided by the recently created Hadassah, the Women's Zionist Organization of America. Shortly after the British occupation of Palestine, Hadassah, ZOA, and JDC cooperated in sending the American Zionist Medical Unit—a pioneer team of doctors, dentists, nurses, sanitary engineers, and administrators—to Palestine, with hundreds of tons of supplies and equipment. In spite of hardships and frequent financial difficulties, they were able to establish preventive and curative medical services and institutions throughout the disease-ridden country. In 1921 the Medical Unit became a permanent institution—the Hadassah Medical Organization—which rendered services both in the cities and the countryside, and expanded its network of clinics and laboratories for the prevention and treatment of disease, particularly for maternity and child health work, malaria, and eye diseases. In September 1927, Hadassah assumed the entire burden of providing the budget for the maintenance of its programs in Israel.[12]

The promise of a Jewish National Homeland in Palestine, proclaimed in the Balfour Declaration and sanctioned in the Mandate, increased Jewish immigration and quickened efforts to develop the country. The Palestine Foundation Fund (Keren Hayesod) was formed in 1921 as the financial arm of the World Zionist Organization. Under its direction, agricultural training camps were installed in Europe and transportation was arranged for immigrants to Palestine. Reception centers and vocational retraining facilities were set up for the newcomers; new colonies were established on JNF land; loans were made to artisans and shopkeepers; and nascent industry, land development companies, school systems, public works, and unemployment relief programs were subsidized. The Keren Hayesod was active in over seventy countries and during the years 1921–1940 American Jewry contributed over $18,500,-000 or almost half of its net income.[13]

NEW CRISES AND CONTINUED NEED FOR AID

Distress in Poland

In 1925, JDC began to consider liquidating its operations in Palestine and Eastern Europe, and did in fact transfer many of its activities to local committees in Palestine. It turned over almost $2,000,000 worth of assets to the Palestine Economic Corporation, which had been formed to further the country's economic development. However, the economic crisis which swept Poland and other areas during this period compelled JDC to continue its work in Eastern Europe. Half of the Jewish workers in Poland were unemployed; in Warsaw the figure was as high as 80 percent. To cope with the increased needs, fund-raising campaigns in the United States were intensified and considerable amounts were spent by JDC to expand the free loan societies in Eastern Europe to make available small loans without interest to hundreds of thousands of shopkeepers and merchants. The precarious state of Jewish economic life was highlighted by the fact that the loans averaged eleven to sixteen dollars! And the loans were repaid, delinquency totalling less than 6 percent. These free loan societies subsequently became entirely self-supporting and were an important factor in Jewish economic survival in Eastern Europe during the 1920's and 1930's.[14]

The Nazi Era

At the beginning of the 1930's, the strength of the communal agencies abroad and the continuing economic crisis in the United States, with a resultant decrease in amounts collected by Jewish fund-raising organizations, made it seem realistic for JDC to plan for an orderly liquidation after eighteen years of activity and a record of well over $80,000,000 of expenditures. But the rise of Hitler ended any prospect of liquidation. American Jews whose interest in overseas needs had been diverted by the depression to the more visible needs on their own doorsteps, were stimulated to renewed efforts by Nazi atrocities. A special JDC campaign to provide help for the 600,000 Jews of Germany yielded well over a million dollars in cash and pledges.

As Nazi terror mounted, and as the Jews were progressively isolated and prevented from earning a livelihood, emergency aid was provided by making JDC funds available to local committees throughout Germany through a central committee in Berlin. The aid was not restricted to meeting economic needs; allocations were also made for cultural and educational projects. In 1935, one-fifth of the Jews in Germany received JDC assistance; by 1937 it was one-third! However, it quickly became evident that emigration—flight—was the only hope for German Jewry. With the cooperation of HIAS, ICA, and the Central British Fund for German Jewry, JDC initiated extensive migration and resettlement programs and ORT helped organize trade and vocational schools which prepared the people for emigration. Finding havens for the masses of oppressed Jews was a colossal problem and many of those who were resettled had to be helped until they could establish themselves. It was estimated that by the beginning of World War II almost half a million Jews had fled from Germany to some eighty-seven countries on the five continents and, significantly, more than half of them found homes in Palestine. JDC mobilized local resources and subsidized refugee-aid committees to provide food, clothing, medical aid, child-care services, and vocational training both on the continent and in the countries of destination.

RESCUE EFFORTS DURING WORLD WAR II

By September 1940, JDC was reaching four hundred localities in Nazi-occupied areas through the network of local organizations it had developed during the preceding two decades. Its European headquarters were moved to Lisbon and there were American representatives in France, Spain, Hungary, Shanghai, and South America. The number of Jewish victims of Nazi barbarism and the stream of Jewish refugees swelled as a result of the successive German occupation of Austria, Czechoslovakia, Poland, the Baltic States, White Russia, and the Ukraine—the areas of the greatest Jewish concentration in Europe. By the end of 1941, practically all of the eight million Jews on the European continent were inexorably trapped as a result of the Nazi ban on the emigration of Jews between the ages of 18 and 60. The Transmigration Bureau, which had been opened by JDC in the United States in 1940 to accept payment by relatives in America for transportation requirements of overseas kin, was closed.

During the war great ingenuity and resourcefulness were employed to distribute funds and supplies to the refugees. With the knowledge of the Departments of State, Treasury, and Justice, "clearance transfers" enabled Jewish emigrants from the occupied countries to transfer their resources to the local Jewish relief organizations in return for transportation; and money was borrowed in local currency to support local programs on the strength of promises of post-war repayments. Both programs made available the funds required for JDC welfare operations in the occupied countries without benefiting the enemy. Another ingenious arrangement made it possible for refugee Jews in Soviet Asia to obtain food and other necessities by sending them parcels of scarce merchandise to be used for barter. In spite of war-time shortages of goods and shipping, JDC distributed hundreds of thousands of parcels containing items purchased mainly in Palestine, but also in South Africa, India, and the Middle and Far East.

The United States admitted about 100,000 Jewish refugees between 1933-1939 and about an equal number during the war years—considerably less than the aggregate quotas for the Nazi-occupied countries. To coordinate aid to these refugees, the principal Jewish-supported immigrant-service agencies created a National Coordinating Committee for Aid to German Jewry, which was superseded in 1939 by the National Refugee Service. The new immigrants were resettled in various cities throughout the country and local Jewish community services were made available to facilitate their integration and absorption. Thousands received financial assistance, loans, vocational guidance, retraining, and placement, and like previous generations of refugees subsequently made valuable contributions to the Jewish and national communities.[15]

TOWARDS UNITY IN FUND-RAISING

American Jewry was united in its desire to aid oppressed Jews everywhere, but ideological differences mainly over Zionism and the Jewish National Home resulted in multiple fund-raising drives. In 1925, various Palestine-centered organizations in the United States merged their fund-raising efforts in the United Palestine Appeal (UPA), and in its first year UPA raised over $2,500,000—more than the total receipts of its member organizations the previous year. Four years later, the Jewish Agency was established to enable non-Zionists to cooperate with Zionists in the building of Palestine. The Keren Hayesod, the chief source of funds for the Jewish Agency, became a leading member of the UPA. Subsequently, repeated efforts were made to bring the UPA and JDC together in one consolidated nationwide drive for funds for overseas causes. In 1930, an Allied Jewish Campaign was launched, but the combined drive fell short of the quota, largely because of the worsening economic crisis, and the Palestine funds received less than $1,000,000. UPA and JDC therefore resumed their separate competitive campaigns. Other short-lived attempts at cooperative fund-raising were made in 1934 and 1935, but not enough money was raised to meet the needs of the partner agencies, and they returned to running independent campaigns.

Hitler focused the attention of American Jews on the central problem of rescue—a global concern which made all differences unimportant. In November 1938, when the German *Kristallnacht* pogroms were headlined in American newspapers, Palestine ceased to be an ideology and became a necessity; and it ceased to be solely the concern of Zionists. Early in 1939, the three major Jewish overseas agencies, JDC, UPA, and the National Coordinating Committee Fund, merged their fund-raising functions into a single new fund-raising organization—the United Jewish Appeal for Refugees and Overseas Need (UJA). In its first campaign, UJA received almost $15,000,000, or more than twice the amount which American Jewry had donated to the separate appeals in 1938.[16]

For the first few years of its existence, the cooperative campaigns were repeatedly menaced by disagreements about the distribution of UJA income, mainly because contributions in 1940 and 1941 did not reach the 1939 level. In 1945, the partners were unable to agree on distribution terms and carried on individual campaigns until the middle of the year, when a reconciliation was effected on the basis of an acceptable distribution formula. By the time the war came to an end and the news of the German massacre of six million Jews was confirmed, UJA had become the undisputed leader in American Jewish overseas fund-raising and could be counted on to raise sums of unprecedented magnitude to meet the needs of the two million survivors of one of the starkest tragedies in the history of mankind.

SINCE WORLD WAR II

Refugee Camps

It is not known how many Jews were in the concentration and death camps when the Axis collapsed; a census taken about a year later found 80,000 to 100,000 in the camps of Germany, Austria, and Italy. Most of the nationals of the Western countries had made their way home but many of those from the East felt they no longer had homes to go to because entire Jewish communities had been wiped out by the Nazis and their collaborators, and because the East European peoples, so long exposed to vicious anti-Semitic propaganda, did not welcome returning Jews who were likely to demand restitution of jobs and property. During the first half of 1946, the Soviet Union repatriated to Poland about 140,000 Jews who had fled eastward before the invading German army. The Kielce pogrom of July 4, 1946, convinced those who had not immediately continued westward that Poland was no longer habitable for Jews, and by the end of the year almost half of them had fled the country. Anti-Semitic demonstrations, inflation, and famine later precipitated a similar exodus from Roumania and Hungary. By the end of the year, one out of every six surviving Jews in Europe was a refugee. On their flight, the fugitives were provided with food, medicines, and transport by JDC.

After the liberation, the Allied Armies assembled the homeless remainder of the concentration camps in Displaced Persons (DP) Centers in Germany, Austria, and Italy, and the new Jewish refugees from Eastern Europe also found shelter there. During the summer of 1945, a study mission headed by Earl Harrison, President Truman's special emissary and American member of the Inter-Governmental Committee on Refugees, made the first on-the-spot survey of the plight of the survivors of Nazism. In his report to President Truman, Harrison recommended that separate camps be set up for the Jews because of the hostility of the other (mainly Eastern European) DP's whose traditional anti-Semitism had not been modified by their own suffering at the hands of the Nazis. He further recommended the transfer of the administration of the DP camps to the United Nations Relief and Rehabilitation Administration (UNRRA). When both recommendations were implemented, conditions in the camps improved, although standards remained far below the requirements of people who had suffered years of starvation and torture. Both the army and UNRRA recognized the need for supplementary aid by voluntary agencies, and JDC, as well as other organizations, made available tons of food, clothing, and medicines and furnished medical, educational, cultural, and recreational facilities for over 230,000 men, women, and children.[17] In the camps there were kindergartens and *yeshivoth*, newspapers and magazines, sports and theatrical groups. ORT schools, factories, and training centers prepared prospective migrants for their new lives overseas by teaching them trades, and the Jewish Agency prepared them for life in Palestine through language courses and *Hakhshara*. Both JDC and HIAS helped with emigration to other countries.

Settlement in Palestine

Harrison's most important recommendations from the point of view of the rapid resettlement of the DP's was the immediate issuance of 100,000 certificates to Palestine and an equivalent gesture from the United States, but immigration to Palestine remained restricted despite the subsequent support of the Harrison recommendations by the Anglo-American Committee of Inquiry. Therefore, Bricha, the group which had been responsible for illegal immigration to Palestine during the war, expanded its activities. The DP camps became way stations between Eastern Europe and the ships which were waiting at French and Italian ports and beaches to run the gauntlet of British gunboats and attempt illegal entry into the promised land. At first the human cargoes intercepted by the British patrols were confined to prisons and detention camps in Palestine. One year after the war and a few weeks after the Kielce pogrom, the British Government announced and implemented a decision to deport illegal immigrants to internment camps in Cyprus, and some 50,000 were herded there before they were finally admitted to independent Israel. During the immigrants' stay in Cyprus, JDC sent doctors, nurses, teachers, dieticians, and social workers to help set up community programs. Minimum needs were supplied by the British, but supplementary food rations, medical care, educational and recreational facilities were provided by JDC, which also built a nursery for the newborn infants and a special camp for orphans.

Financing of the mass movements from Europe to Israel was shared by the Jewish Agency, which selected the immigrants and carried the responsibility for their absorption in Israel, and JDC, which paid for transportation and expenses en route. The decision to subsidize the illegal immigration was described by Herbert Agar in his history of JDC as "the most difficult in its career."[18]

With the establishment of the State of Israel in May 1948, hope was born overnight for a speedy end to homelessness. In seven months some 50,000 Jews left the camps of Germany, Austria, and Italy; other thousands left from Eastern and Western Europe, from Aden, and Shanghai. By the year's end, some 105,000 Jews had reached their promised land—their transportation in nearly every instance paid by American Jewry through JDC.

One month after the proclamation of the State of Israel, the United States Congress finally approved the admission of 400,000 Displaced Persons over a period of four years. The low restrictive quotas which discriminated against Eastern Europeans were not altered, and so many new restrictions were imposed that only one out of every six visas was issued to Jews.

American Jewry taxed itself nearly $500,000,000 in the four post-war years (1945 through 1948) to pay for these mass movements, for the resettlement and absorption of newcomers in the United States and Israel, and for the relief and rehabilitation of those who remained in Europe. This was the most significant philanthropic effort a Jewish community had ever known. Just as the United States had emerged from World War II a leader among the nations of the world, so the leadership of world Jewry had devolved upon American Jewry. Similarly, just as the war-stricken Europeans looked to America for aid, so did the surviving Jews look to the American Jewish community for help in rebuilding their shattered lives. And they were not disappointed. About three-quarters of the $470,000,000 budgeted by Jewish Federations and Welfare Funds from 1945 through 1948 was assigned to UJA for overseas needs. Contributions to UJA which had more than doubled between 1941 and 1945 (from $14,500,000 to $34,700,000) almost tripled in the single year 1946 ($101,000,000) and reached a peak of $147,000,000 in 1948. This extraordinary achievement is even more remarkable when it is noted that the potential contributing public, including children, was only five million persons, and that "UJA collections in 1948 exceeded the entire national collections of the American Red Cross by as much as 400 percent."[19]

Eastern Europe

In 1949, as the major costs of the programs shifted from Europe to newly created Israel, the JDC share of UJA funds declined in favor of the United Israel Appeal. The Jewish DP camps emptied as transports left for Israel in the most dramatic exodus of modern times.

By the end of 1949, all the international Jewish welfare organizations had either withdrawn from or been asked to leave the countries of Eastern Europe in which they had rescued millions of Jews from darkest despair during their decades of service. However, JDC was permitted to continue assisting the aged and children in Hungary until the fraudulent "Moscow doctors' plot" terminated those programs as well. No American Jewish welfare agencies were permitted to work in Eastern Europe until October 1957, when the Polish Government invited the help of JDC and ORT in an effort to establish programs for the physical and economic rehabilitation of a new group of Jewish repatriates from Russia.

The emigration policies of the East European countries were intermittently liberalized after the establishment of the State of Israel, and Austria was the transit station for small numbers of emigrant Jews from Hungary, Poland, and even the Soviet Union. However, the small Austrian Jewish community was totally unprepared for the 20,000 refugees who poured out of Hungary after the revolt of November 1956, and called upon JDC for funds and for food, clothing, and medical care. The Jewish Agency arranged for emigration to Israel, and emigration to all other countries was the task of the United HIAS Service, the organization formed through the merger of the United Service for New Americans (the successor organization of the National Refugee Service), JDC migration services, and HIAS.

Western Europe

During the first four years after the liberation, considerable American aid—an average of about $6,000,000 annually—was given to the Jews of France, the Benelux countries, Spain, and Portugal. Children's homes, feeding stations, and hostels for the homeless met the emergency needs of a population which returned from concentration camps or came out of hiding. Synagogues, dispensaries, and schools were rebuilt and a network of credit and producers' cooperatives and loan funds was established. As economic conditions improved this type of assistance diminished, and after 1948 American-Jewish financial support, which had contributed to the renascence of Jewish social, cultural, and economic life in France, was gradually reduced.

However, professional and technical help was required to rebuild Jewish community life destroyed by the Nazis. The lack of local leadership was responsible for a change in the operating methods of the overseas welfare agencies, which of necessity became more functional. Public health and welfare experts, immigration and child care specialists, administrators, technicians, and office workers were recruited in the United States to supervise the programs and develop and train new leadership among the survivors.

In 1949 JDC established the Paul Baerwald School of Social Work in Paris to train students from Europe, the Moslem countries, and Israel in modern social work methods to be applied in welfare programs in their own communities,[20] and the National Council of Jewish Women sponsored scholarships in American and Canadian schools of social work. American fund-raising and welfare administration methods were adopted by local community organizations in their efforts to become self-supporting. The most notable example is the Fonds Social Juif Unifié (FSJU)—the French version of UJA—which through annual fund drives has assumed an increasing proportion of the obligation for French Jewish welfare—36 percent in 1953; almost 50 percent in 1962.

Since the establishment of the State of Israel, economic and political upheavals and anti-Semitic outbreaks in the Arab Middle East and North Africa have precipitated the exodus of thousands of Jews, especially to Israel and France. At the end of 1961, the Jewish population of France was 375,000. During the summer of 1962, almost 100,000 Algerian Jewish refugees were added to the thousands who came from other parts of North Africa and Eastern Europe. These additions made the French Jewish community, with half a million Jews, the fourth largest in the world, exceeded only by the United States, the Soviet Union, and Israel.

Upon arrival in France, those refugees who are French citizens are eligible for government grants and loans and require only supplementary aid from the voluntary agencies. Those who do not have French nationality are completely dependent on the aid of Jewish organizations for cash grants, feeding, and medical care. The number of beneficiaries of American Jewish subsidized organizations in France doubled from 1961 to 1962; over two-thirds were from North Africa.

In view of the manpower shortages in France, many newcomers found employment readily, but the extreme housing shortage remained a difficult problem. In 1961, the FSJU, the Central British Fund, ICA, and JDC cooperated in establishing a special fund to grant loans to the refugees to help alleviate their housing problems.[21]

Moslem Countries

Not all the million Jews who lived in the Moslem countries at the time of the establishment of the State of Israel were able to emigrate, and a large proportion of those who remained required assistance which the local Jewish communities were unable to provide without outside aid. When the first pleas were made to the West during World War II, JDC had to overcome the hesitation of some of the American Jewish donors who were not even aware of the existence of these communities, with their age-old and seemingly insoluble problems. In certain regions, the death rate for children was among the highest in the world, and those who survived a deadly triad of diseases—diarrhea, tuberculosis, and malaria—generally grew up in a primitive world of ignorance, persecution, and crippling poverty.

JDC planned and carried out a frontal attack on disease and illiteracy. A substantial child-care program was set up with the help of OSE; pre- and post-natal care and baby milk stations were part of an organized assault on the high incidence of infant deaths. Preventive and curative medical services were expanded to include school children, and nursery schools and kindergartens were built in order to get the young children off the streets and out of their filthy hovels. A hot noonday meal was served in all the schools under Jewish auspices.[22] ORT vocational courses prepared the youth for life in industrial society, either in their own countries or elsewhere. Local personnel was trained to carry on the programs established and supervised by American professionals, and every effort was made to enlist community interest and financial participation in all the projects.

Despite residence in Moslem countries for many generations, Jews were frequently unable to acquire citizenship, were treated as second-class citizens and were systematically deprived of economic opportunities. In addition to being accused of disloyalty as Israelites, they were attacked as foreigners, and entire communities—those of Libya, Iraq, Egypt, and Yemen—had to be evacuated (in Operation Flying Carpet) as the result of outbreaks of violence and pogroms. Fortunately, Israel underwrote its traditional promise to end homelessness by offering broad immigration opportunities to all.

Immigrant Absorption in Israel

Philanthropic funds were formerly an important source of Israel's foreign currency, accounting for about 20 percent of foreign currency income in 1954–1955. With the rise of foreign currency reserves since 1959, this source is no longer as significant. The sale of Israel Bonds, United States governmental assistance, and German reparations and restitution are the other major external sources of economic assistance. Philanthropic funds have come mainly from UJA, which provided about $660,000,000 to the United Israel Appeal—for the Jewish Agency programs from 1948 through 1962.[23] Jewish Agency expenditures have been primarily for the transportation, initial reception, and absorption of new immigrants. The latter includes investments in agricultural settlements, immigrant housing, long-term loans, and supplementary employment—all aimed at enabling the newcomer to become economically independent. The Jewish Agency has shared the cost of education, health, and employment services with the respective government departments, and the costs of Youth *Aliyah* (immigration) programs have been shared with Hadassah and to a lesser extent with other women's groups such as the Mizrachi Women's Organization of America and Pioneer Women.

JDC, the second largest partner in UJA, has spent over $200,-000,000 in Palestine and Israel since 1914[24] and, although it has consistently avoided any ideological label, objective analysis of the effect of its activities, if not their intent, must lead to the conclusion that some of its most enduring accomplishments have been linked to Israel. This is one of the most eloquent testimonials to its effectiveness and importance for World Jewry.

Since World War I, JDC has supported *yeshivoth,* rabbis, and scholars in Palestine. In 1949 a new chapter was added when the Israel Government called upon JDC to set up programs for handicapped and aged newcomers. A new organization known as Malben (derived from the first letters of four Hebrew words meaning "Organization for the Care of Handicapped Immigrants") was created to restore the productive capacity of such immigrants through rehabilitative social services and to provide custodial care for those unable to live in the community. The number of persons helped by Malben has almost tripled from 1958 to 1962. The services have ranged from mental health programs, TB hospitals, and sheltered workshops to interest-free loans; from a school for nurses and a center for mentally retarded children to welfare grants for the aged in their own homes. Malben has built two villages for the aged and one for the blind. From its inception it was intended to integrate Malben services into the respective government welfare agencies, and today most Malben programs function in cooperation with the Ministries of Health, Welfare, and Labor and with the Jewish Agency, the municipalities, and local councils.

Since 1947, JDC by agreement with ORT has made substantial grants for vocational training programs in Europe and North Africa. In 1953 for the first time, JDC also agreed to include ORT's program in Israel in its subvention. Women's American ORT has been the second largest contributor to the ORT budget and has quadrupled its income, which comes only from membership, in the last ten years. Over $1,000,000 was raised in 1962.

Hadassah is the most important source of American philanthropic funds for Israel after the UJA. It unites over 300,000 members in branches throughout the United States and has been raising about $10,000,000 annually to support the Hadassah-Hebrew University Medical Center and Medical School, as well as its other medical services and Youth *Aliyah* programs.

Many other American organizations are devoted to raising funds for projects in Israel. Among the more important are the National Committee for Labor Israel and the Pioneer Women, which have raised about $45,000,000 since the establishment of the State, mainly from trade union and Labor Zionist groups. Their funds support the vocational training, health, and immigrant welfare programs of the Israel General Federation of Labor (Histadrut).

The institutions of higher learning—Weizmann Institute, Hebrew University, and the Technion—also receive financial support from American committees as do some forty Israeli agencies in the fields of music, theater, dance, art, and literature through contributions to the America-Israel Cultural Foundation.

American Jewry rose to the challenges of rescue and reconstruction posed by the dislocations of World War I, the ravages of Nazism, and the constructive efforts of the State of Israel. It furnished some $94,000,000 to JDC alone during the years 1918–

1938, and almost an equal amount to UJA from 1939 to 1944. When the effects of Nazi barbarity became known after World War II, there was an outpouring of funds which brought the total contributions to UJA to over $1,400,000,000 by the end of 1962. The consistency and continuity of support has been most impressive and is a testimonial to the fact that this community can be depended on to measure up to its challenges. Communal giving has become a universally recognized expression of Jewish identification in the United States and, as has been demonstrated in the past, can clearly be relied upon to call forth prodigious efforts whenever they become necessary.

X

Zionism, Israel and American Jewry

JUDD L. TELLER

In history, truth is at times no match for myth. A strikingly resilient popular myth depicts American Zionism as a foreign importation which drew its support from East European immigrants while American Jews of German descent and Reform belief were implacably opposed to it. It contends also that almost all financial support from American Jewry between the two world wars came from the lower-income Zionist rank and file and that the affluent German Jews, then disdainfully called *Yahudim,* stuffed their ears and snapped their purses to all pleas for the Palestine effort.

The myth draws from the strong animosity of the East European newcomer for his German predecessor. To a second and third generation American Jew, these "ethnic" distinctions, based in their day on real economic, social and cultural differences, are wholly meaningless, as is the term *Yahudi,* which had once been a battle cry. Yet the false impression persists, despite the testimony to the contrary by veterans of American Zionism of East European descent.[1]

From the very first, some of the ranking leaders of American Zionism came from the Reform pulpit, even though the overwhelming majority of the Reform rabbinate and laity opposed the movement.[2] Some of the substantial practical undertakings in Palestine might not have been realized without the philanthropies of Felix Warburg, Louis Marshall, Oscar Straus; of Nathan Straus, who openly espoused Zionism, and Jacob Schiff, who supported its practical efforts while dissenting from its principles, and who once, in 1917, unguardedly committed himself to the proposition that ". . . the Jewish people should at least have a homeland of their own. . . . And naturally that land should be Palestine."[3] It is possible to marshal impressive support for the thesis that pre-Herzlian American Zionism originated with the *Yahudim* and Sephardi Jews, and that from those early gropings a distinct Anglo-American Zionist tradition evolved, which is today boldly defended by "East European" heirs.

THREE TRADITIONS

Zionism is compounded of three distinct traditions—the East European, the Central European and the Anglo-American. We must consider the movement's beginnings to comprehend the three "schools." Zionism properly began with the Jews who wept for Zion by the rivers of Babylon. However, the movement we know by that name today began to assume shape early in the nineteenth century. Seven decades before the appearance of Theodor Herzl, its formal founder, schemes were already in circulation to settle Jews in Palestine.[4] Several of the most persistent proponents were Christians from America and Britain. The impulse behind this proto-Zionism was the desire to relieve the plight of persecuted Russian Jewry.

The incentive of anti-Semitic persecution is common to all three Zionist traditions, but it is by their supplementary incentives that they may be distinguished one from the other. East European Zionism sought not only security but a distinct identity for the Jew. Russian national culture would not accept the Jew. He was restricted in its schools, and physically, economically and socially segregated in The Pale. So that he might retain a sense of his own worth, he was compelled to acclaim his own tradition. This forced many who had repudiated their religious custom to bethink themselves, retrieve elements of this religious culture and secularize and bend them to contemporary uses. The result was a Hebrew and Yiddish renaissance which merged eventually into the movement for territorial sovereignty.

The Central European Jew, conversely, was confident of his identity. He had completed his experience with the Enlightenment at least one century before the Russian Jew. He had accommodated his ritual and theology to the Central European pattern. His eruption into German literature and science had been so vigorous that his effect upon them could not be eradicated. He regarded German culture as completely his own, and superior to other cultures of that era. Herzl's utopian novel, *Altneuland,* merely transplanted Central European shape and substance to the Jewish state and endowed all Jewry with its beneficence. The Central European Jew sought the dignity of status which anti-Semitism denied him.

The East European tradition provided Zionism with a mass following, the urgency of despair and the dynamics of a distinctive culture. Central European Zionism articulated Jewry's needs and demands in terms comprehensible to the Central and West European nations of that day. Neither the Central European Herzl, nor his Russian predecessor, Leo Pinsker, were at first Palestine-oriented. They sought a territory, any territory, in which Jewry might establish its sovereignty, obtain security and acclaim its dignity. Their East European followers did compel them, however, towards Palestine as the only acceptable territory.

The Anglo-American tradition, conversely, was from the first Palestine-oriented, optimistic, and the most romantic of the three. It envisioned the restoration on a biblical scale. The reason for this is that it was born less of Jewish need than of Christian millennial vision. Its early proponents included those who were eager to hasten Christ's rule on earth by restoring the Jews to their land and converting them there. Its advocates included also Anglo-American travelers and British colonial officials with experience in the East. The latter envisioned the restored Jewish state as fulfilling a dual function—solving for all times the problem of Jewry's displacement and standing guard over the crossroads to Britain's Asian and African possessions.[5] These Christian Zionists endowed their vision with the enormous vigor and intellectual conceit that characterized their two nations at that juncture in history. The British had convinced themselves, as they consolidated their eastern empire, that theirs was a God-ordained "white man's burden." The Americans, pushing westward, celebrated the illimitable capacities of man, especially the American Man.

AMERICAN PROTO-ZIONISM

This high optimism, Palestine-orientation and prescience about Mediterranean affairs also characterized the first Jewish Zionist in America, Mordecai Manuel Noah,[6] a Sephardi Jew, journalist, playwright, United States consul, Tammany politician, orator and synagogue trustee. His "Discourse on the Restoration of the Jews," delivered in 1843, adumbrated the Herzlian blueprint more than a half-century before Herzl. He proposed that Palestine be purchased from the Sultan and populated by Jews, with the aid of America and other great Christian powers. Jewry did not respond to his plan, perhaps because he was too flamboyant, as were most American public figures of that day; perhaps because his call was couched in a language and addressed from a country that were then still remote and alien to the overwhelming majority of Jewry. But similar proposals by revered European Orthodox rabbis were no better received at that time.

In 1852, Michael Boaz Israel,[7] a retired American farmer and resident of Jerusalem, published a call for the "restoration and consolidation of all Israel on their own land." He formed an international committee which proposed to establish Jewish settlements in Palestine under American protection through special arrangements with the Sultan. His plan, like Noah's, met no response. But he had already found his fulfillment. Born Warder Cresson, a Quaker, he had converted to Judaism and become a leader of the Sephardim in Jerusalem.

It was not till the tide of Russian Jewish immigration began to converge on Britain and the United States that American Zionism acquired the incentive of pressing need. Emma Lazarus,[8] poetess, journalist, translator from the Hebrew, mediated between dream and poignant need in a series, "An Epistle to the Hebrews," published in *The American Hebrew* (1882–83). References and quotations in the epistles show that her awareness of the need was sharpened by reading Leo Pinsker's *Auto-Emancipation,* published a quarter of a century before Herzl's *Jewish State,* and her Zionist dream was nurtured by correspondence with Oliver Oliphant, an early British advocate of Palestine settlement, and by George Eliot's Zionist novel *Daniel Deronda* published in 1876, a quarter century before Herzl's *Altneuland.*

American Zionism has always contended that its incentives are purely compassionate and religio-cultural. Yet acceptance of Zionism no doubt was facilitated by an uneasy feeling among American Jews about the effects of continued Jewish mass immigration to this country. There is a faint hint of this in Emma Lazarus' statement that "for the mass of semi-Orientals, Kabbalists and Chassidim who constitute the vast majority of East European Israelites, some more practical measure of reform must be devised than their transportation to a state of society [the United States] utterly at variance with their time-honored customs and most sacred beliefs."

She was perhaps the first Zionist to be accused by Jewish critics of advocating something akin to dual allegiance. Her reply to the charge also adumbrated American Zionism's contemporary retort to Ben Gurion's contention that a Zionist true to his creed must settle in Israel. "We possess the double cosmopolitanism of the American and the Jew," she proclaimed.

There is not the slightest necessity [she wrote], for an American Jew, the free citizen of a republic, to rest his hopes upon the foundation of any other nationality soever, or to decide whether he individually would or would not be in favor of residing in Palestine. All that would be claimed from him would be a patriotic and unselfish interest in the sufferings of his oppressed brethren of less fortunate countries, sufficient to make him promote by every means in his power the establishment of a secure asylum.[9]

OLD ROOTS OF PRESENT CONTROVERSIES

The issues that are of major contention today between Ben Gurion and American Zionism—is America only another Diaspora, and how far is the Zionist committed by his creed—asserted themselves early in intramural Zionist polemics in this country. Perhaps wholly unaware of the Emma Lazarus *cause célèbre,* recent arrivals from Eastern Europe independently founded in 1884 an American branch of Hoveve Zion (Lovers of Zion) dedicated to establishing and supporting agricultural settlements in Palestine. The Russian parent organization, founded two years earlier, already claimed several colonies to its credit. By 1886, the American Lovers of Zion had split.[10] One faction defined as its purpose "the *mitzvah* of aiding . . . the colonization of the Holy Land by our poor and persecuted *Yehudim*"; another addressed itself to those who "wish to settle in Palestine and to join an organization for that purpose." The latter faction advanced a pessimistic determinist thesis wholly alien to American proto-Zionism. The state of exile, it argued, was a morbid condition, and the sole corrective for the aberrations it had conduced in the Jew was his resettlement in Palestine where, secure from persecution, restored to his own estate, he would sustain and expand his spiritual sovereignty. Given the classical set of circumstances, this faction contended, America would turn on the Jew as all other Diasporas had done.[11]

European events were impinging on American Jewry as if to support the determinist view. President Harrison referred to the problem of refugees from Russia in a message to Congress in September, 1891, warning that their influx was "likely to assume proportions which may make it difficult to find homes and employment for them here and to seriously affect the labor market. . . ."[12]

That same year President Harrison was petitioned to convene an intergovernmental conference to "consider the condition of the Israelites and their claims to Palestine as their ancient home, and to promote, in all other just and proper ways, the alleviation of their suffering condition."[13] The petition was originated by William E. Blackstone, and signatories included John D. Rockefeller, Melville E. Fuller (Chief Justice of the United States Supreme Court) and William McKinley, the future President.

In 1896, when Herzl began to claim universal attention, three ranking American Jews—Cyrus Adler, Mayer Sulzberger and Oscar S. Straus—agreed to support a scheme for settling Jews in Mesopotamia. It would have disposed of all problems. It would have provided the Jews with a sanctuary and deflected mass immigration from America. It would also have mollified that segment of American Christian opinion which opposed the restoration of Palestine to an unconverted Jewry. However, the letter which Adler addressed to Herzl was never acknowledged.[14]

Thus Christians and Jews in America had already committed their attitudes towards Zionism, and American Zionism had acquired a distinctive personality even before Herzl launched his movement. Its posture has altered little since then. Like their precursor, Emma Lazarus, American Zionists have maintained the posture of noble concern, defended American "exceptionalism" and argued that they are not committed, by creed, to settle in the Jewish state.[15]

After the first World Zionist Congress the Hoveve Zion societies were reconstituted as Zionist societies. In November, 1897, a Federation of New York Zionists was formed, and in July, 1898, a national body called the Federation of American Zionists was founded at a conference in New York City, attended by Zionists from fourteen cities. The Executive Board included seven rabbis—Orthodox, Conservative and Reform.[16]

INTER-DENOMINATIONAL UNITY

This was unprecedented in many respects. Almost to a man, the Central European rabbis either opposed or abstained from Zionism. The East European rabbis, overwhelmingly Orthodox, were split on the issue. That rabbis of the three denominations should maintain a close working relationship on a governing body was almost inconceivable. It even proved difficult for the World Zionist movement to maintain cordial relations between the non-clerical rank-and-file of Central (Western) and East European Jewry. The East-West differences repeatedly threatened to tear the movement apart, even at the Zionist congresses which were intended to demonstrate solidarity. The Russian Zionists, deprecating diplomatic effort, demanded that the movement concentrate primarily on cultural activity and on establishing colonies in Palestine. The western Zionists led by Herzl contended that unless there was a charter from the Sultan permitting Jewish colonization, all such effort would be impeded, frustrated and wasted. These disagreements over principle and tactics were exacerbated by environmental factors—differences in custom, habit and condition.

American Zionism was no wiser but more fortunate than the others. It was situated in an unsettled milieu. All America was in flux. The East and Central European Jews in America were influenced by the overall American circumstance which disarranged class distinctions, by the peculiar immigrant circumstances which undermined religious dogmatism, and by geographic placement which compelled the *Yahudim* and East Europeans into daily awareness of each other. The great majority of American Jewry was concentrated in New York and several other large cities. The vigor and restiveness of the new immigrants embarrassed the *Yahudim,* who had cultivated a public image of the Jew as a pillar of conformity. The East European radical immigrants, having claimed for the Jew a predilection for socialism, were in turn disconcerted by the *Yahudi's* political and economic conservatism. The philanthropies of the *Yahudim* were perhaps meant to serve as a bridle on the new immigrants and they, in turn, hoped to bend the philanthropic institutions to their own audacious purpose. The result was daily confrontation, recurring controversy and reluctant but constant collaboration between the two camps. Thus the *Yahudim* and East Europeans were familiar with each other even before they met in the Federation of American Zionists.

The Zionist Reform rabbis were frequently also social rebels. The Reform Rabbi Bernard Felsenthal had been a vigorous and bold Abolitionist;[17] Stephen S. Wise, the first secretary of the Federation of American Zionists, became one of the major voices of social protest in the American pulpit,[18] and Judah L. Magnes was an incorrigible dissenter throughout his life.[19] Because of their stature, and no less because of their association with mass causes, the Zionists became the most prominent public figures of the Reform rabbinate, whose overwhelming majority denounced Zionism and obliged Zionists to resign from posts in central Reform institutions.[20] Men of graver demeanor were also attracted to the movement. Gustav Gottheil, senior rabbi of Temple Emanu-El, was one of the first exponents of Herzl's cause in America, and his son, Richard Gottheil of Columbia University, was the first president of the Federation of American Zionists.

The effect was that American Zionism, almost unnoticeably by example rather than by design, emerged as mediator between European Zionism's East and West wings.[21] It took the middle ground in the major controversies, the Reform leadership addressing itself to the Central Europeans, the East European majority addressing itself to the Russian Zionists. Some of the latter, notably She-maryahu Levin, stranded here by World War I, and Isaac Ben-Zvi and David Ben-Gurion, political fugitives from Turk-ruled Palestine, observed this cooperation firsthand.

FORMATION OF PARTIES

American Zionist harmony was less constant, of course, than it retrospectively appears to have been. The Federation was harassed by factionalism that was neither ideological nor related to the East-West conflict; it was inherent in the federative structure, its component organizations and their leaders simultaneously seeking un-circumscribed autonomy and hegemony of the whole.[22] Indeed, the wrangling within Zionism diminished when ideological factions were formed and accorded the status of parties by decision of the World Zionist Congress of 1907. Their differences clearly and lucidly stated, they were better able to cooperate on issues of common agreement.

The American Mizrachi (religious Zionists)[23] was founded in 1903, and the American Poale Zion (Labor Zionists) in 1905, although each had its precursors in the Federation of American Zionists. Hadassah, The Women's Zionist Organization, was founded in 1912 as a virtual auxiliary of the Federation. In 1921, it too left the Zionist Organization of American (ZOA), the new name of the Federation after it had lost its federative character. Hadassah, not a party in the same sense as the others, was content to leave ideological polemics and diplomatic efforts in the male domain and concentrated its attention and energies on Palestine's health and welfare needs.

The Zionist parties, like the estates in medieval society, each performed a distinct and indispensable function in the parallelogram that was the Zionist movement. Mizrachi promoted the cause among a resistant Orthodoxy, Poale Zionism's[24] small forces of doughty warriors advanced on the Jericho walls of the solidly anti-Zionist Jewish labor movement, and the Federation ZOA addressed itself to public opinion at large, engaged the *Yahudim* in polemics and led the movement's diplomatic sorties on Washington. The ZOA was eminently qualified for the three tasks, because it advocated broad principles without ideological interpolations, possessed the lion's share of membership, and included among its leadership men from the higher socio-economic strata, some of whom had acquired a reputation in American public affairs, or in their professions, before turning to Zionism. The mere presence of the latter added luster to the movement.

THE BRANDEIS ERA

American Zionism's golden age was between 1914 and 1921. It was paralleled only by the 1940's, when the Zionists led American Jewry in enlisting United States government support for immediate Jewish sovereignty in Palestine. In 1914, a Provisional Executive Committee for Zionist Affairs was formed under the chairmanship of Louis D. Brandeis, a recent convert to Zionism and to Jewish causes generally. It dissolved two years later. Yet, in that brief interval, it managed to dramatize the Zionist demands before American opinion, to act as a spokesman for a Zionist leadership which was dissevered between the two warring camps of Britain and Germany, and to make a strong impression on the central powers and allies alike. Before the United States entered the war, France sent an emissary to America to woo United States Jewry.[25] Because of Czarism's persecutive policy against Jewry, the immigrants were at first patently pro-German, and United States Zionist leadership included pro-Germans and neutralists.[26]

Brandeis and Wise, supported by a United Zionist movement, and subsequently by the American Jewish Congress, a broad "parliamentary" coalition of all American Jewry, frustrated State Department opposition, enlisted warm public and congressional support and won the slow, considered endorsement of President Wilson for the Jewish National Home. The American Jewish Congress,[27] conceived by the Poale Zion as the supreme representative of American Jewry and championed by Brandeis and Wise, was composed of delegates elected in nationwide balloting and supplemented by appointed representatives from the national organizations, in-

cluding the American Jewish Committee which had opposed the
elections, but, impressed by the voters' turnout, decided to join
the coalition. The Committee, nonetheless, sent its own separate
but not separatist delegation to the Peace Conference. However, its
president, Louis Marshall, shared the leadership of the American
Jewish Congress delegation. Thus spurred by Zionist initiative,
American Jewry (with the exception of a small minority led by
Henry Morgenthau, Sr.), almost unanimously demanded of the
Peace Conference international endorsement of the Balfour Declaration, and for the Jews in the newly formed and enlarged Balkan,
Baltic and East European states, assurance of the same guarantees
and rights as all other minority nationalities.[28]

Two other striking achievements of American Zionism at this
time were the Hadassah Medical Unit to Palestine (1916–1918)
and the considerable number of volunteers from America and
Canada who served with the Jewish Legion. The Legion was conceived by Vladimir Jabotinsky, author, orator, and later founder of
the Zionist-Revisionist party and godfather of Irgun. Volunteers
were recruited in this country by Ben-Zvi and Ben-Gurion, leaders
of Mapai, Israel's dominant moderate labor party.

Although his official tenure in Zionism was brief, Brandeis nonetheless played a crucial role in achieving the Balfour Declaration,
the movement's greatest single triumph before the United Nations
resolution of 1948 sanctioning the establishment of the State of
Israel. The significance of Brandeis' influence upon a vacillating
Wilson is conceded unenthusiastically by Weizmann, who surpris-
ingly and generously credits him, however, with an inordinate influence on Balfour.[29] Another result of Brandeis' leadership was
the influx into the ZOA of a new corps of men of astonishing
capacities. Intellectuals—Harry Friedenwald of Johns Hopkins
Medical School, Gustav Gottheil, rabbi of Temple Emanu-El, his
son Richard Gottheil of Columbia University, and Henrietta Szold
—had led the Zionist movement from the start; but all these leaders
had deep roots in Jewish tradition. Brandeis attracted men of established reputation in American society, or of imminent prominence who, like himself, had no such roots, or at any rate, no
previous familiarity with the East European immigrant multitudes.
The roster of enrolled Zionists at that time included Felix Frank-

furter, Ben Cohen, Bernard Flexner, Lawrence Steinhardt, later a United States diplomat in crucial posts, Eugene Meyer, Jr., later a Federal Reserve Bank governor and publisher who served in various capacities under five presidents, the banker-merchant-maecenas Sol M. Stroock, L. M. Kirstein, and Maurice Wertheim.[30]

When the first golden age came to an end, breaches appeared in American Zionism. The internal struggle within the Labor Zionist movement was not surprising, since schisms are inherent in all dialectical movements. But the acrimonious dissension which tore the ZOA apart had no apparent ideological basis. Even a close scrutiny of the minutes of the Cleveland convention of 1921, at which the followers of Brandeis broke away from the ZOA, fails to disclose any truly irreconcilable differences over principle.[31] The official reasons for the schism were Brandeis' opposition to the co-mingling of philanthropic and investment funds and the diversion of some of the Zionist revenue to Jewish education and other purposes not patently related to the economic development of the Jewish National Home; his insistence that the Zionists suspend their diplomatic sorties and concentrate all their energies on practical efforts in Palestine; and his alleged plan to place the Jewish National Home in the custody of private investors. The dispute over the co-mingling of funds should not have been beyond amicable settlement. Nor should it have been difficult to persuade Brandeis that the application of Zionist funds to Jewish education outside the United States was not a perversion of the donors' purpose. And none can consider seriously the charge that Brandeis, the Elijah in the war on bigness in American business, advocated corporate control of Palestine. Today the Mapai-led Israel government offers at least as good an incentive to business entrepreneurs as Brandeis proposed at a time when only utopists would dream of investing their monies in Palestine. Furthermore, soon after his triumph over Brandeis, Weizmann adopted the latter's policy of placing practical effort before diplomatic posture.

The true differences between Brandeis and the ZOA majority were of psychological origin, hence both elusive and insurmountable. The schism also had "ethnic" overtones relating to the indigenous and the immigrant Zionists, although there were both kinds in each camp. Both Brandeis and the immigrant Zionists subscribed

to the Emma Lazarus tradition, implying that I am my brother's
keeper, but I am not my brother. The immigrants, however, were
shamefaced about it. Their public posture for a purist Zionism con-
tradicted a private decision implicit in their failure to leave America
for Palestine. They escaped the agony of inner conflict by a rationale which offered absolution through public ritual and afforded
verbal and vicarious participation in the *Halutzic* passion. Brandeis
and his followers were driven by a Calvinist compulsion, as it were,
and could not and would not evade their commitments. They
launched the Palestine Economic Council (later Corporation)
which was the precursor of Ampal, Israel Bonds and other invest-
ment-aid programs. Some who had at one time or another gravitated
around Brandeis were impelled even beyond the limits of their commitments. America's first ranking Zionists to settle in Palestine were
Henrietta Szold (whose Hadassah disaffiliated from the ZOA but
otherwise kept aloof from the conflict after Brandeis' departure[32]),
and Judah L. Magnes, first president of the Hebrew University, who
independently broke with Brandeis and the masses. None of their
stature among the immigrant Zionists felt similarly compelled towards "self-realization." Of course, both Henrietta Szold and Judah
L. Magnes had been Zionist leaders long before Brandeis joined the
movement.

Weizmann's triumph in the struggle for hegemony of world
Zionism cost the movement that cadre of novitiates—intellectuals
and maecenases who had been attracted by the Brandeis name. Although very few of them could completely cast off the Zionist
spell (they joined non-Zionist organizations and led the latter into
cooperation with the Zionists, or became engaged in such apolitical,
overtly unideological projects as the Hebrew University), nonetheless, in losing them as members, the Zionist movement no doubt
lost untold others whom they might have brought into its ranks.

DECLINE OF INTELLECTUALISM

Indeed Brandeis' defeat signaled the decline of American Zionism
as an intellectual force, although men like Maurice Samuel and
Ludwig Lewisohn continued to hover on its periphery. But intellectuals were never again at the center, except for Louis Lipsky, an

early leader of the Federation of American Zionists and Weizmann's spokesman in America, and Emanuel Neumann, another
aide in the Weizmann assault on the Brandeis camp. Neither
Lipsky nor Neumann, however, was concerned with the movement's intellectual condition.

The various components of American Zionism settled down each
to its specific task. Mizrachi concentrated on reconciling tradition
with the new times and, directly or obliquely, contributed perhaps
more than any other single agency to the evolution of the modern
American Jewish Day School. Its Hebrew Teachers Institute,
affiliated to Yeshiva University, used from the start Hebrew as the
language of instruction and included medieval philosophy and modern Hebrew literature in its curriculum. In the 1920's, this constituted courageous defiance of the Orthodox dogmatists. The Labor
Zionists also engaged in education. Farband, the Labor Zionist
Order, founded the first Yiddish-language secular schools in this
country. Peculiarly, the Poale Zion were perhaps the least Americanized of all Zionist parties, and yet they were those most concerned with serving the American *Golah's* needs. Unfortunately,
many of their programs and remedies, tailored to East European
conditions, were of only transient relevance to American Jewish
life. One of their leaders even proposed putting forth Jewish slates
of candidates in American elections,[33] a rational procedure only in
the context of East European politics.

No component of American Zionism seemed less concerned with
the needs of American Jewish life than the ZOA. Many of its members, of course, were profoundly and zealously committed to the
furtherance of Hebrew studies. The Herzliah Teachers Institute
was founded by them. But ZOA financial support for such cultural
enterprises as the Hebrew weekly, *Hadoar,* and the Yiddish weekly,
Dos Yiddishe Folk, was doled out reluctantly and parsimoniously.

With prominent political figures on its board, and a larger proportion of English-speaking orators than all the other parties together could claim, the ZOA continued to be Zionism's chief in-
terpreter to the community at large. Weizmann, wary of excessive
and public political demands, reluctantly conceded, even on such
occasions as British White Papers and Arab riots in Palestine, that
mass rallies were necessary[34] to keep governments, and especially

Britain, aware that Zionism had a popular mandate from the Jewish people. The ZOA led in staging these rallies with the solid support of the Zionist Yiddish daily press, a formidable force in the 1920's and 1930's. Yet the ZOA, although its ranks at that time were Yiddish-speaking, never courted the Yiddish intellectual. Weizmann's primary desire was that American Zionists provide the funds for the Palestine undertaking.[35] The other parties participated, of course, but the ZOA was instigator and chief custodian of the effort which required two components, executives who were primarily promoters and fund-raisers, and big donors who could be enlisted largely from among the immigrant newly rich. It was a combination allergic to the disconcerting presence of intellectuals.[36] Concern with American problems was beyond the purview of ZOA preoccupation and personnel. There was, of course, another reason, the then unuttered conviction, and today the credo of most American Zionists, that American Jewry was inordinately blessed and not really a *Golah,* and hence had no problems.

Hadassah, removed from political battle, has built a powerful membership organization and has pursued as its primary, although not exclusive task, the expansion of its medical facilities in Israel. Pioneer Women—The Women's Labor Zionist Organization—and Mizrachi Women, both founded in the mid-1920's, have concentrated on general social welfare service. They work through Israel agencies, unlike Hadassah which has its own apparatus. They are boldly ideological as are the agencies through which they work in Israel, and although distinct and separate corporate entities, they both maintain an interrelationship with the Mizrachi and Mapai, their parent organizations. Hadassah, too, has in recent years digressed from its ideological and structural neutrality by affiliating, globally, with the progressive wing of general Zionism. Somewhat parallel to Pioneer Women is the Women's League for Israel founded in 1928, which also concentrates on the needs of the Israel working mother and cooperates with Histadrut agencies.

The responsibility for sustaining Zionism in America as an ideology and not merely as a political aim, fell to Mizrachi and the Labor Zionists. The Yiddish and indigenous American Jewish intellectual, displaced in the ZOA, began to incline in the direction of Poale Zion. They were attracted by its social philosophy and by

the engaging personality of the late Chaim Greenberg, editor of the
Jewish Frontier (Poale Zion monthly), and *Der Yiddisher Kemfer*
(Poale Zion weekly). However, Greenberg was a reluctant figure in
politics, and real power in American Labor Zionism gradually began to slip into more parochial custody. This process, completed
with Greenberg's passing, caused the decline of Labor Zionism as
an influence in American Jewish life, and was no less adverse for
the evolution of American Zionism than the departure of Brandeis
from the ZOA. Another disadvantage was that Labor Zionism's
ideological guidance from Palestine was self-centered, not appreciative of the needs of American Jewry, and not conversant with its
tides.

However, even after its intellectual élan had passed, Poale Zion
still made significant contributions. The ZOA sustained in United
States Jewry the obligation to support the Jewish National Home
financially and politically, and kept Zionism alive before the public
imagination. Farband, the fraternal order founded by Poale Zion,
contended for the loyalties of the Yiddish-speaking laboring masses
against the Workmen's Circle, the affluent Socialist fraternal organization, and the Jewish Fraternal Order, a Communist agency.
The Farband and the Israel Histadrut Campaign eventually
eclipsed Poale Zion in numbers, resources and corresponding prestige, even as the ZOA was dislodged from its central position by
the fund-raising agencies it had brought into being. The Israel
Histadrut Campaign, originally launched as the Gewerkschaften
Campaign, breached the seemingly impregnable anti-Zionist Jewish
labor movement, and eventually won all American labor for the
cause of Israel. The Campaign is now gaining as a cause to which
liberals rally because of the effective application by many of
the underdeveloped states of Histadrut's pragmatism—trade unionism combined with government-scaled social welfare programs
and cooperative economic initiative.

THE PANIC OF THE 1930's

The strengths and weaknesses of the American Zionist movement
were strikingly revealed in the turbulent 1930's when American
Jewry's concern for its brethren overseas was exacerbated into

alarm over its own future by native American fascist groups.

American Zionism was eminently prepared and successful in the area of philanthropy but failed completely in the then equally important domain of dialectics. Both the Zionist apparatus and its rank and file were well apprenticed in the techniques of fund-raising. Yet the American Joint Distribution Committee (JDC), from its founding in 1914 and through the 1920's, did eminently better for several reasons: the requirements of the Zionist blueprint could not be equated with the agony of East European Jewry's persecuted and deprived millions, and, furthermore, American Jewish wealth was still primarily in the hands of the *Yahudim,* and although Zionism had enlisted many of them, the majority of their class were concentrated around JDC. In the 1930's this changed. The East European immigrants brought forth their own upper-middle class, more responsive to Zionist ideology than the *Yahudim,* and even the latter began to comprehend the interrelationship between the Jewish refugee problem, presented by Nazi Germany, and the Jewish National Home, to which the Jews could post legal claim based on contemporary pledges and covenants. United States Zionism pressed the advantage. In 1939, to rationalize allocations and prevent competitive fund-raising, the United Jewish Appeal was established by tripartite agreement among the (Zionist) United Palestine Appeal, the JDC, and the National Refugee Service which looked after refugees in the United States. However, it should have been apparent to American Zionism that its services as a philanthropic spur would soon become unnecessary.

Alarmed by the double-pincer movement of Nazism and domestic fascism, American Jewry's attention turned to "defense activities." This was the great "expansionist" period of the Anti-Defamation League, the American Jewish Committee and the American Jewish Congress. The Congress, a Zionist creature supported by the then vigorous Yiddish press, led mass demonstrations against Nazism, filed petitions for United States intervention against Hitler, and launched a boycott of German goods and services, the latter over the shocked protests of the American Jewish Committee which believed Hitler could be persuaded to temporize. This Zionist commitment to militancy in the anti-Nazi struggle should have attracted large numbers of campus youth to its banners. How-

ever, because it functioned through a proxy, the American Jewish
Congress, because Stephen S. Wise, its central figure, had a liberal
prominence apart from Zionism, and because its major public activity at this time was fund-raising, American Zionism did not present itself to the youthful imagination as a relevant factor in the
anti-Nazi struggle.

The Jewish intelligentsia was then drawn largely to the dialectical
left of center movements which offered panaceas for all domestic
and global ills. American Zionism had three faces, all somewhat re-
pulsive to the young intelligentsia. The ZOA and Hadassah, with
their formal fund-raising dinners, were unrelieved "bourgeois" in
the eyes of depression-conditioned youth, oriented towards socialist
doctrine and bohemian morals. Mizrachi was sheer "medievalism,"
and Poale Zionism's Yiddish emphases placed it in the "ghetto"
from which the young were leaping to freedom. Nonetheless, because of their socialist dialectics, the Labor Zionist youth movements (Hashomer Hatzair and Poale Zion's Habonim) did succeed
in some measure where other Zionists failed completely; they recruited sufficient numbers to populate several *kibbutzim.*

ZIONIST-LED UNITED FRONT

The 1940's imposed on American Zionism its greatest responsibilities since the days of the Balfour Declaration. Chaim Weizmann
and David Ben-Gurion hurried to the United States. The American
Zionist Emergency Council was formed, a united front of all Zionist
parties for political effort, on the pattern of the Provisional Executive Committee for Zionist Affairs of 1914. In 1943, B'nai B'rith
president Henry Monsky convened, on Zionist initiative, the American Jewish Conference (a coalition of Zionists and non-Zionists)
successor to the American Jewish Congress of 1918. Its purpose
was to draw up Jewish demands and map Jewish strategy for a
post-war Peace Conference.[37] The American Jewish Committee,
dissenting from the demand for a Jewish commonwealth in Palestine, left the Conference. However, B'nai B'rith, a non-Zionist mass
organization and co-convener of the Conference, remained within
until 1948, when the Conference dissolved.[38]

The Zionists were bold. They initiated in camera fund-raising for

clandestine immigration into Palestine and arms-running for the
extra-legal defense force, *Haganah*. They also gauged accurately
American Jewry's new prosperity and readiness to donate, and led
the United Jewish Appeal to set audacious annual goals.

Zionism's bold initiatives in Palestine compensated American
Jews for the trauma of shock and humiliation that afflicted them
following the European catastrophe. Hitherto uncommitted American Jews, of the highest socio-economic strata, responded to the call
for funds and political support required in the struggle for a sovereign Jewish state. The excitement communicated itself even to
the intellectuals, who briefly were again intrigued by Zionism's purpose and valor. But as in 1921, when it suffered the departure of
the Brandeis group, American Zionism once more failed to score
permanently with the intellectuals, and, instead, soon suffered a
general setback in numbers and influence. Some of the reasons
were inherent in the movement; some were beyond its control.

By its very nature, American Zionism has been a middle-class
movement, lacking intellectual élan. The affections of even veteran
Zionists were, after 1948, deflected from the movement to the State
of Israel, Zionism's embodied purpose. The recognition conferred
upon them by Israel has affected the status of all agencies and individuals in American Jewish public life. Zionism has not enjoyed
warm recognition from Israel. The latter, of necessity, has been
concerned with those who best serve its immediate purposes, financial and political. The Zionist apparatus and membership have been
regarded by some of Israel's leadership as not particularly relevant
to their country's immediate purpose. In the political arena, all the
major Jewish organizations have responded promptly and alike, if
not always jointly, whenever Israel has appeared to be threatened.
The United Jewish Appeal and Israel Bonds have assumed former
Zionist responsibilities in the financial field. Zionism has created its
own replacements.

American Zionists have yet to explain convincingly how they
differ ideologically from non-Zionists, now that the State of Israel
has been established. They contend that non-Zionists would not
risk public embarrassment in supporting Israel. The one test to
which this contention was put, the Sinai campaign of 1956, found
the non-Zionists as critical as the Zionists of United States govern-

ment policy. Ben-Gurion's test of Zionist loyalty is whether one studies Hebrew and settles in Israel. This test has probably been met by as many, or as few, non-Zionists as Zionists.

FUNCTION FOR ZIONISM

Zionism might recover its relevance to Israel by re-establishing its relevance to American Jewry. Unfortunately, here too Zionism has become least relevant in the one field in which it had in the past made an appreciable contribution. That field is "defense activity," which is now called "human relations." Zionists provided this effort with stimulus and a *raison d'etre* when they called for militant preventive action against Nazism in the early 1930's, whereas non-Zionist agencies advised temporizing with Berlin. But "human relations" has since turned to more subtle targets and problems, and it is the preserve of leading non-Zionist organizations, serviced by technocrats—lawyers, sociologists and copy writers. The new techniques are beyond the range of a mass movement which Zionism was intended to be.

The American Zionist movement has been casting about for some other area of activity that might re-establish its relevance. It has been trying to stake out a claim to Jewish education. But that field too has been pre-empted by others, including Zionist-oriented educators whom American Zionism previously and outrageously ignored.

It is sometimes proposed that American Zionism's true function is to prevent a future alienation between American Jewry and Israel. Symptoms of estrangement have been detected in the younger generation's alleged apathy to appeals for funds for Israel. But this is hardly a proper gauge. Indeed, this kind of one-dimensional relationship between donor and beneficiary is detrimental. A more integral relationship is necessary, but it cannot evolve until American Jewry becomes fully visible and identifiable. Its concerns today are diversified and departmentalized and convey the impression of incoherent, disjointed functioning. Israel does not address itself to American Jewry in its totality, but to its separate functions, which is an absurd circumstance.

What American Jewry requires, both for its own good and for

its relations with Israel, is a coordination of its functions, concerns and interests. This does not mean the type of operational centralization which Zionist leaders propose. It means synthesis. World Zionism's historic contribution, apart from bringing the State of Israel into being, has been its ability to extract the survivalist elements from all movements that deeply stirred contemporary Jewry and to synthesize them into a Zionist totality. It adopted the Yiddish and Hebrew literary renaissance; some of its segments espoused socialist principles; and it impressed itself even on the realm of religion by splitting the Reform rabbinate over the issue of a Jewish National Home, and by producing an Orthodox *kibbutz* movement. There is no evidence, however, from its utterances, that American Zionist leadership is endowed with the total comprehension which this task requires in America.

Since movements and organisms can outlive their usefulness, it would be absurd to predict the longevity of the American Zionist movement. However, one may state with some degree of certainty that the Zionist women's organizations may outlive all the others because they have retained their relevance through their social welfare projects in Israel. This cannot be said of the others. American Zionism in its totality has long been what Chaim Arolosoroff, the martyred Labor Zionist, accused the ZOA, in 1929, of being—mediocre, conventional and correspondingly adverse to the intellectualism that made Zionism a force in recent Jewish history. There is an inescapable co-relationship, of course, between the condition of the world Zionist movement and the pathology of its parts.

The Problems of Coordination and Unity[1]

ABRAHAM G. DUKER

DEVELOPMENT AND PROLIFERATION OF JEWISH ORGANIZATIONS

THE socio-economic forces which have influenced the development of Jewish communal institutions have been described in preceding chapters. Charity was dispensed in the early (Sephardi) period by the synagogue. The German Jews fashioned their own charitable societies, beginning in New York in 1844. Jewish hospitals were established in the 1850's and 1860's in the large cities independently of the synagogues. Fraternal orders and educational institutions emerged. The leadership of these institutions was predominantly German.

The increase in East European immigration after 1865 and especially after 1881 compelled the Jewish communities to expand their charitable and welfare services. Because of the Jewish tradition of charity, communal pride, fear of anti-Semitism, and concern about Gentile criticism and acceptance, the established German-Jewish leadership provided family aid, hospital facilities, orphan asylums, shelters for transients, settlement houses, old age homes and similar services.

The East European immigrants brought with them a strong tradition of self-help, close family ties, appreciation of learning and communal cooperation. After the 1890's certain elements among them also professed labor and Zionist ideologies that emphasized the westernization of Jewish culture rather than its abandonment through assimilation or through a form of "Americanization" which was equivalent to assimilation. The East Europeans developed their own institutions, and two separate Jewish communities emerged—the "uptown *Yahudim*" and the "downtown" immigrants.

For decades there existed a deep chasm between the German "established" leadership and the East Europeans or "Russians." It was due mainly to differing self-images, resulting from the contempt of the Germans for East Europeans in general and that of emancipated Jews for the non-emancipated. It expressed itself mainly in far-reaching differences over the definition of the Jewish group (religion versus peoplehood), as seen in the struggle over Zionism and over religious adjustment (Reform versus Orthodoxy). Other less articulated positions involved disagreement concerning the desirability of a Jewish culture beyond the limits of the reduced modern forms of religion, as seen in attitudes to Yiddish, Hebrew and continuity of customs. Important also were differences in economic status and economic ideologies.

In time, however, the Jewish "melting pot" and the traditional drive for Jewish solidarity during periods of emergency overcame many differences. Anti-Semitic accusations led to the establishment of the New York Kehillah, in which German and East European Jews cooperated for a time. During World War I, the desperate situation of the Jews of Eastern Europe and Palestine helped bring the two communities together in joint fund-raising campaigns under the JDC and even for the defense of minority rights in Europe.

The great changes in American Jewry which have occurred since World War I have likewise been described earlier: a predominantly immigrant population has been transformed into an overwhelmingly native one; proletarian occupations have given way to middle-class, upper-class, and professional pursuits; the crowded immigrant neighborhoods have been abandoned for new settlements in the suburbs.[2] The same period witnessed a proliferation of national Jewish organizations. Nineteen such bodies were listed in 1900 in the *American Jewish Year Book,* 71 in 1914, 116 in 1925–26, and 247 in 1962. The number of rabbinical seminaries rose from three to five during 1900–25, but no less than 25 were functioning in 1962. There was only one community relations agency in 1900, five in 1925 and 12 in 1962. Nine domestic welfare agencies and three overseas aid organizations were listed in 1925; in 1962, the corresponding numbers were at least 30 domestic and 15 overseas bodies. Only one Zionist ideological group was recorded in 1900, five in 1925, and 22 in 1962. Similarly, the number of Holy Land reconstruction agencies was four in 1925 and twenty-odd in 1962. Women's organizations increased from six in 1925 to over 30 in 1962. Finally, cultural and educational institutions independent of synagogues increased from three in 1925 to over 30 in 1962.

Today the national organizations and the local communal bodies which some of them represent or service consist of a congeries of groupings or establishments, some dependent on one another or with some points of contact and areas of common work or policy, others aloof from, indifferent to or in competition with similar organizations. Most, if not all, are competitive to some degree in fund-raising and in the desire to attract leadership of status and influence.

Status and power of board membership vary from city to city. The prestigious major groupings may be identified as first the welfare agencies, the core of the Federation and therefore also the Welfare Funds, some community relations (overseas defense) agencies, and non-sectarian causes. Some national fund-raising agencies for overseas or American causes wield great power. Religious central bodies have managed to maintain a good deal of independence. Less status and influence is enjoyed by the Zionist groupings. The Jewish (not non-sectarian) educational, cultural, and research bodies are in the least advantageous positions. The importance of status and control in Jewish communal enterprise should not be minimized. Its welfare aspects alone involve an annual expenditure of $200,000,-000. The Jewish communities and organizations are said to employ about 100,000 persons. Executives usually manage them in the style of large corporations, a vivid illustration of the "managerial revolution" in Jewish communal life. The role of the civil services is therefore paramount in the evaluation of the strength of an organization or agency. In many functional areas, national and local coordinating organizations have arisen which service the local bodies and consult with them in the formulation of policy.*

COORDINATION IN FUND-RAISING

Coordination has been most evident in fund-raising, and this form of united effort began in the local communities in the area of the social services. It will therefore be helpful to examine briefly the development of local coordinating communal agencies.

The Welfare Funds and Community Councils

After World War I, inter-sectarian Community Chests emerged for the support of social services of all faiths. They were joined by many Jewish Federations because of a feeling of communal unity and responsibility for the welfare of all needy, and also because of a desire to work with non-Jews. The relief needs of the Jewish population declined with its economic rise and with the restriction of immigration. Many Federations therefore began to limit themselves primarily to the distribution of Chest allotments to the Jewish agencies. Eventually, however, it became clear that the Chests could not take care of special needs of the Jewish clients, such as *Kashrut*, Hebrew school fees, higher rents in Jewish districts, and the financing of religious, cultural, and overseas needs. Besides, allotments from Community Chests declined steadily. The Federations, therefore, had to re-emphasize their fund-raising activities.

---

* A number of these have been discussed in appropriate chapters of this book—the synagogue and rabbinic associations in Chapter Five, and the coordinating bureaus and commissions in Jewish education in Chapter Six. The National Jewish Welfare Board, the central service agency of the Jewish community centers, has been dealt with in Chapter Eight, and the recently organized National Foundation for Jewish Culture in section II of the Conclusion. In this chapter, attention is focussed upon two themes, namely: (1) the achievement of coordination in fund-raising; and (2) the repeated but thus far unsuccessful attempts to fashion a roof agency for the entire Jewish community (ed.).

The communities also faced the ordeal of annual campaigns by numerous and competing national and overseas organizations. The campaign difficulties were eventually resolved by the emergence of the Welfare Funds (first in Detroit in 1925) that raised funds for both local and national causes, with allocation committees distributing the funds. Five Welfare Funds were established in 1926. By 1929 there were also sixty-three Federations. In twenty-four other cities, family agencies served as the central organizations. The 1929 Depression, increasing acculturation in the 1930's, and overseas needs in that decade stimulated the growth of the Welfare Funds, so that 23 were organized during 1934–36.[3]

Democratic influences and the Kehillah tradition also stimulated in the 1930's the growth of Community Councils, based on the representation of groups rather than on individual donors. The Councils' interests originally included fund-raising, social services, community relations, representation, and cultural and educational activities. Starting in New Haven and Cincinnati (1928, 1930), it seemed during the 1930's that the local communities would become organized under these new democratic roof bodies, American versions of the Kehillah.[4]

However, the growth of the Welfare Funds changed the trend. The Depression of 1929 again posed basic relief as a problem for the Jewish community. The rise of Hitler, too, soon underscored the urgency of raising more funds for overseas needs. The Federations and Welfare Funds therefore assumed increasing importance. Because the Federations and the social services had generally been headed by the established leaders and serviced by professionals, the communities turned to this experienced leadership for help in fund-raising for national and overseas causes.

This trend weakened the democratic drive in the Community Councils and deprived them of their financial base. The established leadership had not been partial to the ideas of Jewish unity or Kehillah-form of organization.[5] The professionals usually followed the established line of assimilationist liberalism which had been tinged with extreme leftist ideology in the 1930's and 1940's, especially in the social work field. The established lay leadership showed little awareness of this orientation among professionals, and the partnership of leftist and rightist assimilationists worked well.[6] In some intermediate and in many smaller communities, the Community Councils developed into central agencies, but in the large cities, the functions of Community Councils were generally reduced to community relations, cultural activities, or forums on community problems.

Meanwhile, local coordinating and fund raising organizations under various names, mainly Community Councils, Welfare Funds, or Federations, grew in number. In 1961, there were over 200 such organizations covering some 800 communities in the United States. New York and Washington remained the two important communities without Welfare Funds, with the New York Federation and UJA functioning as fairly independent establishments.

National Coordination—UJA and CJFWF

National coordination in fund-raising has developed along two lines, namely: (1) unified efforts under the United Jewish Appeal; and (2) mutual consultation through the Council of Jewish Federations and Welfare Funds (CJFWF).

The fashioning of the UJA has been traced briefly in Chapter Nine. Until 1933, overseas needs had been represented by the JDC, with its emphasis on relief and reconstruction within Europe, and the Zionist United Palestine Appeal which championed the building of the Jewish National Home in Palestine as a permanent solution of the Jewish problem. By the mid 1930's, a new need had arisen when German-Jewish refugees began to arrive in the United States, and the established leadership organized in 1934 the National Coordinating Committee for German Refugees (later, National Refugee Service—NRS; United Service for New Americans—USNA). This agency expanded rapidly and appealed for funds in the local Jewish communities.[7]

The communities preferred united campaigns and voiced their demands at the annual assemblies of the CJFWF. This was attempted repeatedly with varying success. By 1937 a ratio of national allocation with priority to JDC (rather than the UPA) had been agreed upon. This was continued in 1938, when a third partner, the National Coordinating Committee, was added. In 1939, the UJA was established as the joint campaign and allocation instrument of the three bodies, again with priority to non-Palestinian causes. The joint effort was menaced during the war years by disagreements over the distribution of the monies raised, and it was temporarily disbanded in 1945. After World War II, however, when American Jewry learned about the effects of the Nazi holocaust, the world's indifference to the rescue of European Jewry, and the desire of the Jewish survivors to settle in the Jewish homeland, the UJA was reconstituted and it became the leading national fund-raising body in the United States.[8] Since then, allocation priority has been going to the UPA (UIA—United Israel Campaign).

The CJFWF had its origin in the National Appeals Information Service, which was organized by Federations in 1927 to supply the need for guidance and information in fund-raising campaigns. Five years later, it became the nucleus of the CJFWF, which was organized to provide services in fund-raising, budgeting and other aspects of community organization. In 1963, it embraced associated central community organizations, Federations and Welfare Funds in the United States and Canada in 210 cities. Its strategic position in rendering advice on fund-raising and budgeting and as an employment service for professionals in the local and national institutions raised it to its present position of great influence in Jewish communal life, particularly in the disposition of funds for national and local causes.

Within the CJFWF, an inner group known as the Large City Budgeting Conference (LCBC) wields a great deal of power. Organized in 1948 for the purpose of developing joint policies in connection with the defense agencies, it has become a most important factor in resolving campaign and allocations problems. It now consists of representatives of the Federations and Welfare Funds of 23 important cities, and its recommendations are generally followed by the local fund-raising bodies.

Attempts have been made to introduce "national budgeting," that is control or supervision through the CJFWF of the budgets of Jewish national organizations. This has not been achieved, but spearheaded by the LCBC, the CJFWF has succeeded in attaining mutual "discussion" of budgets. The Jewish Agency for Israel, for example, has agreed to budgetary consultation with the LCBC, but without "validation."[9] In 1963, the LCBC was further strengthened by the participation of the powerful Anti-Defamation League.

Effects of Coordination in Fund-Raising

During the past three decades, the Federations and Welfare Funds have organized the communities for fund-raising and promoted efficiency through the elimination of rival campaigns. They have served as the local communities' voice in national affairs, thus curbing unbridled campaign tactics. They have developed a corps of lay leaders and professional workers with experience in fund-raising and certain areas of community organization. Above all, they have strengthened the feeling of identification with the Jewish people (*Klal Yisrael*) through philanthropic activities.

The combined or united annual campaigns have become routine in the Jewish communities, and the results have been unprecedented in the history of philanthropy, transcending such campaigns as that of the Red Cross. In sixteen post-war years (1946–1961), over $2,160,000,000 were raised by central organizations through organized Jewish campaigns, with an annual average of $118,000,000 in the 1950's and with some $125,000,000 in 1961.[10]

However, there is a debit side to coordinated fund-raising. The tradition in Jewish communal philanthropy has been to succor the sick and the poor, and while in recent years the emphasis has been on service rather than charity, the preference for the social and health services still prevails among the established leadership. Thus, the allocations for various local services included the following percentages in 1961: Family and Child Services, 21.7 percent of total funds appropriated for local services; Health Services, 22.1 percent; Recreation and Culture (a catch-all for the group-work agencies), 24.8 percent.[11]

In contrast to these proportionally large allocations, the share of Jewish education and culture has been scandalously small. Jewish education received only 12.6 percent of allocations for local services in 1961, and cultural institutions fared even worse. The American Academy for Jewish Research had in 1961 a total income of $16,954, of which $4,394 were secured from Welfare Funds, and the Conference on Jewish Social Studies had a total income of $24,721, including only $2,704 from Welfare Funds. In the same year, the Jewish Publication Society received from Welfare Funds a total of $15,404, and the Yivo Institute for Jewish Research the sum of

$34,025. Altogether, 14 "cultural" agencies received in 1961 some $662,000, including $478,000 allotted to the B'nai B'rith National Youth Service Appeal and $25,000 to the Zionist Organization of America. Similarly, 18 religious agencies received in 1961 a total of $434,000 from Welfare Funds out of the $5,637,000 distributed to domestic organizations.[12]

In recent years, Jewish cultural institutions have begun to elicit the interest of the CJFWF. In 1954, the latter sponsored a partial study of agencies of social and historical research, and in 1960 it encouraged the establishment of the National Foundation for Jewish Culture.[13] The response of the Welfare Funds, however, indicates that the influence of the Federations is still very strong. Hence the emphasis on non-sectarian services and the lack of readiness to assume responsibility for all Jewish communal needs.

The neglect of Jewish education and culture by the Welfare Funds[14] is frequently explained by the lack of money or by the assumption that only the synagogues or educators are responsible for these areas, or in other words, for Jewish cultural and religious survival. This, however, fails to reckon with the basic changes which have occurred in recent years. The development of welfare state policies has led to the assumption by the government of many of the charitable functions of Jewish communal institutions. Furthermore, the rapid economic advance of the Jewish population and its shift to the suburbs have reduced the number of Jewish clients for the services of Jewish institutions. As a result, the clinics in most Jewish hospitals cater predominantly to non-Jews, and the national hospitals have overwhelmingly non-Jewish clientele. Jewish family services, child guidance agencies, employment services, and settlement houses are likewise becoming increasingly non-sectarian. And the ideological justification of Jewish communal sponsorship of such institutions has been found in the thesis that the prime obligation of the organized Jewish community is the care of the welfare of all the needy.[15] The problem of training for Jewish social work has likewise not met with the proper interest of the large Federations and top professionals.[16]

The neglect by the coordinated fund-raising agencies of Jewish educational and cultural services which are the mainstay of Jewish survival but cannot claim government funds, and their generous support of services which have become increasingly the responsibility of government or the total community, warrants the basic question of whether the traditional policies of Federations and Welfare Funds have not become obsolete.[17]

THE QUEST FOR A CENTRAL ROOF AGENCY

Critical situations generally induce the desire for effective central representative bodies. Such has been the experience of American Jewry since the fourth decade of the nineteenth century. However, the efforts to organize a permanent roof body have come to naught because of divergent ideologies, group interests, and unbridled individualism.

Prior to the twentieth century, the chief obstacles to unity consisted of differences between the East and Midwest leaders, Reform and Orthodoxy, and the seemingly unbridgeable chasm between the East Europeans and Germans. During the first two decades of the twentieth century, differences over Zionism, Jewish nationalism and labor ideologies constituted additional stumbling blocks. After World War I, a new issue arose: reconstruction in Europe versus the building of Palestine. The labor movement became sharply split between Communists and anti-Communists and between pro- and anti-Zionists. The threat of Nazism produced sharp clashes on tactics in the anti-Nazi struggle. During World War II, there were divisions over issues such as a Jewish army, pressure for the rescue of European Jewry, and finally, Jewish statehood. After World War II, the struggle continued particularly about the statehood of Israel and later about its defense.[18] At present that disagreement has been reduced on the surface to the voices of the isolated American Council of Judaism and the extreme Orthodox elements. However, beneath the surface there are grave struggles between proponents of local and overseas causes, between the religious groupings and secularist agencies and between the advocates of continued involvement in non-sectarian services and those who would give priority to survivalist cultural, educational, and religious causes. To all these doctrinal and tactical discords must be added the vested interests of the individual organizations and leaders which militate against the achievement of effective unity.

Projects Prior to the Twentieth Century

A proposal by Isaac Leeser in 1841 for a "Sanhedrin" of the New World failed to materialize. Synods of congregations proposed in 1848 and 1865 likewise came to naught because of factional religious and regional objections. The emergency situation created by the forced baptism of the Mortara child in 1858 brought into existence the Board of Delegates of American Israelites (1859–78). The Board functioned for several decades in defense, research, education and the "regulation" of emigration. However, its Reform leadership was more interested in the Union of American Hebrew Congregations, which eventually absorbed the Board through its own Board of Delegates on Civil Rights.[19]

The influx of Russian Jews in the 1880's produced a desire to unite the old and the new elements through the Jewish Alliance of America, established in 1891 "for the purpose of more effectively coping with the grave problem presented by enforced emigration." It was the first bid of the East European elements for their share in national communal leadership. However, the Alliance faded quickly because of the maneuverings of the established leadership.

The American Jewish Committee

A new emergency, the Kishinev pogrom (1903), underscored the need for a representative body, both American and international, for the protection of European Jewry. Attempts were made to fashion local federations of Jewish organizations which, it was hoped, would form the basis for a national roof organization. The American Jewish Committee was organized in 1906, with limited representation and emergency character. However, its powerful leadership and the prestige it enjoyed in the general community soon won it a preponderant influence in Jewish life.[20]

World War I and First American Jewish Congress

The suffering of the Jews in the Russian war zone and in Palestine, and the war idealism generated by President Wilson, stimulated demands for Jewish unity in order to protect Jewish rights in the post-war settlement. The Zionists favored a popular and representative American Jewish Congress to speak for the Jewish community. The American Jewish Committee and the anti-nationalist labor groups offered vigorous resistance, but their cooperation was finally secured and the first American Jewish Congress was held in December 1918. This body represented almost all important American Jewish elements, including the American Jewish Committee, and its delegation played a prominent role in inducing the Paris Peace Conference to accord international protection to the minorities (including the Jews) of Poland and other new and enlarged states. This Congress disbanded in 1920, in accord with a prior agreement.[21]

Since World War I

In 1922, the present American Jewish Congress was organized, but it failed to win support as the overall roof organization. Other plans for a permanent representative body of American Jewry likewise failed.

With the rise of Hitler to power in 1933, and the consequent menace of international anti-Semitism, the movement for American Jewish unity became equated, to a large extent, with the struggle against anti-Semitism. This focussed attention upon the defense or community relations organizations, and public opinion demanded the coordination of the competing defense activities of the "Big Four"—the American Jewish Committee, the B'nai B'rith Anti-Defamation League, the American Jewish Congress and the Jewish Labor Committee. In 1933, a Joint Consultative Council was formed, but disagreement over tactics in the anti-Nazi struggle (militancy versus caution, and discord over the boycott of German goods) disrupted the Joint Council in 1937. In the following year, a semblance of cooperation was restored by the establishment of a General Jewish Council representing the four organizations.

The oubreak of World War II and the intensification of Nazi persecution of Jews, as well as isolationist and anti-Semitic propaganda in the United States, led to the expansion of the activities of Jewish defense organizations, which in turn brought more rivalry in fundraising. Suggestions by Welfare Funds that combined allocations be made to the "Big Four" failed to get approval and, instead, the American Jewish Committee and the Anti-Defamation League formed in 1941 their own fund-raising instrument, the Joint Defense Appeal. This led to the withdrawal of the American Jewish Congress from the General Jewish Council, which lingered on until 1944, when a new attempt was made to coordinate the defense agencies on a broader base.

In 1944 the National Community Relations Advisory Council (NCRAC) was established at the General Assembly of the CJFWF. It included the "Big Four," the Union of American Hebrew Congregations, the Jewish War Veterans, and fourteen local community relations councils. Other national organizations and additional community relations councils joined subsequently. However, the NCRAC, involved as it was in community relations problems, and insufficiently representative, could not meet the demand for an overall body to act for the American Jewish Community in matters affecting the future of the Jewish National Home, the rescue of surviving Jews and their protection in the postwar world.[22]

The American Jewish Conference

During World War II, an attempt was made to organize a unified and broadly representative body to deal with current and post-war overseas problems. The precedent of World War I, when American Jewry did achieve unity, gave encouragement to the proponents of the plan, and the mass murders of Jews at the hands of the Nazis appeared reason enough to induce all Jewish organizations to cooperate.

In the fall of 1942, the leading Jewish organizations formed, on the initiative of the American Jewish Congress, the Conference on the Jewish Situation in Nazi Europe, which developed into the Joint Emergency Committee for European Affairs. In 1943, community pressures were sufficient to effect the organization of the American Jewish Conference to promote the rescue of Jews and the defense of Jewish rights in Palestine and to prepare for the inevitable problems of postwar reconstruction. To mollify opponents, it was agreed that the Conference would be a temporary organization limited to overseas problems, but even this assurance proved insufficient to effect unity. The American Jewish Committee and the Jewish Labor Committee, which had participated reluctantly in the initiating conference, withdrew: the first because of objections to statehood; the second because of resentment against the admission of a leftist fraternal order. At the close of World War II, there was, therefore, no united Jewish representation, as had been the case when World War I came to an end. The partially representative American Jewish Conference endured until 1948, when it was disbanded.[23]

The MacIver Report

The end of the Conference centered attention on the large community relations agencies and on NCRAC as an instrument of at least partial coordination. Expenditures for community relations mounted steadily: the combined expenses of the "Big Three" (American Jewish Committee, Anti-Defamation League and American Jewish Congress) rose from about $100,000 annually in the early 1930's to $5,312,000 in 1949; and the pressures for funds especially by the Joint Defense Appeal created discord within the welfare funds. It was also felt that much money might be saved if rival programs and overlapping functions could be eliminated through coordination. The Large City Budgeting Conference therefore proposed that an impartial study be made of the programs and financing of the community relations agencies. This was approved by the NCRAC and Robert M. MacIver was engaged to make the study. MacIver's report, submitted in 1951, favored the ideological position of the American Jewish Committee and the Anti-Defamation League, but it recommended joint planning, a division of the fields of activities, and other coordinating procedures. When the NCRAC accepted the recommendations (1951), the American Jewish Committee and the Anti-Defamation League withdrew from the NCRAC.[24] The fragmentation of the American Jewish community was thus increased.

The Pros and Cons of Communal Unity

Various proposals have been made for a unified roof organization. The Conservative rabbinate has proposed an American Jewish Assembly. Suggestions have been made to transform the CJFWF into a roof organization by expanding its functions. Perhaps the most far-reaching plan has been advanced by Mordecai M. Kaplan, who favors a central organization based on "organic communities," or democratic community councils. But the latter vary in constituency, leadership and democratic structure.

The opponents of a unified representative agency argue that historically such bodies have generally been imposed from above. They assert that such coordination would constitute "a state within the state"; that it might have been suitable for Eastern Europe but is contrary to the ideal of "voluntarism" and, therefore, un-American; that it would breed an uncontrollable bureaucracy and stifle free expression. Finally, organic unity has been dismissed as unattainable, and it has been urged that voluntary coalitions, though weak and unstable, are the most that can be achieved.

The Present Situation

Unable to fashion an effective roof organization, American Jewish leadership has resorted to *ad hoc* agencies for consultation on overseas problems. Arab agitation against Israel and Jewry, and its support by the Soviet Union, prompted the rise in 1954 of the informal Conference of Presidents of Major Jewish Organizations. This body, comprising the heads of seventeen Jewish national organizations, has functioned through national and regional meetings. It has spoken for American Jewry before agencies of the American Government. But it is a voluntary conference, activated during emergencies, and, while it includes the major organizations, the American Jewish Committee stands aloof.

Occasionally, special conferences of Jewish organizations are called to meet special emergencies. A recent example was the conference on Soviet Jewry held in April, 1964, with the participation of some 24 national organizations, including the American Jewish Committee. Finally, several major American Jewish organizations cooperate with similar bodies of the Western world on problems of international import. But here, too, there is no unity. The American Jewish Congress, B'nai B'rith and the Jewish Labor Committee are members of the World Conference of Jewish Organizations (COJO), which was formed in 1956, whereas the American Jewish Committee cooperated until 1964 with a rival organization known as the Consultative Council of Jewish Organizations (CCJO). The American Jewish Congress is also a constituent of the World Jewish Congress.

Thus, for nearly a half century, individuals and groups have sought repeatedly to coordinate the efforts of the numerous agencies of the American Jewish community and to fashion a roof organization that could speak in its name. To a considerable degree, co-ordination has been achieved in fund-raising. Within functional areas in welfare and along "denominational" lines in religion and education, progress has also been made.[25] But overall unity has thus far proved unattainable. This objective remains on the agenda of American Jewry as an item of high priority.

XII

Ideologies of American Jews

Harold Weisberg

The preceding chapters have noted significant changes in the American Jewish community since the last war.[1] Corresponding ideological changes have been equally impressive: the disappearance of assimilationism as a serious ideological option, the abandonment of secularist ideologies, the replacement of Marxist, humanist, and liberal ideologies with existentialist theologies and ideologies, the effective armistice in the warfare between science and theology, the enormous growth of organized Jewish religion coupled with the serious decline of liberal theologies, the success of political Zionism and the subsequent, perhaps consequent, failure of Zionist ideologies and parties. In fact, so much has happened and we are so close to it that it is quite impossible to give a satisfactory account of all major developments or avoid partisan treatment of questions which are still at issue. However, one can get a good sense of what has transpired and where matters stand now by examining and contrasting two divergent ideological trends: the growth and success of the ideologies of the organized community,[2] and the emergence of new ideological patterns among Jewish intellectuals and theologians. Clearly, such an approach has obvious disadvantages. It appears to provide a very narrow perspective from which to view the complex

development of the Jewish community since the war. It may encourage over-simple classifications of "the community" and "the
intellectuals" and exaggerate the importance of the antagonism between the community and its alienated critics. One must also exercise great care in comparing the programmatic ideologies of the vast
majority of American Jews with the ideological brooding of a small
group of sensitive and articulate men. Nevertheless, the comparison
may be sufficiently instructive to permit a fruitful evaluation of the
ideological situation within and on the borders of the American
Jewish community.

JEWISH INTELLECTUALS IN THE POST-WAR WORLD

As is well known, the dominant response of Jewish intellectuals to
the cumulative experience of the depression, fascism, the Soviet
betrayal of democracy and socialism, the extermination of European
Jewry, and the war itself was part of a thorough re-evaluation by
western intellectuals of the major ideological assumptions and institutionalized values of the liberal culture of the past one hundred
years. This story is familiar and requires no extended narrative
treatment here. It suffices for our purposes to note only a few
features of this re-evaluation which greatly influenced the post-war
attitudes of many Jewish intellectuals toward Judaism. So complete
was the disenchantment of many with what they once thought was
the fruit and flower of western civilization, and so intensely
pursued was the indictment of this civilization, that within five
years after the war, the language, the concepts, the heroes, the
gambits, indeed the entire universe of pre-war intellectual discourse
had been radically transformed. Rationalism, humanism, secularism, Marxism, radicalism, liberalism, faith in progress, science and
intelligence, in the perfectability or cumulative improvement of
human nature were replaced wholesale by irrationalism and existentialism, recognition of the mythical and absurd, belief in the
imperfectability of man, the incompetence of intelligence in human
affairs, and the impossibility of significant progress. The misery,
terror and destruction that had been visited upon the world since
the beginning of the twentieth century were such that intellectuals
became profoundly convinced that liberal culture itself was at fault,

and that even such seemingly innocent ideas as the belief in progress and the use of intelligence in human affairs might, in their own
way, be responsible for the tragic history of the century. A more
anxious yet more sophisticated generation demanded a rupture with
what they believed had been the naive optimism and liberalism of
the past and insisted on a more realistic ideology which was
prepared to cope with the neglected but powerful determinants of
the "human condition"—power, terror, the irrational, the mythical,
the existential.

Though there was a general disenchantment with liberal culture
and a kind of existentialist mood among Jewish intellectuals in the
years immediately following the war, it would be incorrect to conclude that they thought alike or manifested a common position on
Jews and Judaism. Attitudes were quite diverse and motivations
differed. Some had clearly articulated interests and moved in the
direction of theology; others dimly saw in Judaism (a reinterpreted
Judaism of course) a possible counter to what they believed were
the disastrous trends of western civilization. Some thought that
the long and rich Jewish tradition provided an abundant source of
the mythic and non-rational attitudes which could form the basis of
a fresh approach to the problems of the "human condition," while
others, for a variety of reasons, were simply nostalgic and moved,
in David Riesman's phrase, from a "vindictive and aggressive and
contemptuous attitude towards tradition [to] a honeyed and sentimental one."[3] Still others hoped to overcome the general alienation
of modern man through reidentification with the seemingly well-
integrated historic Jewish community, or if they were not quite up
to this, by searching out those elements in Jewish tradition which
appeared to suggest appropriate alternatives to the predicament of
alienation. There were also those who used Judaism, in its existential, largely individualistic interpretation, as a foil against liberal
and radical political ideologies, and some who professed to see in it
an irreproachable source for their anti-Stalinism. Nor should we
forget that there were some, very few alas, who were unmoved by
what they called a "new failure of nerve" and persisted in their
metaphysical naturalism or political radicalism.

Jewish intellectuals were working out their post-war reactions
to Judaism and Jewish identification with the methods and attitudes

of what may be called the "post-modern temper." They were among the leaders of the ideological revolution in the United States and it would be a mistake to assume that they were so intimately involved in it because they were searching for new directions in Jewish ideology. Some of them, no doubt, were, but the revolution was a general one that suggested more congenial interpretations of Judaism and Jewish identification than seemed to be available before the war. But, whatever the primary motivations of Jewish intellectuals, a substantial number of them were recasting the image of pre-war Judaism or were preparing a new and more existential set of ideological requirements which they hoped a reinterpreted Judaism might satisfy.

The Jewish intellectual's wrestle with his Jewish identity had considerable influence throughout the Jewish community, though, as we shall see, a large portion of that community remained almost totally impervious to any ideology save that which emanated from organizational programs and policies. What intellectuals and independent theologians[4] were struggling over and writing about in the years immediately following the war radically changed the dialectic of ideology in the American Jewish community. This can readily be seen even if we only catalogue the changes in ideological attitudes for which they were primarily responsible. We need not minimize other contributory factors, nor overlook the widespread distribution of the new winds of doctrine to recognize that the intellectual's encounter with Judaism and the Jewish community was a significant factor in the developments which follow.

SOME CONSEQUENCES OF THE POST-WAR IDEOLOGICAL REVOLUTION

(1) Assimilationism could no longer be a viable ideology in the Jewish community. It wasn't simply that a kind of cultural *realpolitik* developed in the community after the Hitler experience. Rather, it was that Jewish intellectuals began to look upon their Jewish identification or "Jewishness" as a basic constituent of their existence. What many described as their "human condition" was inextricably bound up with their relations to Jews, Judaism, Jewish tradition, the Jewish community, etc. One could not dismiss the

Jews and Judaism as relics or fossils. One had to account for them, or as the more existentialist-minded would have it, had to come to grips with the existential fact of being, in some way, a Jew. Of course, there were other important reasons for the general disappearance of assimilationism in the Jewish community during the past two decades, not the least of which were the profound changes in the social and economic status of American Jews, and undue causal weight should not be assigned to the role of the intellectuals in bringing about the widespread self-acceptance which has characterized American Jewry since the war. But, the intellectuals provided a special ideological justification for self-acceptance, or at least made respectable the attempt to discover such justification.

(2) Another development which stemmed largely from the intellectuals and their ideological broodings, and not unrelated to the disappearance of assimilationism, was the reorientation to religion and theology. The post-war re-evaluation of liberal culture actually produced more than an armistice in the warfare between science and theology. It suggested to many that there could be no conflict at all because theology and religious belief no longer required the sanction of reason or science. For the more irrationally oriented, theology was a "scandal" to science and intelligence; to the less, there was no conflict because, as they saw it, there could be no conflict. It was almost like adding apples and pears—a confusion of categories. Jewish religion and theology became intellectually respectable to a generation that was unafraid of myth and had little concern with proofs for the existence of God, the authentication of miracles and other theological responsibilities of the true believer a generation or two ago. The reinterpretation of Jewish theology along non-rationalist lines brought to the attention of the American Jewish community such neglected theologians as Martin Buber and Franz Rosenzweig and radically reshaped the gambits of Jewish theological discourse.

(3) This counter-ideology was most successful in its opposition to liberalism and humanism in religion and theology. The liberal temper of much pre-war Jewish theology has almost completely disappeared. Reform Judaism, though it prefers to be called Liberal Judaism, seems to have abandoned theology altogether, and Reconstructionism, once the last word in humanistic Jewish theology,

appears to be the last gasp of an enfeebled liberalism. Religious existentialism and other anti-liberal theological approaches may not be all-conquering today, but they have succeeded in routing liberal religious thought as a serious ideological contender in the Jewish community. To a lesser extent, the intellectuals and the independent theologians in the years immediately following the war also contributed to the abandonment of secularism as a live option for American Jews. But not all Jewish intellectuals were sympathetic to religion despite the general existentialist mood they seemed to share. By no means all of those who participated in the reorientation of western thought after the war advocated a return to religion and an abandonment of certain dominant features of secularism; few indeed advocated reidentification with the Synagogue. Moreover, the disappearance of secularism was more directly the result of the changing social structure of the American Jewish community and the emergence of religious institutions as a dominant mode of Jewish identification in the great suburban centers of Jewish population.

(4) The revolt against liberal theology and religion accompanied an equally hostile opposition to political liberalism and radicalism as ideologies. This is a familiar story which requires a different setting for adequate treatment. It need only be observed here that this opposition was compounded of many elements, among them a deep and somewhat guilt-ridden anti-Stalinism, ambivalence toward McCarthy and the irresponsible anti-Communism of the 1950's, and a suspicion that political liberalism was not entirely innocent of responsibility for the social and political disasters of the twentieth century. Marxism and radicalism were completely discredited and the radical ideologies and programs of the 1930's were buried under a new "search for roots." What passed for social and political discussion in the late 1940's and early 1950's was a continuing condemnation of earlier radical political positions (an exercise in *mea culpa* which many intellectuals now lament) or an attempted demonstration of the irrelevancy or impossibility of political thought and action in the "post-modern" world. Some flirted with a non-political conservatism, stressing tradition, community, and the organicity of society. Others inclined to a more theological condemnation of man as sinner. Still others demanded

greater recognition of the place of myth, power, terror, and the irrational in contemporary social systems. Generally, political and social concerns were subordinated to psychological and existential ones. Emphasis shifted from social conditions to the "condition of man."

(5) This last development had particular relevance to Jewish ideology. The abandonment of programs of reform and the profound disenchantment with Marxism helped bring about a decisive shift from the social and political to the individual and the psychological. If progress is suspect, intelligence incompetent in human affairs, and man's nature the source of evil, attitudes and ideologies directed toward the individual will predominate. Positions, stances, attitudes, convictions and existential choices become more important than programs, reforms, social changes, and, of course, revolutions. Attention was thus directed from the allegedly peripheral and palliative programs of social and economic reconstruction to the "real" problem—the nature of man. Once again, there were various permutations and combinations of positions, but for more than a decade after the war there was widespread suspicion of political activism and grave doubt that political ideologies were significant in the great business of understanding and managing human existence. This meant that one must seek a non-political standpoint, a kind of existential locus from which to appraise the meaning of one's own life and the age in which he lived. From this it seemed to follow that ideologies which were not directed to an assessment of the "post-modern" condition of man were irrelevant where they were not harmful. The "right" attitude or the "authentic" commitment involved an act of personal choice which need have no programmatic social consequences. The institutional aspects of existence were minimized or dismissed and the ideological question of the age became not the political "What is to be done?" but the more existential "Where do I stand?" or "What do I believe?"

(6) Mention of belief suggests another dimension of the rejection of the social. A recent writer put it clearly: "The confession with which I begin is a statement of existential dogma—that is what *I* say here *I* must believe, because without it there is nothing

I consider *ultimately* relevant or meaningful to believe."[5] The emphasis in Jewish theological thought after the war, especially among the existentialist-oriented theologians, was more upon the act of believing than the content of belief. Having a belief which one holds dearly, having, in Tillich's overworked phrase an "ultimate concern"[6] became the hallmark of modern man. But this implies an emphasis on what your convictions are, not on how you behave. To put the matter differently, the preferred predicates of the post-war period were "is a believer," "is committed," "is authentic." The condemned predicates were "is a revolutionary," "is a Marxist," and the despised, "is a liberal," "is a social reformer."

(7) This leads to a final point. Jewish intellectuals and independent theologians were able to do something which their immediate liberal predecessors could not. They reduced, and perhaps eliminated the gap between Judaism and contemporary ideology. Thirty or forty years ago, it was the difficult task of liberal theologians to show that Judaism was not incompatible with the world of humanism, Marxism, secularism, science, etc. Even the most successful of the liberal theologies, that is the ones that most directly came to grips with the world of the early twentieth century and worked out what appeared to be a satisfactory cultural and intellectual rapprochement, could only do so by "giving in" on the most crucial points—God, resurrection, miracles, etc. Judaism was recast in various molds—Deweyian, Marxian, Darwinian, Freudian —but it still was uncomfortable and essentially estranged from what was triumphantly called the modern world.

Today, and for the past fifteen years, Judaism is no longer estranged. What Jewish theology teaches is at one with the most "advanced" thought. What is "authentic" in Judaism is what the "post-modern" world considers to be generally "authentic." It isn't simply that cultural conditions change and the heroes and values of one generation are replaced by those of another, but that the new conditions are exceptionably favorable to Judaism. Jewish ideologies and theologies are fashioned in a much more hospitable cultural and intellectual environment, and reinterpretations of Jewish tradition appear much less forced than they were thirty and forty years ago. One need not approve of current ideological and theological attitudes to recognize that there has been a significant change in the intellectual status of Judaism in the "post-modern" world.

There is, of course, much more to be said about Jewish intellectuals and their ideological struggles, and we shall briefly return to another aspect of this issue later; but enough has been said to indicate general tendencies and common directions. However, in all of these developments we should not assume that there were schools of thought with clearly articulated ideological programs, or that large numbers of men were involved. Nor can it be said that most of those involved knew where their ideological brooding would lead, or whether it could ever be anything more than an individual statement. They were marginal and alienated men who shared common dissatisfactions, not unified goals. Programmatic thinking was utterly foreign to those who helped fashion the ideological revolution in Judaism and organizational activity was almost inconceivable. Generally there was no plan for the reform of specific practices and organizations or a program for the radical reconstruction of the Jewish community.

THE IDEOLOGY OF THE ESTABLISHED COMMUNITY: THE
CULTURE OF ORGANIZATIONS

But, programs, plans, and organizations are precisely what appeal to most American Jews. Not only are their ideological ambitions considerably less demanding than those of the intellectuals and independent theologians; they usually can be fulfilled in an institutional manner. In fact, one of the most distinguishing features of community ideologies is their capacity for programmatic translation. The search for community and identity among most American Jews is a very practical undertaking and the genius of the Jewish community is organization. Jewish life in the United States is expressed primarily through a culture of organizations. To be a Jew is to belong to an organization. To manifest Jewish culture is to carry out, individually or collectively, the program of an organization. Of course, there is a perfectly good sense in which this claim is false; there are many less public and less formal individual manifestations of Jewish culture. Nevertheless, the activity which overwhelmingly dominates American Jewish life is organizational and the ways in which most Jews are "Jewish" are the institutional ways of the synagogue, the center, the welfare fund and the service agency.

What is most striking, perhaps, is the identification of neutral organizational tasks with Jewish culture. It is already standard practice to identify attending meetings, raising funds, distributing organizational literature, speaking or listening to speeches and participating in testimonial dinners with what was once called "a Jewish way of life." These activities do not exhaust Jewish life, but they come quite close to it. What distinguishes the Jew from the non-Jew is, increasingly, not a special ethic, religious discipline, or language, but the intensity and pervasiveness of his organizational commitments and activities. That part of Jewish culture which was once expressed in face to face situations, in the home, in the street, or through the medium of a special group language has largely disappeared and, as we shall soon see, the great religious discipline which in the past permeated every aspect of individual and communal life is missing. At present Jewish culture in the United States is predominantly what Jews do under the auspices of Jewish organizations.

It won't do to object that the activities which most concern the community are only a continuation and extension of traditional community interests, or that the causes which are served are only contemporary expressions of traditional Jewish values. Of course, they are that, but to argue in this way is to miss the point. Unlike earlier Jewish societies, our organizational programs and responsibilities are almost the whole of Jewish culture. In fact, they may well be *the* Jewish culture of the United States. Communal organization and its maintenance has been a central preoccupation of Jews for a very long time in a variety of Jewish communities, but the programs of the organizations and the activities involved in sustaining them did not previously suffice for or pre-empt Jewish culture.

A number of factors have contributed to the development of the culture of organizations: the "coming of age" of the American Jewish community and the increased welfare and community institutional apparatus it has required; the enormous burden of overseas responsibilities undertaken by American Jews and the organizational machinery which has been developed to do the job; the striking growth of religious institutions and organizations; and the changed social status of most American Jews. The last point deserves comment here because it has influenced the structure and style of the organizations created by the developments just noted, and also because it has provided some interesting ideological ramifications which have helped justify the culture of organizations.

American Jews reflect the general social and economic changes since the war and possess strikingly similar institutional apparatus and ideological attitudes to those of the general American leisure-consumption-status class. They manifest so many of the traits which sociologists and social critics attribute to the new American bourgeoisie (the familiar "affluent society") that they may be said to epitomize it. But, for our purposes we need emphasize only one aspect of this development—the emergence of new Jewish communities. A large number of American Jews, enjoying considerable leisure time and on the whole something very close to affluence, have moved out of the urban centers in which pre-war Jewry largely resided to a variety of suburbs, some no more than mediocre mass "developments," others quite substantial and "residential." In these new communities they have had to create organizations and community apparatus where none existed before. Many Jews of the large urban centers never before thought about communal organizations like schools, centers, synagogues and welfare agencies. In the pre-war urban centers such apparatus, if recognized at all, was identified with the culturally reactionary immigrant generation. It was just there and was usually regarded with disdain by those who were seeking greater assimilation into the general American community.

However, the move to the suburbs cannot by itself explain the incredible organizational achievements of the new communities. The development of these communities was part of a broader manifestation of the culture and society of the leisure-consumption-status class. These broader manifestations, some of them paralleling doctrinal movements among intellectuals and independent theologians, included a rapprochement with religion, greater acceptance of bourgeois values, such as a reorientation to the family and to private property, and a general conservatism which stressed institutional stability and, in the broadest sense, social security. Moreover, in the case of the Jews, all those events which, as we have noted, combined to alter pre-war attitudes of Jewish intellectuals to Judaism, were also powerful ideological forces among the masses of Jews. Desire for Jewish identification ran deep, convictions of group loyalty were strong, and concern for the "Jewish life" of future generations was almost an obsession. Jewish communal organizations became a necessity and their development and maintenance became the uniquely American Jewish "way of life."

SOME IDEOLOGICAL CONSEQUENCES OF THE CULTURE OF ORGANIZATIONS

The ideological presuppositions and consequences of this culture may now be sketched.

(1) Caring for the organization and living through it becomes, as we have already observed, the culture of the Jews. It also produces ideologies which seek to justify this pattern of behavior. Primarily, they take two interrelated forms. The first promotes identity with the established community and sanctions the activity of the community as essential to group survival. So much is at stake in the established community organizations that one is obliged to feel loyalty and to commit himself to the destiny of the community. The second suggests that the programs of particular organizations are indispensable to achieving the group purpose, and consequently they must also be encouraged and supported.

(2) This means, in effect, that the various and presumably compatible organizational programs constitute the ideologies of the community. The justification of Jewish identity and involvement in the community often, perhaps too often, consists of a recital of organizational and communal programs, which in turn appear to require no further justification. The "charter" of the community is the program of its organizations. And it is this which directly leads to the identification of organizational tasks and responsibilities with "the Jewish way of life."

(3) Another consequence is that the organization and its program reduce and often eliminate the need for individual ideo-

logical concern. The organization provides an ideology which one may assume when he joins it. (And let us recall here that one cannot join *the* Jewish community in the United States, only the Jewish organizations which function as a quasi-community.) This is neither unique nor necessarily bad. A culture that cannot provide ideology through institutional means and which must depend on constant individual ideological re-evaluations is in serious difficulty. However, in the American Jewish community this has had the effect of stifling criticism and re-evaluation within the community and of producing hostility against those who practice it outside the community.

(4) Also worth mentioning is the increased status of formal identification with the Jewish community. This is a direct result of the social and economic changes we noted above. What it means is that part of the ideology of Jewish identification may now be justified on grounds of status. It is part of the preferred pattern of American leisure-consumption-status class life to join religious organizations and to be active in the community. This is the institutional counterpart of the intellectuals' and independent theologians' success in making Judaism less estranged from "postmodern" thought. Active Jewish communal identification is no longer sneered at. It is very acceptable. In fact, it is a definite status achievement.

(5) What is often overlooked is that the preponderance of organizational activity is surrogate activity. By that I mean that participation in the organization usually involves doing something for others. Many Jewish organizations are purely service organizations. However, even among those which are not, service to others forms a major part of the organizations' purpose. Obviously, this is a commendable orientation, but it has interesting ideological ramifications. If what I argued earlier is substantially correct, namely that Judaism in the United States is what Jews do under the auspices of Jewish organizations, then a good deal of American Judaism is essentially philanthropic. Granted that some organizational service is cultural as well as philanthropic, the fact remains that involvement in the organization encourages what may be called a "philanthropic attitude." And this is precisely what may make it so attractive to many people. This point can be pushed too

far. I am not unmindful of what the organizational involvement provides for the member, nor have I forgotten the various other motives for organizational identification mentioned earlier. But this only serves to reinforce the point. The activity of the organization provides satisfaction in doing something for others and this may well be what contemporary Judaism is all about. I cannot over-look, but I don't know if I can satisfactorily explain the fact that the two largest and most active non-religious Jewish organizations in the United States, Hadassah and B'nai B'rith, are overwhelmingly service organizations.*

(6) This leads to a final observation. All the factors which have repeatedly been mentioned as components of new social and ideological conditions for American Jews since the war coalesce to make Jewish identification and what may be called "Jewish be-havior" considerably less demanding than it was a generation or two ago. This is not a perverse nostalgic reflection. Most of the conditions which contributed to the widespread hostility toward Jewish identification and Judaism before the war have disappeared. Religion is socially and intellectually respectable, Jewish culture is not identified with immigrant culture, and most Jews can now economically afford to participate in a community life which is more than socially acceptable. In addition there is so much less that is behaviorally expected of a Jew today. Bilingualism has declined, dietary laws are not observed by the masses, and a rigorous religious discipline is not considered normative. There were major breaks with tradition thirty and forty years ago of course, but not, I suspect, with such an absence of guilt or with the organizational means to substitute communal activity for religious discipline that we have today. Moreover, the intellectual and emotional demands of the culture of organizations are not burden-some. They are precisely what appeals to the leisure-consumption-status orientation of most American Jews. There is no agony, no turmoil, no anguish. Community ideologies, like middle-class life

* The failure of Zionist parties and ideologies after the establishment of the State of Israel further illustrates this point. The welfare of the State of Israel is among the chief concerns of American Jews, but it is over-whelmingly a *welfare* concern; hence the success of Hadassah and the failure of the ZOA.

in the United States, seek to overcome doubt through activity and loneliness through organization. *Angst,* despair, even inconclusiveness, are not part of the ideology of the community.

RELIGIOUS IDEOLOGIES IN THE CULTURE OF ORGANIZATIONS

One would expect that matters would be quite different in the field of religion. Religious ideologies are far more demanding than other community ideologies, and in religion the new winds of existential doctrine have had considerable effect. Moreover, religion deals with the great crises in the life of the individual and his community; it sanctifies the important events in the history of the group and it provides an ethical system. In Judaism there is also a pronounced behavioral emphasis which stresses doing as well as believing. Nevertheless, while there are obvious differences between the religious and non-religious community ideologies, the former are essentially not successful alternatives to the latter. In fact, they have become increasingly only another manifestation of the culture of organizations.

That this is not as disastrous an overstatement as it may appear to be can be seen if we examine several developments in Jewish religion since the war.

The first, which we have mentioned repeatedly, has been the general revival of religion in America or, more accurately, the revival of religious affiliation. This has been part of a general attitudinal and institutional change in this country and it has been equally manifest in the Jewish community. It is by now patently clear that the religious revival has been primarily institutional and has had little effect on individual religious behavior and, most probably, on religious belief as well. The most impressive accomplishment of the religious revival in the United States may not be the amazing recovery of theological ideas from the intellectual débacle of the past half century, but the organizational form the revival has taken. If there has been a theological revival among intellectuals, there has been an institutional resurrection within the general community.

This essentially organizational accomplishment suggests that religious beliefs and theological convictions are not taken seriously in the general American community and in the Jewish community. This for at least two reasons. All that we have said concerning the habits and attitudes of the leisure-consumption-status class in America indicates that organized religion is just one of several components which make up that comfortable culture. But, what is often overlooked, is that the new theologies which were presumed by many to provide the impetus and foundation for the institutional religious revival cannot be accepted by the vast majority of the newly identified, certainly not in the Jewish community. The new theologies demand the kind of belief and behavior which is utterly incompatible with the dominant culture patterns of most American Jews. Whatever form these theologies have taken —neo-Hasidic, mystic, or existential—they have not altered these culture patterns in religion and elsewhere.

The independent theologians have emphasized authenticity, commitment, piety, humility, awe and a large number of familiar and unfamiliar virtues. The Jewish community has not been able to subscribe to them. Of course, Jews can mouth them or trot them out on particular occasions, but the culture pattern which dominates their lives precludes their taking them seriously. Increasingly, in fact, the organizational commitments of synagogue membership have made the realization of these virtues and values more difficult. The community culture pattern is reflected in the synagogue and the vulgarities of the leisure-consumption-status class which have infiltrated the synagogue are too well known to repeat here. The new theologies have been at most pulpit theologies and have not become serious religious ideologies in the community.

It may be objected that this was forever so, that all serious theologies do not affect the great mass of religious communicants who most desperately require them. This is no doubt true, though there are many exceptions: classical Reform Judaism, for example. But even if true, this objection does not affect the point made here. I am not criticizing the theologians for this condition; I am trying to establish the organizational character of religion in the Jewish community by emphasizing the gap between theological expectation and religious performance.

This point underscores two further developments. The first, that no new theology has come from the official religious groups (Reform, Conservative, and Orthodox); the second, that the success of the religious groups is usually measured by the groups themselves in terms of number of congregations, number of synagogues, number of men's groups, etc. In the former case, Jewish theology since the war has come from such non-Americans as Buber, or those I have called independent, i.e., non-organizational theologians in America, or to some extent from small Hasidic communities. In the latter case, there is no doubt that the most formidable successes of Jewish religion are in organizational structure, membership, plant, etc. It has been notably unsuccessful in introducing a religious and ethical discipline into the lives of the thousands who formally affiliate and are more or less active in the institutional life of the synagogue.

Some comment is in order on two points discussed earlier concerning the decline of religious liberalism and the emphasis on religious belief. It is quite true that religious liberalism has declined, but it is still behaviorally significant. That is, the major religious groups may officially and unofficially pay homage to existentialist theologies, but their institutional religious practices are not illiberal. This is even true of Conservative groups who have permitted ritual changes (especially in the service) which they did not introduce when more left-wing theologies were in vogue. As for Reform Judaism, despite the recent emphasis on ritual and the increasingly existentialist theology of its more thoughtful rabbis, it is, as its preferred name hopes to suggest, a liberal religious movement. All of this only serves to indicate the absence of any institutional theologies and the relative independence of organized religion and its institutional requirements from any theology. Institutional religious behavior is considerably to the left of the theology which is alleged to support it. This, not because the Jews are Reform or Reconstructionist Marranos, but simply because the culture of organizations is hospitable to such behavior.

Concerning religious belief, it was argued earlier that the intellectuals and independent theologians emphasized beliefs, positions and attitudes rather than behavior. In the community, emphasis is also not on a discipline of religious behavior affecting the ordinary as well as the extraordinary aspects of existence, but on the discipline of organizational obligation and institutional responsibility. Essentially the Jewish community follows a Protestant pattern: it has a set of beliefs, not too strongly held about God, man, destiny, life after death, etc., which are basically independent of a discipline of religious behavior. The decline of immigrant Jewish culture and the emergence of the culture of organizations serve only to emphasize the emerging Protestant pattern of Jewish religious life. One behaves regularly as an American, believes as a Jew, and hopefully what he holds in the latter will affect what he does in the former.

CURRENT DISENCHANTMENT AND THE NEW ALIENATION

During the past few years evidence has been accumulating that ideological changes are forthcoming in the United States and in the American Jewish community. How serious they are and how successful they will be is difficult to determine, but they are worth remarking in passing. One may discern the beginnings of disenchantment with existentialism and similar ideologies. Existentialism and the related attitudes it generated are losing their force because many of the conditions which prompted men to abandon political and naturalistic ideologies and programs are gone and no longer concern the present generation. Almost two decades of talk about the permanent condition of man, the futility of social change, and the need for the psychological-moral-theological reorientation of man himself seems more a litany than an intellectual challenge. A good portion of the post-war ideological revolution reflected the dissatisfactions and disenchantments of the generation of the depression. These are all but forgotten now and the contemporary college generation snickers at professorial evocations of "the thirties." The great issues in their lives are disarmament and desegregation, and here the outlook is decidedly political and activist. We have come a long way from the immediate post-war debasement of politics, and almost as far from the bleak days of McCarthyism. Perhaps today's youth are more concerned with the humanitarianism of peace and integration. They may not have a political ideology which dictates particular attitudes. They also may be too innocent and overlook the political associations and complications of the humanitarian causes they espouse. Nevertheless, they are interested in social change and in the use of political means to achieve it.

In the Jewish community there is another development not unrelated to the above. If there are signs of disenchantment with the ideologies of the post-war intellectuals, there are signs of new alienation from the post-war Jewish community. After the war many Jewish intellectuals were nostalgic for the immigrant Jewish culture from which they had been thoroughly alienated because it was no longer a threat. They had overcome it. But there is one major and disturbing difference between the two generations of alienated. The earlier generation was alienated from an immigrant culture which it once felt should be rejected because it was hostile to what it thought was the best in America. But soon after the war many realized that there were elements in this culture which were valuable precisely because they were not the values of the middle-class America which they disdained. They could not return to such a culture; in fact it was fading away when they began to romanticize it, but they were able to compare it not unfavorably with the leisure-consumption-status culture. The current generation of alienated has no such Jewish culture to look back on. Jewish culture is so much like American culture or more so that there is no great gap between Jewish culture and "America" as there was thirty and forty years ago. Nostalgia will be difficult under such circumstances. There appears also to be some sense of betrayal among the newly alienated. After all the promises of a new and greater Judaism—a Judaism which was supposed to alter the character of our existence—what we really have produced is only the culture of organizations.

SOME CONCLUSIONS

We have discussed two antagonistic ideological postures. One emphasizes loyalty, communal tasks, organizational responsibility, group survival. The other, largely the product of incurable alienation, is doubtful and often scornful of these values and searches for "something more." The one is at home in the world and represents attitudes toward history, culture, society, value, religion, and reality which, in addition to being essentially bourgeois, are vaguely or clearly, remotely or directly assumed to promote loyalty to the Jewish people and foster its survival and growth. The other is self-consciously radical (not necessarily in a political sense) in that it seeks to transform the lives of those who subscribe to it. It is more an ideological quest than a fulfillment, and usually cannot be satisfied—certainly not through the culture of the established community.[7] One is an ideology of acts and tasks—the communal and the institutional—of affirmation and participation, of belonging and conforming. The other is an ideology of thought and feeling— the private and the individual—of doubt and disenchantment, alienation and non-conformity.

This discussion has implied serious misgivings about the established Jewish community (and its ideology) which overwhelmingly dominates American Jewish life. But one should not minimize its importance or overlook the striking fact that it is this community which keeps the Jews and Judaism alive in America. Furthermore, it is undoubtedly true that, despite some grumbling, most American Jews are quite satisfied with their culture of organizations.

On the other hand, the ideological posture of the Jewish intellectuals is also inadequate. Their criticisms of the established Jewish community and their own ideological investigations are of considerable value and serve to point up the hollowness of much of organized Jewish life in the United States. But, *Angst* cannot be institutionalized and alienation is inadequate as a sustained ideological stance. Similarly, theological positions and existential attitudes are also insufficient. Throughout Jewish history, creeds, beliefs, "positions," and theologies were never enough. Significant Jewish ideologies require institutional embodiments and forms of communal identification. Jewish ideologies which are predominantly expressions of dissatisfaction with Judaism and the Jewish community, or are largely positions emphasizing the anxiety of the age and the perils of existence will not be significant alternatives to the dominant direction of American Jewish ideology without the institutionalization and communal identification characteristic of the best in traditional Judaism and modern (not contemporary) Jewish ideologies.

What is lacking in our community is the opportunity to develop significant ideologies in opposition to the ideologies of the established community which have institutional manifestations and a communal identification. A contemporary Jewish community of reasonable distinction would have room for small sub-groups or sub-communities whose ideologies are free of the banality of much of organized Jewish life and who possess their own institutionalized apparatus and communal structure within the historic Jewish community. Unfortunately we possess few such groups who can sustain such ideologies. There are the Lubovich and similar Hasidic communities (and they tend to separatism and fanaticism) and to a considerably lesser extent, some non-Hasidic Orthodox groups and, perhaps, the bona-fide Reconstructionists.

At one time Zionist and secularist Yiddish groups offered important ideologies which ran counter to prevailing attitudes and were not simply the anguished personal expressions of alienation and disenchantment. Nor were communal identification and organizational structure the exclusive attributes of the conforming community. Socialist groups, labor groups, Zionist groups, dissident religious groups, all maintained their own institutional forms. But the circumstances under which such groups developed cannot be duplicated, and in our own day the most distinctive non-conformist groups—the Hasidic communities—can only be continued by rigid cultural isolation. Given the social structure of the Jewish community in the United States and its almost uniform culture, it is extremely doubtful if sharply divergent minority ideologies and institutions manifesting them can be sustained by small sub-communities within the broader community. A community need not be ideologically polarized between accepted conformist ideologies and institutions and the individualistic radical ideologies of those who remain outside it, but it is increasingly apparent that this is what is happening in the American Jewish community.

XIII

Conclusion

1. Leadership in the American Jewish Community

EDWIN WOLF 2ND

AMERICAN Jews within the freedom of a democracy have been able to assimilate themselves to a remarkable degree into American life. Except for certain vestigial remains of their past, they have become Jewish-Americans, given recognition and—to a certain extent—status equal to that of Protestant-Americans and Catholic-Americans. The tripartite division of the country into religious groups, although having far less to do with religiosity than membership, is an accepted fact. Prejudice in many areas of American life has disappeared; economic discrimination is being whittled away; social discrimination has lost its importance; anti-Semitism is bad business, bad manners and bad Americanism. Consequently, Jews have been able to adopt the ideals, the mores and the coloration of their individual socio-economic classes within American society. Some Jews are organization men or follow that pattern; others are intellectuals and expound the varied "isms" of the day. Most of them act and react in accordance with their situation in life, very few philosophically as Jews. "Jewish" has become a respectable American tag denoting membership in an organization

or in a social group which differs from other similar organizations
and social groups in the United States only because of the origin,
religion or interests of its members.

While the exceptions to the above statement are many, some
specious, others significant, it holds true for most American Jews
outside the fast-dwindling, heavily populated quasi-ghettoes in a
few large cities. Even in these cities, which still contain a majority
of the Jews in the country, the distinctive islands of Jewishness are
largely in the process of dissolution. In brief, the standards of
American Jewish life are derived from and mirror—*mutatis
mutandis*—American life. So, too, does the quality and type of
leadership.

In the era of Morgan, Rockefeller and Ford, when men with
strong individuality, a Puritan sense of being "the elect," and even
eccentricity formed the power elite, when a Theodore Roosevelt, as a Franklin Delano Roosevelt several decades later, put
his personal impress upon the office of the president, the American
Jewish community had its Marshall, Schiff, Warburg and Adler.
It is probably true that retrospection magnifies stature, and that no
generation sees its great men in the same perspective as it sees
its heroes of the past. Yet it would seem that the leaders of yester-
day were bigger, bolder, more individualistic and more imaginative
than their successors today. The obvious rebuttal to such a statement is that it is easier to be a big frog in a little pond, and the
American Jewish community was a little pond in those days.
Nevertheless, there was an acceptance then of the leadership of the
individual which does not exist today.

As American Jews have become acculturated, they have created
their semi-mythical American Jewish giants: Haym Salomon, Rebecca Gratz and Commodore Uriah P. Levy. But the first man who
had a real influence on national Jewish life was Isaac Leeser. A
rabbi and a bulwark of traditionalism in religion, Leeser, personally, as an individual and without organizational backing, promoted
the establishment of an all-day Hebrew school, an orphan asylum,
a publication society, a national Jewish sounding board, a periodical
which circulated all over the country, a theological seminary, an
interest in the up-building of Palestine, and much else. Some of his
creations have survived to this day; others were seeds which never

blossomed, but from whose roots many of today's flourishing trees grew. He and his bitter opponent, the religious liberal, Isaac Mayer Wise, were personalities. They and their followers fought over the future of American Jewry, and each tried to mold it to his specifications. These men had glamor and that charismatic touch which attracted disciples. They fought; they thought; and they created.

It was in the path of Leeser that a generation followed which built the skeletal structure of American Jewish life as we know it today. Aaron Dropsie, influenced by Leeser, was the major influence on Mayer Sulzberger, who in turn influenced Cyrus Adler, who, as he matured, became the advisor of Louis Marshall, Jacob Schiff, Felix Warburg, Julius Rosenwald and others. At the same time, among the immigrant group, there rose Abraham Cahan, who politically and intellectually exerted an unparalleled influence upon the Yiddish-speaking Jews of the United States. In the area of Zionism, it was the personal magnetism of Stephen Wise which crystallized a movement politically and emotionally oriented, and it was Judah Magnes who helped build the cultural foundations for Jewish life in Palestine. No woman in American Jewish history made the impact on the life of the community which Henrietta Szold did. It was symptomatic of the times that Joseph Duveen and A. S. W. Rosenbach dominated the art and rare-book worlds as no individuals have since. In the years before the depression, American Jewry was led in most of its aspects by a handful of men, those named above and others.

The modern history of American Jewry really dates from the end of World War II. Hitler and his atrocities and the petty *Führers* of Yorkville proved to be a concentric force which broke down, almost instantaneously, the slowly disintegrating barriers between German and Eastern European Jew, between Reform Jew and Orthodox, between worker and boss. The separate organizations did not merge. Jewish hospitals continued to carry on their work; Zionists stepped up their programs; the defense organizations became urgent; the saving and care of refugees assumed a priority they had not had since the founding of the Joint Distribution Committee several decades earlier. Synagogue membership began to grow; a concern for Jewish education was felt where earlier passivity had existed. American Jews in the spell of a mass psychology rushed toward a manifestation of Jewish identity.

First, it was important to stand as Jews against Nazism and its threat of total extermination. Then, it was important—a tiny but vocal minority dissenting—to create an independent state in Palestine so that the surviving remnants of European Jewry could recreate a life for themselves and hopefully create a center of Jewishness for the Diaspora. There was a surge of feeling expressed in material and ideological support scarcely equalled in the long annals of Jewish history. No matter what the special interest of an American Jew was, whether it was centered in service to men in the armed forces or in a *yeshivah,* in a home for the aged or a fraternal organization, the main thrust of his emotions and his dollars was directed toward Israel. And in the wake of aroused Jewish emotion, benefits accrued to every Jewish-sponsored institution.

These masses no longer needed leaders with new ideas. They did not have to be led. All they wanted were mechanisms through which they could give expression to their feelings and into which they could pour their dollars. An historic urge was the force which motivated them, not the eloquence or the thoughtfulness or the imagination of a person. Jewishness, even Judaism, became big business, and as big business it assumed the character of the American corporate structure.

The corporate structure, with its tremendous strengths of discipline, organization, efficiency and success, became the pattern of Jewish life. The leader gave way to the executive; committee action and community action supplanted the initiative of an individual. The tremendous upsurge of Jewishness, aided by the economic rise of Jews, unmatched by any other immigrant group in the United States, was channeled, manipulated, directed, persuaded, exhorted and encouraged by rabbis, fund-raisers, salesmen, entrepreneurs and dedicated idealists. No longer was American Jewry a single candle here and there, but a bed of tinder which flared up. Circumstances—Hitler, Israel, wealth, a sense of guilt and the creative possibilities of Jewishness without prejudice—molded the masses into a dynamic movement, a movement whose own momentum carried it forward.

Membership-getting and fund-raising machines are typical of the era. In most of the cities and towns of the country these have been centralized in federations and welfare funds. The overall community organization has assumed the task of planning, of allocating and of getting money. The world of philanthropy, which includes health and welfare agencies, community relations agencies, aid to Israel, national service organizations, educational institutions and much else, became so big, so complicated and so confusing that, for efficiency and to create a modicum of order in the scramble for support, people banded together to do corporately what they found themselves unable to do individually. In the last twenty years the gain for all causes supported by the central bodies—and the many mavericks swept along by the flood-tide—has been enormous. The operation of agencies by professionals according to professional standards has become a matter of course, and the programs of those agencies have benefited accordingly. The raising of funds in the high-pressure tradition of Yankee salesmanship with all the refinements—or lack of refinements—of a commercial advertising campaign has produced funds of astronomical size. And patterns for the distribution of those funds, crystallized by the priority needs and emotional appeal of Israel, have, with little change, remained fixed for two decades.

The loss has been the submerging of the individual, the individual who gives and the individual who receives. It is the welfare fund, the synagogue or the fraternal group which is the operative factor in Jewish life. That is not to say that individual givers and individual workers are not made much of, but these men and women are the presidents of the organizations this year, or the chairmen of the drives that year, or big givers for many years. Generosity, sincerity, dedication and hard work these people give, but leadership in terms of magnetism—in a charismatic sense—they do not have. Nor are they expected to provide it. The loyalty is toward the organization, not toward the man.

The chair he occupies, the title he holds, or the check he gives becomes the measure of the individual's importance. The head of a national agency or a local federation wields authority and has influence only in the name of the organization he represents. His praises are sung; honors are heaped on him; he is made the "Man of the Year"; he is given testimonial dinners and plaques—as long as he is in office, works or gives. His glory is that which the organization bestows upon him. He is expected to be a company man, to work for the company, to support the company, and to be rewarded by the company.

There are comparatively few men or women in American Jewish public life today who will not be mourned fittingly on their passing, and quickly replaced. Automobiles will be made no matter who is chairman of the board. The show must go on. The community, because of its size and complexity, has become impersonal. An almost anonymous staff is always there; the replacement parts are on hand. In many ways this is good, for it assures continuity of program. It is efficient. It permits progress in slow, steady motion. It provides insurance against the sudden collapse of the whole structure. While the American Jewish community, with its varied and frequently antipathetic elements, is far from monolithic, the foundation stones of organization seem uniform in appearance, if not in size or position. This is true, of course, of many of the patterns of American, middle-class, suburban life of which the Jewish community has become a typical manifestation.

There is no doubt that the organizational methods of the immediate past have been successful. The momentum of Jewishness is still forward. But what of the future? It was external events, rather than internal drive or self-generated ideas, which produced the climate in which the organizations flourished. Pragmatic methods were applied to world-wide circumstances, and they worked. But, now, the circumstances are changing. The emotional appeal which welded American Jewry together is waning, as in American national life the excitement of the Depression, of World War II and of the atomic breakthrough are waning. People, not only Jews, are looking for ideals and leadership of a different kind, for something which will challenge them and at the same time something which will be acceptable within their educated, sophisticated frame of reference.

The trend away from the emergence of individuals into positions of power and influence has been universal. The cult of "the man" which was recreated by Hitler, Stalin and their imitators, even the aristocratic, autocratic ideals of Henry James and T. S. Eliot, fell into disrepute. There is a feeling that something is not quite decent about De Gaulle. Theologically, this feeling was manifest in the dissatisfaction with doctrine as personally revealed religion. Human perfectability came into question in a world which sometimes seemed bent on self-annihilation. As a result the leadership of man, any man, became suspect.

The ideal, in the immediate present at least, is "the organization man" of whom so much has been written. He is a faceless, well-dressed, well-spoken, conventional person, energetic but not aggressive, educated but not intellectual, cultured but not arty. He is efficient, has good common-sense and lives in the suburbs of a large city. It does not matter whether he is the chief executive or low in the white-collar ranks; he is expected to conform. He should have enough flexibility to encourage change, enough imagination to plan for the future, but the change and the future should be evolutionary, not revolutionary. He is the antithesis of the robber baron, the tycoon, the demagogue and the genius.

As in the past people looked to their rulers for bounty, so now the masses look to the organization men for the material comforts and pleasures of life to which, increasingly, they believe themselves entitled—and for the satisfaction of their religious and philanthropic impulses. Henry Ford may have led the world into assembly-line production, but it will be teams of computer experts who will push it into automation. Research organizations—industrial, governmental and academic—are looked to for the kind of leap forward in the field of physics which Einstein made. Cures for the dread diseases of man are being sought by regimented battalions of scientists. Group therapy and group dynamics have become the instruments of psychiatrists and sociologists. The impersonal foundation is taking its place along with the impersonal government as the promoter of welfare. Through organizations men are seeking outlets for doing good.

Although we are in a period of great material advances, we are in an age of moral and social ambiguity. Our knowledge of how to create a better society has not kept pace with our knowledge of how to feed, clothe and entertain that society. We know how to *do* better than how to *think*. As a result, most of the intellectuals and creative artists have placed themselves outside the establishment. They are—and consciously look upon themselves as—the Jeremiahs of our age, the critics, the philosophers, the propounders of presumed verities. Parenthetically, it should be noted that many or most of them have at the same time been assimilated into the academic establishment, which in form differs little from the business, labor, government and military establishments. Yet, in many different ways—as anti-nationalists, as anti-materialists, as symbolists, as non-objectivists—they attack, vilify, satirize, criticize and segregate themselves from organizations and organization men.

To a greater extent than at any time in the immediate past, they have been able to capture the imaginations of those dissatisfied with the status quo. The intellectuals have not come up with a proposition of faith which has been accepted by the majority, but an increasing minority, college-educated, trained to look toward intellectuals for guidance, are adopting their manner of thought, if not their specifics. The basic question is whether the world has not gone too far in its encouragement of similarity, of team-work and of conformity. There is a feeling that new problems cannot be solved with old answers.

The effect on the Jewish community of the bubbling of a new, seeking generation must be great. In proportion to their numbers, Jews to a greater extent than any other group form part of that dissident intelligentsia and its periphery. The Jewish minority boasts of the accomplishments of its fellow-Jews in the fields of science, medicine, art, music, literature and the humanities, but is silent or unmoved by their utter disregard, if not of Judaism, at least of the Jewish community. Jewish leadership is manifest in intellectual, artistic and academic circles, but it has no relation to Jewishness. It is the personal superiority of an individual in his chosen field, and that field has not been, for most of them, anything connected with Jewish life.

That there is a search for leadership is apparent from such a twentieth-century paradox as the surprising resurgence of Hasidism. People are looking for something in which they can believe, something to which they can be loyal, something which sees them as souls. With their business-like methods, the synagogue, the welfare fund and the miscellaneous civic and fraternal organizations are not providing that something. It is not difficult to become a cog in a machine, even a large cog, but the movement in the machine allows little freedom for individual expression. The organizations want and need manpower and money, but they are not adjusted to revolutionary change, to sparkling new ideas or to personal leadership. They can convince, but they can no longer inspire. Soon they must seek men who can inspire, even if it means the sloughing-off of established ways of thought and action. There is plenty of food, perhaps too much, and too little seasoning.

The American Jewish community, bigger, richer, more powerful than ever before in its history, is intellectually passive. Disintegration at the edges—the shift from the centrality of Jewish life to the fringes and from the fringes into non-Jewish, middle-class Americanism—is taking place. Every sociological study affirms this. And many of the best Jewish minds are moving most quickly to the edges. Yet, as before, a vast reservoir of potentiality exists in the new generation which is seeking the kind of leadership which its intelligence deserves. A new model machine is needed. The men to make the new model must be found.

2. Jewish Culture: Transplanted and Indigenous

Judah J. Shapiro

It is a new fact of modern Jewish history that it is possible to regard Jewish culture separately from other aspects of Jewish association and activity. A reading in the *American Jewish Year Book* of the list of National Jewish Organizations in the United States reveals that there is a distinct group of Jewish associations and a variety of Jewish activities that are delineated by their designation as *cultural* from others under the categories of *community relations, political, overseas aid, social, mutual benefit, social welfare* and *Zionist*. Even more significant is the fact that cultural agencies are also separated from the *religious* and *educational* organizations. This reality is the culmination of a century and a half of economic, political and social developments which altered the inner core of the Jewish community and the status and behavior patterns of individual Jews within the general society. A tapestry of the Jewish cultural scene of today must be woven with the threads of these changes and developments for its adequate portrayal.

In earlier periods, historical writing tended to stress the impact of people on the physical and social environment. Modern historians exhibit greater understanding of the effect of environment on people.[1] Our analysis of the Jewish cultural scene similarly reveals that the opportunity for Jews in this country to participate in, and contribute to, the emergence of contemporary America has had an overwhelming impact on their Jewish life. The hundred years following the middle of the nineteenth century represent the effect of American culture and civilization upon the varieties of Judaism brought to this country from Eastern and Western Europe and the gradual blending of these varieties into an American pattern.[2]

It was mainly a German-Jewish immigration, hence from Western Europe, that increased the population of about 3,000 at the beginning of the nineteenth century one hundredfold by 1875 to a quarter of a million. It was this migration that carried distinctive Jewish patterns into the American host-culture, patterns which were already reactions to a German host-culture of great comparability to the American. In the case of the Eastern European migrations, mainly from the 1880's to the mid-1920's, the varieties of Judaism brought were different from those of German Jewry both as internal Jewish expressions and as reactions to the societies in which they emerged.

To consider the cultural dimension of the difference between these two Jewries, we must pause to examine the varying meaning of the term *culture* and take note that it had different meaning for each section, rather than apply the term as an absolute in each instance. The meaning of Jewish culture has been one of the major issues in the perennial polemics among Jews. The debate is itself an aspect of Jewish culture, as are the multiple views and definitions of that term. In general, and apart from any Jewish context, there are currently two accepted concepts of the word *culture*. The first is the anthropological view of culture as the total discernible and describable life-patterns of an identifiable group, including behavior, beliefs, and artifacts. A second definition, more limited, restricts the use of *culture* for such activities as are considered to be intellectual, spiritual and artistic. It may reduce the acrimony of the debate over Jewish culture if it were recognized that the term was applied simultaneously by two separate definitions, the first in reference to Eastern European Jewry, and the second to the Jews in Western Europe. The blending of the two Jewries in America but the continuance of the two separate definitions is the source of confusion in the examination of the contemporary Jewish cultural scene.

Simon Dubnow described the situation in Germany at the beginning of the eighteenth century as one in which the Jews sought "to keep step with their Christian fellow-citizens in cultural progress" and forced them "to reject many traditions as incompatible with reason and conscience." With respect to Eastern European Jews, he described the Jewish community in that period as a "broad and well-ordered social organization" which provided "culture and laws and educated it in the spirit of discipline and self-rule."[3]

In the German situation, that which was specifically Jewish was the spiritual, the intellectual, and what became the Jewish scientific. As early as 1819, in Berlin, there was formed "A Society for the Culture and Scientific Knowledge of Judaism," which was the forerunner of the ultimate conceptual framework of Wissenschaft des Judentums. In general, the preoccupation of German Jews with Jewishness from that time forward was in terms of religion and scholarship, without impinging upon the position of the Jew as a German.

In further contrast, the Eastern European Jew was totally absorbed within the Jewish community, free and under total control, in the sense of Professor Talmon's description of "totalitarian democracy."[4] The politics of the Jewish community of Eastern Europe was the application of a Jewish philosophy to every phase of the Jew's life.

So important are these European backgrounds to an understanding of the contemporary Jewish cultural scene in America that yet another essential concept must be presented. Raymond Williams traces back the use of "culture" and finds that it gained its current use only at the end of the eighteenth century, with the beginnings of the Industrial Revolution.[5] Before then, *culture* was simply "the tending of natural growth," just as *industry* was an attribute of character. When industry became associated with complex "manufacturing and productive institutions," culture became identified with intellectual pursuits and the arts. The logic of the relationship lies in the fact that the hallmark of the Industrial Revolution was "division of labor" by which each separate task became the work of a specialist. In the same way, the intellectual, spiritual and artistic dimensions of the society became specialized areas for individuals who were trained in the associated skills as professionals, or as laity participating as patrons and consumers. It follows, therefore, that in the areas of the West, where the Industrial Revolution originated and held sway, there should have been an increased use of the term *culture* in these specialized terms. In Eastern Europe, where industrialization was long delayed, such specialization would not have occurred. The small segment that could be associated with specialized intellectual and artistic developments in these countries was a function of economic position rather than industry. For the Jews, certainly, this definition enforces the earlier description of the wholeness of Jewish life in the isolated Jewish communities of the East and the segmented and functional quality of Jewish spiritual and intellectual activities in the West.

It goes somewhat further in explaining division of Jews within the community. In the words of John Ruskin in *The Stones of Venice,* "We have much studied and much perfected, of late, the great civilized invention of the division of labor; only we give it a false name. It is not truly speaking, the labor that is divided, but the men. . . ." Jewish affiliations are today so specialized, that Jews are divided by their functional Jewish involvements rather than unified by common Jewish beliefs and convictions.

The panoramic view of Jewish life in America for the past hundred years reveals a shifting Jewish culture from an all-encompassing definition of Jewish activity to a specialized view of Jewish culture as restricted to *intellectual, spiritual* and *artistic* activities and the diminution of the proportion of Jews involved in such activities. The separation of definitions in matters pertaining to culture as between Eastern and Western European Jews is eroded, and those identified with Jewish culture are isolated in a Jewish enclave within the Jewish community. This specialized segment of the Jewish population does not characterize the majority of Jews.

The earliest national Jewish organizations in America, still extant, are in the cultural and religious areas.[6] Understandably, the first are almost exclusively German-Jewish in origin. Hebrew Union College (1875) followed soon after the organization of the Union of American Hebrew Congregations (1873). Reform Judaism, rooted in German-Jewish life, was the major dimension of Jewishness of that era and it was concerned not only with matters of doctrine and practice but with the training of personnel for its pulpits and later for its Sunday Schools when the Gratz College was established (1895). But in addition to these, there were also strictly cultural organizations such as the Jewish Publication Society of America (1888) and the American Jewish Historical Society (1892), though each had overtones of apologetics in its motivations and statements of purpose.

It was at the close of the nineteenth century, with the beginnings of mass migration from Eastern Europe, that the numbers of Jewish organizations in America grew rapidly. As with the German-Jewish migrants, there were a variety of mutual benefit societies first, frequently in the form of *landsmanschaften,* followed by religious associations such as the Union of Orthodox Congregations (1898) and Yeshiva University (1886).[7] At almost the same time the Jewish Theological Seminary was organized (1887). Its congregations having largely postdated the Seminary, the United Synagogue did not come into being until 1913. We thus find that the religious base for Jewish associations was established early and upon it there gradually developed congregational and educational programs divided according to religious profession, generally classified as distinctly Jewish cultural activities.

By far the largest number of associations between 1900 and the mid-twenties were fraternal, health and philanthropic, with the outstanding organization being that of the Joint Distribution Committee, which must be credited not only with its unique traditional service, but with representing one of the first functional Jewish programs coordinating the Reform, Conservative, Orthodox and secular elements of the Jewish population. In their early years, however, these health and welfare organizations could not be classified as purely philanthropic as distinct from cultural. In practically all cases it was clear that the motivation, the sponsorship and the clients served were distinctively Jewish. The cultural dimension of the services was recognizable both in specific activities and programs which were called cultural and made available to participants on the client and sponsors levels, as well as in the clear intent to delineate the Jewish services from comparable programs under non-Jewish auspices. The members of fraternal organizations, *landsmanschaften,* and mutual benefit societies were more often engaged in programs of a cultural nature than in the stated business of the societies.

The earlier distinction between the two broad segments of the Jewish population continues to be seen throughout the first quarter of the twentieth century, with the Eastern European Jewish community continuing to hold to its anthropological definition of Jewish culture as being a distinctly Jewish pattern of life in all sectors; and the German-Jewish population moving outside of the limited Jewish community into the total American society and being associated with *Jewish* philanthropies in terms of client services to poor, sick and infirm. Few were the distinctly cultural organizations developed in this period, for the German Jews found little need for them outside the established religious associations, and the Eastern European Jews had a cultural component in every undertaking by whatever name or purpose. Specific creations were the Histadrut Ivrith (1916) to further the study of the Hebrew language and to publish the weekly journal, *Hadoar;* the Dropsie College for Hebrew and Cognate Learning (1907); the Sholem Aleichem Folk Institute (1918); and national organizations such as the Workmen's Circle (1900) and the Farband-Labor Zionist Order (1913) maintained schools and intense programs of Jewish culture within organizations generally classified under "mutual benefit societies."

The period from the 1920's until the outbreak of World War II represents the gradual extinction of the double definition of Jewish culture—the anthropological and the intellectual. It was the period of the acculturation of the Jewish population to American patterns with the attendant loss of any self-definition as a "total discernible and describable life-pattern of an identifiable group"; it was simultaneously the period of deculturation of the Jewish community from what was considered to be a unique, intellectual, spiritual and artistic Jewish experience. It was also the period of the withdrawal of the Jewish scholar from the mainstream of Jewish organizational activity which was now severed from a definition of Jewishness.

The same period was also characterized by the emergence of the American college and university as a new field for Jewish cultural activity. The children of immigrants were increasingly finding their way to colleges and obtaining opportunities for professional training as well as opportunities to acquire broad cultural education, not characteristic of their parents and grandparents. From this area arose new programs of Jewish intellectuality both through programs for Jewish students and ultimately through appointments of Jewish faculty members.

The first significant program specifically designed for Jewish college students was that of the B'nai B'rith Hillel Foundations (1923), originating at a major mid-Western university (University of Illinois) located within a minor Jewish community, and spreading to other institutions having in common the pattern of a large university and a small town. The absence of the usual Jewish communal institutions in such small communities seemed to justify the creation of the unique concept of a Jewish community on campus for the Jewish college students and the rare number of Jewish faculty members in the 1920's. Though exceptions have occurred, most directors of Hillel Foundations have been rabbis, giving the program a religious context without denominational emphasis. The comparatively small number of Jewish students yet able to attend college in the 1920's made valid the emphasis of the program on the "future leadership" of the Jewish community. With the passage of time, the increase in the proportion of Jewish youth of college age attending college has reached close to 70 per cent at the time of this writing. Jewish students are distributed through the colleges across the country, including small towns and the large urban centers. The process of Jewish acculturation to American life has unquestionably been speeded by the college experience. For those seeking a Jewish experience, the Hillel Foundations provided a variety of programs and services, but its non-denominational basis has been increasingly challenged by student associations related to the several denominations. Hillel's educational services, in turn, are now to be viewed against an increasing number of opportunities for academic Jewish studies provided by the college or university. Two major Jewish student programs—the Menorah Society and the Avukah Society—must also be recorded as having emerged from the college milieu. The former placed great emphasis on an intellectual definition of Jewish life and through its journal did bring to life some outstanding analyses of Jewish life. The Avukah Society was Zionist in its orientation and was active both intellectually and politically on behalf of that cause. Both programs, however, were conducted without major organizational or professional direction.

Jewish academics were relatively few through the 1930's. The organization of the Conference on Jewish Relations (1935), which later became the Conference on Jewish Social Studies, emerged from the university campus at a time when Jewish professors in all subjects numbered under five hundred. In rare instances were professors of Judaica developed by the general universities. It was a role undertaken by the Jewish rabbinical seminaries, which broadened their definition to include the training of Jewish historians, philosophers, and students of literature. The outbreak of World War II required vast numbers of college-trained personnel and these requirements opened the doors to Jewish students on a broad basis. Teachers also being in great demand, Jewish faculty members were appointed with greater frequency in all fields. The number of Jewish faculty members is not known, but must be assumed to be counted in the thousands. Concurrently, there has been a greater increase of Judaic studies. The faculty for such studies has been drawn from European-trained scholars and those receiving their education at the rabbinical seminaries. Only recently have American-born teachers of Jewish subject matter appeared on the college and university level who are products of the general universities. The trend continues with more Jewish departments being created and increasing numbers of Jewish students pursuing doctoral programs for the purpose of teaching Judaica. The combination of such faculty members with specialization in Jewish subjects and the large number of Jewish faculty members in general subjects give some promise of a new and intensified Jewish intellectual life on the American college campus. This has many positive implications for the Jewish community which may possibly be able to avail itself of the intellectual strength and skills of this segment of the Jewish population.

The availability of Jewish scholarship in America has shown

itself increasingly. The *Encyclopedia Judaica* currently being prepared was originally undertaken as an effort of Jewish scholars in Israel, but it has broadened its personnel to include many Jewish scholars in the United States with assignments in the most significant areas. *The Jewish Book Annual*[8] reveals the number of volumes appearing annually in the Jewish field and the high percentage of publications in the scholarly domain. Increasing, too, is the number of publishers issuing volumes on Jewish subject matter, including commercial and university presses. While special works commissioned by the Jewish community itself and books of almost exclusive Jewish interest require financial resources from Jewish sources, a book of Jewish interest or subject matter is no longer dependent upon Jewish publishers alone.

The narrowing of Jewish cultural life into the definition of intellectual activity poses problems new to the discussion of Jewish culture. We can only present a few basic questions as examples and state their implications:

(1) *Language:* There can be little question that the Jews of America are without a distinctive language. There is no Jewish language and no writing or creativity in a language considered to embody the flavor or constructs of Jewish thought. Knowing that "the very language one speaks conditions the style and structure of thought and experience,"[9] we must wonder whether there can be a uniqueness of Jewish thought and experience, or whether it can be fully expressed.

(2) *Ideology and polemics:* The large struggles within the Jewish community of the past involved variations in ideology with respect to the relationship of the Jew to the general society. Even the arguments about inner communal matters were, in the main, reflections of the attempts to open the door of the Jewish community to the outer world or the desire to seal it. Out of these struggles the polemical works of the leading intellectual and spiritual personalities emerged. The polemical literature represents a significant part of the Jewish books published in contemporary Jewish history. These struggles and polemics are minor in an American Jewish commonality which has in reality left warring positions in the realm of membership adherence and fund-raising efforts. Intellectuality

and spirituality cannot be sustained in the absence of a cause which they further or demolish.

(3) *Responsibility for Jewish scholarship:* Insofar as Jewish intellectual, cultural life becomes dependent upon Jewish scholars who are in turn increasingly dependent for their development and professional opportunities upon the American university, the Jewish community will not itself have any hold upon Jewish scholarly personnel. This can only mean that Jewish academic scholarship will become esoteric and Jewish communal life will not be directly nourished by the fruits of such scholarship. We face the discomfiting paradox of Jewish scholarly efforts becoming the province of the American milieu rather than of the Jewish community.

(4) *The* raison d'être *of Jewish communal life:* Since 1933, the year of the rise of Hitler to power in Germany, the financial philanthropic burdens of American Jewry have been overwhelming. Rescue of Jews from Germany and other Nazi-occupied countries, relief and assistance during World War II, post-war rehabilitation and migration, development of Israel, and the development of programs and facilities for various Jewish social services in America have required funds of staggering magnitude.[10] The standards of leadership that prevailed earlier—personality, knowledgeability, intellectuality—in the Jewish community were supplanted by the one major consideration of financial support. No challenge to the criterion could have been made by any who were aware of the urgency of the requirements, but for this reason thirty years of fund-raising priority in Jewish communal life have well done away with an older, intellectual definition of Jewish leadership which existed independently or sometimes in tandem with financial leadership. The *raison d'être* of Jewish communal life itself has become fund-raising, and for this end, intellectual leadership is not seen as contributory to success.

(5) *Israel as the surrogate of Jewish culture:* The emergence of a Jewish state has tended to have many American Jews ascribe to that Jewish community the responsibility for defining Jewishness and providing the intellectual material and behavior patterns to make it viable. Implicit in this, too, is the recognition that a Jewish pattern of behavior requires a distinct language, which in this instance becomes Hebrew. What is overlooked is that in anthropolog-

ical terms the blending of Jewish cultural patterns from Europe, Africa, Asia and the western hemisphere will produce an *Israeli culture* which may be different from what was called *Jewish culture* in the past. The quality lacking in the Jewish community of Israel is the challenge in daily living requiring answer to the question of what is Jewish about the Jew in contrast to the members of the general society who are not Jewish. In any event, Jewish culture in America, conceived as import from abroad, from Israel, is novel. The role of surrogate in this field, assigned to Israel by those who are largely severed from Jewish intellectual enterprise, tends to sanction the avoidance of Jewish intellectuality in America. The logical fallacy, of course, is that even were such a policy to be followed it could only result in a situation whereby the elimination of Jewish intellectual efforts from Jewish communal life in America now would provide no receptive community later were Israel to have cultural wares for export to this country.

New circumstances have altered the questions requiring answers in the discussions of Jewish culture, as they have made the term itself different. Some of these can be summarized briefly.

Jews have been drawn into the support of American university programs, mainly by certain Jewish efforts in higher education. Brandeis University, defining itself as a Jewish-sponsored American university, has given large numbers of Jews the sense of identification with university support and management. Yeshiva University, moving outside a narrower definition of rabbinical and Jewish teacher-training, has similarly brought philanthropists to the support of higher education in the graduate schools and medical schools which are not governed by any commitment to Jewish learning, *per se*. The easier crossing onto university ground provided by such Jewish-sponsored university efforts has moved many Jews into the ambit of learning and scholarship. This is a potential for the support of Jewish intellectual efforts as part of the university scene, rather than of the Jewish communal scene. This may help to overcome the prospect of finding Jewish scholars and their efforts within the exclusive preserve of the American university without relationship to Jewish life.

Fund-raisers, pragmatically oriented, have begun to be confronted with the finality of death, and the finality of the contributions of those who formerly lived. It is no longer an abstraction to suggest that with the bodies of major philanthropic supporters are oft interred Jewish commitments not replaced by those who inherit the funds. Jewish culture as producer of such commitments, at least in part, therefore takes on a practical role for those whose *raison d'être* of Jewish communal life had acquired a fund-raising context. With a focus on the survivors, the younger segment of the Jewish community, the organized Jewish community and the major philanthropic agencies are offering Leadership Training Institutes, seminars, field visits in the expectation and hope that there may be restored the Jewish motivations which were the original sources of Jewish philanthropy. These learners, in their later ascendancy in Jewish communal affairs, may be expected to restore the Jewish communal role of their Jewish teachers as leaders. These latter are in the main academic personalities.

Finally, the organized Jewish communities whose essential role has been to acquire and distribute funds for Jewish social services, have seemingly been learning both lessons. On the one hand, the Jewishness of the constituency is the greatest potential of continued and expanded support of Jewish philanthropy. Secondarily, it has become apparent that to a younger, college-educated constituency the place of knowledge and those who develop and interpret it must be assured within the Jewish scheme. No more obvious demonstration is needed of the beginnings of bringing Jewish cultural activity within the framework of the Jewish community than the National Foundation for Jewish Culture. The significance and the challenge of this development is described by one scholar as follows:

The all-important question is whether the Jewish community as a whole can be awakened in time to meet its cultural responsibilities. Evidence of improvement in the outlook of the American Jew can be seen in the establishment of the National Foundation for Jewish Culture. Some of the most prominent leaders of the Jewish communities in the United States, meeting in 1959 in the annual assembly of the Council of Jewish Federations and Welfare Funds, brought the new foundation into being. It was assigned the tasks of assisting cultural institutions already in existence and of stimulating the development of new facets of Jewish cultural activity. It remains to be seen whether those who voted for the establishment of the foundation will provide it with the means to realize these objectives. The American Jew's response to this effort will be an index of the cultural maturity of Jewish leadership in the United States.[11]

3. The Image of the American Jewish Community

OSCAR I. JANOWSKY

THE aims of this book have been indicated in the Preface—to marshal the available data and stimulate thought on the nature of the American Jewish community. To this end, the Historical Introduction has traced the evolution of American Jewry, while individual chapters have delineated the development of specific institutions and the functions which motivate their programs. The demographic, economic and social patterns which characterize the Jews as a group, and some aspects of inter-community relations have been discussed, the religious and educational trends noted, philanthropic achievements outlined. Special efforts have been made to appraise the currents of thought and cultural expression in the American Jewish community. Implicit in all these analyses are the conceptions underlying the efforts of American Jewry to further the continuance and welfare of the group.

The image of American Jewry evoked by this book will no doubt vary with the reader—his interests, predilections, biases, scale of values. What follows are the conclusions of one person who has studied the contents of this book with special care. It should be noted, however, that my views do not necessarily represent those of the individual contributors to the volume or of the publisher.

INTEGRATION, ACCULTURATION, HOMOGENEITY

To appraise an object or a group, it is often instructive to view it first from a distance. Detail falls away, the exceptional and divergent elements grow dim, while the prominent features stand out. Viewed thus from a distance, the image is imposing and formidable: American Jewry appears prosperous, acculturated, increasingly homogeneous.

In less than half a century, a mass of poor immigrants have become integrated in the American economy and attained a high level in its occupational and income structure. The Jews are concentrated in the servicing industries—commerce, the professions and other white-collar occupations—with a large percentage of proprietors, managers, and professional practitioners whose income is markedly higher than the national average. This economic concentration, formerly viewed with misgivings as "abnormal," is now recognized as consistent with American economic trends: the occupational shift to the service industries is evident among non-Jews too.

American Jewry is highly urbanized: over 87 percent live in towns or cities of 250,000 population or more; 84 percent in metropolitan areas of a million or more inhabitants. This too is in harmony with the rapid urbanization of the country as a whole, for nearly 70 percent of the American people live now in urban areas.

Two generations ago, the image of American Jewry was that of an immigrant enclave with transplanted institutions, ideologies, customs and mores which appeared to have little relevance to American life. Today, the Jews are integrated in the American economy, extensively involved in the processes of American government and at home in the American milieu. In dress and appearance, in language and education, in fashions and recreation, conceptions of status and material values they conform to the prevailing norms of the dominant culture. In the language of the sociologist, they have become acculturated. Predominantly (at least three-quarters of them) native born, the great majority are the products of the American public school.

All this and other factors have created the image of homogeneity

—a middle-class community, the large majority of whose members are essentially alike in character, aspirations, modes of thought and patterns of behavior. The birth rate among American Jews is lower and the size of the family smaller than the national average—a feature of an urban middle class. That general education is in high favor among American Jews is evidenced by the fact that at least two-thirds of the Jewish youth of college age are enrolled in institutions of higher education—again a symptom of an urban middle class accentuated by the traditional Jewish propensity for education.

The aspect of homogeneity has been enhanced as disparities among segments of American Jewry have faded. The barriers between German and East European Jews have been leveled by the increase in wealth among the latter, and intermingling of these elements has been accelerated by the menace of Nazism and the stupendous efforts undertaken for the relief, resettlement and reconstruction of displaced European and other Jews. The shrill ideological disharmonies in the American Jewish community have likewise been muted. The clamorous debates over Zionism have been reduced to a whimper of dissent from an insignificant minority, while Zionists and non-Zionists cooperate in constructive efforts on behalf of the people of Israel. The conflicts between Yiddishists and Hebraists, between secularists and religionists have likewise subsided. Indeed, the American Jewish community is rarely stirred by ideological controversy. What we hear is the sound and bustle of organizational activity.

Viewed from a distance and in broad outline, American Jewry presents the image of respectability, conformity and moderation—the qualities generally evinced by well-to-do, complacent groups.

AMERICAN JEWRY AS A FUNCTIONING COMMUNITY

Closer study reveals that the bulk of American Jewry constitutes a community as defined in the Preface to this book. The great majority have a sense of belonging together, with common interests which are served by special organizations and institutions. The latter relate to religion, education, civic defense or community relations, philanthropic and welfare services, social and recreational activities, Zionism and Israel, overseas aid, cultural expression.

Furthermore, as one reads the contents of this book, it becomes clear that the increasing and vaunted homogeneity of American Jewry does not mean structural or functional unity. The Jewish community is voluntarily constituted and maintained. There is no central authority over individual Jews or their organizations and institutions. The individual is free to identify himself with such communal agencies as attract his interest or fancy or to remain aloof entirely. The organizations and institutions, too, are autonomous: they may or may not join central bodies; they will honor the decisions of the latter only in so far as their presumed interests are served. As a result, numerous associations have come into being, and the American Jewish community embraces more than 300 national organizations and thousands of local bodies. The services rendered by these units are fragmented and often competitive, for there is no clear division of function. American Jewry has neither a representative spokesman nor a central address. The attempts which have been made to devise a representative congress or conference have been thwarted by the "Liberum Veto" of the autonomous organizations.

Yet, something resembling a "super-structure" does exist in the American Jewish community. Certain bodies enjoy the status of "major" organizations or coordinating agencies because of the wealth and influence of their leadership, because of mass membership, because of the popularity or assumed importance of their work. In the local town or city, these are apt to be the federation of philanthropies or community services, the central fund-raising agency and the community relations (civic defense) council. On the national scene, too, the "major" organizations are as a rule concerned at least in part with community relations, overseas aid, and fund-raising on a large scale. The best known or most influential of the national organizations are the American Jewish Committee, the American Jewish Congress, B'nai B'rith, the central congregational associations and rabbinical bodies, Hadassah, the Zionist Organization of America, JDC, the Jewish Labor Committee, and several others.

The "super-structure" is especially evident in fund-raising, for American Jewish lay leadership, schooled in the practical realm of business and finance, has succeeded to a marked degree in rationalizing and coordinating campaigns for funds. The United Jewish

Appeal and the Council of Jewish Federations and Welfare Funds
come nearest to a central address in fund-raising. However, it must
be noted that even in this field there is no complete unity. A number of large organizations and many small ones campaign for funds
independently of the UJA.

The functions performed by Jewish organizations and institutions are manifold, embracing the varied interests of American
Jewry. This is often overlooked by censorious critics because the
activities which attract the public eye and ear are the ballyhoo
and blandishments of fund-raising drives. In the quiet functioning
of the institutions much significant work is done, as is evidenced by
the record of this book. Large numbers attend religious services
regularly or intermittently. Close to 600,000 children are enrolled
in Jewish schools; active youth movements are maintained; adult
lectures, study and discussion groups are organized in numerous
communities. Small circles devote themselves to Hebrew and Yiddish literature. The community services provide medical and health
facilities, family and child care, aid to the aged, vocational guidance, organized recreation and informal education. Civic defense
and human rights have been advanced by the efforts of Jewish organizations. The achievements in overseas aid and the contribution
to the building of Israel have been stupendous.

When a balance is struck, however, the distinctive feature of
American Jewry emerges as organized philanthropy. The word
"charity" has been expunged from Jewish communal usage. The
patronizing notion of "uplifting" the immigrant masses has vanished. With increasing provision for relief of the needy by government, a marked trend has developed to orientate communal services to "the whole community" rather than exclusively to the poor.
Yet, the big donors—the mainstay of central communal funds—
still make their contributions for the succor or welfare of others.

RELIGIOUS COMPLEXION OF THE JEWISH COMMUNITY

A striking development of the past two decades has been the in-
creasing identification of American Jewry as a religious community.
Religion has always been the distinguishing characteristic of the
Jew, especially in the Diaspora. The vogue of rationalism in the

eighteenth and nineteenth centuries, the repudiation of religion by socialism as the "opium of the people," the spread of nationalism, all contributed to the belief among segments of American Jewry that the theological and ritualistic aspects of Judaism might be dispensed with; that ethnic cohesion and national-cultural traditions and institutions would suffice for a flourishing Jewish group life in America.

During the early decades of the twentieth century, there were considerable elements in the Jewish community who repudiated Judaism as a religion or found it superfluous. It is estimated that a generation ago, a majority of American Jews were unaffiliated with the synagogue or temple.

The trends of recent decades reveal that the non-religious conception of Jewishness has become a far less significant force in the Jewish community. Today, perhaps two-thirds of American Jews are affiliated with congregations. Except for a small fraction, the Jewish schools have come under congregational influence; that is, Jewish education is under religious auspices. Symbolic of this development is the increasing tendency to employ the term "religious school" instead of "Hebrew school." In fact, this is more than symbolic, for there is today greater emphasis in Jewish schools upon prayer and ritual. The reader of this book will recall that Jewish art in America is basically synagogue art and Jewish music synagogue music. The Yiddish schools which formerly shunned "religion" have moved closer to the traditional ways. The anti-religious enclaves, which were vociferous during the early years of this century have dwindled and are heard no more. Recent surveys have shown (as C. Bezalel Sherman has indicated) that today American Jews regard themselves as primarily a religious group. The image of the American Jewish community is assuming a definite religious complexion.

However, when the adjective "religious" is applied to the Jewish community, its meaning must be properly identified. The Protestant Reformation and the rise of national states tended to confine "religion" to theology, ethics and ritual. Many Americans therefore employ the term in this limited sense. But the American Jewish community is far more embracing, as this book has indicated.

Moreover, when Jews say that they regard Jewishness as primarily religious, it does not necessarily imply a commitment to a body of doctrine or a code of ritual. For some it *is* a confession of deep faith and strict observance. Others are non-observant in the ritualistic sense and they are neither rejected nor misprized by synagogue and temple. Many turn to the synagogue only on special occasions, such as the High Holy Days or Bar Mitzvah. Synagogue affiliation may be no more than a formality, an expression of "togetherness" or a means of finding companionship. For such Jews, religion is a symbol of identification rather than an expression of faith in Divine Providence.

The synagogue has responded to this quest for identification under religious auspices. It does, of course, concern itself with worship and ritual. It also engages in activities which some would regard as secular, and in many instances the synagogue has the appearance of a recreational and social center. The functions of the rabbi, too, have changed. Traditionally a scholar and judge of religious law and usage, he has become a representative figure in inter-community relations, a family relations counselor, an administrator, a director of education.

RELATION TO AMERICAN SOCIETY

The increasing identification of Jewishness with religion raises a number of questions. As a rule, the qualification is made that the Jews regard themselves as *primarily* a religious community. This means either that religion is of the first order of importance in characterizing the Jewish community, or that it is the factor from which the other Jewish interests are derived. If religion is only the most important feature of Jewishness, the implication must be that the Jewish community is concerned with other, "non-religious" elements. If, however, religion is the *source* of the other Jewish activities, then Jewish communal life becomes indeed a function of religion or, in Mordecai M. Kaplan's words, "a religious civilization." This has important bearing on the question: What is the relation of the Jewish community to American society?

It is customary to explain the relationship of Jews to American society in terms of "cultural pluralism." But this is an oversimplification. The term "culture" in its limited sense relates to language, art forms and the intellectual and spiritual aspects of life. Cultural pluralism, therefore, can mean the existence of distinctive groups in a country with *parallel* linguistic, artistic, intellectual and spiritual institutions but with no *all-embracing* language, literature or the other factors which compose a common heritage. In some respects, this obtains in Switzerland; it does not prevail in the United States.

On the other hand, cultural pluralism may mean no more than the existence in a free society of a variety of linguistic, intellectual, spiritual and social sub-groups who are part of an all-encompassing milieu but who maintain their singular institutions *in addition* to those shared with the population as a whole. In large measure, this is the situation in the United States.

Another distinction must be noted. Culture includes religion, but the term "cultural pluralism" cannot be employed in the same sense when speaking of differences in the United States in religious belief and observance and differences in other aspects of culture. There is no *all-embracing* religion in America. Government and society sanction the existence of *parallel* religious groupings, each of which is fully independent in doctrinal belief, ritual observance and church organization and functioning. In matters of faith, the interest of each group is primary, all-absorbing and exclusive. The Roman Catholic or Methodist or Jew does not accept the body of doctrines or usages of another denomination, and the separation of church and state precludes special privileges for any group. Therefore, *religious pluralism* is truly descriptive of prevailing conditions in America in the sphere of religion.

Cultural differences beyond the range of religion (in its limited sense of theology, ritual, etc.) are in a different category. While we have no all-embracing religion, we do have an all-embracing English language, an American history and a literature which are presumed to be the shared cultural assets of all Americans, national holidays, like Independence Day, which all observe, ideals and symbols which are regarded as the common heritage of all Americans. In other words, there is a predominant and all-embracing American cultural pattern.

There are groups in American society which have *additional* cultural interests. In the case of the Jews, these relate to the experiences of a long history, the Hebrew and Yiddish languages, distinctive folkways, symbols, traditions and customs, a sense of kinship with Jews in other parts of the world, and concern with the Jewish cultural center in Israel. We must underscore, however, that these distinctive Jewish cultural interests are *additional* to the all-embracing American cultural pattern with which the American Jews are identified. In religious faith and usage, the distinctiveness of the Jew is complete and parallel with other religious denominations. In language and other aspects of culture, the uniqueness of the Jew is partial. The English language is his idiom, American history, literature and ideals are his cultural values as they are the values of other Americans. His unique Jewish cultural assets are *additional* or *supplementary* to the all-embracing American cultural pattern.

Therefore, the term "cultural pluralism," when applied to the totality of Jewish distinctiveness, is misleading. If employed in the sense of "religious pluralism," (that is, a distinctiveness which is complete, as in faith and ritual), it assumes too much, because the concern of Jews with the Hebrew and Yiddish languages or with Jewish history and literature is supplementary; they accept the all-embracing English language, American history and literature. If, on the other hand, "cultural pluralism" connotes the supplementary relationship which obtains in language, history and literature, it embraces too little, for it fails to define the situation governing religious doctrine and ritual.

The distinctiveness of American Jews and their relationship to American society cannot be defined by a single term. A substantive difference must be recognized between faith and ritual on the one hand and other aspects of culture on the other. "Religious pluralism" describes properly the relationship respecting religious doctrine and usage. In the area of language, history, literature and the like, a more realistic characterization would be "cultural supplementation."

JEWISH CULTURE IN AMERICA

Jewish cultural activities relating to the intellectual, spiritual and artistic have received much attention in this book. Jewish literature, art and music have been surveyed, religion and education discussed, the role of the Zionist idea assayed, current Jewish ideologies appraised. The resultant image, however—the cultural image of American Jewry—is unimpressive.

In numbers, wealth and influence, American Jewry has attained a stature unequalled in any land of the Diaspora during two millennia. The mantle of leadership has fallen to America's Jews as the European communities succumbed to war, revolution and Nazi savagery. America has become the center of Diaspora Jewry, and even Israel depends in long measure upon its assistance. The world's Jews, however, look to their American brethren for financial aid and to a lesser extent for political influence and managerial skill. Cultural leadership is neither proffered nor invited. Indeed, American Jewry is disdained as culturally barren.

The Jewish center of the New World does indeed suffer grievously by comparison with the celebrated Diaspora communities of the past. Babylonia left a Talmud and Gaonic learning as a cultural legacy. Spain's Golden Age still dazzles us with its amazing cultural versatility and brilliance. The relatively small medieval communities along the River Rhine produced Rabbenu Gershom ("Light of the Golah"), Rashi and others. Poland and (later) Russia became the centers of traditional learning and pietistic lore; more recently, these lands were the home of modern Hebrew and Yiddish literature and of the Zionist ideal. What of comparable significance has American Jewry wrought in the realm of the spirit that will merit remembrance in years to come? What cultural influence can it exert upon its own youth, when it cannot even supply sufficient numbers of qualified Jewish teachers?

To the older generation, the image of cultural barrenness in American Jewry looms especially portentous because the assets of former years have disappeared. The rich and stimulating Yiddish milieu and Hebrew letters have languished in the wake of acculturation, while the Jewish home has been emptied of Jewish content. The American Jewish masses are strangers to the Jewish heritage, ignorant of Jewish values, unconcerned with Jewish cultural efforts.

It has been asserted that the Jewish masses of former eras were likewise ignorant. This is no doubt true, if ignorance is equated with lack of learning. But unlike American Jews, the masses of the past respected Jewish learning, and they were not alienated from the Jewish heritage nor unconcerned with Jewish values.

Moreover, until our own age the masses had neither the means nor the leisure for education: the elementary needs of food, clothing and shelter absorbed all their energies. Today, American Jewry is more fortunately situated. Technological advances have reduced both the length and the exhausting toil of the work day. Leisure time is abundant and general (non-Jewish) educational opportunities plentiful. That these opportunities have not been neglected by American Jews is evidenced by the fact that at least two-thirds of American Jewish youth of college age are enrolled in colleges and universities. It is doubtful if any Jewish community, that of present-day Israel included, ever attained a higher level of *general* education than that of American Jewry. America's Jews are far from an uneducated community, but they are illiterate in things Jewish.

Even more discouraging is the image of American Jewish leadership. The men and women who are prominent in Jewish organizations and institutions are able and often cultivated persons. They have achieved stature in large business affairs, in the arts, sciences, and the professions, in government service or social welfare work. They are generally highly intelligent, well-informed and articulate. But not many possess even a modicum of Jewish learning or are appreciative of Jewish cultural endeavors.

Critics have characterized American Jewry as a cultural void filled with organizational activity. The latter has been concerned primarily with social services, the relief of the needy and the menace of anti-Semitism at home and abroad, and with aid to Israel. These purposes have required vast sums of money, especially overseas relief and aid to Israel which have won almost unanimous sanction in the American Jewish community. Continuing or repeated crises, with consequent and urgent pleas for money, have resulted in a disproportionate emphasis upon fund-raising drives and membership campaigns. American Jewry has, therefore, been stigmatized as a community preoccupied with little more than "campaign Judaism." This is, of course, an exaggeration, for in the areas of philanthropy and social welfare, vision and scope have been manifested. But it is true that in Jewish education and culture the efforts of organization leadership have been puny and myopic.

This view that the weakness of the cultural component in American Jewish life is due at least in part to the world situation which has dictated the emphasis upon fund-raising is frequently overlooked. It has been argued with considerable force that the cause is inherent in the American environment. Learning and culture are neither felt needs in America nor primary factors determining status; wealth and success are, and political stature or professional recognition. Education is prized primarily as a means of achieving "success." The average person does not read serious matter which requires concentration. As a rule, even the schooled person, the college graduate, does not devote leisure time to study or reading. Entertainment is preferred and, although such instrumentalities abound, boredom often contrives strange means of "killing time." In such an intellectual climate, there is even less inclination for Jewish learning or culture. The need is less evident, the motivation weak, if present at all. Therefore, discouragement is rife among the small circles which are concerned with Jewish culture. Some have pronounced a sentence of doom upon American Jewry. They see no future for it other than disintegration and ultimate extinction.

This mood is understandable but hardly justified. American Jewry is a vital and generous community with good potentialities for the future. Those who condemn it because of its deficiencies betray their own impatience. They expect too much too soon.

The great centers of Jewish population of the past did not blossom into cultural communities in a few generations. Jews were in Babylonia in the sixth century B.C.E., but they did not achieve cultural leadership until eight hundred years later. In Spain and in Western Germany, Jews lived in considerable numbers for at least six hundred years before cultural life assumed significant proportions in the tenth century C.E. Poland, too, had its Jewish communities for hundreds of years before it became a center of learning in the sixteenth century.

To appraise the present situation, American Jewry must be viewed in historical perspective. While Jews have lived in this land since 1654, the great masses did not begin to arrive until the last decades of the nineteenth century. Two million Jews immigrated into the United States between 1880 and 1914, and we forget too soon that they suffered hardship and heartache. The first concern of the immigrants was with the needs of food and shelter, which had to be earned in an environment of rugged individualism. The government was then distant and aloof, for notions of social security were utopian dreams. The struggle for a livelihood was rugged indeed. It was "each for himself and the devil take the hindmost." The devil often did, and the immigrant was the hindmost.

The newcomers transplanted the religious, educational and cultural institutions of Eastern Europe. They fought here the battles of the old home: Bundism *versus* Zionism, Yiddish *versus* Hebrew, Orthodoxy *versus* freethinking. The new life seemed rich and colorful. It had a stimulating, dynamic quality. But it was a mirage to which memories of the old home gave a semblance of reality. Many of the transplanted institutions and ideas failed to take root in American soil. The older generation tried to preserve the heritage but the children, who craved acceptance in American society, rejected the traditional way of life as alien and outlandish. Parents and children ceased to speak the same language, literally as well as figuratively. They lost spiritual contact. Only physical contact remained as an irritant. The conflict was not one of generations but of centuries. Parents and children no longer lived in one world. Jewishly speaking, the generation of immigrants was largely without issue.

For the second generation, the very rejection of the Jewish heritage lent color to Jewish living. The synagogue, the Jewish school, the Yiddish and Hebrew languages were at least objects of attack. But for many of the third generation, the heritage became irrelevant, for it was no longer even a memory. It had become an echo of the distant past, without meaning or purpose or personal concern. Thus did Jewishness become a cultural vacuum for large numbers of American Jews.

It was only in recent decades that American Jewry began to stir with new life. Many who had drifted away or were poised for flight from Jewishness were driven back into the fold by the menace of Nazism. Others were inspired by the rise of Israel. These spiritual refugees yearned for rootage and identification. Since genuine cultural expression was beyond their reach, they sought refuge in organizational activities. They enlisted en masse in the counter-attack on anti-Semitism, and when this menace subsided, they took on the struggle for equal rights. They joined in drives for funds and buildings. And they groped vaguely for some means of rendering Jewishness more meaningful to their children.

Today, the stream of Jewish spiritual and cultural life is shrunken and shallow, but it has not ceased to flow. The American Jewish community is not a cultural void. There are Jewish institutions of learning—rabbinical seminaries, a few Jewish colleges and universities and chairs of Jewish studies in general universities, academies of research and learned societies, libraries and museums. Hillel Foundations function throughout the country. Important books of Jewish interest are published by the Jewish Publication Society and by others. We have Jewish newspapers and periodicals, radio programs, lectures, forums, occasional music and dance recitals. Zealous groups devote themselves to the Hebrew language and to Yiddish. Synagogues and Jewish centers provide recreational and some cultural activities for large numbers.

These cultural agencies must not be disdained. Nor should one disregard the spiritual and cultural ferment among American Jews. The flight from the synagogue, so evident a generation ago, has ceased, and the new generation is seeking anchorage in religious identification. That parents recognize the need of Jewish education for their children is witnessed by the 600,000 children who are enrolled in Jewish schools. The phenomenal growth of the Day School confirms a desire for some depth in Jewish education. The concern of community leadership was recently indicated by the establishment of the Jewish Culture Foundation with the enthusiastic approval of the Council of Jewish Federations and Welfare Funds.

These stirrings of interest do not necessarily foreshadow a Jewish cultural renaissance in America. The unique ideas and institutions of a relatively small minority absorbed in the prevailing culture of a country require unstinted support and stimulation. This might be forthcoming if educational and cultural needs received much higher priority than now prevailing in the allocation of Jewish communal funds. The increasing concern of government with charitable and welfare work underscores the possibility for a shift of emphasis in Jewish communal services from the philanthropic to cultural. There is no firm evidence that Jewish leadership is ready for so drastic a change.

It would be idle to attempt to forecast the future that American Jewry will fashion for coming generations. But one may venture the conclusion that the vitality and dynamism which enabled Jews to master destructive forces in the past are far from spent. The colorful parade of Jewish organizational life, with its bustle, its slogans, its rival claims and touted accomplishments, is not a procession of ghosts of the past. It is part of the unending march of the centuries. Frustration there is aplenty, but despair is unwarranted. American Jewry is not disintegrating. It is in the process of becoming.

Notes and Bibliographies

LIST OF ABBREVIATIONS

AAJE	American Association for Jewish Education
AJYB	American Jewish Year Book
CJFWF	Council of Jewish Federations and Welfare Funds
HIAS	Hebrew Sheltering and Immigrant Aid Society
JCA	Jewish Colonization Association
JDC	American Jewish Joint Distribution Committee
JEC	Jewish Education Committee of New York
JJCS	Journal of Jewish Communal Service
JSSQ	Jewish Social Service Quarterly
JWB	National Jewish Welfare Board
NCJE	National Council for Jewish Education
PAJHS	Publications of the American Jewish Historical Society
UJA	United Jewish Appeal
YM and YWHA	Young Men's and Young Women's Hebrew Association

Preface   (pp. vii–x)

BY OSCAR I. JANOWSKY

Notes

1. See G. A. Hillery, "Definitions of Community: Areas of Agreement," *Rural Sociology*, XX, 2 (June, 1955), 111–123. See also L. Nelson, *Rural Sociology* (New York, 1952), p. 71; R. M. MacIver, *Community: A Sociological Study* (London, 1917), pp. 22–24 and *passim; idem, Society* (New York, 1937), pp. 8–12; I. T. Sanders, *The Community* (New York, 1958), pp. 14–20, 120, 189.

Background of American Jewry   (pp. 1–25)

BY JACOB RADER MARCUS

Bibliographical Note

There are, unfortunately, as yet far too few worthwhile books surveying the entire field of American Jewish history. The distinguished German Jewish historian, Ismar Elbogen, who spent his last years on these shores, described the American scene—within the framework of world Jewish history—in *A Century of Jewish Life* (Philadelphia, 1944). Jacob R. Marcus has summarized the colonial period in *Early American Jewry*, II (Philadelphia, 1955), 377–553. The first writer to pay due regard to Jews of East European origin in the United States was Peter Wiernik in his *History of the Jews in America* (New York, 1931), and this concern with the experience and ideals of the immigrants from beyond the Vistula is reflected also in Rufus Learsi's *Jews in America* (Cleveland, 1954). Lee J. Levinger's high-school textbook, *History of the Jews in the United States* (New York, 1954) is both useful and readable, while Anita Libman Lebeson's *Pilgrim People* (New York, 1950) and Oscar Handlin's

Adventure in Freedom (New York, 1954) contain keen historic insights. The four volumes of *The Jewish People: Past and Present* (New York, 1946–1955)—volume four deals entirely with Jewry in this country—offer much information and solid material. A somewhat similar work ranging through virtually all aspects of Jewish life since antiquity is the two-volume *The Jews: Their History, Culture, and Religion* (New York, 1960), edited by Louis Finkelstein.

For a sociological study of Jewish religious life on this continent, one may turn with profit to Nathan Glazer's *American Judaism* (Chicago, 1957). It is a particular pleasure to recommend here for diversity of content and high quality of presentation, *The American Jew: A Composite Portrait* (New York, 1942), edited by Oscar I. Janowsky. Finally, students of American Jewish history are unable to dispense with the by now more than fifty volumes of *Publications of the American Jewish Historical Society* (renamed *American Jewish Historical Quarterly* since the appearance of volume 51 in 1961–1962) and the fifteen volumes of *American Jewish Archives* which have been issued since 1948.

Demographic and Social Aspects (pp. 27–51)

BY C. BEZALEL SHERMAN

Notes

1. U.S. Department of Commerce, Bureau of the Census, *Current Population Reports: Population Characteristics,* Series P-20, no. 79, p. 7.
2. D. J. Bogue, *The Population of the United States* (Glencoe, Illinois, 1959), p. 697.
3. *Current Population Reports,* p. 6.
4. For figures on Jewish population, see A. Chenkin, "Jewish Population in the United States, 1960," *AJYB,* vol. 62 (Philadelphia, 1961), 62–63. For figures on Foreign White Stock, see U.S. Department of Commerce, *Statistical Abstracts of the United States,* 83rd ed., prepared by Edwin D. Goldfield (Washington, 1962), p. 33.
5. Migration of Negroes from the South or of white underprivileged groups from other areas has had little effect on Jewish geographic mobility.
6. While the growth of the Washington community reflects in part the greater participation of Jews in government service, that of Los Angeles, Miami Beach and Tucson reflect in part the aging of the American Jewish population, with many removing to those cities for reasons of health after retirement.

7. H. Cohen, *Jewish Population Trends in New York* (Federation of Jewish Philanthropies of New York, 1955), mimeographed.
8. M. C. Horowitz and L. J. Kaplan, *The Jewish Population of New York Area, 1900–1975* (Federation of Jewish Philanthropies of New York, 1959).
9. A. Chenkin, "Jewish Population in the United States, 1961," *AJYB*, vol. 63 (Philadelphia, 1962), 136.
10. I. Dijour, "Jewish Immigration to the United States Since 1944," *ibid.*, vol. 62, pp. 63–66.
11. N. Goldberg, "Demographic Characteristics of American Jews," in *Jews in the Modern World*, ed. by Jacob Freid, vol. 2 (New York, 1962), p. 688.
12. *Ibid.*, p. 690.
13. E. Rosenthal, "Jewish Fertility in the United States," *AJYB*, vol. 62, p. 4.
14. N. Goldberg, *op. cit.*, p. 663.
15. *Ibid.*, p. 696.
16. *Ibid.*, p. 696.
17. Bogue, *op. cit.*, pp. 696–97.
18. N. Goldberg, *op. cit.*, p. 670. Figures for non-Jewish population are from 1950 U.S. Census; the Jewish data are based on the various community studies.
19. *Ibid.*, p. 705.
20. D. M. Liberson, "Causes of Death Among Jews in New York City in 1953," *Jewish Social Studies*, XVIII, 2 (1956), 99, 101.
21. L. Srole, T. Langer, S. Michael, M. Opler and T. Rennie, *Mental Health in the Metropolis, Midtown Manhattan Study*, vol. 1 (New York, 1962).
22. J. Drachsler, *Democracy and Assimilation* (New York, 1920), p. 128.
23. For a summary of available material on intermarriage among Jews, see C. B. Sherman, *The Jew Within American Society—A Study in Ethnic Individuality* (Detroit, 1960), pp. 183–89.
24. R. Shosteck, "Our Youth in College," *National Jewish Monthly* (November, 1956), p. 9.
25. Bogue, *op. cit.*, p. 700.
26. *Ibid.*, p. 704.
27. D. Young, *American Minority Peoples* (New York, 1932), p. 296.
28. *Ibid.*, p. 318.
29. V. Packard, *The Status Seekers* (New York, 1961, paper), p. 181.
30. Quoted in *ibid.*, p. 171.
31. B'nai B'rith Hillel Foundations, *Jewish Identification and the Jewish College Student* (Washington, 1959, pamphlet), p. 8.
32. M. Shapiro, *The Bayville Survey* (Miami, 1961, pamphlet), p. 2.

33. Southville Jewish Community Relations Committee and the American Jewish Committee, *Summary of Highlights from the Southville Survey of Jewish Attitudes* (New York, 1959), p. 4 (mimeographed).
34. *The Bayville Survey*, p. 1.
35. *Jewish Social Studies*, XXIV, 1 (January, 1962), 30–48.
36. *The Bayville Survey*, p. 1.
37. *Southville Survey*, p. 5.
38. For an evaluation of the attitudes toward Israel, see: *The Bayville Survey*, p. 3; *Southville Survey,* p. 7; H. T. Lipman, *The White Plains Jewish Attitudes Survey* (New York, 1958), p. 6; M. Sklare and M. Vosk, *The Riverton Study* (New York, 1957), p. 21; M. Sklare and B. Ringer, "A Study of Jewish Attitudes Toward the State of Israel," in *The Jews*, edited by M. Sklare (Glencoe, Illinois, 1958), p. 437; A. G. Duker, "Impact of Zionism on American Jewry," *Jewish Life in America*, edited by T. Friedman and R. Gordis (New York, 1955), p. 316; and C. B. Sherman, *op. cit.*, pp. 213–15.
39. H. T. Lipman, *The White Plains Survey*, p. 4.
40. *Jewish Identification and the Jewish College Student*, p. 23.

Bibliographical Note

Demography: Annual summaries of Jewish population trends are available in A. Chenkin, "Jewish Population in the United States," in recent issues of the *American Jewish Year Book*. M. C. Horowitz and L. J. Kaplan, *The Jewish Population of New York, 1900–1975* (New York, 1959), is based on the "Yom Kippur Method" and also contains projections on the future. N. Goldberg, "Demographic Characteristics of American Jews" in *Jews in the Modern World*, Jacob Freid ed., vol. II (New York, 1962), pp. 638–711, is a comprehensive study based on original research.

Mortality and fertility among Jews are analyzed in D. M. Liberson, "Causes of Death Among Jews in New York City in 1953," in *Jewish Social Studies*, 18, 2 (1956), pp. 83–117; E. Rosenthal, "Jewish Fertility in the United States," *AJYB*, vol. 62 (Philadelphia, 1961), pp. 3–27. Socio-economic mobility of American Jews is discussed in B. Seligman, with the assistance of A. Antonovsky, "Some Aspects of Jewish Demography," in *The Jews—Social Patterns of an American Group*, M. Sklare ed. (Glencoe, Illinois, 1958), pp. 45–93.

The following works, based on U.S. Government census figures, contain much material on American Jews and are invaluable for comparison with other ethnic and religious groups: D. J. Bogue, *The Population of the United States* (Glencoe, Illinois, 1959); E. D. Goldfield, *Statistical Abstracts of the United States,* prepared for United States Department of Commerce, 83rd edition (Washington, D.C., 1962); E. P. Hutchinson, *Immigrants and Their Children 1850–1950* (New York, 1956).

Suburbia: A. J. Gordon, *Jews in Suburbia* (Boston, 1959), is the most comprehensive survey of Jewish life in the suburbs; and H. J. Gans, "A Study of the Jews of Park Forest," in *The Jews,* M. Sklare ed., pp. 205–248, is a pioneering study of Jews in a planned suburb.

Intermarriage: U.S. Department of Commerce, Bureau of the Census, *Current Population Reports,* Series P-20, no. 79, February 2, 1958, includes statistics on intermarriage. J. Drachsler, *Democracy and Assimilation* (New York, 1920) is a monumental study of intermarriage in New York City during 1908–1912, which still has validity. W. J. Cahnman ed., *Intermarriage and Jewish Life,* a Symposium (New York, 1963) includes the proceedings of the Conference on Intermarriage convened by the Theodor Herzl Institute in 1960, and deals also with the problems of intermarriage involving Jews in other lands.

Social Aspects of Acculturation: B'nai B'rith Hillel Foundations, *Jewish Identification and the Jewish College Student* (Washington, 1959) contains brief summaries of surveys of Jewish attitudes among Jewish students. A. G. Duker, "Emerging Culture Patterns in American Jewish Life," *Publications of the American Jewish Historical Society,* no. 39, part 4 (June, 1950), pp. 351–88, reviews patterns of behavior and the attempts to fit Jewish traditional practices and values into general American mores. L. H. Fuchs, *The Political Behavior of American Jews* (Glencoe, Illinois, 1956), analyzes Jewish voting practices in political elections in a number of Jewish districts. M. Sklare ed., *The Jews—Social Patterns of an American Group* (Glencoe, Illinois, 1958), includes a number of essays dealing with attitudes and social trends in American Jewry.

C. B. Sherman, *The Jew Within American Society* (Detroit, 1960), deals with all facets of American Jewish life functioning against the background of the general processes operating in American society.

Economic Status (pp. 53–74)

BY NATHAN REICH

Notes

1. B. Lazrewitz, "A Comparison of Major United States Religious Groups," *Journal of the American Statistical Association* (September, 1961), p. 574.

2. *Ibid.*, p. 256.
3. F. Masarik, *A Report on the Jewish Population of Los Angeles*, Research Service Bureau of the Jewish Federation-Council of Greater Los Angeles (Los Angeles, 1959), p. 23.
4. Cited by N. Glazer in "Social Characteristics of American Jews," *AJYB*, 1955, p. 28.
5. D. J. Bogue, *The Population of the United States* (Glencoe, Illinois, 1959), p. 702.
6. B. Lazrewitz, "Jews In and Out of New York City," *Jewish Journal of Sociology* (December, 1961), p. 256.
7. *Ibid.*, p. 259.
8. Adapted from Committee on Economic Adjustment, *Industrial Classification of Jewish Gainfully Employed Workers in New York City,* Conference on Jewish Relations (1938), 13 pp., mimeographed: cited by N. Reich, "Economic Trends," *The American Jew,* O. I. Janowsky ed. (New York, 1942, Harper and Brothers), p. 163.
9. *United States Statistical Abstracts,* 1962, p. 224.
10. Figures pertain to New York City only.
11. Editors of *Fortune,* "Jews in America" (New York, 1936).
12. J. R. Kramer and S. Leventman, *Children of the Gilded Ghetto* (New Haven, 1961), p. 130.
13. *Kultur un Dertziung* (May, 1962), p. 14.
14. M. Newcomer, *The Big Business Executive* (New York, 1955), p. 48.
15. N. Goldberg, *Occupational Patterns of American Jewry* (New York, 1947) p. 11.
16. "A Business Elite: German Jewish Finance in Nineteenth Century New York," *The Business History Review* (Summer, 1957), p. 170.
17. *Ibid.*, p. 176.
18. Goldberg, *op. cit.*, pp. 15–16.
19. *Reports of the Immigration Commission,* vol. 28, Senate Document no. 282, 61st Congress, 2nd Session (Washington, D.C., 1911), pp. 272, 277, 280, 362, 367, 370: cited in S. Kuznets, "Economic Structure and Life of the Jews," in *The Jews,* Louis Finkelstein, ed., vol. II, 3rd ed. (1960), 1639.
20. Goldberg, *op. cit.*, pp. 29, 38, 52; Reich, *op. cit.*, pp. 162–167.
21. Memo to the author from Louis Rosenberg, research director, Canadian Jewish Congress.
22. Cited by W. Duckat, *Contributions of Jews to the American Economy* (New York, 1955), p. 4.
23. Reich, *op. cit.*, p. 172. Quoted with permission of the publisher.

Bibliographical Note

There is no comprehensive work on Jewish economic life in the United States. Brief summaries or surveys of developments are given in: Editors of *Fortune, Jews in America* (New York, 1936); N. Glazer, "Social Characteristics of American Jews, 1654–1954," *AJYB,* vol. 56 (Philadelphia, 1955), 3–41; W. M. Kephart, "What Is the Position of Jewish Economy in the United States," *Social Forces,* 28, 2 (December, 1949), 153–164; N. Reich, "Economic Trends," *The American Jew,* O. I. Janowsky, ed. (New York, 1942), pp. 161–182. Occupational trends are discussed in N. Goldberg, *Occupational Patterns of American Jewry* (New York, 1947); J. Kramer and S. Leventman, *Children of the Gilded Ghetto* (New Haven, 1961); J. S. Fauman, "Occupational Selection Among Detroit Jews," *Jewish Social Studies,* 14 (1952), 17–50.

Good studies of earlier periods are available in J. R. Marcus, *Early American Jewry,* 2 vols. (Philadelphia, 1951, 1953). (Vol. II, ch. 17, pp. 395–428 contains excellent material on economic activity to 1790); M. K. Freund, *Jewish Merchants in Colonial America* (New York, 1939); M. Whiteman, "The Colonial Jewish Peddler," *Studies and Essays in Honor of Abraham A. Neuman,* M. Ben Horin and others, eds. (Philadelphia, 1962), pp. 503–515; G. Davidson, "The Jew in Agriculture in the United States," *AJYB,* vol. 37 (Philadelphia, 1935), pp. 99–134; A. Tarshish, "The Economic Life of the American Jews in the Middle-Nineteenth Century," *Essays on American Jewish History,* under direction of J. R. Marcus (Cincinnati), 1958), pp. 263–293.

On the Jewish labor movement, the following works are recommended: A. Antonowsky, ed., *The Early Jewish Labor Movement in the United States* (New York, 1961), based on *Di Geshikhte fun der Yiddisher Arbeterbavegung in di Fareynikte Shtaten,* edited by E. Tcherikover, 2 vols. (New York, 1943, 1945); M. Epstein, *Jewish Labor in the United States,* 2 vols. (New York, 1951), 1953; J. B. S. Hardman, "Jewish Workers in the American Labor Movement," *Yivo Annual of Jewish Social Science,* vol. VII, 1952, pp. 229–254; N. Reich, "The Americanization of Jewish Unionism: A Two-Way Process," *Jewish Quarterly Review* (April, 1955), 540–561; M. Rischin, *The Promised City* (Cambridge, Mass., 1962) contains excellent material on Jewish labor movement in New York City to 1914.

Special subjects are treated in the following: E. Rivkin, "A Decisive Pattern in American Jewish History," *Essays in American Jewish History,* under direction of J. R. Marcus (Cincinnati, 1958), pp. 23–61, is a well-written essay on the favorable climate provided by

American capitalism for the economic advance of American Jewry; G. Lensky, *The Religious Factor* (New York, 1961), is a penetrating sociological study of the impact of Jewish religious tradition on the economic career of the Jew in modern times. D. J. Bogue, *The Population of the United States* (Glencoe, Illinois, 1959), provides valuable material for comparative analysis of the economic characteristics of the various denominational groups. Particularly relevant is chapter 23, pp. 688–709.

Inter-Group Relations (pp. 75–100)

BY MILTON R. KONVITZ

Notes

1. L. Gumplowics, *Der Rassenkampf* (1883).
2. M. R. Konvitz, *Civil Rights in Immigration* (Ithaca, New York, 1953), p. 10.
3. *Ibid.*, p. 11.
4. A. and C. Rose, *America Divided* (New York, 1948), pp. 39–40.
5. R. Weintraub, *How Secure These Rights?* (New York, 1949), p. 89.
6. *Ibid.*, pp. 92 ff.
7. *Fortune,* February, 1946; *Fortune,* October, 1947.
8. G. E. Simpson and J. M. Yinger, *Racial and Cultural Minorities* (New York, 1953), p. 293.
9. N. C. Belth ed., *Barriers* (New York, 1958), p. 119.
10. D. Caplovitz and D. Rogers, *Swastika 1960* (New York, 1961), pp. 7–8.
11. "The Ultra-Conservative Movement," memorandum by American Jewish Committee (New York, 1961); M. Sherwin, *The Extremists* (New York, 1962); R. Burlingame, *The Sixth Column* (New York, 1962).
12. M. R. Konvitz and T. Leskes, *A Century of Civil Rights* (New York, 1961); The People Take The Lead.
13. "The Future of Law," 47 *Yale L. J.,* 1, 13.
14. Dissenting opinion in W. Va. State Board of Education v. Barnette, 319 U.S. 624 (1943), at pp. 670–671.
15. Otis v. Parker, 178 U.S. 606, 609 (1902).
16. H. S. Bettenson, *Documents of the Christian Church* (New York, 1943), p. 27.
17. Memorandum on the topic by American Jewish Congress, June 3, 1958.
18. McGowan v. Md., 366 U.S. 420 (1961); Two Guys from Harrison—Allentown v. McGinley, 366 U.S. 582 (1961); Gallagher

v. Crown Kosher Super Market, 366 U.S. 618 (1961); Braunfeld v. Brown, 366 U.S. 599 (1961).

19. *Weekly Rest in Commerce and Offices,* ILO (Geneva, 1955).
20. The New York Legislature amended the law in 1963 to allow local option in New York City.
21. Cited in opinion by Justice Frankfurter, 366 U.S. 514, 515.
22. See opinion of Justice Frankfurter, *ibid.,* at 518. W. Hodgkins, *Sunday—Christian and Social Significance* (London, 1960).
23. Hodgkins, *op. cit.; supra,* note 22, at 141 ff.
24. Engel v. Vitale, 10 New York 2d 174 (1961). The Supreme Court citation is 370 U.S. 421 (1962). Justice Frankfurter was ill, and Justice White had not yet taken his place on the Court when the case was argued. Justice Douglas wrote a concurring opinion. Justice Stewart dissented. The decision in the Schempp and Murray cases in June 1963 essentially reaffirmed the 1961 decision.
25. *New Leader,* August 6, 1962. *Christianity and Crisis,* July 23, 1962.
26. *New York Times,* June 27, 1962; June 29, 1962; July 1, 1962.
27. *New York Times,* June 28, 1962.
28. *New York Times,* July 1, 1962.
29. *Article in Newark Star-Ledger,* July 22, 1962.
30. *New York Times,* July 28, 1962.
31. *Jewish News,* Essex County, New Jersey, September 7, 1962.
32. *America,* September 15, 1962.
33. *Commonweal,* September 7, 1962.
34. *Commonweal,* September 28, 1962.
35. *The Pilot,* September 1, 1962.
36. Quoted in *New York Times,* September 2, 1962.
37. The Lutherans are the only Protestant denomination that have developed their own parochial schools for a substantial number of pupils. The total enrollment in non-Catholic parochial schools in 1958 was estimated at 500,000. N. G. McCluskey, *Catholic Viewpoint on Education* (New York, 1959), pp. 35, 176. The same author stated that the enrollment in Roman Catholic elementary and secondary schools for 1958–59 was 4,900,000. The Legal Department of the National Catholic Welfare Conference reported that in 1960 there were 4,400,000 pupils in Roman Catholic elementary schools, and 885,000 in secondary schools. Memorandum, "The Constitutionality of the Inclusion of Church-Related Schools in Federal Aid to Education," 50 *Georgetown L. J.,* 339 (Winter, 1961).
38. See *Jewish Education in the United States,* Report of the Commission for the Study of Jewish Education in the United States, AAJE (New York, 1959).
39. In 1961 such bills were introduced in 28 state legislatures. See *AJYB,* 63, (Philadelphia, 1962), p. 195.

40. B. Epstein and A. Forster, *Some of My Best Friends* . . . (New York, 1962).

Bibliographical Note

For the most comprehensive and general bibliography, see Alexander D. Brooks, *A Bibliography of Civil Rights and Civil Liberties*, Civil Liberties Educational Foundation (New York, 1962).

For an extensive bibliography on church-state problems, see Anson Phelps Stokes, *Church and State in the United States* (New York, 1950), vol. III. A shorter bibliography is in Leo Pfeffer, *Church, State and Freedom* (Boston, 1953).

For a bibliography on immigration policy, see Milton R. Konvitz, *The Alien and the Asiatic in American Law* (Ithaca, New York, 1946).

For surveys of anti-Semitism in the United States, see the reports prepared by the Anti-Defamation League, especially Arnold Forster, *A Measure of Freedom* (New York, 1950); Benj. R. Epstein and Arnold Forster, *Some of My Best Friends* . . . (New York, 1962); Ruth G. Weintraub, *How Secure These Rights?* (New York, 1949).

For an over-all view of civil rights, see Milton R. Konvitz and Theodore Leskes, *A Century of Civil Rights* (New York, 1961). See also, Arnold M. Rose, ed., *Race Prejudice and Discrimination* (New York, 1951); Geo. Eaton Simpson and J. Milton Yinger, *Racial and Cultural Minorities* (New York, 1953).

The American Jew and His Religion   (pp. 101–119)

BY ARTHUR HERTZBERG

Notes

1. See my article, "Religion," *AJYB,* vol. 59 (Philadelphia, 1958), pp. 114–15.
2. See A. M. Dushkin and U. Z. Engelman, *Jewish Education in the United States* (New York, AAJE, 1959), pp. 39–44.
3. See M. Sklare and M. Vosk, *The Riverton Study* (New York, 1962), p. 11. In that community, three out of ten did not observe the High Holidays; only two out of ten came to synagogue on other occasions.
4. The most recent study of intermarriage is that of E. Rosenthal, "Studies of Jewish Intermarriage in the United States," *AJYB,* vol. 64 (Philadelphia, 1963), pp. 3–53. Jewish college students in relation to their religion have been studied recently in a survey

that appeared in *The National Review* (October 8, 1963), pp. 279–302. The survey came to the radical conclusion that "students raised as Jews tend to abandon the tenets of their faith, regardless of what kind of college they attend." This must be qualified by the fact that Jewish allegiance is not necessarily measurable by the kind of theological commitment that the editors of *The National Review* had in mind. It is nonetheless true that the intensity of Jewish concern has been lessening in the college community.

5. See the best study of a large Jewish community, S. K. Bigman, *The Jewish Population of Greater Washington in 1956* (Washington, 1957), pp. 114–15. This finding is consonant with what was discovered about the religious behavior of the leadership, i.e., the most committed part, of Conservative synagogues: see E. Lehman, *National Survey on Synagogue Leadership* (New York, n.d.), pp. 13–15. The members of Conservative synagogue boards keep *kosher* at home as follows: 37% "strictly," 27% "partially," i.e., they buy *kosher* meat but have no separate dishes, and 36% are not *kosher* at all. This survey found that a majority of the synagogue leaders did not attend Sabbath services. No question was asked regarding personal observance of the Sabbath. The best discussion of the current estate of Jewish observance is still that in A. Gordon, *Jews in Transition* (Minneapolis, 1949), pp. 71–147.

6. There is considerable conflict of scholarly opinion as to the size of the Jewish community in the United States in the Revolutionary period. The estimate that has generally been given is 2,500 to 3,000, for 1790, the date of the first census of the United States. See figures in S. Wolf, *The American Jew as Patriot, Soldier and Citizen* (Philadelphia, 1895), p. 12, and J. R. Marcus, *Early American Jewry*, vol. 2, p. 393. This estimate has been scaled down in more recent writing. The lowest figure is that given by I. Rosenswaike in "An Estimate and Analysis of Jewish Population in the United States in 1790," *PAJHS*, vol. 49, p. 34. He concludes that "in the entire country there were possibly 1,300 to 1,500 Jews."

7. D. de Sola Poole, *An Old Faith in a New World* (New York, 1955), pp. 258–301.

8. H. B. Grinstein, *The Rise of the Jewish Community of New York* (Philadelphia, 1947), p. 334.

9. Poole, *op cit.*, p. 459. Until 1700 the Sephardim were twice as numerous as the Ashkenazim. In the course of the eighteenth century the Ashkenazim grew to outnumber Sephardim. See also M. Stern, "Function of Genealogy in American Jewish History," *Essays in American Jewish History* (Cincinnati, 1958), pp. 79–81, 85; and the Preface to the same author's *Americans of Jewish Descent* (Cincinnati, 1960). Stern's researches have shown that by 1840 the early Sephardim had disappeared almost entirely as a

separate group, either through marriage with Ashkenazim or because of a rate of intermarriage of at least 15%. In re the provenance of the clergy of Shearith Israel, see Poole, *op. cit.*, pp. 158–210.

10. Poole, *op. cit.*, pp. 437–38.
11. R. Learsi, *The Jews in America* (Cleveland, 1954), pp. 64–78.
12. For a summary of the statistical information in this area, see U.Z. Engelman, "Jewish Statistics and the United States Census of Religious Bodies (1850–1936)," *Jewish Social Studies*, 9 (1947), pp. 127–174.
13. Grinstein, *op. cit.*, pp. 243–51.
14. M. Weiner, *Abraham Geiger and Liberal Judaism* (Philadelphia, 1962), p. 18.
15. D. Philipson, *The Reform Movement in Judaism* (New York, 1931), pp. 335–36.
16. C. Reznikoff and U. Z. Engelman, *The Jews of Charleston* (Philadelphia, 1950), p. 128.
17. One famous incident was the serving of *trefah* food at the graduation banquet in 1883 for the first four graduates of the Hebrew Union College. See M. Davis, *The Emergence of Conservative Judaism* (Philadelphia, 1963), pp. 219–20. See also Philipson, *op. cit.*, p. 379.
18. Davis, *op. cit.*, pp. 317–18.
19. J. R. Rosenbloom, "The American Jewish Community," in B. Menkus, ed., *Meet the American Jew* (Nashville, 1963), p. 8.
20. See the most recent discussion in N. Glazer and D. P. Moynihan, *Beyond the Melting Pot* (New York, 1963), p. 139.
21. Davis, *op. cit.*, p. 322.
22. The Schechter-Schiff controversy over Zionism is described by C. Adler, *Jacob H. Schiff: His Life and Letters*, vol. 2 (New York, 1929), pp. 163–69. Schiff wrote Schechter on September 22, 1907: "The political doctrine brought forth and advocated by Zionism has nothing in common with the Jewish messianic hope." Earlier Schiff had maintained that Zionism was incompatible with American patriotism.
23. Rosenbloom, *op. cit.*, p. 10.
24. See my essay, "The Conservative Rabbinate: a Sociological Study," *Essays in Jewish Life and Thought*, J. L. Blau *et al.*, ed. (New York, 1959), p. 331.
25. This description of the role of the rabbi in America agrees with that presented by M. Sklare, *Conservative Judaism* (Glencoe, Illinois, 1955), pp. 159–95, and by J. E. Carlin and S. H. Mendlovitz, "The American Rabbi: A Religious Specialist Responds to the Loss of Authority," *The Jews* (Glencoe, Illinois, 1958), pp. 377–414.

Bibliographical Note

There is, as yet, no monograph on the history of Jewish religion in America. The best recent statement is a long essay by Moshe Davis in *The Jews: Their History, Culture and Religion*, Louis Finkelstein, ed., I, 3rd edition (New York, 1960), pp. 488–587. Information and insights on various aspects of the subject will be found in the one-volume works on the Jews in America; in that mine of information which is the quarterly, *Publications of The American Jewish Historical Society;* in the several collections of documents published by Jacob Marcus and by Salo W. Baron and Joseph L. Blau; and in an early volume by Max J. Kohler, *Phases in the History of Religious Liberty in America* (Baltimore, 1905). The monographic studies of the various individual cities, some of which are mentioned in the notes, are rich in material.

On the history of Reform Judaism in America, the following two volumes are the most useful: David Philipson, *The Reform Movement in Judaism* (New York, 1931), and Sylvan D. Schwartzman, *The Story of Reform Judaism* (New York, 1953). The key figure in the history of American Reform Judaism, Isaac Mayer Wise, has been the subject of a recent biography: *Rabbi in America*, by Israel Knox (Boston, 1957).

Conservative Judaism has recently been treated by Moshe Davis in *The Emergence of Conservative Judaism* (Philadelphia, 1963). There is as yet no history of the Conservative movement after 1902. The career of Solomon Schechter has been described in a biography, *Solomon Schechter*, by Norman Bentwich (Philadelphia, 1938). Though in this bibliographical note only historical studies are listed, an exception needs to be made for one book that does not fit that category, the volume in which the Reconstructionist position was announced and defined: Mordecai M. Kaplan, *Judaism As A Civilization* (New York, 1934).

The greatest dearth of published historical writing is in relation to Orthodox Judaism in America. Its history is yet to be written. It is revealing that Leo Jung in *Guardians of Our Heritage* (New York, 1958) does not discuss a single American figure. The ultra-Orthodox community in Brooklyn has recently been the subject of study. The best book is Solomon Poll, *The Hasidic Community of Williamsburg* (Glencoe, Illinois, 1962).

Jewish Education: Achievements, Problems and Needs

BY OSCAR I. JANOWSKY   (pp. 121–173)

Notes

1. I am indebted to a number of educators who made available important sources: to Dr. U. Z. Engelman for the manuscript of his latest (1962) study of enrollments; to Dr. J. Kaminetsky and I. Toubin for material on the Day Schools; to Professor A. I. Katsh and J. Lapson for information on Hebrew courses in high schools and colleges; to Dr. I. Margolis for the manuscript of his study of teachers colleges; and to Dr. G. Pollack for the manuscript of his study of Day School graduates. I am especially grateful to Dr. Louis L. Kaplan and to L.L. Ruffman who read the entire chapter and made valuable suggestions.

2. The talmudic source is in the tractate Baba Batra 21a. For differing views on the development of school systems in ancient Palestine, see N. Drazin, *History of Jewish Education from 515 B.C.E. to 220 C.E.* (Baltimore, 1940), ch. III, and N. Morris, *Toledot ha-Hinuk Shel Am Yisrael,* vol. I (Tel Aviv, 1960), chs. II–III. For education in biblical times, see M. Radin, *The Life of the People in Biblical Times* (Philadelphia, 1929), ch. V.

3. See S. W. Baron, *The Jewish Community,* vol. II (Philadelphia, 1942), pp. 169–200 for an account of Jewish education up to the eighteenth century. Israel Abrahams, *Jewish Life in the Middle Ages* (Philadelphia, 1896), chs. XIX–XX, contains graphic descriptions of the medieval schools and the scope of education they provided.

4. See Z. Scharfstein, *Toledot ha-Hinuk be-Israel be-Dorot ha-Ahronim,* second revised edition, 3 vols. (Jerusalem, 1960–1962), especially vol. I, ch. XI on Russia and Poland, and pp. 389–410 on the *Heder Metukan;* vol. II, pp. 28–30, 183–88 ff. on the development of the Yiddish school. For general background, see S. M. Dubnow, *History of the Jews in Russia and Poland,* 3 vols. (Philadelphia, 1916–1920).

5. Philadelphia, 1955–56, 3 vols. See I, pp. 12–13; II, pp. 74, 76, 111, 283–284; III, p. 9.

6. See Marcus, *op. cit.,* II, p. 74. See also I, pp. 277–78, 281 ff. For Jewish education prior to the 1880's, see H. B. Grinstein, *The Rise of the Jewish Community of New York* (Philadelphia, 1945), ch. XII; A. M. Dushkin, *Jewish Education in New York City* (New York, 1918), part I, pp. 39–62; M. Davis, *Yahadut Amerika be-hitpathutah* (New York, 1951), pp. 101–106; E. Wolf and M. Whiteman, *The History of the Jews of Philadelphia from*

Colonial Times to the Age of Jackson (Philadelphia, 1957), pp. 141–142, 245, 255; U. Z. Engelman, "Jewish Education in Charleston, S. C., During the Eighteenth and Nineteenth Centuries," *PAJHS,* XLII, 1 (September, 1952), pp. 43–70; J. I. Hartstein, "The Polonies Talmud Torah of New York," *ibid.,* XXXIV (1937), pp. 123–141.

7. For a detailed account of Jewish schools in New York City from 1881 to 1917, see Dushkin, *op. cit.,* part I, chapter III.

8. "Report of Committee on Jewish Education of the *Kehillah* (Jewish Community) . . . ," *Jewish Education,* XX, 3 (Summer, 1949), pp. 113–116.

9. Dushkin, *op. cit.,* part II, chs. I–IX; see also summaries by S. Benderley and A. M. Dushkin in *The Jewish Communal Register of New York City, 1917–1918* (New York, 1918), pp. 349–370 ff.

10. H. Bricker and S. Marcson, *Jewish Education in Chicago* (Jewish Charities of Chicago, 1940), pp. 6, 16 (mimeographed); U. Z. Engelman, "Jewish Education in Facts and Figures," *Jewish Education Register and Directory* (New York, AAJE, 1951), p. 27.

11. For the work of the Bureau and the influence of Benderley, see *The Jewish Communal Register,* pp. 1143–46; Dushkin, *op. cit.,* part I, ch. IV; and *Jewish Education,* 20, 3 (Summer, 1949).

12. See J. H. Greenstone, "Jewish Education in the United States," *AJYB,* 5675 (New York, 1914), p. 118; A. M. Dushkin and U. Z. Engelman, *Jewish Education in the United States* (New York, AAJE, 1959), p. 44; Engelman, "Jewish Education," *AJYB, 1963,* vol. 64, p. 152. See also I. S. Chipkin, *Twenty-five Years of Jewish Education in the United States* (New York, 1937), pp. 34–37. The figures include only the proportion of enrolled children during a given year. The National Study estimated that over 80 percent of the Jewish child population received some Jewish instruction during the elementary school years.

13. This table presents data gathered in surveys before World War II and in annual canvasses by the Jewish Education Committee of New York since the 1950's. The information is generally more reliable than that for the country as a whole. Yet comparative analysis presents difficulties. For example, the first three items relate only to the five boroughs of New York, whereas the figures for the 1950's and early 1960's include the counties of Westchester, Nassau and Suffolk, in which large numbers of New York Jews have settled, and which are closely linked to the central city. The omission of the counties would present a distorted picture of Jewish education in New York. On the other hand, New York Jews have also settled in considerable numbers in other suburban areas which are not included. Our purpose, however, is to examine trends, and this can be done despite the difficulties.

14. See *JEC Bulletin* (October, 1959), p. 9.

15. See *Jewish Education Register and Directory, 1951*, p. 27. For New York City, see *Jewish Education* (Summer, 1949), p. 115; Dushkin, *op. cit.* p. 182.

16. Girls exceeded the number of boys in Sunday Schools and in Institutional Schools; they composed over 28 percent of the enrollments of Congregational Schools and over 12 percent of the *Talmud Torahs*. See "Report of Committee on Jewish Education of the *Kehillah*," *Jewish Education* (Summer, 1949), p. 115.

17. Engelman, "Jewish Education," *AJYB*, 1963, p. 151; *Jewish Education in the United States*, p. 51.

18. Dushkin, *op. cit.*, p. 168. For conditions in the 1950's, see *Survey of Jewish Education in Greater New York, 1951–1952, Quantitative Studies* (JEC, 1957), pp. 117–24 ff; *Jewish Education in the United States*, pp. 92–94.

19. See *ibid., pp.* 52–54; *Jewish Education Register and Directory, 1951*, p. 15; S. Dinin, "Democracy and Jewish Education," *The Reconstructionist* (January 29, 1954), pp. 13–14; L. L. Ruffman, "Trends and Recent Developments in the Field of Jewish Education," *JSSQ* (Fall, 1952), p. 32; Engelman, "Jewish Education," *AJYB*, 1963, p. 154.

20. The schools of the International Workers Order were more concerned with communist-line propaganda than with Jewish education. For detailed descriptions of the Yiddish schools, see A. Penn, *Yidishkeit in Amerike* (New York, 1958), part II, chs. 30–33; *Shul Almanakh* (Philadelphia, 1935), pp. 27–164; L. Lehrer, "The Jewish Secular School," *Jewish Education*, VIII, 1 (1936), pp. 33–42.

21. See *Jewish Communal Register and Directory, 1951*, p. 28; *Survey of Jewish Education in Greater New York, 1951–1952*, pp. 35–36; *JEC Bulletin* (September, 1962), pp. 6–11; *Jewish Education in the United States*, pp. 57–58; I. B. Berkson, *1936 Jewish Education Study: Summary and Conclusions* (New York, May 31, 1936), section IV, pp. 8–10 (unpublished); Engelman "Jewish Education," *AJYB*, 1963, p. 160; Engelman, *Jewish Education* (1962), p. 14 (ms).

22. See *Jewish Education Register and Directory*, p. 35; *Jewish Education in the United States*, pp. 47–48.

23. Engelman's figure, however, included Sunday Schools which provided one additional week-day session. See Engelman, "Jewish Education" *AJYB*, 1963, p. 151; *Jewish Education in the United States*, p. 45; *Jewish Education Register and Directory, 1951*, p. 27.

24. See *Jewish Education Register and Directory, 1951*, p. 13; *Jewish Education in the United States*, pp. 60 f.

25. See J. Kaminetsky, *Torah Umesorah, Dynamic Force for Torah*, unpublished.

26. See United Synagogue Commission on Jewish Education, *Objectives and Standards for Congregational Schools,* revised edition (New York, 1958), p. 22.
27. About 600,000 children attend 1,800 private preparatory schools (*New York Times,* April 9, 1963) and over four million attend parochial schools.
28. G. Pollak, *The Graduates of the Jewish Day Schools: A Followup Study* (June, 1961), unpublished. For other aspects of the Day School, see U. Z. Engelman, *All-Day Schools in the United States, 1948–1949* (New York, AAJE, 1949); J. Kaminetsky, "Evaluating the Program and Effectiveness of the All-Day Jewish School," *Jewish Education,* XXVII, 2 (Winter, 1956–57), pp. 39–49; I. Toubin, *The Relationship of the Jewish Welfare Fund to the Jewish Day School: An Informal Survey* (New York, AAJE, November 1961); I. Toubin and U. Z. Engelman, *Summary and Interpretation of the Study on Financing Jewish Day Schools* (New York, AAJE, November, 1962); L. Rosenfeld, *The New York Story*—Memorandum on Day-School Movement in New York City (New York, JEC, November, 1962); *Survey of Jewish Education in Greater New York, Qualitative Studies,* pp. 50–58; *Jewish Education in the United States,* pp. 46–49, 57–59, 62–64, 206–212; Engelman, "Jewish Education," *AJYB,* 1963, pp. 151, 160–164. See also A. Eisenberg and L. L. Ruffman, *A Hard Look at the JEC on the Eve of Its Twenty-fifth Anniversary* (New York, 1963), mimeographed.
29. On the teachers colleges, see the survey by L. Hurwich, *Bate Midrash le-Morim* (New York, AAJE, 1949), and "Hebrew Teachers' Colleges in the United States: Digest of Survey," *Jewish Education,* XXII, 1–2 (1950–51), 73–96; *Our Teacher* (AAJE, Spring, 1958). A recent doctoral dissertation by I. Margolis, *An Abstract of a History of Teacher-Training Schools . . . in the United States in the First Half of the Twentieth Century* (New York: N.Y. University, 1960), unpublished, contains a detailed description of six schools established during 1897–1924. See also Z. Scharfstein, ed., *Sefer ha-Yobel shel Agudat ha-Morim ha-Ibrim . . .* (New York, 1944), pp. 249–313; L. L. Honor, "Comparative Study of Hebrew Teacher Training Schools in the United States," *Jewish Education,* VII, 2 (1935), 71–90; S. Dinin, "Twenty-five Years of Teacher Training," *ibid.,* VII, 1 (1935), 25–33.
30. National Board of License, *Requirements and Procedures,* 1963; *idem, Criteria for the Evaluation of Hebrew Teachers Colleges,* n.d.
31. See AAJE, *A Model Code of Practice* (New York, 1963). For an estimate of the situation in 1952, see report of survey by M. M.

Edelstein, "The Status of the Jewish Education Profession," *Jewish Education*, XXIV, 1 (Spring, 1953), 23–38, 63.

32. This Study was sponsored and financed by the American Association for Jewish Education. To insure full independence, it was placed under the auspices of a Commission for the Study of Jewish Education in the United States, of which Oscar I. Janowsky was chairman. The latter and Uriah Z. Engelman were named professional directors of the Study. The Study was planned as a three-year project. A Prospectus outlining the point-of-view and scope of the Study was prepared by Janowsky; Engelman and he drafted a volume of research instruments; a 10 percent random sample of communities was designated for study; and pilot communities were studied in depth.

The Study encountered difficulties. The promised funds could not be raised, adequate staff could not be employed, and the work began to lag. For these and other reasons, Janowsky resigned in 1955, but he was induced to continue as chairman of the Commission. In 1957, he felt impelled to withdraw completely from the Study, and he declined to write the final report. Milton R. Konvitz succeeded to the chairmanship of the Commission; Engelman served as sole director after 1955; and Alexander M. Dushkin was invited to cooperate with Engelman in the interpretation of the data and the writing of the Report. Only volume I of the Report was published—*Jewish Education in the United States*, by A. M. Dushkin and U. Z. Engelman.

33. The standard work on the bureaus is A. P. Gannes, *Central Community Agencies for Jewish Education* (Philadelphia, 1954); see especially ch. III. *Jewish Education in the United States*, pp. 157–169, which contains a good summary of the work of the bureaus. O. I. Janowsky, *The Cleveland Bureau of Jewish Education, 1924–1953*, unpublished, is a study in depth of one bureau based on the original sources.

34. See, for example, *Curriculum Outline for the Congregational School*, revised edition (New York, 1959), prepared by L. L. Ruffman and A. Segal for the United Synagogue Commission on Jewish Education. See also J. B. Stern in *Sheviley Hahinuch*, XXII, 1 (Fall, 1961), 18–22.

35. See *Jewish Education in the United States*, pp. 70–72 ff; 84, 87–88.

36. See CJFWF, *Yearbook, Jewish Social Work: Jewish Education* (New York, 1948), p. E-4; *idem, Jewish Communal Services: Programs and Finances* (New York, March, 1963), Table 6. See also U. Z. Engelman, *Federation Allocations for Jewish Education, 1941–1959* (New York, AAJE, 1962); H. L. Lurie, *A Heritage Affirmed: The Jewish Federation Movement in America* (Philadelphia, 1961), pp. 73–75, 100–101, 309–312, 364–365.

37. Courses in Yiddish language and literature have likewise been introduced in a number of colleges and universities.

38. On Hebrew in colleges and universities, see A. I. Katsh, "Current Trends in the Study of Hebrew in Colleges and Universities," *The Modern Language Journal*, XLIV, 2 (February, 1960), 64–67; *idem, Hebrew Language, Literature and Culture in American Institutions of Higher Learning* (New York, 1950); *idem, Hebrew Culture in American Secular Institutions of Higher Learning* (New York, 1947); J. Lapson, *Hebrew in Colleges and Universities* (New York, 1958). On Hebrew studies in public high schools, see J. Lapson, "A Decade of Hebrew in the High Schools of New York City," *Jewish Education*, XIII, 1 (1941), 34–45; *idem*, "New Challenges Facing Hebrew in the Public Schools," *ibid.*, XXVII, 1 (1956), 38–42, 56. Recent enrollment figures secured from Judah Lapson, director of Hebrew Culture Council of JEC of New York, and from Board of Education, New York City.

39. This section is a revision and amplification of several articles which appeared in *The National Jewish Monthly*.

40. E. Lehman, *National Survey on Synagogue Leadership* (New York, 1953) (mimeographed), pp. 6–7.

41. S. Dinin, "Democracy and Jewish Education," *The Reconstructionist* (January 29, 1954), p. 19; *Jewish Education in the United States*, p. 66. It should be noted that we are speaking of the "average child." The best schools retain a larger proportion of their pupils for more than three years.

42. See, for example, O. I. Janowsky and U. Z. Engelman, *The Study of Jewish Education in Cleveland* (New York, 1953), pp. 41–42 ff., 68–70 ff., 108–112, unpublished; U. Z. Engelman, *The Jewish Educational System of Rochester* (New York, 1955), p. 20, unpublished. See also, *idem, The Study of Jewish Education in Greater Los Angeles, 1956*, part I (New York, 1958), pp. 36 ff., 44–45 ff., unpublished; *Jewish Education in the United States*, pp. 66–67.

43. *Ibid.*, p. 67.

44. *Ibid.*, p. 96. See also O. I. Janowsky and U. Z. Engelman, *The Study of Jewish Education in Savannah, Ga.* (New York, 1955), pp. 1–2; U. Z. Engelman, *Partial Draft of Study of Jewish Education in Akron, Ohio* (New York, 1955), p. 1; *idem, The Jewish Educational System of Rochester*, Table I; *idem, The Study . . . in Greater Los Angeles*, pp. 30 ff. (all unpublished).

45. See U. Z. Engelman, *The Study of Jewish Education in Detroit, 1956: The United Hebrew Schools* (New York, 1957), unpublished; L. Crohn, "Detroit's Communal School System," *The Reconstructionist* (November 27, 1959), pp. 22–27.

46. See *Survey of Jewish Education in Greater New York, Quantitative Studies* (New York, 1957), pp. 61–62, 64, 66.

47. *Ibid., Qualitative Studies*, pp. 22–38. See also *Jewish Education in the United States*, pp. 178–195.
48. However, these young people, and apparently the graduates of the Day Schools too, do not subscribe to the *Hadoar*, the one Hebrew weekly in America. A partial survey in 1950–1951, chaired by the present writer and conducted by Engelman, found that the journal was then issued in "over 8,000" copies which were read by perhaps 20,000 persons. Today, the *Hadoar* prints 9,200 per issue and the estimated number of readers is still about 20,000. The average age of the *Hadoar* following is said to be 55. For a realistic appraisal of the effects of the teaching of Hebrew, see S. Dinin, "The Future of Hebrew in America," *Congress Bi-Weekly* (October, 1961), pp. 7–10.
49. For a penetrating analysis of the necessary elements of a common Jewish school program, see I. B. Berkson, "Jewish Education—Achievements and Needs," in O. I. Janowsky, *The American Jew: A Composite Portrait* (New York, 1942), pp. 76–91.
50. Attention has been focussed upon the basic economic problem, but other measures are, of course, necessary. Several concrete and realistic proposals were presented by Louis L. Kaplan in *Major Issues Facing Jewish Communities: A Symposium Prepared for the General Assembly of CJFWF*, November 6–10, 1963.
51. See *The JEC School Accreditation Program*, June 1963; L. L. Ruffman, "School Accreditation in Greater New York," *Jewish Education*, XXXII, 2 (Winter, 1962), pp. 85–95.
52. *Jewish Education in the United States*, p. 85.
53. See A. Eisenberg and L. L. Ruffman, *A Hard Look At the JEC*, pp. 51 f.

Bibliographical Note

The most comprehensive works on the contemporary situation in Jewish education are the reports of two surveys: A. M. Dushkin and U. Z. Engelman, *Jewish Education in the United States* (New York, AAJE, 1959) (Report of National Study); and *Survey of Jewish Education in Greater New York, 1951–1952*, 2 vols. (New York, JEC, 1957–1959). The latter survey was conducted by I. S. Chipkin and the report was edited by L. L. Ruffman. I. B. Berkson, "Jewish Education—Achievements and Needs," in O. I. Janowsky, ed., *The American Jew* (New York, 1942), ch. III, is an incisive account of conditions and needs in the early 1940's.

A well-documented survey of Jewish education in the United States is available in Z. Scharfstein, *Toledot ha-Hinuk be-Israel be-Dorot ha-Ahronim*, vol. 3, second revised edition (Jerusalem 1962), pp. 9–235. But their is no history of the subject in English. Brief summaries are available in I. S. Chipkin, *Twenty-five Years of Jewish Education in the United States* (New York, 1937)—reprint from *AJYB*, vol. 38 (Philadelphia, 1936), pp. 27–116; by the same author, *Jewish Education in the United States at the Mid-Century* (New York, 1951); and L. L. Honor, "Jewish Education in the United States" in *The Jewish People: Past and Present*, vol. II (New York, 1948), pp. 151–171.

For Jewish education in New York City during earlier periods, two studies are recommended: H. B. Grinstein, *The Rise of the Jewish Community of New York, 1654–1860* (Philadelphia, 1945), ch. XII; and A. M. Dushkin, *Jewish Education in New York City* (New York, 1918).

Special subjects in Jewish education have been treated in a number of books. *Curriculum Outline for the Congregational School*, rev. ed. (New York, 1959), prepared by L. L. Ruffman with the assistance of A. Segal, is the best study of the subject. The standard work on Bureaus of Jewish education is A. P. Gannes, *Central Community Agencies for Jewish Education* (Philadelphia, 1954). *Readings in Jewish Educational Philosophy*, compiled and edited by J. Pilch (New York, American Association for Jewish Education, n.d.), is a useful collection of essays by leading figures in Jewish education. The study of Hebrew in American colleges and universities is surveyed in A. I. Katsh, *Hebrew Language, Literature and Culture in American Institutions of Higher Learning* (New York, 1950), and in J. Lapson, ed., *Hebrew in Colleges and Universities* (New York, 1958).

A series of Bulletins, prepared by U. Z. Engelman for the American Association for Jewish Education, furnish invaluable statistical information on Federation allocations for Jewish education, budgeting and financing of central agencies for Jewish education, tuition fees and other matters.

The memoirs of Jewish educators shed light on the problems and struggles in Jewish education. One of the best is L. Hurwich, *Zikronot Mehanek Ivri*, 3 vols. (Boston: Bureau of Jewish Education, 1960).

The Journal *Jewish Education* is a storehouse of material on every aspect of Jewish education, and recent issues of the *American Jewish Year Book* contain annual summaries of current developments.

Development and Decline of Hebrew Letters   (pp. 175–191)

BY EISIG SILBERSCHLAG

Notes

1. See Eisig Silberschlag, "Hebrew Literature in America: Record and Interpretation," *Jewish Quarterly Review*, XLV (April, 1955), 415.

2. M. Weinberger, *ha-Yehudim we-ha-Yahadut be-New York* (New York, 1887), p. 31.

3. A. Malachi, *Iggrot Soferim* (New York, 1931), p. 133.

4. From *Minhat Yehudah*, translated into English by F. DeSola Mendes, in B. Drachman, "Neo-Hebraic Literature in America," *Proceedings of the Seventh Biennial Convention of the Jewish Theological Seminary Association* (New York, 1900), p. 106.

5. M. Weinberger, *op. cit.*, p. 5. The reference to tanners is an obvious allusion to the talmudic saying in *Kiddushin* 82b: The world cannot exist without a perfume-maker and without a tanner. Happy is he whose craft is that of a perfume-maker, and woe to him who is a tanner by trade.

6. *Ibid.*, p. 36.

7. H. Malachovsky, *Ketabim ba-Sefer* (Philadelphia, 1902), p. 69.

8. B. Drachman, *op. cit.*, pp. 60–61.

9. Benjamin II, *Three Years in America*, I (Philadelphia, 1956), p. 88.

10. Malachovsky, *op. cit.*, p. 89.

11. G. Rosenzweig, *Masseket America Min Talmud Yankai* (New York, 1907), p. 13.

12. E. Silberschlag, "Naphtali Herz Imber," *Judaism*, 2 (Spring, 1956), p. 158.

13. B. N. Silkiner, *Shirim* (New York, 1927), p. 99.

14. E. Lisitzky, *Ele Toledot Adam* (Jerusalem, 1950), p. 5. Translated from the Hebrew by Moshe Kohn and Jacob Sloan under the title *In the Grip of Cross-Currents* (New York, 1959), unpaginated after introduction.

15. S. Halkin, *'Arai we-Keba* (New York, 1942), p. 43.

16. See *Sefer ha-Shanah il-Yehude America*, edited by M. Ribalow, X–XI (New York, 1949), pp. 249–256.

17. For a recent and highly encomiastic evaluation of Noah's personality, see Robert Gordis, "Mordecai Manuel Noah: A Centenary Evaluation," *PAJHS*, XLI (September, 1951), 1–26.

18. The Hagrite is a *double entendre:* in Hebrew it alludes to a root, the meaning of which is emigrate. In the Bible, the name Hagri, the Hagrite, occurs almost exclusively in the Book of Chronicles. He is mentioned among officials who "were the rulers of the substance which was King David's" (I Chronicles 27.31). It is no mere coincidence that the name Yehiel, son of Hachmoni, occurs in the same chapter, in verse 32. And Hachmoni alludes to wisdom. Thus the title of Halkin's first novel—*Yehiel the Hagrite*— is rich in theological and secular connotations.

19. See R. Wallenrod's collection of stories, *ba-Deyotah ha-Shelishit* (On the Third Floor) (New York, 1937), p. 130.

Bibliographical Note

There is no monograph on the history of Hebrew literature in America, nor even an anthology of American Hebrew prose. An anthology of Hebrew poetry in America, edited by M. Ribalow, was published in 1938. Anthologies of Hebrew literature, such as Hayyim Toren's *Sifrutenu ha-Yafah* (Our Belles-Lettres) in three volumes (Jerusalem, 1953–54), contain selections of American Hebrew writers in prose and poetry. See vol. I, pp. 176–189, 221–227; II, 209–232; III, 168–225, 271–294, 309–343.

Few books deal with the subject. Abraham Epstein's two-volume work in Hebrew, *Soferim 'Ibrim ba-America* (Hebrew Writers in America) which appeared in 1952, is a sensitive evaluation of the significant Hebrew writers in America from the end of the nineteenth century to the present day. Also useful is *Toledot ha-Sifrut ha-'Ibrit be-Dorenu* (The History of Hebrew Literature in Our Generation) (Tel Aviv, 1954), by Aaron Ben Or who gives an insight into Hebrew letters in America within the context of contemporary Hebrew literature; see vol. I, pp. 99–154, 311–316; II, 157–170, 276–282, 367–370, 383–388. The bibliographical articles of A. R. Malachi, scattered in books and periodicals, are very useful.

In English the dearth of books and articles on the subject is even greater than in Hebrew. Reuben Wallenrod's *The Literature of Modern Israel* (New York, 1956), devotes a chapter to American-Hebrew writers. Meyer Waxman devotes considerable space to Hebrew literature in America in *A History of Jewish Literature* (New York-London, 1960). See vol. IV, part two, pp. 1048–1191, 1251–1305; V, 187–272.

Guidance to the subject may be found in Jacob Kabakoff's "Hebrew Culture and Creativity in America," *Judaism*, 3 (1954), 391–407, and Eisig Silberschlag's "Hebrew Literature in America: Record and Interpretation," *Jewish Quarterly Review*, XLV (1955), 413–433.

Yiddish Literature (pp. 193–209)

BY HASYE COOPERMAN

Notes

1. See, for example, E. Wolf and M. Whiteman, *The History of the Jews of Philadelphia from Colonial Times to the Age of Jackson* (Philadelphia, 1957), pp. 7, 39, 42, and n. 31, p. 393.
2. For the origins of the Yiddish press, see M. Soltes, *The Yiddish Press, An Americanizing Agency*, 2nd edition (New York, 1950);

Y. Shatzky, ed., *Zamlbukh tzu der Geshikhte fun der Yiddisher Presse in Amerike* (New York, 1934); Y. Glatshtein, S. Niger, H. Rogoff, eds., *Finf un-zibetzik Yur Yiddishe Presse in Amerike* (New York, 1945).

3. New York, 1877, 36 pp.
4. Other dailies, no longer in existence, were *Der Teglekher Yiddisher Kurier*, established in Chicago in 1877; *Die Yiddishe Velt*, launched in Cleveland in 1908; and *Die Yiddishe Velt*, established in Philadelphia in 1914.
5. See N. B. Minkoff, *Pionern fun der Yiddisher Poezye in Amerike: Die Sotzyale Poetn*, 3 vols. (New York, 1956).
6. L. Wiener, *The History of Yiddish Literature in the Nineteenth Century* (New York, 1899), p. 130.
7. See I. Goldberg, *Great Yiddish Poetry* (Girard, Kansas, 1923), pp. 24–27.
8. See H. Cooperman, "The Poet of the Sweatshop," *The Jewish News*, April 20, 1962.
9. *Poems of Yehoash*, selected and translated by I. Goldstick (London, Canada, 1952), pp. 24, 49.
10. A. A. Roback, "Yiddish Literature, 1933–61," *The Institute Anniversary Volume* (New York, 1962), p. 242.

Bibliographical Note

There is a rich bibliography in the Yiddish language on Yiddish literature in the United States. Especially noteworthy is the three-volume work on the social poets by N. B. Minkoff, *Pionern Fun der Yiddisher Poezye in Amerike* (New York, 1956), which contains individual biographies, analyses of each poet's contribution, and a colorful depiction of the times. Two articles in the *Zukunft* by the same author deal with the early writings in the United States, and with trends and currents: "Di Unhoibn Fun der Yiddisher Literatur in Amerike," April, 1954; and "Tendentsn Un Shtremungen in der Yiddisher Literatur in Amerike," December, 1954. S. Niger's, *Dertzeiler un Romanisten* (New York, 1946), and his *Bletter Geshikhte Fun der Yiddisher Literatur* (New York, 1959), are highly recommended. E. Shulman's *Geshikhte fun der Yiddisher Literatur in Amerike, 1870–1900* (New York, 1943), covers the early period.

The English reader will find invaluable M. Soltes' *The Yiddish Press, an Americanizing Agency*, second edition (New York, 1950), and as a supplement, A. A. Roback's "The Epic of Yiddish Periodicals," *Jewish Forum* (Chicago, 1959). L. Wiener's *The History of the Yiddish Literature of the 19th Century* (New York, 1899), is limited and dated but still useful, especially the anthology. Chapters on Yiddish literature are included in vol. IV of M. Waxman's *A*

History of Jewish Literature from the Close of the Bible to Our Own Days (New York, 1930–1941), and in *The Jewish People Past and Present,* vol. III (New York, 1952). A. A. Roback's *The Story of Yiddish Literature* (New York, 1940), devotes attention especially to recent writing.

Good translations from the Yiddish are available in I. Howe and E. Greenberg, *A Treasury of Yiddish Stories* (New York, 1954), and in J. Leftwich, *The Golden Peacock, an Anthology of Yiddish Poetry* (London, 1939, revised edition New York and London, 1961).

Jewish Awareness in American Literature (pp. 211–233)

BY MARIE SYRKIN

Bibliographical Note

The bibliography for the subject under discussion is essentially contained in the article itself. The most significant books directly relevant to the theme have been named in the body of the essay. As far as general works of a critical nature are concerned, few are available though there are many scattered articles by various writers in various periodicals. For further reference the reader may find the following books useful: *The American Jew,* a collection of essays edited by Oscar Janowsky (New York, 1942), particularly the essay on "The Cultural Scene," by Marie Syrkin which discusses in detail American Jewish writing till 1940; *The Jew in the American Novel* by Leslie A. Fiedler, the noted critic (pamphlet published by the Herzl Institute, 1959), which provides a stimulating appraisal of some American Jewish novelists; *A Treasury of Jewish Poetry,* edited by Nathan and Marynn Ausubel (New York, 1957), an anthology of Jewish poets in English translation.

Art and the American Jew (pp. 235–244)

BY ALFRED WERNER

Notes

1. A typical example is the Wilshire Boulevard Temple in Los Angeles.
2. Outstanding American Jewish architects who designed synagogues include, in alphabetical order: Sigmund Braverman, Sidney Eisenshtadt, Percival Goodman, Moses Halpern, Fritz Nathan and Louis Gordon Redstone. Non-Jewish architects of American

synagogues include Philip Johnson and the late Frank Lloyd Wright.

3. American craftsmen who have produced ritual objects include Calvin Albert, Judith Brown, Earl Krenzin, Victor Ries, Herman Roth, Ludwig Y. Wolpert, and the late Ilya Schor (*hanukkah menoroth, kiddush* cups, spice boxes, *mezzuzzoth*); Evelyn Applebaum, Belle Quitman, Amalie Rothschild; Louise D. Kayser, Perli Pelzig and Robert Sowers (stained glass windows). Other artists and craftsmen who have lent their talents to the decoration of synagogues include Max Finkelstein, Alfred Van Loen, Robert Motherwell, Bernard Rosenthal, Sigmund Rothschild and Elbert Weinberg. Modern Jewish ritual art has been exhibited repeatedly at New York's Jewish Museum.

4. The discussion of the concept "Jewish art" is beyond the scope of this brief article. For a detailed treatment of this subject, see Cecil Roth's introduction to *Jewish Art* (New York, 1961). See also, "Jewish Art as a Minority Problem" by Heinrich Strauss, *The Jewish Journal of Sociology,* London (November, 1960), and "The 'Second Commandment' and the Image in Judaism" by Joseph Gutmann, *Hebrew Union College Annual,* XXII (1961).

Bibliographical Note

The literature on Jewish art and the contribution of Jews to the space arts is extensive, but it has appeared mainly in scholarly magazines of limited circulation, a good deal of it in languages other than English. All major books and articles published prior to 1945 can be found in the extensive bibliography of *A History of Jewish Art* by Franz Landsberger (Cincinnati, 1946). In this book several American Jewish artists, all born before 1900, are discussed—the painters Max Weber, Bernard Karfiol, Samuel Halpert, Abraham Walkowitz, Maurice Sterne, Leon Kroll, and A. Raymond Katz, and the sculptors Jacob Epstein, Jo Davidson and William Zorach. Only one American architect is mentioned: Dankmar Adler (1844–1900), and only one American synagogue, Anshe Ma'ariv of Chicago, built by Adler in collaboration with his non-Jewish colleague, Louis Sullivan. A much larger number of American Jewish artists are treated in *Jewish Artists of the 19th and 20th Centuries* by Karl Schwarz (Tel Aviv, 1949), and in *Jewish Sculptors* (1954) by the same author. In the latter work, contributions to American synagogue art by American sculptors are illustrated: Milton Horn's "Cherub" (West Suburban Temple, River Forest, Illinois); Herbert Ferber's "Burning Bush" (B'nai Israel Synagogue, Millburn, New Jersey); and Ibram Lassaw's "Pillar of Fire" (Temple Beth-El, Springfield, Massachusetts).

A good up-to-date account of contributions by Jews to American art is given by Edouard Roditi, "The Jewish Artist in the Modern World," in *Jewish Art,* edited by Cecil Roth (New York, 1961). The same volume contains "The Architecture of the Contemporary Synagogue," by Edward Jamilly, which illustrates the aforementioned Anshe Ma'ariv synagogue, as well as Erich Mendelsohn's Park Synagogue of Cleveland, Ohio, Percival Goodman's B'nai Israel Temple of Millburn, New Jersey, and his Beth-El Temple of Springfield, Massachusetts, and the building of the Hillel Foundation of Evanston, Illinois, designed by Harrison and Abramovitz. Highly recommended is *Synagogue Architecture in the United States* by Rachel Wischnitzer (Philadelphia, 1955). A large number of important American synagogues and major works of ritual art are also described and illustrated in *A Jewish Tourist's Guide to the U.S.,* by Bernard Postal and Lionel Koppman (Philadelphia, 1954). No book on modern ritual art since the end of the last war is as yet available. *Jewish Ceremonial Art* by Stephen S. Kayser and Guido Schoenberger (Philadelphia, 1955), is a valuable guide to the treasures of the Jewish Museum in New York, but it does not deal with present-day accomplishments beyond stating, in a brief sentence, that "an attempt is being made to reshape the Jewish ceremonial objects in the artistic terms of our own time." Modern Jewish ritual art is, however, displayed both in the Jewish Museum, and in the as-yet-small museum established on the campus of the Hebrew Union College–Jewish Institute of Religion in Cincinnati, Ohio.

Music and the Jew   (pp. 245–251)

BY JUDITH K. EISENSTEIN

Notes

1. However, the vernacular and songs brought by Sephardi immigrants during the twentieth century have not been entirely abandoned.
2. The purely oral tradition of the Shearith Israel Congregation of New York has been amended by a number of nineteenth century melodies composed by David Aaron de Sola of the Bevis Marks Synagogue, London, and others. Choral arrangements have also been added, principally from the volume *Sephardi Melodies,* originally assembled by Aguilar and de Sola in 1857, and re-issued with additional material edited by E. R. Jessurun in 1931. Choral arrangements also occur in *Kol Shearith Israel* by O. Guttmann and L. M. Kramer (New York, 1942).
3. The music of Sulzer, Lewandowski and others has become practically traditional in Ashkenazi services of all denominations.

4. See, for example, O. Loeb, *Israelitische Tempel Gesänge und Hymnen für Fest Tage, mit Deutschen und Englischen Text* (Chicago, 1870).

5. A number of English hymnals preceded the first edition of the *Union Hymnal,* edited by Alois Kaiser (Cincinnati, Union of American Hebrew Congregations, 1897).

6. A number of famous cantors either migrated to or visited the United States before World War I. Each cantor sang his own improvisations based on the traditional chant. Frequently the chant was heavily overlaid with operatic and martial tunes.

7. See S. Schack–E. S. Cohen, *Yiddish Folk Songs* (New York, 1927); A. Shomer–Rothenberg, *Songs Heard in Palestine* (New York, 1928); Th. Goldfarb, *Echoes of Palestine* (New York, 1929).

8. Among the choral groups were The Poale Zion Singing Society, Hadassah Choral Union, Freiheit Singing Society, Workmen's Circle Chorus and Orchestra. The conductors were Platon Brounoff, Abraham W. Binder, Leo Low, Lazar Weiner.

9. Specifically for schools or for young children were: I. and S. E. Goldfarb, *The Jewish Songster,* in two volumes (New York, 1925, 1928); J. K. Eisenstein, *Gateway to Jewish Song* (New York, 1939), and others. For community singing by all ages: H. Coopersmith, *Songs of My People* (Chicago, 1937) and *Songs of Zion* (New York, 1942); M. Nathanson, *Manginoth Shirenu* (New York, 1939), and others.

10. A. Z. Idelsohn, *Jewish Music in Its Historical Development* (New York, 1929). Other musicologists were Solomon Rozowsky, Lazare Saminsky, Alfred Sendrey, Eric Werner, Joseph Yasser. A book of essays by L. Saminsky appeared under the title *Music of the Ghetto and the Bible* (New York, 1934). Curt Sachs, in his *History of Musical Instruments* (New York, 1940), included a substantial chapter on the instruments of ancient Israel.

11. Among these were Joseph and Isidore Achron, Moshe Rudinow, Jacob Weinberg. Others of the group migrated to Palestine. Some stayed in Russia, and continued to function as Soviet composers.

12. Mailamm (*Makhon Eretz Israeli le-Madaey ha-Musika*) combined the forces of musicians and laymen. It raised money to support the research of Solomon Rosowsky in Palestine, and it sponsored concerts in New York. Ha-Shofar sponsored concerts in Detroit. The Jewish Music Forum was formed in 1940 after the closing of Mailamm, and consisted mainly of musicians at the beginning. At its meetings new music was read or auditioned and papers on various aspects of Jewish music were presented. Other influences which stimulated some interest among the general public were

productions of the Yiddish Art Theatre under the direction of
Maurice Schwartz, and the visiting Habima Theater.

13. For several years an annual concert called "A Festival of Jewish
Arts" was presented in New York, through the almost single-
handed efforts of Jacob Weinberg. These programs included
the dance as well. Similar events were sponsored in other cities.

14. Idelsohn became Professor of Music at Hebrew Union College,
and he was followed by Eric Werner. Binder became Professor of
Music at the Jewish Institute of Religion; Saminsky was music
director of Temple Emanu-El, N.Y., and Rudinow was its cantor;
Weiner became music director of the Central Synagogue, N.Y.;
and Fromm was made director at Temple Israel, Boston. Among
the composers whose works appeared in this period were Achron,
Binder, Freed, Fromm, Jacobi, Helfman, Schalit, Weinberg,
Weiner.

15. This development has been furthered by new professional attitudes among the cantors, who united in order to improve their
own status, and incidentally that of their art. Three organizations
were formed along denominational lines: The American Conference of Cantors (Reform); The Cantors' Assembly of America
(Conservative); The Cantorial Council of America (Orthodox).

16. Gershon Ephros' five volume *Cantorial Anthology* was begun in
the 1930's, but reached completion only in the 1950's. Other
examples of Conservative-sponsored activity are: the publication
of *The Seventh Day* by Chemjo Vinaver; the annual service of
new music at the Park Avenue Synagogue of New York (instituted by Cantor David Putterman), which resulted in the
volume, *Synagogue Music by Contemporary Composers* (New
York, 1951). This volume is distinguished by music of composers
who are known principally in the general world of music, and
who were induced to compose especially for this series—Lukas
Foss, David Diamond, Morton Gould, Leonard Bernstein and
others. More recently, music was commissioned for the High
Holy Days by the Cantors' Assembly, and published in 1961.

17. These are: The School for Sacred Music, Hebrew Union College-
Jewish Institute of Religion, with Binder and Werner as directors; The Cantors' Institute and College of Jewish Music, Jewish
Theological Seminary, with Hugo Weisgall as director; and
courses for cantors within the Music Department of Yeshiva University. It is appropriate to mention also the secular experiment
being made on the elementary level: The Hebrew Arts School
of Music and the Dance, with Tz. Jochsberger as director, is a
school for general music instruction of children, which includes
training in some aspects of the Jewish music tradition, and in
the music of Israel.

18. See P. Gradenwitz, *The Music of Israel* (New York, 1949); A. Sendrey, *Bibliography of Jewish Music* (New York, 1951); A. Weisser, *The Modern Renaissance of Jewish Music* (New York, 1954); A. Rosowsky, *The Cantillation of the Bible* (The Five Books of Moses) (New York, 1957); E. Werner, *The Sacred Bridge* (New York, 1959). Articles have appeared in learned journals and encyclopedias.

19. Dr. Johanna Spector of the faculty of the College of Jewish Music (Jewish Theological Seminary) is the leading ethno-musicologist in the Jewish field in this country.

20. Examples of such services are: I. Freed, *Chassidic Service* (New York, 1959); Ch. Davidson, *Chassidic Service* (New York, 1962). This "Hasidic" trend may be credited in part to the neo-Hasidic inclination of many religious leaders in recent years, and in part to the presence of large Hasidic communities whose on-going musical tradition has filtered through to the larger public via Orthodox day-schools, Hebrew speaking summer camps, and some commercial recordings. The most serious operatic work thus far composed is *Athalia* by Hugo Weisgall.

21. The operas are *Isaac Levy,* with music by F. Picket; *Chelm,* with music by R. Strassberg; *The Golem,* with music by L. Weiner; *Sons of Aaron,* with music by S. Landau; *The Last Sabbath* and *Time for Choosing,* with music by Ch. Davidson. The director and moving spirit of the theater, Ray Smolover, has written all the librettos.

22. The Schwann Catalogue of Long Playing Records lists these under: "Folk Music—Israel" or "Popular Music of other countries—Israel." Art music of Israel may be found under the name of the composer. Records of religious content may be found under "Popular Music—Religious."

Bibliographical Note

For general background information on the music of the Jews, the basic text is A. Z. Idelsohn's *Jewish Music* (New York, 1929). Information about contemporary Jewish music, which includes the American scene and brings it more nearly up-to-date, is provided in the latter chapters of P. Gradenwitz, *The Music of Israel* (New York, 1949); A. Weisser, *The Modern Renaissance of Jewish Music* (New York, 1954); and A. M. Rothmuller, *The Music of the Jews* (New York, 1954). Some nuggets of information of special interest may be found in the discursive essays by I. Rabinowitch, in *Of Jewish Music,* translated from the Yiddish by A. M. Klein (Montreal, 1952). Succinct, factual summaries may be found in *The Jewish People, Past and Present, Encyclopedic Handbooks,* published by the

Central Yiddish Culture Organization (New York, 1952): vol. 3 contains an article on "Jewish Music" by A. W. Binder, and vol. 4 incorporates music in an article entitled "American Jewish Scholarship" by J. Trachtenberg.

The bibliographies, biographical material and program guides issued by the National Jewish Music Council, sponsored by the National Jewish Welfare Board, give a very concrete account of Jewish musical activity and of the material available for study and performance.

Jewish Communal Services: Health, Welfare, Recreational and Social   (pp. 253–276)

BY CHARLES S. LEVY

Notes

1. H. D. Stein, "Jewish Social Work in the United States, 1654–1954,"*AJYB*, 1956 (Philadelphia, 1955), pp. 7 ff; see also H. L. Lurie, "Jewish Communal Life in the United States," *The Jewish People: Past and Present*, vol. IV (New York, 1955), 191–192.
2. B. Rabinowitz, *The Young Men's Hebrew Associations (1854–1913)* (New York, 1948), pp. 9–11.
3. H. Silver, "Jewish Communal Services: Historical Perspectives," *JJCS*, XXXIX, 1 (Fall, 1962), 10; see also H. L. Lurie, *A Heritage Affirmed* (Philadelphia, 1961), pp. 16–18, 52–56.
4. See M. Wischnitzer, *Visas to Freedom: The History of HIAS* (New York, 1956).
5. Stein, *op. cit.*, pp. 38 ff.
6. I. Sobeloff, "The Changing Jewish Community: An Appraisal," *JJCS*, XXXIII, 1 (Fall, 1956), 14.
7. Stein, *op. cit.*, pp. 62–63.
8. CJFWF, *1961 Yearbook of Jewish Social Service* (New York, 1961), p. 2.
9. Sobeloff, *op. cit.*, p. 17.
10. CJFWF, *Jewish Communal Service: Programs and Finances* (New York, March 1963), pp. 33–34.
11. *1961 Yearbook of Jewish Social Service*, p. 7; S. P. Goldberg, *Jewish Communal Services: Programs and Finances* (New York, March 1963); see also CJFWF, *The Community Plans for Its Chronically Ill and Aged* (New York, 1961).
12. *1961 Yearbook of Jewish Social Service*, pp. 7–9.
13. See W. Posner, "Aging with a Future," *Jewish Life*, XXVIII, 4 (April, 1961), 17–26; *idem*, "Socio-Cultural Factors in Casework with Adult Children and Aged Parents," *JJCS*, XXXV, 2 (Winter, 1958), 193–201; H. Silver, "The Effect on Family

Agencies of Developments in Services to the Aged," *ibid.*, XXXIV, 4 (Summer, 1958), 391–395.

14. See for example "Serving the Aged Outside Institutions," Workshop Session, Council of Jewish Federations and Welfare Funds (General Assembly, Philadelphia, November 16, 1962), mimeographed; D. Rabinowitz, "Coordinated Planning for Economic Opportunities for Jewish Aged," *JJCS*, XXXVI, 2 (Winter, 1959), 181–185, and I. Barshop, "Planning Constructive Economic Opportunities for the Jewish Aged," *ibid.*, pp. 186–191.

15. *1961 Yearbook of Jewish Social Service*, pp. 5–6.

16. *JWB Year Book, 1960–1961: Jewish Community Center Field* (New York, ca., 1962), Appendices, pp. I, II. See also pp. 7–8.

17. *Ibid.*, Appendices, p. VI. With allowances for changes in the price index, the increase would be about 112%.

18. *Ibid.*, Tables 18–20.

19. O. I. Janowsky, *The JWB Survey* (New York, 1948).

20. *Ibid.*, p. xxiii.

21. *Ibid.*, p. 8.

22. Sobeloff, *op. cit.*, p. 18.

23. See D. M. Goldenberg, "Practice of Group Work in a Synagogue Setting," *JSSQ*, XXXI, 2 (Winter, 1954) 233–239; *Selected Articles: Jewish Community Center Relationships with Synagogues*, 2 vols. (New York, National Jewish Welfare Board, 1956 and 1959), mimeographed.

24. "The Center and the Synagogue: A Symposium," *Conservative Judaism* (Winter-Spring, 1962). See also S. Solender, "The Vital Future of the Jewish Community Center in America," *JJCS*, XXXIX, 1 (Fall, 1962), 42–54.

25. See for example *News Service*, Federation of Jewish Philanthropies of New York, vol. 5, no. 1 (September-October), *passim*. See also A. Amsel, "The Case for Distinctively Jewish Social Work," *Tradition*, 5, 1 (Fall, 1962), 58–70; and "The Values of Jewish Family Service to the Client and the Community: A Rationale for the Jewish Family Agency," Council of Jewish Federations and Welfare Funds (April, 1954).

26. Stein, *op. cit.*, p. 75.

27. "A National Profile of Changes from Old to New Centers and Implications for the Years Ahead," *Perspective for the 1960's, Seminar of Center Executives of Intermediate Cities* (May 25–26, 1961, New York, JWB), mimeographed; H. Millman, "Jewish Community Centers, 1946–1955," *AJYB*, 1956, p. 266.

28. *Ibid.*, Exhibit A.

29. See for example M. B. Blanchard, "The Effect of Social Trends and Population Mobility on the Jewish Center," *JJCS*, XXXII, 1 (Fall, 1955), 49–60; M. Cohn, "Jewish Community Planning in Suburban Areas," *ibid.*, pp. 71–84; and Council of Jewish

Federations and Welfare Funds, "Social Planning for Shifting Jewish Population," *Proceedings of Professional Social Planners' Workshop* (May 26–27, 1956), mimeographed.

30. H. Millman, *op. cit.*, p. 271; B. Warach, in *JWB Yearbook*, 1960–61, pp. 38, 59.
31. M. B. Hexter, "Jewish Health and Welfare in the '60's: Reappraisal and Planning," *Assembly Papers*, 30th General Assembly, CJFWF (New York, 1961), pp. 34–36.
32. Lurie, *op. cit.*, p. 39.
33. H. L. Lurie, "The Council's First 25 Years," *Assembly Papers*, 25th General Assembly (CJFWF, New York, 1956), pp. 4–5.
34. Lurie, *op. cit.*, pp. 83–84 and notes pp. 416–417.
35. Adapted from Lurie, *op. cit.*, pp. 5–6.
36. See M. R. Ephraim, "The Impact of the Conference on the American Jewish Community," *JJCS*, XXXV, 1 (Fall, 1958); *NAJCW at Forty* (New York, 1959).
37. E. V. Hollis and A. L. Taylor, *Social Work Education in the United States* (New York, 1951).
38. For an extensive review of professional education for Jewish communal services, see M. Freund's report on *The Training Bureau for Jewish Communal Service*, Parts I and II (New York, Council of Jewish Federations and Welfare Funds, 1956), mimeographed.
39. Janowsky, *op. cit.*, pp. 31–32, 212–214.
40. See Ph. Bernstein, *A Study of Training for Jewish Social Work* (New York, Committee on Training for Jewish Social Work, 1944), mimeographed.
41. See "Use of Public Funds by Jewish Agencies," *Assembly Papers* (New York, CJFWF, 1958); M. K. Selig, "Implications of the Use of Public Funds in Jewish Communal Services," *JJCS*, XXXVI, 1 (Fall, 1959), 48–58.
42. See for example CJFWF, *The Value of Jewish Family Service to the Client and Community: A Rationale for the Jewish Family Agency* (New York, April, 1954); "The Responsibility of the Jewish Agencies in the American Community," *Assembly Papers*, General Assembly (New York, CJFWF, 1959); and G. Berger, "Professional Training for Jewish Communal Services," *Adult Jewish Leadership*, 6, 3 (Spring, 1960), pp. 17–27.
43. See for example references to Berger and Hexter cited above. On the question of the needs of those left behind when Jewish agencies remove their facilities to follow their Jewish clientele, see I. Brodsky, "The Changing Neighborhood: The Opportunity for Service in Old and New Neighborhoods," *JSSQ*, XXXI, 2 (Winter, 1954), 240–246; B. Lambert and H. Alpert, "Problems of Jewish Centers in Changing and Mixed Population Neighborhoods," *ibid.*, XXX, 2 (Winter, 1953), 152–157.

44. See R. Dolgoff, *Gentile Leaders and Jewish Programming in Single Adult Social Groups, The Jewish Social Work Forum,* I, 1 (Fall, 1963), pp. 76–89; *idem,* "The Viewpoint of a Graduate of a School under Non-Sectarian Auspices," *The Role of the Jewish School of Social Work in Preparing Social Work Practitioners for Jewish Communal Services,* C. S. Levy, ed. (New York, Wurzweiler School of Social Work, 1962), p. 21.

Bibliographical Note

Relatively brief descriptions of the social work disciplines of social casework, social group work and community organization are included in: Arthur E. Fink et al., *The Field of Social Work,* fourth edition (New York, 1963).

For more extensive discussions of each of these disciplines, see: G. Hamilton, *Theory and Practice of Social Case Work,* second edition, revised (New York, 1951); G. Konopka, *Social Group Work: A Helping Process* (Englewood, N.J., 1963); M. G. Ross, *Community Organization: Theory and Principles* (New York, 1955). The development of social work as a profession is treated in E. V. Hollis and A. L. Taylor, *Social Work Education in the United States* (New York, 1951).

A review of the development of Jewish communal services is afforded in H. D. Stein, "Jewish Social Work in the United States, 1654–1954," *AJYB,* 1956 (Philadelphia, 1956), pp. 3–98. For the Jewish Federation Movement see H. L. Lurie's *A Heritage Affirmed: The Jewish Federation Movement in America* (Philadelphia, 1961). An extensive account of attempts to provide special training opportunities for social workers in Jewish communal services is given in Michael Freund, *The Training Bureau for Jewish Communal Service* (New York, CJFWF, December, 1956) (mimeographed and bound in two volumes).

The Jewish Community Center movement is discussed in: B. Rabinowitz, *Young Men's Hebrew Association* (1854–1913), New York, 1958; L. Kraft and C. S. Bernheimer, eds., *Aspects of the Jewish Community Center* (New York, 1954); O. I. Janowsky, *The JWB Survey* (New York, 1948); *Let's Get to the Center of Things* (New York, National Jewish Welfare Board, undated).

A rich variety of articles on the Jewish communal services will be found in the quarterly *Journal of Jewish Communal Service,* published by the National Conference of Jewish Communal Service.

Overseas Aid   (pp. 277–299)

BY JOSEPH J. SCHWARTZ AND BEATRICE I. VULCAN

Notes

1. M. J. Kohler, "The Board of Delegates of American Israelites, 1859–1879," *PAJHS*, no. 29 (1925), p. 77.
2. C. Adler, ed., *The Voice of America on Kishineff* (Philadelphia, 1904), p. 468.
3. For the origin and early history of JDC, see *JDC Primer* (New York, 1945), pp. 12–14 (mimeographed); "Jewish War Relief Work," *AJYB*, 1917–1918 (Philadelphia, 1917), pp. 194–226. For annual or accrued figures on JDC income or expenditures, see "Summary Statement of Income and Expenditures," for the pertinent year in the *JDC Annual Reports* published annually since 1930. For figures up to and including 1930, see the *JDC Annual Report, 1930*.
4. H. Hoover, *The American Epic*, vol. II (Chicago, 1960), p. 220. For JDC programs in Eastern Europe during World War I, see F. Warburg and A. Lucas, *Reports Received by the JDC* (New York, 1916), pp. 11–108.
5. F. Warburg, "History of the War Relief Fund," *The American Hebrew* (September 14, 1917), pp. 482–484.
6. Fuller accounts of these relief activities are given in JDC Executive Committee, *Report on the Activities of the JDC* (Chicago, 1927), pp. 9–22; B. Bogen, *Report of JDC Activities in Poland* (New York, 1920), pp. 11–35; JDC, *Brief Summary of the Child Care Department in the Various Countries in Europe for Period 1922–1925* (Berlin, 1925); J. J. Golub, "The JDC and Health Programs in Eastern Europe," *Jewish Social Studies*, V, 3(1943), 293–304.
7. D. A. Brown, *Report to the Special Commission* (New York, American Jewish Relief Committee, n.d.); see also M. A. Leavitt, *The JDC Story: Highlights of JDC Activities, 1914–1952* (New York, 1953), pp. 8–9; J. Billikopf and M. Hexter, *The Jewish Situation in Eastern Europe* (Chicago, 1926), pp. 7–37.
8. Hoover, *op. cit.*, II, pp. 214–223; III, pp. 76–161.
9. For the reconstruction programs, see JDC Executive Committee, *Report on the Activities*, p. 24. JDC, *1930 Annual Report* (New York, 1931), pp. 18–23; American Joint Reconstruction Foundation, *Report of Activities* (Berlin, 1927), pp. 5–14.
10. J. C. Hyman, *Twenty-five Years of American Aid to Jews Overseas: A Record of the JDC* (New York, 1939), p. 33. See also J. B. Rosen, *Jewish Colonization Work in Russia under the*

Auspices of the JDC (Philadelphia, 1925), *passim;* JDC, *1937 Annual Report* (New York, 1938), pp. 13–14; D. A. Brown, *The New Exodus: The Story of the Historic Movement of Russian Jewry Back to the Soil* (New York, 1925), *passim.*

11. I. E. Rontsch, "The Present State of the *Landsmannschaften,*" *The Jewish Social Service Quarterly,* XV, 4 (June, 1939), p. 369. For a detailed picture of European immigration to the U.S., see M. Wischnitzer, *To Dwell in Safety* (Philadelphia, 1948).

12. Until 1927, Hadassah received contributions from organizations which raised money throughout the world, but two-thirds of its budgets from 1922–1927 were raised in the United States.

13. On American Jewish aid to Palestine before World War II, see S. Hoofien, *Report to the JDC Concerning Relief Work in Palestine from August 1, 1917 to May 31, 1918* (New York, 1918), pp. 28–38; J. de Haas, *Secretary's Report of the Provisional Executive Committee for General Zionist Affairs* (Pittsburgh, 1918), pp. 9–10; E. Radinsky, *Jewish National Fund Program* (New York, 1929), pp. 5–18; I. Goldstein, *President's Message to the 35th Anniversary Conference, Jewish National Fund* (New York, 1937), pp. 4–19; A. Boehm and A. Pollack, *The Jewish National Fund: Its History, Function and Activity* (Jerusalem, 1939), *passim;* A. Ulitzur, *Two Decades of Keren Hayesod* (Jerusalem, 1940), pp. 131–132; M. C. Taub, "Hadassah's Medical Work," in J. Hirsch, ed., *The Hadassah Medical Organization* (New York, 1956), pp. 9–22.

14. D. M. Bressler and J. C. Hyman, *Report to the JDC on Present-Day Conditions of the Jews in Eastern Europe* (New York, 1930), pp. 21–22.

15. For the American-Jewish contribution during the Nazi era and the war years, see Wischnitzer, *op. cit.,* pp. 210–221, 289; *idem, Visas to Freedom: The History of HIAS* (New York, 1956), pp. 135–198; JDC, *Annual Reports,* 1931–1945; United Service for New Americans, *The USNA Story* (New York, 1954), *passim.*

16. In 1938, JDC raised about $4,750,000 and the UPA about $2,150,000 from independent campaigns, a combined total of less than $7 million. UJA figures here and subsequently were made available by UJA Accounting and Research Departments. For early efforts to effect unity in fund-raising see E. Neumann, "The United Palestine Appeal: A Brief Review of Its Formation and Results," *UPA Report for 1925–1926* (New York, 1926), pp. 14–20; E. Ginzberg, *Report to American Jews on Overseas Relief, Palestine, and Refugees in the United States* (New York, 1942), pp. 14–89; S. Halperin, *The Political World of American Zionism* (Detroit, 1961), pp. 195–217, 310–311; H. L. Lurie, *A Heritage Affirmed* (Philadelphia, 1961), pp. 136–143.

17. Ten thousand children attended schools in DP camps in 1947. On the aid rendered in the DP camps, see E. G. Harrison, *The Plight of the Displaced Jews in Europe* (Washington, 1945), pp. 10–14; U.S. Displaced Persons Commission, *Memo to America: The DP Story* (Washington, 1952), pp. 27, 39; JDC, *Annual Reports,* 1947–1951; The *AJYB* for 1946 through 1951 contains valuable articles and summaries.
18. H. Agar, *The Saving Remnant* (New York, 1960), p. 201.
19. S. Halperin, *op. cit.,* p. 212. On the migration to Israel, see *Reports of the Zionist Organization and the Jewish Agency* (Jerusalem, 1960), pp. 75–97.
20. In 1953, the school was closed and the program transferred to in-service training. In 1958, JDC with the cooperation of the Israel Government, re-established the school in Jerusalem as part of the Hebrew University.
21. On post-World War II developments and aid, see JDC, *Annual Reports* 1945–1962; *AJYB,* 1945–1962; *ORT: A Record of Ten Years of Rebuilding Jewish Economic Life* (New York, 1956), *passim;* Wischnitzer, *Visas to Freedom,* pp. 205–234.
22. Since the second half of the nineteenth century, the Alliance Israélite has maintained a network of schools serving thousands of Jewish children in North Africa and the Near East. JDC subsidizes these schools as well as those of religious groups such as Ozar Hatorah and the Lubavitcher.
23. The Jewish National Fund has been receiving annual allocations in Israel from the Jewish Agency since 1952 and has discontinued all fund-raising in the United States, except through traditional collections up to a predetermined ceiling.
24. JDC Accounting Department figures. JDC received almost half of its budget, about $350 million, from UJA between 1948 and 1962. The balance came mainly from the Conference on Jewish Material Claims Against Germany and other types of restitution income, with contributions from Canadian and various South American appeals. See also *Reports of the Zionist Organization and the Jewish Agency* for the work of the Jewish Agency.

Bibliographical Note

There is no comprehensive account of the American Jewish contribution to the relief and rehabilitation of Jewish communities overseas or of the effect of this contribution on Jewish communal life.

A number of the organizations working abroad have produced official histories or summaries of their work and achievements:

JDC's contribution has been described in J. C. Hyman, *Twenty-Five Years of American Aid to Jews Overseas: A Record of the Joint*

Distribution Committee (New York, 1939); in M. A. Leavitt, *The JDC Story: Highlights of JDC Activities, 1914–1952* (New York, 1953); and, in a more popularized version, in H. Agar, *The Saving Remnant: An Account of Jewish Survival* (New York, 1960).

The principal agencies raising money in the United States for welfare programs in Israel made extensive reports to the 25th Zionist Congress which were published under the title, *Reports of the Zionist Organization and the Jewish Agency* (Jerusalem, 1960). Earlier reports or studies are: A. Boehm and A. Pollack, *The Jewish National Fund* (Jerusalem, 1939); A. Ulitzur, *Two Decades of Keren Hayesod* (Jerusalem, 1940); J. Hirsch, ed., *The Hadassah Medical Organization: An American Contribution to Medical Pioneering and Progress in Israel* (New York, 1956); and L. Levensohn, *Vision and Fulfillment: The First Twenty-Five Years of the Hebrew University, 1925–1950* (New York, 1950).

M. Wischnitzer, *Visas to Freedom* (Cleveland, 1956), has recorded the history of HIAS. *To Dwell in Safety* (Philadelphia, 1948), by the same author, is one of the most comprehensive studies of the mass population movements since 1800. The efforts and achievements of the American Ort Federation are outlined in *ORT: A Record of Ten Years of Rebuilding Jewish Economic Life* (New York, 1956).

The contributions of the Jewish labor movement are available in several fine histories, notably in YIVO's *Geshikhte fun der Yiddisher Arbeter Bavegung in die Fareinikte Staten,* E. Tcherikower, ed., 2 vols. (New York, 1943–1945), which has been translated by A. Antonovsky under the title *The Early Jewish Labor Movement in the United States* (New York, 1961).

Among the first serious attempts at evaluation and appraisal of the programs and needs of the Jewish fund-raising organizations for overseas welfare was that of E. Ginzberg, *On Overseas Relief, Palestine, and Refugees in the United States* (New York, 1942). This work analyzed the organizations which had agreed to coordinate their appeals in the UJA and the reasons for the creation of the UJA. Another point of view about the forces which led to the creation of the UJA was presented in S. Halperin's well-documented, if partisan, *The Political World of American Zionism* (Detroit, 1961). Still another viewpoint, that of the Federation movement as the propellant for merged fund-raising activities, has been presented by H. L. Lurie, *A Heritage Affirmed* (Philadelphia, 1961).

For the relationship of overseas welfare activities to the Jewish social work scene, the reader is referred to H. D. Stein, *Jewish Social Work in the United States, 1654–1954, AJYB* (Philadelphia, 1956). For their relationship to Jewish history and culture, the best sources are the two compendia of essays: L. Finkelstein, ed., *The Jews: Their History, Culture, and Religion,* 2 vols., rev. ed. (Philadelphia, 1960), and *The Jewish People: Past and Present,* 4 vols. (New York, 1946–1954).

Basic sources of information about the organizations are their own reports, which are summarized annually in the *AJYB* (Philadelphia, 1917), seriatim, in the sections on the "Survey (or Review) of the Year," or in the special articles on communal affairs in the United States and abroad. Summaries are also included in the annual publications of the Council of Jewish Federations and Welfare Funds—*Jewish Communal Services and Programs* (New York, 1956), seriatim, and *Budget Digest—Overseas Organizations* (New York, 1943), seriatim.

Summaries of the work of the organizations are also available in the material prepared for employee training courses: JDC, *The JDC Primer* (New York, 1945), mimeographed; and HIAS, *Training Course on Migration Problems,* 2 vols. (New York, 1944), mimeographed.

Most general works on governmental or voluntary overseas welfare programs include a section on the activities of the Jewish organizations. Especially useful are H. Hoover, *The American Epic* (Chicago, 1960), about the World War I period; the report of the United States Displaced Persons Commission, *Memo to America: The DP Story* (Washington, D.C., 1952), for an important part of the World War II story; and M. Curti, *American Philanthropy Abroad* (New Brunswick, 1963), which gives an excellent account and appraisal of the work of the principal Jewish overseas agencies in a historical and organizational framework.

Zionism, Israel and American Jewry   (pp. 301–321)

BY JUDD L. TELLER

Notes

1. B. G. Richards, "Zionism in the United States," in I. Cohen, *The Zionist Movement* (New York, 1946), p. 345.
2. M. Davis, *Yahadut Amerika* Be-hitpathutah (New York, 1954), pp. 267–68. See also I. Knox, *Rabbi in America: The Story of Isaac M. Wise* (Boston, 1957), pp. 112–15.
3. Quoted in J. Rappaport, "Zionism as a Factor in Allied-Central Power Controversy (1914–1918)" in I. S. Meyer ed., *Early History of Zionism in America* (New York, 1958), p. 306. See also Ch. Weizmann, *Trial and Error* (New York, 1944), pp. 311–12; H. Parzen, "The Federation of American Zionists (1897–1914)," in Meyer, *op. cit.,* 263, 267.
4. N. Sokolow, *History of Zionism 1600–1918,* vol. I (London, 1919), pp. 206–12; I. Cohen, *op. cit.,* General Introduction and

chapter 11; Richards, *op. cit.*, pp. 326–27; F. Manuel, *The Realities of American-Palestine Relations* (Washington, 1949), pp. 2–3, 44–46, 48–51.

5. Sokolow, *op. cit.*, vol. I, pp. 155–60, vol. II, addenda pp. 405–12; Manuel, *op. cit.*, p. 53.
6. S. H. Levine "Palestine in the Literature of the United States to 1867," in Meyer, *op. cit.*, p. 32; Manuel, *op. cit.*, p. 2.
7. N. M. Gelber, *Hassidei Umot ha-Olam* (Tel Aviv, 1931), pp. 81–86; Sokolow, *op. cit.*, vol. 1, pp. 136–37; A. J. Karp, "The Zionism of Warder Cresson," in Meyer, *op. cit.*, pp. 1–20; *Universal Jewish Encyclopedia*, vol. III, p. 410; Manuel, *op. cit.*, pp. 10, 11.
8. A. Zeiger, "Emma Lazarus and Pre-Herzlian Zionism," in Meyer, *op. cit.*, pp. 77–108.
9. See *ibid.*, pp. 90–92.
10. Sh. Noble, "Pre-Herzlian Zionism in America as Reflected in the Yiddish Press," in Meyer, *op. cit.*, pp. 39–42.
11. See *ibid.*, pp. 40–41, 43–47. On the split among American *Hoveve Zion*, see also I. Klausner, "Adam Rosenberg: One of the Earliest American Zionists," in R. Patai, ed., *Herzl Year Book*, 1 (New York, 1955), *passim.*
12. Quoted in I. Elbogen, *A Century of Jewish Life* (Philadelphia, 1944), p. 231.
13. Quoted in C. Adler and A. M. Margalith, *With Firmness in the Right: American Diplomatic Action Affecting Jews, 1840–1945* (New York, 1946), p. 43; Manuel, *op. cit.*, p. 71.
14. Parzen in Meyer, *op. cit.*, pp. 245–46.
15. M. M. Kaplan, *A New Zionism* (New York, 1956), pp. 82–89; B. Halpern, *The American Jew* (New York, 1956), pp. 89–90; H. M. Kallen, *Utopians at Bay* (New York, 1958), pp. 287–89; N. Rotenshtreich, *Hanahot be-Inyan Shelikhut ba-Amerika*, in B. Dinaburg (Dinur), A. Bone, and Binyamin, eds., *Shivat Zion*, vol. 1 (1950); *Forum* (for the problems of Zionism, Jewry and the State of Israel), Jerusalem (Spring, 1958), especially section II of issue; J. L. Teller, "Zionism Moves Toward Clarity, To Be or Not To Be Ingathered," *Commentary*, November, 1951.
16. Parzen, in Meyer, *op. cit.*, p. 247.
17. B. W. Korn, *American Jewry and the Civil War* (New York, 1951), pp. 22–23, 29, 30.
18. S. S. Wise, *Challenging Years* (New York, 1949), *passim.*
19. N. Bentwich, *For Zion's Sake, a Biography of Judah L. Magnes* (Philadelphia, 1954), *passim.*
20. *Ibid.*, pp. 33–35; Parzen, in Meyer, *op. cit.*, pp. 246, 268.
21. Parzen, in Meyer, *op. cit.*, p. 257.
22. *Ibid.*, pp. 25–53.

23. S. Rosenblatt, *The Mizrachi Movement* (New York, 1940), *passim.*
24. L. Shpizman, "Poale Zion in Der Arbeter Bawegung," in vol. I, and "Oifn Arbeter Front," in vol. II of L. Shpizman and Baruch Zuckerman, *Geshichte fun der Tzionistischer Arbeter Bawegung in Tzofen America";* C. B. Sherman, "The Beginnings of Labor Zionism in the United States" in Meyer, *op. cit., passim.* For environmental roots of Labor Zionism, read the first 153 pages of O. I. Janowsky, *The Jews and Minority Rights* (New York, 1933).
25. M. Syrkin, *Nachman Syrkin, Socialist Zionist* (New York, 1961), pp. 160–61; Manuel, *op. cit.,* p. 154; J. Rappaport, in Meyer, *op. cit.,* p. 304.
26. See Wise, *op. cit.,* p. 184.
27. See Janowsky, *op. cit.,* pp. 160–90.
28. Janowsky, *op. cit., passim;* Wise, *op. cit., passim;* I. Elbogen, *op. cit.,* pp. 505–06; Adler and Margalith, *op. cit.,* pp. 138–39, 165–67.
29. Weizmann, *op. cit.,* pp. 193–94, 208; Manuel, *op. cit.,* pp. 164–70 and *passim.*
30. Manuel, *op. cit.,* p. 207; J. Haber, *The Odyssey of an American Zionist* (New York, 1956), p. 159.
31. See *Report of the Proceedings of the 24th Annual Convention of the ZOA Held in Cleveland, June 5–8, 1921* (New York, August 1921), *passim;* J. L. Teller, "America's Two Zionist Traditions," *Commentary* (October, 1955); *idem,* "Chaim Weizmann, A Retrospective View," *Rehovot* (Quarterly of Weizmann Scientific Institute) (Autumn, 1962). For slightly different evaluations, see Manuel, *op. cit.,* pp. 206–11, 261–66; J. B. Schechtman, *Rebel and Statesman, the Vladimir Jabotinsky Story,* vol. I (New York, 1956), pp. 320–21, 374, 390; J. de Haas, *Louis B. Brandeis* (New York, 1929), *passim.*
32. I. Fineman, *Woman of Valor, the Life of Henrietta Szold* (New York, 1961), pp. 329–30.
33. Shpizman and Zuckerman, *op. cit.,* vol. II, p. 378, reports Borochov opposing this view. See also Sherman in Meyer, *op. cit.,* pp. 285–86.
34. Weizmann, *op. cit.,* pp. 327, 337.
35. Teller in *Commentary,* and in *Rehovot;* Ch. Arlosoroff, *Surveying American Zionism,* a privately circulated letter, April, 1929 (New York, September, 1929), pp. 9–10.
36. *Ibid.,* pp. 6–7, 14.
37. *American Jewish Conference, Its Organization and Proceedings of the First Session (1943)* (New York, 1944), *passim.*
38. *The American Jewish Conference, Proceedings of the Fourth Session* (December, 1947) (New York, 1948), *passim.*

Bibliographical Note

Origins and Development of Zionism: Nahum Sokolow's two-volume *History of Zionism 1600–1918* (London, 1919), is the best reference work on the origins of Zionism. Although written for the British public, and a pioneer work, it is still unmatched in style and exhaustiveness. Likewise valuable is the two-volume work (prepared by I. B. Berkson for the Esco Foundation for Palestine), *Palestine: A Study of Jewish, Arab and British Policies* (New Haven, 1947), which analyzes the origins and development of Zionism and the Jewish National Home up to the eve of Israel's independence. It also contains an exhaustive bibliography.

American Zionism: There is as yet no history of Zionism in America. Two volumes may be recommended as partly filling this gap: Isidore S. Meyer, ed., *Early History of Zionism in America* (New York, 1958), is a collection of papers on various aspects of the subject. Frank E. Manuel, *The Realities of American-Palestine Relations* (Washington, 1949), is primarily a diplomatic history from 1832 when the United States appointed its first consular agent in Jerusalem through the establishment of Israel in 1948. However, it embraces more than diplomatic material. Especially recommended are its chapters on the Wilson-Wise-Brandeis relationship, and the discrepancies between State Department and White House policies from Wilson's day onwards.

Peace Conference: A complementary volume, dealing with broader aspects, not encompassed by Manuel's book, is Oscar I. Janowsky, *The Jews and Minority Rights* (New York, 1933). It portrays the formulation of a nearly unanimous American Jewish policy at the end of World War I, the struggle at the Peace Conference for Jewish minority rights and Zionism's crucial role in that struggle, and is prefaced by a 153-page review of the ideological impulses behind the demands for minority rights.

Zionist Ideological Crisis: For the evolution of an "American" Zionist ideology since establishment of Israel, M. M. Kaplan's *A New Zionism* (New York, 1956), and Ben Halpern's *The American Jew* (New York, 1956), are recommended. On the defects in American Zionism, Chaim Arlosoroff's brochure, *Surveying American Zionism* (New York, 1929), although concerned with conditions in 1929, is equally relevant today.

Indispensable, of course, are the autobiographies of Chaim Weizmann, *Trial and Error* (New York, 1944), and S. S. Wise, *Challenging Years* (New York, 1949); and the following biographies: Norman Bentwich, *For Zion's Sake: A Biography of Judah L. Magnes* (Philadelphia, 1954); Jacob de Haas, *Louis D. Brandeis* (New York, 1929);

Irving F. Fineman, *Woman of Valor: the Life of Henrietta Szold, 1860–1945* (New York, 1961). Louis Lipsky's *A Gallery of Zionist Profiles* (New York, 1956), includes sketches of American Zionist leaders.

Problems of Coordination and Unity (pp. 323–338)

BY ABRAHAM G. DUKER

Notes

1. Thanks are due to Messrs. Victor Geller of the Community Service Division of Yeshiva University, S. P. Goldberg of the CJFWF, Drs. Judd Teller of the Israel Histadrut Campaign and Yehuda Hellman of the Presidents Conference and COJO for their generous aid in the clarification of some important points.
2. For a terse outline and ample bibliography of the organizational aspects of the different periods in American Jewish history, see my "Jews in the United States," in L. A. Feldman, ed., *Aspects of American Jewish Life* (New York, 1961), pp. 13–29.
3. The most detailed coverage will be found in H. L. Lurie, *A Heritage Affirmed* (Philadelphia, 1961).
4. See I. Franck, "The Changing American Jewish Community," in E. Kohn, ed., *American Jewry: The Tercentenary and After* (New York, 1955), pp. 35–43.
5. Critical periods produced much discussion on expanding the Federation into a *kehillah*-like democratic institution primarily with Jewish purposes. There is ample material on this in the *JSSQ*, particularly the *Proceedings* issues and in Lurie, *op. cit.*, esp. pp. 57 ff., 100, 126 ff., 252–53, 237–43, 247–48, 342, and others. However, the large city Federations generally followed the path leading to nonsectarianism and thus set the pattern for other communities.
6. This aspect has been left out of the histories and anthologies of the social work field in general. For a Labor Zionist reaction, cf. *The Jewish Social Worker*, Conference Issue, New York (June 1941), particularly the article, "Blitzkrieg against Zion," p. 3.
7. See L. C. White, *300,000 New Americans. The Epic of a Modern Immigrant Aid Society* (New York, 1957).
8. See Lurie, *op. cit.*, pp. 139–43; on UJA at its height, see E. Ginzberg, *Agenda for American Jews* . . . (New York, 1950); on the struggle, see S. Halperin, *The Political World of American Zionism* (Detroit, 1961), pp. 189–217. See also M. Curti, *American Philanthropy Abroad: A History* (New Brunswick, N.J., 1963),

and H. Agar, *The Saving Remnant: An Account of Jewish Survival* (New York, 1960).

9. See Lurie, *op. cit.*, index, pp. 472 and 476.

10. See S. P. Goldberg, "Jewish Communal Services," *AJYB*, vol. 64, 1963, pp. 7, 191.

11. *Ibid.*, p. 197.

12. *Ibid.*, pp. 197–202.

13. On cultural services, see Lurie, *op. cit.*, pp. 207–08; CJFNF, *Survey Report—National Jewish Cultural Services in America—Appraisals and Recommendations* (New York, Sept. 20, 1959).

14. On the support of Jewish Education, see "Long Term Trends in Federation and Chest Allocations for Local Jewish Agencies and Federation Allocations for Jewish Education 1941–1959," AAJE, *Information Bulletin,* no. 26 (New York, March 1962); Z. Slesinger, "Financing Jewish Education," *The Reconstructionist*, XXVIII, 19 (Jan. 25, 1963), pp. 10–15.

15. On the diversity of views on the direction of Jewish social welfare institutions, see P. Bernstein, "Current Developments in Jewish Communal Service," *JJCS*, XXXIX (1962), pp. 20–28; M. B. Hexter, "The Next Twenty-five Years in Jewish Communal Service," *JSSQ*, XXXII (1955), pp. 30–48; H. L. Lurie, "The Approach and Philosophy of Jewish Social Welfare," *ibid.*, XXIX (1953), pp. 255–64; *idem, A Heritage Affirmed*, pp. 381–400; J. Shapiro, "Jewish Communal Services for a Native-Born Community—Values, Changes, and Perspectives," *JJCS*, XXXVII (1960), pp. 5–20; M. S. Shapiro, "An Appraisal of the Current Needs of the American Jewish Community," *JJCS*, XL (1963), pp. 36–47; M. Sklare, "The Future of Jewish Giving," *Commentary*, XXXIV, 5 (Nov. 1962), pp. 416–426; J. Willen, "The Challenge of Equality," *Issues* (American Council for Judaism), XIV, 6 (Summer 1960), pp. 15–28.

16. Resistance to Jewish training checked efforts to teach Jewish background to Jewish social workers, a problem which could not conceivably be raised in a Christian denomination. The literature is vast. See M. Freund, *The Training Bureau for Jewish Communal Service*, 2 vols. (New York, CJFWF, 1956), mimeographed.

17. The survivalist point of view in Jewish social work has been heard much more frequently during the past decade, sometimes, however, under the pressure of synagogue and rabbinical leadership. See *News Service* published by the Commission on Synagogue Relations of the Federation of Jewish Philanthropies of New York, and *The Jewish Social Worker,* published by the Alumni Association of the Wurzweiler School of Social Work of Yeshiva University. See also Conference issues of *JSSQ* and *JJCS*.

18. On the history of roof organizations, see J. Buchler, "The Struggle for Unity: Attempts at Union on American Jewish Life, 1654–1868," *American Jewish Archives*, II, 1 (June 1949), pp. 21–46; A. G. Duker, "Efforts to Build an Overall Jewish Body in the United States," *The Record*, The American Jewish Conference, July 1947, pp. 5–7; Sept. 1947, pp. 12–15; B. G. Richards, "Organizing American Jewry," *Jewish Affairs*, II, 2 (May 1, 1947) (American Jewish Congress); Z. Szajkowski, "The Alliance Israelite Universelle in the United States, 1860–1949," *PAJHS*, XXXIX (June 1950), pp. 389–443; M. Davis, *The Emergence of Conservative Judaism* (Philadelphia, 1963), pp. 114–46.

19. See M. J. Kohler, "The Board of Delegates of American Israelites, 1859–1878 . . ." *PAJHS*, XXIX (1925), pp. 75–135; A. Tarshish, "The Board of Delegates of American Israelites (1859–1878)," *PAJHS*, XLIX (1959), pp. 32–39.

20. See N. Schachner, *The Price of Liberty* (New York, 1948); F. E. Robin and S. Hirsh, *The Pursuit of Equality* (New York, 1957).

21. See O. I. Janowsky, *The Jews and Minority Rights (1898–1919)* (New York, 1933), pp. 161–90, 245–47, 254–390.

22. See Lurie, *op. cit.*, pp. 48, 201–03.

23. On Zionist efforts, see S. Halperin, *op. cit.*, pp. 29 ff.

24. See R. M. MacIver, *Report on the Jewish Community Relations Agencies* (New York, Nov. 1951); [A. G. Duker], "The Significance of the MacIver Report," *The Reconstructionist*, XVII, 14 (Nov. 16, 1951), pp. 7–13; *idem, Jewish Community Relations —An Analysis of the MacIver Report* (New York, 1952); Lurie, *op. cit.*, pp. 149, 202–03. For recent proposals, see M. Davis, "Centres of Jewry in the Western Hemisphere: A Comparative Approach," *The Jewish Journal of Sociology*, V, 1 (June 1963), p. 22.

25. Close coordination, as in the Federation-Welfare Fund field, does not exist in other areas because of ideological differences, vested interests, and the absence of a closely knit professional leadership. Religious and educational institutions are divided along "denominational" lines, with strongly consolidated roof organizations in both the Conservative and Reform groups, The Jewish Theological Seminary of America and the Union of American Hebrew Congregations. The tendency has been to build a separate "denominational" apparatus in every area—central rabbinical, cantoral and congregational bodies, men's and women's auxiliary organizations, educational commissions, and even agencies for community relations. Spokesmanship for the variegated Orthodox community is claimed by the Union of Orthodox Jewish Congregations. Orthodox Jewry is also served by the Community Service Division of Yeshiva University. Unlike the single organizations of Reform and Conservative rabbis, there are some eight Orthodox

rabbinical associations, ranging from the Hasidic to the "Neo-Orthodox" Rabbinical Alliance of America, and some twenty-odd ordination granting *yeshivot*. Orthodoxy is also divided politically into groupings ranging from the extremist opponents of Israel to the Religious Labor Zionists. The Synagogue Council aims to represent all Jewish religious elements, but its powers are limited.

"Denominationalism" has reduced the strength of communal schools, local education bureaus, and the central bodies in education (American Association for Jewish Education and the National Council for Jewish Education). The Day Schools, a result of the Orthodox emphasis in education, present additional problems in coordination: there are at least six categories of higher *yeshivot;* and the elementary and secondary Day Schools are served by Torah Umesorah and by the National Council for Torah Education of the Religious Zionists of America.

During World War II the Zionist movement was united in the American Zionist Emergency Council, with regional and local groups. Efforts to reorganize the American Zionist Council after the rise of Israel have not been entirely successful, and coordination in the Zionist movement has become increasingly less effective.

Bibliographical Note

The *vade mecum* to the dynamics of Jewish community organization is the *American Jewish Year Book,* now (1963) in its sixty-fourth volume, published annually by the American Jewish Committee and the Jewish Publication Society of America. Essential to our subject are the various directories and summaries, especially the annual reports on "Jewish Communal Services: Programs and Finances," of late authored by S. P. Goldberg of the CJFWF and, based on the annual publication of the same title issued by that organization. Other publications of the CJFWF are also recommended, among them *The Jewish Community,* a quarterly; "The General Assembly Papers" (now in 32nd year); *The Year Book of Jewish Social Work;* and *Notes and News.*

Among the histories and commentaries of Jewish community organization the most important is H. L. Lurie, *A Heritage Affirmed: The Jewish Federation Movement in America* (Philadelphia, 1961). Other useful works are: A. G. Duker, "Structure of the Jewish Community," in O. I. Janowsky, ed., *The American Jew: A Composite Portrait* (New York, 1942), pp. 134–160; I. Franck, "The Changing American Jewish Community," in E. Kohn, ed., *American Jewry: The Tercentenary and After* (New York, 1955), pp. 18–45; M. J. Karpf, *Jewish Community Organization in the United States: An Outline of Types* of *Organizations, Activities and Problems* (New York, 1938); S. C. Kohs, "The Jewish Community," in L. Finkelstein, ed., *The Jews,* vol. II (New York 1949), pp. 1267–1324; H. L. Lurie, "Jewish Communal Life in the United States," in *The Jewish People, Past and Present,* vol. IV (New York, Jewish Encyclopedic Handbooks, 1955), pp. 187–227; A. Penn, *Yiddishkeit in Amerika* . . . (New York, 1958); I. M. Minkoff, "Development of Jewish Communal Organization in America 1900–1956," in H. Schneiderman, ed., *Two Generations in Perspective: Notable Events and Trends 1896–1956* (New York, 1957), pp. 110–38; M. Taylor, "Jewish Community Organization and Jewish Comunity Life," in *YIVO Annual of Jewish Social Science,* vol. IX (New York, 1954), pp. 179–204.

On communal leadership, see *Papers and Proceedings of The Tercentenary Conference on American Jewish Sociology, Jewish Social Studies,* XVII (1954), pp. 179–204.

Ideologies of American Jews   (pp. 339–359)

BY HAROLD WEISBERG

Notes

1. For an account of pre-war Jewish ideologies in the United States see Milton Steinberg's "Current Philosophies of Jewish Life in America," in O. I. Janowsky, ed., *The American Jew: A Composite Portrait* (New York, 1942), pp. 205–230.
2. I use the terms "organized community" and "established community" interchangeably throughout this chapter.
3. D. Riesman, Introduction to *Commentary on the American Scene* (New York, 1953).
4. By "Independent Theologians" I mean those theologians who are not official representatives of, or spokesmen for, any of the formal religious organizations. I have in mind such men as Will Herberg, Emil Fackenheim, and Maurice Friedman, and a younger man, Arthur Cohen. A. J. Heschel is also an independent theologian despite his affiliation with the Jewish Thelogicial Seminary. His theology can scarcely be called a theology of Conservative Judaism.
5. A. A. Cohen, *The Natural and the Supernatural Jew* (New York, 1962), p. 5.
6. A succinct statement of Tillich's views on "Ultimate Concern" can be found in his *Dynamics of Faith* (New York, 1956).
7. The kind of ideological quest I have in mind is something like Erik Erikson's concept of the ideology of young people. See his *Young Martin Luther* (New York, 1962), esp. p. 41.

Bibliographical Note

The following are good introductory works for the study of the American Jewish community and its ideologies: J. Agus, *Modern Philosophies of Judaism* (New York, 1941); N. Glazer, *American Judaism* (Chicago, 1957); B. Halpern, *The American Jew: A Zionist Analysis* (New York, 1956); M. Steinberg, "Current Philosophies of Jewish Life," in O. I. Janowsky, ed., *The American Jew* (New York, 1942), pp. 205–30.

Liberal and Reconstructionist ideologies are well presented in M. M. Kaplan, *Judaism As a Civilization* (New York, 1934), and *The Future of the American Jew* (New York, 1948), which are the best introductions to Kaplan's thought; I. Eisenstein and E. Kohn, *Mordecai M. Kaplan: An Evaluation* (New York, 1952); M. Steinberg, *A Partisan Guide to the Jewish Problem* (Indianapolis, 1945). A. A. Cohen, ed., *Anatomy of Faith* (New York, 1960) presents a later and quite different Steinberg.

Non-liberal ideologies are elucidated in M. Buber, *I and Thou* (Edinburgh, 1937), and in a collection of Buber's shorter pieces, *Israel and the World* (New York, 1948); N. N. Glatzer, *Franz Rosenzweig: His Life and Thought* (New York, 1953)—a fine anthology and helpful introduction. For Heschel's views, the reader is referred to A. J. Heschel, *Man Is Not Alone* (New York, 1951) and *God In Search of Man* (New York, 1955); and Fritz Rothschild, ed., *Between God and Man: From the Writings of Abraham J. Heschel* (New York, 1959).

Perhaps the best, and the most dogmatic statement of "postmodern" theology is W. Herberg, *Judaism and Modern Man* (New York, 1951). E. E. Cohen, ed., *Commentary on the American Scene* (New York, 1953) is a good example of post-war "nostalgia." Interesting illustrations of the ideological gropings of two generations of Jewish intellectuals are contained in two symposia: "Under Forty: Literature and the Younger Generation of American Jews," in *Contemporary Jewish Record* (February, 1944); and "Jewishness and the Younger Intellectuals," in *Commentary* (April, 1961).

Jewish Culture: Transplanted and Indigenous   (pp. 373–384)

BY JUDAH J. SHAPIRO

Notes

1. See for example Frederick Jackson Turner's address entitled "The Significance of the Frontier in American History" delivered before the American Historical Society in 1893.

2. J. L. Blau, *"The Spiritual Life of American Jewry, 1654–1954,"* *AJYB*, vol. 56 (Philadelphia, 1955), pp. 99–170.
3. S. Dubnow, *Nationalism and History,* K. S. Pinson, ed. (Philadelphia, 1961), pp. 133, 315–316.
4. J. L. Talmon, *The Origins of Totalitarian Democracy* (New York, 1960), p. 2.
5. *Culture and Society* (New York, 1959).
6. The first national Jewish organizations, apart from local synagogues, were mainly those called "mutual benefit societies," such as B'nai B'rith (1843) and the Free Sons of Israel (1849).
7. Originally this was only a rabbinical seminary under the name Rabbi Isaac Elhanan Theological Seminary, preparing rabbis and laymen as in Eastern Europe.
8. Published annually by the Jewish Book Council and the National Jewish Welfare Board.
9. J. S. Bruner, *On Knowing* (Cambridge, Mass., 1962), p. 116.
10. See above, chapter IX.
11. S. Grayzel, *A History of the Contemporary Jews* (New York, 1960), p. 169.

Index

Aden, 292

Adler, Cyrus, 110, 114, 306, 307, 364, 365

Adler, J. P., 203

Agar, Herbert, 292

Aged, services to, 261–262

Agro-Joint, work of, 283–284

Akron, Ohio, 157

Albany, N.Y., 107

Alcalay, Albert, 243

Algeria, 295

Alliance Israélite Universelle, 17, 278

Allied Jewish Campaign, 289

Amalgamated Clothing Workers Union, 69, 70

America, 96, 97, 98

America-Israel Cultural Foundation, 298

American Academy for Jewish Research, 330

American Association for Jewish Education, 21, 148, 149

American Civil Liberties Union, 86, 91, 93

American Council for Judaism, 47, 114, 332

American Hebrew, The, 304

American Jew, The, 235

American Jewish Agricultural Association. *See* Agro-Joint

American Jewish Archives, 21

American Jewish Committee, 18, 19, 20, 21, 22, 23, 46, 48, 50, 51,

American Jewish Committee (*cont.*) 94, 97, 278, 285, 310, 311, 317, 318, 333, 335, 336, 337, 388

American Jewish Conference, 22, 318, 335–336

American Jewish Congress, I, 19, 311, 333–334

American Jewish Congress, II, 20, 21, 23, 93, 94, 96, 97, 317, 318, 334, 335, 336, 337, 388

American Jewish Historical Society, 21, 377

American Jewish Joint Distribution Committee. *See* JDC

American Jewish Relief Committee, 278

American Jewish Year Book, ref. to, 33(n), 39(n), 134, 325

American Labor Zionists, 316. *See also* Poale Zion

American Mizrachi, 309

American Reconstruction Foundation, 283

American Relief Administration, 281, 282

American Zionist Emergency Council, 318

American Zionist Medical Unit, 285

Anglo-American Committee of Inquiry, 292

Anti-Defamation League of B'nai B'rith, 22, 94, 317, 329, 334, 336

Antin, Mary, 213, 215

[455

THE JACOB R. SCHIFF LIBRARY
OF JEWISH CONTRIBUTIONS TO AMERICAN CIVILIZATION